FATHERS *and* SONS

FATHERS
and SONS

The Autobiography
of a Family

Alexander Waugh

NAN A. TALESE

DOUBLEDAY

New York   London   Toronto   Sydney   Auckland

For Bron

PUBLISHED BY NAN A. TALESE
AN IMPRINT OF DOUBLEDAY

Published in the United States by Nan A. Talese, an imprint of The Doubleday
Broadway Publishing Group, a division of Random House, Inc., New York.
www.nanatalese.com

DOUBLEDAY is a registered trademark of Random House, Inc.

Cataloging-in-Publication Data is on file with the Library of Congress

ISBN 978-0-385-52150-5

PRINTED IN THE UNITED STATES OF AMERICA

1   3   5   7   9   10   8   6   4   2

First U.S. Edition

Contents

Dr Alexander Waugh FRCS
'The Brute'
1840–1906
m. Anne Morgan

Arthur Waugh
1866–1943
m. Catherine 'K' Raban
1870–1954

Constance Waugh
'Connie'
1870–1951

Alick Waugh
1871–1900
m. Florence Webster
1 child

Beatrice Waugh
'Trissie'
1872–1927

Elspeth Alice Waugh
'Elsie'
1875–1952

Alec Waugh
1898–1981
m. Joan Chirnside
(second wife)

Evelyn Arthur St John Waugh
1903–1966
m. Laura Herbert (second wife)
1916–1973

Andrew Waugh
b.1933
m. Vivienne Gorges
2 children

Veronica Waugh
b.1934
m. Christopher
Keeling
3 children

Peter Waugh
b.1938

Teresa Waugh
b.1938
m. Prof. John
D'Arms

Auberon
Alexander Waugh
'Bron'
1939–2001
m. Teresa
Onslow

Mary
Waugh
1940–1940

Margaret Waugh
'Meg'
1942–1986
m. Giles
Fitzherbert
5 children

Harriet Waugh
'Hatty'
b.1944
m. Richard
Dorment

James Waugh
b.1946
m. Rachel
D'Abreu
1 child

Septimus Waugh
b.1950
m. Nicola
Worcester
3 children

Sophia Waugh
b.1962
m. Julian Watson
4 children

Alexander Evelyn Michael Waugh
b.1963
m. Eliza Chancellor

Daisy Waugh
b.1967
m. Peter De Sales La Terriere
2 children

Nathaniel Waugh
'Nat'
b.1968
w. Natalie Muller
2 children

Mary Waugh
b.1993

Sally Waugh
b.1995

Auberon Augustus Ichabod Waugh
'Bron'
b.1998

I

Pale Shadows

I shall begin with a telephone call. It was half past seven on the morning of 17 January 2001 – *annus horribilis* – when I was woken by the ringing.

'He's dead,' my mother said.

'I'll be right over.'

Quivering with excitement I told Eliza to break it to our children and to ring her father who, as planned, would act as conveyor of this dread information to the press.

Fifteen minutes later I was at Combe Florey, turning under the Elizabethan archway, looking up at my father's house. Unless I am very much mistaken, it was sulking. A gaping ambulance was parked by the perron. My elder sister was waiting for me by the front door. In the kitchen I was greeted by my mother and two sheepish paramedics. All three were ashen. Then the telephone rang – already, the first shoot of my father-in-law's grapevine: reporters from the Press Association seeking verification and a quotation.

My mother answered: 'It is hard to sum up someone so wonderful,' I heard her telling them, 'but I've been hanging around for forty years, so that says something.'

I slunk out of the kitchen and shimmied up the stairs.

In his room the curtains were drawn, but there was just enough light to acknowledge the effect: open mouth, closed eyes; face a tobacco-stain yellow. The spectacle was disconcerting but, for the first time at least, I understood what 'He's dead' really meant. I sat on the armchair facing his bed and, for a short while, thought about death, endings, termini . . . There was no communication between us, not even in my imagination, and after a couple of minutes the stillness of the room began to oppress me. Now what? I wondered. A prayer? Should I speak to the corpse? Am I supposed to touch it?[1]

'No. That is not Papa, just a gruesome remnant.' I slunk back down the stairs to the kitchen, glad, at least, that I'd seen it.

The night before was the last time we had talked together. There was a brief exchange, until he lost consciousness.

'Ah, a little bird has come to see me. How delightful!'

'No, Papa it's me. I suppose you must have thought I was a bird because I was whistling as I came up the stairs.'

'It's a bit more complicated than that,' he replied, with a hint of the old twinkle.

I could not be surprised that the last words he spoke to me were intended as a joke: he was always funny, but those drawn-out deathbed days were – despite our finest efforts – not particularly amusing. It is not true that the dying are more honest than the living – I agree with Nietzsche about that: 'Almost everyone is tempted by the solemn bearing of the bystanders, the streams of tears, the feelings held back or let flow, into a now conscious, now unconscious comedy of vanity.'

'Everything is going to be dandy,' Papa had insisted, as he lay uncomfortable and bemused with the skids well underneath him. 'Isn't life grand?'

On the next day the papers were full of it: 'Waugh, scourge of pomposity, dies in his sleep,' trumpeted *The Times*; 'End of Bron's Age' was the *Express*'s more comic effort. His death was lamented by the Australians on the front of their *Sydney Morning Herald*, by the Americans with long obituaries in the *Philadelphia Inquirer* and the *New York Times* ('Auberon Waugh, witty mischief maker, is dead'),

---

[1] When she read this passage Eliza told me that she had kissed his forehead; a valiant deed that never occurred to me as an option.

and as far afield as Singapore, India and Kenya. At home, all of Fleet Street rallied. Even the tabloid *Sun*, victim of his mockery for over three decades, sounded a plucky Last Post. Here is a typical broadside from earlier days:

> The *Sun*'s motives in whipping up hatred against an imaginary 'elite' of educated cultivated people are clear enough: 'Up your Arias!' it shouted on Saturday in its diatribe against funding which put 'rich bums on opera-house seats.' If ever the *Sun*'s readers lift their snouts from their newspaper's hideous, half-naked women to glimpse the sublime through music, opera, the pictorial and plastic arts or literature, then they will never look at the *Sun* again. It is the *Sun*'s function to keep its readers ignorant and smug in their own unpleasant, hypocritical, proletarian culture.

Undeterred, Britain's best-selling tabloid gallantly mourned his passing. 'Good Man' was the heading in its leader column that day:

> *Auberon Waugh, who has died at the age of 61, was a writer and journalist with a unique and wonderful talent.*
> True he occasionally used his talent to attack the *Sun*. But his wit shone like a beacon. We suspect he loved us as much as we loved him.
> *Our sympathies are with his family. His was a great life lived well.*

If this was remarkable the *Daily Telegraph*, a paper for which he had worked for nearly forty years, elected to treat his death as though it were the outbreak of World War III. A top front-page news story ('Auberon Waugh, Scourge of the Ways of the World, Dies at 61') propelled its readers on a five-page binge-tour of his life and work, complete with portraits, obituaries, quotations, adoring reminiscences and amused commentaries.[2] A. N. Wilson, in a piece entitled

[2] A reader's letter in the next day's paper: 'SIR – I wish to protest, in the strongest possible terms, at your decision to devote five pages to an appreciation of Waugh. Anyone with an ounce of decency would expect no fewer than 10.'

'Why Genius Is the Only Word to Describe Auberon Waugh', put down a marker for his immortality:

> He will surely be seen as the Dean Swift of our day, in many ways a much more important writer than Evelyn Waugh. Rather than aping his father by writing conventional novels, he made a comic novel out of contemporary existence, and in so doing provided some of the wisest, most hilarious, and – it seems an odd thing to say – some of the most humane commentary of any contemporary writer on modern experience.

I was pleased by these sentiments, even though Wilson's use of the word 'important' spoils the thing a little. My father, who spent his life vigorously lobbing brickbats at the whole muddled notion of 'importance', would have laughed at the idea of himself as an 'important' writer.

> My various solutions to the problems which beset the nation are intended as suggestions to be thrown around in pubs, clubs and dining rooms. If the Government adopted even a tenth of them, catastrophe would surely result. . . . The essence of journalism is that it should stimulate its readers for a moment, possibly open their minds to some alternative perception of events, and then be thrown away, with all its clever conundrums, its prophecies and comminations, in the great wastepaper basket of history.

If journalism was not 'important' to him he nevertheless held it, as a profession, in high regard. It was only when journalists took their jobs too seriously, when they tried to play an active part in shaping events, that he began to lose his enthusiasm for the press. The sole purpose of political journalism, he always insisted, was to deflate politicians, the self-important and the power mad: 'We should never, never suggest new ways for them to spend money or taxes they could increase, or new laws they could pass. There is nothing so ridiculous as the posture of journalists who see themselves as part of the sane and pragmatic decision-taking process.'

One such figure was Polly Toynbee, a hardened campaigner of the 'liberal left', whom Papa had long regarded as the preposterous embodiment of all that is most self-important, humourless and wrong-headed within his own profession. She was stung by the glowing obituaries he received and decided, while his body was still awaiting interment on a mortuary slab in Taunton, to launch an impassioned counterblast in the *Guardian*. The effect of this could not have been more explosive or more satisfactory. Just as I feared the press was about to wander from the subject, as the bleak prospect of a January burial was all that lay ahead by way of comfort to the grieving, a new fire was ignited: Papa was briefly revivified.

Toynbee's piece cannot be easily summarised because its gist was clouded by too many swipes at her enemies among the living. If her readers were either hoping for or expecting a prize-fight between Ms Toynbee and a dead man they must have been disappointed: all they got was a bewildering mêlée of emotional ringside scraps. What was it all about? Well, at the root of Ms Toynbee's article could be heard a distant wail of indignation, not so much at Auberon Waugh himself as at his influence. This she termed 'the world of Auberon Waugh', and characterised as 'a coterie of reactionary fogeys ... effete, drunken, snobbish, sneering, racist and sexist'. Her article caused a nationwide explosion of support for the deceased. 'Never,' wrote the eminent Keith Waterhouse in his *Daily Mail* column, 'never in a lifetime spent in this black trade have I read a nastier valedictory for a fellow scribe.' 'Polly put the kettle on,' howled the *Telegraph*'s leader writer, while the *New Statesman* hit back with: 'Polly Toynbee is wrong. The writer she reviled as a 'ghastly man' should be celebrated alongside George Lansbury and Fidel Castro as a hero of the left.'

I swung my own fist into the ruckus with a riposte published on the letters page the following day:

In an earnest piece (Ghastly Man, January 19) Polly Toynbee registered her views on the death of a humorous journalist a few days ago. 'We might let Auberon Waugh rest in peace,' she heaved, 'were it not for the mighty damage his clan has done to British political life, journalism and discourse in the post war years.'

This was illustrated by a drawing of my father's corpse being washed down a lavatory, in much the same way as pee, paper and faecal matter is sluiced on a daily basis. Regular readers, who respect the Comment & Analysis pages, may have thought that the illustration was to be taken equally seriously as Ms Toynbee's high-minded and heartfelt article. Rest assured.

Auberon Waugh's 'clan' does not intend to compound the 'mighty damage' it has already done to this country by disposing of his body in this unhygienic manner. We shall ensure that all health and safety regulations are observed when the great man is buried in Somerset on Wednesday.

If you judge my letter to have been a little low on emotion, consider another from someone called Eamonn Duffy from Welwyn in Hertfordshire which appeared next to mine on the same day:

My immediate reaction on hearing of Waugh's death was to punch the air and exclaim, 'Good riddance!' But Polly Toynbee's reply to all the sickly and sycophantic obituaries put into words exactly how I really felt about this vile man.

The funeral was not as sombre as perhaps it might have been. The service took place three miles from Combe Florey in an Anglican church that was big enough to accommodate the hordes of friends, family, fans and newspapermen who were expected to attend. Many of them had been reminiscing about my father in the bar of the Paddington to Taunton express and arrived as a gabbling pack under a warm halo of intoxication. The sun shone as the cortège proceeded through Bishop's Lydeard where, every forty yards, a stationed police officer bowed his head in deference to its passing. Two sergeants saluted the coffin from either side of the churchyard gate as it entered. Papa, I know, would have been thrilled by this:

The police, like most government departments nowadays, are chiefly concerned to look after themselves. They have no interest in apprehending burglars, tending to blame the householder, and small enough interest in the victims of mugging. When they rush around in vans, nine times out of ten they are rushing to the relief of a colleague who has reported threatening behaviour from a drunk — the offence itself provoked by the presence of a policeman in the first place.

For forty years the police were a target of his ridicule. Now the very force he had lambasted as idle, cowardly, oafish and self-serving had assembled itself in great style, and on overtime pay, to salute his coffin.

Uncle James Waugh dignified the proceedings by reading in an aptly lugubrious, *basso* tone from the Book of Wisdom:

> The virtuous man, though he die before his time, will find rest.
> Length of days is not what makes age honourable,
> Nor number of years the true measure of life;
> Understanding, this is man's grey hairs . . .

One of Papa's favourite songs — a ghost's courting ode from Offenbach's *Orphée aux Enfers*, which he used to sing out of tune with a glass of port balanced on his head — was sublimely sung in the tenor register from the pulpit: 'Oh, do not shudder at the notion, I was attractive before I died.' After that my brother and I took it in turns to read passages from Papa's journalism. Originally I wanted a piece from his diaries in which he had lamented the summer invasion of Somerset by tourists from the Midlands. On consideration, it was probably not such a grand idea for a funeral:

> The roads of West Somerset are jammed as never before with caravans from Birmingham and the West Midlands. Their horrible occupants only come down here to search for a place where they can go to the lavatory free. Then they return to Birmingham, boasting in their hideous flat voices about how much money they have saved.

> I don't suppose many of the brutes can read, but anybody who wants a good book for the holidays is recommended to try a new publication from the Church Information Office:

The Churchyard Handbook. It laments the passing of that ancient literary form, the epitaph, suggesting that many tombstones put up nowadays dedicated to 'Mum' or 'Dad' or 'Ginger' would be more suitable for a dog cemetery than for the resting place of Christians.

The trouble is that people can afford tombstones nowadays who have no business to be remembered at all. Few of these repulsive creatures in caravans are Christians, I imagine, but I would happily spend the rest of my days composing epitaphs for them in exchange for a suitable fee:

> He had a shit on Gwennap Head,
> It cost him nothing. Now he's dead.

> He left a turd on Porlock Hill
> As he lies here, it lies there still.

In the end I chose a more fitting epicedium, one that rails against the young, against television and against junk food. I remember his coming into the kitchen asking what modern muck young people were currently eating. It was always a thrill to be able to help him with information for his articles. 'Brilliant! Goodness, you are brilliant!' he would say, if I succeeded. Usually I failed and he would leave the room with a look of disappointment, but on this occasion I clearly remember his delight. The result, a simple list, was painfully funny to a fifteen-year-old at the time and to a packed church of mainly middle-aged mourners twenty years later, it shone in pristine glory:

The best things on television this summer are the National Health Council advertisements warning parents not to over-feed their disgusting, football-like, toothless children.

Over half the population of Britain is overweight. The main reason is that it sits in front of the television all day, watching advertisements. This is the average diet of your typical, spherical, $14^1/_2$-year-old British kiddy, usually of indeterminate sex:

Breakfast: 4 Crunchie bars; 3 fish fingers; 1 pkt Coca-Cola flavour Spangles; 1 tin condensed milk; 2 btles Fanta.

Elevenses: 3 Mars bars; 2 artificial cream buns; ½ pt peppermint-flavoured milk; 3 pkts Monster Munch multi-flavoured crisps.

Luncheon: 3 fish fingers; 2 Twix bars; 1 tin fruit salad; 17 tea biscuits; ½ pt brown sauce; frozen peas.

Afternoon subsistence: 2lb Super-Bazooka chocolate flavour bubblegum cubes; 1 tin condensed milk; 2 small btles strawberry flavoured Lip-Gloss.

Evening meal: 7 fish fingers; ¾ pt tomato ketchup; 2 btles cherry-flavoured Panda pop; 9 digestive biscuits; frozen peas.

TV snacks: 17 Mars bars; 2 pkts Birdseye cake mix; 1 pkt raspberry jelly cubes; 1 old rubber balloon; 3 cigarette ends; 2oz (approx) dog shit; 1 tube toothpaste; 1 can Pepsi-Cola; 1 elastic band.

Needless to say, there is nothing wrong with this diet which contains everything a growing child needs. It is watching television advertisements which causes the trouble. That is what makes these National Health Council advertisements the only effective piece of satire which television has yet produced.

We had entered the church in bright January sunshine and left it in a blizzard. Banks of press and paparazzi had formed outside. A police officer at the church gate asked me if I would like them all forcibly removed. He was champing a little and foaming round the edges of his lips. It occurred to me that nothing would have given Papa greater pleasure than the prospect of a riot at his funeral, the policeman clearly wanted it also, but I was dazed, not thinking straight, and told him not to bother.

As anyone who has experienced a bereavement will remember, the months after a funeral are generally more difficult than the numb and busy week running into it so I was lucky to have had a distraction — a book to finish, which was a biography of God. When Papa died it was almost done, but a fortnight later, over eighty thousand words were scrambled into an impossible computer puzzle and inadvertently copied in that condition on to all of my back-up files. If God seriously thought He could prevent publication of His biography by killing my father and scrambling my work, He was in error. All He succeeded in doing was to set my heart against His ways so that I produced a portrait which, in the end, was far less flattering to Him than it might otherwise have been.

Unscrambling *God* was a fret and an effort that retarded my bereavement by several months. When at last it was done and the manuscript safely delivered to the publishers, I set about reading anything I could find that my father had written. The exercise was therapeutic, or 'cathartic', as some people prefer. I could hear his voice in every sentence, which was a comfort. As I went along I copied down quotations and filed them under headings: Bossiness, Interesting Observations, Sound Advice, the Royal Family, etc. Then I read through twenty years of his *Spectator* articles — how many hundreds of thousands of words was that? — indexing every point he had made on any subject, then started the process all over again, in the same grimly tunnel-visioned vein, with sixteen years' worth of his *Private Eye* diaries. What was I doing it all for? Was it homage, filial piety, or a dementia that needed checking? I do not remember what was going through my head at the time: when I should have been working, earning money to feed the chicks and pay the mortgage, I was instead leading my family on a pointless journey of impoverishment. I was becoming what in England is defined, with contempt, as an Anorak — sad.

In September I was asked to make a speech at a ceremony in London, an annual prize-giving at which my father had officiated every year for the past decade. Afterwards a lady came up to me and stroked my cheek with her soft prelate's hand[3]: 'Oh, that was so wonderful, to hear you speaking — just as though your father were alive again.' She meant well but made me morose. I could not carry on in this way, poring over his writing and giving cheap-jack imitations for

[3] Germaine Greer, philosopher and feminist.

those of his friends and fans who missed him. If the Boswellian labour of indexing all his works had failed to prick my conscience, this lady's passing remark had at last done the trick. I had to get a life!

And so, with paternal obsessions wilfully swept to one side, I started to plan books about other things – big things: the world and how it works, the meaning of life, the riddle of the universe. A mood of renewed hope set in. Then the telephone rang. A frosty voice from the newspaper that was planning to run extracts of *God* said: 'Actually, we've been having a think about this, and what we really want is an article by you on your family, you know, something about your father and your grandfather but mixing it in with a bit of stuff from your book, yeah?' Red rag to a bull. It had been the same when I published my previous book – a history of Time – but *God* as well? 'Surely *God* is of greater interest to your readers than Auberon or Evelyn Waugh?' I demanded. A long, chilly silence emanated from the other end of the line. So I was wrong.

The effect of that irritating telephone conversation was catalytic. How could I write interesting or amusing things about the world if they all had to be passed through the Evelyn–Auberon masher before I could publicise them? If I accepted this newspaper's rotten offer, would I be clutching crudely at the coat-tails of my illustrious ancestors to draw attention to my own work? These issues troubled me. So did an annoying point Ben Jonson once made: 'Greatness of name in the father often-times overwhelms the son; they stand too near one another. The shadow kills the growth.' This whole Waugh thing needed sorting. If Papa and Grandpapa had left their clobber in my path it would have to be cleared out of the way. But time was ticking and I was unsure how to set about it. I could adopt my younger sister's wilful stance and refuse to answer any questions about my ancestors in connection with my books – or I could retrench, return to the navel-gazing Papa obsession from which I had recently extricated myself and blow the whole thing out in one almighty *atchoo*. My instinct was to go for the sneeze. Of course, there were other factors.

The critical reception for *God*, published exactly a year after my father's death, was, for the most part, as I had hoped it would be.

Those who had understood its simple message were elated; those who hadn't tried at least to pretend that they had. Some were injured at the rough way I had handled this most delicate of subjects. I did not mind which way the critics fell as long as they showed evidence of having concentrated, just a little bit, on the text. The lazy ones invariably hadn't: instead of taking issue with the contents of the book, they chose instead to rabbit on about my family.

A typical example. One critic, invited to supply his views on *God* to a national newspaper north of the border, submitted, instead of a conventional review, a long essay on the Waugh family. It started with Evelyn as 'founder, or at least, reviver of the dynasty', then moved to my father, describing him, among other things, as a 'professional snob'. From Papa the piece went to unnamed and non-existent uncles and aunts accusing them of having written 'tight-lipped, smart-arsed little social comedies of the kind that friendly reviewers call "delightfully astringent"'. Only after several hundred words in this vein did the wretched fellow finally get round to parking his critical bottom on the seat where it was originally commissioned to be: 'Now we are into the third 20th-century gener-ation of the family firm, the children of Auberon,' he puffed. 'Really the kindest one can say of them – and, on this evidence, of Alexander in particular – is that *we kent their faithers*. Talent, sadly, does not operate upon the homeopathic principle that the greater the dilution, the greater the strength.'

Now I do not wish to take issue, especially as I have no idea if talent operates homeopathically or not; nor do I recognise the activity embraced by the term *'we kent their fathers'* – though I suspect it to be something disgusting that Scotch people do to each other in bed. No, the only reason I raise this matter is to identify a tic – one that has persisted now for three generations.

When my father published his first novel, *The Foxglove Saga*, in 1960, he was twenty years old. The temptation among critics to compare it with his father's novels proved irresistible. Reviews with titles like 'Chip Off the Old Block', 'Pale Shadow', 'Dad Waugh Had Best Move Over', 'New Writer on the Waugh Path', 'One Waugh Leads to Another' were ubiquitous. Papa's publishers were partly to blame. The dustjacket blurb, which he had originally drafted to read 'The Foxglove Saga is Mr Waugh's first novel', was changed at proof stage by a canny editor into 'The Foxglove Saga is a first novel by the youngest member of a distinguished family.' And on the back cover they printed a full-page advertisement for Evelyn Waugh's latest book, Tourist in Africa.

Most publishers believe that commercial value can be extracted by vaunting these connections, and although they do not insist upon them, it is often hard for the young author to paddle with his pride against the welling drift of their professional opinion.

When The Foxglove Saga came out in the States, American publishers Simon and Schuster invited direct comparison between father and son by invoking Evelyn Waugh's most successful comic novel on the inside flap of the jacket: 'Here, in a word, is this decade's Vile Bodies!' It was a mistake that gave several critics in America, such as the unfortunately named Mollie Panter-Downes of the New Yorker, something solid to push against:

> Since the comparison has been made for us, we may now ask ourselves if the book can really be described as 'this decade's Vile Bodies,' and the answer seems to be no . . . There is no reason for the description to be used. The champ is still the champ, and perhaps it would be a good thing if Auberon Waugh wrote his next book as Arthur Wagstaff.

My father's next novel, Path of Dalliance, was published in 1963. He did not heed Ms Pants-Down's counsel in naming himself Arthur Wagstaff, but tried another tack. This time the jacket blurb made no mention of Evelyn Waugh, or of his 'distinguished family', but brazenly asserted: 'Auberon Waugh is a born writer and writes like himself and nobody else.'

'That was an attempt to put off the critics dragging in my father,' he admitted to an interviewer at the time. 'It is all so pointless — what use is it to say the book isn't as good as Brideshead Revisited?' But his protestations fell predictably on deaf ears as all the critics continued to compare his books, for the rest of his life, to the novels of Evelyn Waugh. In America, Simon and Schuster put out a series of advertisements that read: 'Auberon Waugh writes like himself, but as clearly, and in the pleasantest possible way, he also echoes his father, Mr Evelyn Waugh.'

Even those who had clearly understood the heavy hint contained in the jacket blurb were reluctant to let it drop: '*Path of Dalliance* is Mr Waugh's second novel,' wrote Isabel Quigly in the *Sunday Telegraph*, 'and although he is no doubt tired of comparisons, it does rather vividly recall his father's early novels. Indeed he . . .'

The situation had not been significantly different for Evelyn Waugh a generation earlier. His father, Arthur (about whom I shall have a great deal to say in the chapters that follow), was a distinguished man of letters, a publisher, a poet, a critic and biographer; his brother, Alec, became a best-selling novelist while Evelyn was still at school, and Alec's first novel *The Loom of Youth* created a scandal by implying that homosexuality was normal in most English boys' public schools and was consequently banned in all of them. When Evelyn was at Lancing anyone caught with a copy of *The Loom of Youth* hidden under his bed was caned. Being the brother of such a famous rebel made him especially interesting to all his schoolfriends. Under these circumstances it is hardly surprising that when he first came to try his own hand at a novel, as an insecure seventeen-year-old schoolboy, he was apprehensive of the adverse effect that his father's reputation and his brother's fame might have on his ambitions. 'And all this will be brought up against you,' he wrote in a dedication to himself at the time. '"Just another of these precocious Waughs", they will say.'

In reviews of his early books Evelyn was introduced by critics as the 'son of Arthur and brother of Alec', which irritated him greatly. After a few years the tables turned and Alec's books were compared unfavourably with Evelyn's. 'Mr Evelyn Waugh is very intelligent and a great wit,' wrote one critic, in a review of Alec's eighth novel, *Three Score and Ten*. 'He has already written two or three books that are far funnier than those of anybody in England – his posthumous fame is assured . . . but while the gifted author of *Decline and Fall* was still in the nursery, his far less intelligent brother was writing *Loom of Youth* and since that time Mr Alec Waugh has never looked back – or would it be more correct to say, he has never looked forward?'

'I do not repine'– a saying that my grandfather and great-grandfather used frequently. 'Comparisons are odious' – that was another.[4]

'He failed to break from beneath the heavy yoke of his forebears.' That is what will be said of me when I am gone and I shall not repine for that either. It is inevitable, just as they said of my father, or at least as one of his obituarists (who I think might have been called Gutteridge, or something similar) wrote of him: 'He never quite escaped the long shadow of his father, Evelyn Waugh. Consciously or unconsciously, he tried to emulate his celebrated parent, one of the 20th century's greatest comic novelists.' Of course, nobody is free from the influence of those who have brought them up and every son who has whiled his youth at his father's table subconsciously emulates him. Yes, we are all *formed* by the tastes of our parents. It is surely part of the charm of life that nobody starts from nowhere – but 'escape' and 'shadow'? What hidden emotion lies behind these words! Was Evelyn Waugh's 'shadow' (why not call it his 'radiating light'?) really such a terrible thing that his own son needed to flee it? Is it wise to flee the shadow of 'one of the 20th century's greatest comic novelists'? Do people 'consciously emulate' the shadows they are fleeing? I think not. Back to the drawing-board, Gutteridge.

> Oh, don't the days seem lank and long
> When all goes right and nothing goes wrong,
> And isn't your life extremely flat
> With nothing whatever to grumble at?

Papa often said that when he died he hoped either to be blown up

[4] 'Comparisons are odious' is a simple twisting of Shakespeare's 'Comparisons are odorous' from *Much Ado About Nothing*. My father and grandfather said it often but I have no idea who invented it. 'I do not repine' has been identified by Anthony Burgess and others as a personal cliché of Evelyn Waugh. He and his father may have used it often – too often – but they took it from Psmith, an early P. G. Wodehouse character. In 1935 my great-grandfather wrote to Wodehouse: 'There was a time in Alec's schooldays when we used to read your books together with enormous enjoyment; and, although we are never long enough together nowadays – to read more than a telegram – we have still preserved a sort of freemason's code of Psmithisms, which continually crop up in our letters. Indeed, I can truly say, in emulation of Wolfe, that I would rather have created Psmith than have stormed Quebec.'

by an atom bomb or to fade out on his bed at home, surrounded by groups of adoring family and friends. He succeeded in the latter. After a sudden dip in late December he found himself half-conscious on a hospital bed in Taunton. I shed no tears for him when he died because I had exhausted the supply in the run-up to that event. My brother and I had composed a stage musical that was being performed in London during December. 'If I should go during the run,' he told us, 'the show must go on.' I heard that Leonard Bernstein once lost his footing during a concert in New York, and as he fell backwards from the podium, clasping his baton in both hands, shouted, 'Carry on, guys!' to the orchestra. Papa fell seriously ill on the last night of *Bon Voyage!*. He had warned us and, to be frank, his decline was so rapid and debilitating that I was relieved when it was all over.

He looked pathetic lying on his hospital bed – a broken reed in stripy silk pyjamas. The man I had looked upon all my life as a fount of wisdom and civility, a pillar of strength, a paragon dad – even, in the last two years, as a friend – lay before me, in those bitter weeks, a thin, depressed, vulnerable shadow, a fragile desperado. His short-term memory had, for some reason to do with his blood circulation, ceased to function, and it was for this reason that he thought he was going mad. He wanted to die.

I sat by his bed each day, first at the hospital and later in his bedroom at Combe Florey. It was difficult to know what to say to him. I read passages from Sidney Smith, told him the day's news, tried to make a joke or two. He in turn made an enormous effort to show that he was amused and alert, but he wasn't. From the depths of our gloom many false notes were struck: we could put a lift into Combe Florey; he could retire from his work and enjoy drinking his way through the thousands of bottles of wine stored in his cellar; we could play croquet in the summer; find a publisher to produce a smart library edition of his works. 'Ah,' he said to that one, 'you mean build a Waugh factory?' But it was all hollow hopefulness since we both knew that, at most, only a few months were left to him. He was passing in and out of consciousness each half-hour and time was running thin.

We had the opportunity in those last solemn weeks to put our final points to each other. It was a chance – enviable to those whose parents die suddenly and without warning – that perhaps I flunked. Our relationship was never perfect, but it was probably better than many; strong enough at any rate, I felt, to allow its embers to extinguish themselves naturally. People assume that the deathbed-side moment provides the perfect arena for exchanging ideas like 'I love you', forgiving ancient wrongs or eliciting from the dying some flattering or memorable quotation. Nothing of this kind occurred to me.

Like many English sons I had not kissed my father since I was twelve years old and had never said, 'I love you,' to him, even as a boy. Nor, for that matter, had he said anything like that to me and neither of us intended to break the taboos of our tribe for this occasion. The closest I came was during a visit to the hospital. When I arrived he was asleep so I scribbled a damp-eyed tribute on a small scrap of paper and dropped it into the mailbox at Reception for him to read when he awoke. His name was not on it and, anyway, I think I put it in the wrong box. Perhaps it was delivered to the perplexed old gaffer with an ingrowing toenail in the ward across the hall. I shall never know.

As far as I remember we never, in all our time together, had a single serious conversation. He had not trained me for it. In the last week there was a brief moment – not a conversation precisely but a few words of paternal advice: I must always be kind to Eliza (he adored her) and, something I already knew, that I was extremely lucky to have married her. He listed a few possessions that he wanted me to have after his death, but I was too rattled to remember what they were.

If Papa's autobiographical account is to be trusted, the news of his own father's death, on Easter Sunday 1966, came to him as a relief: 'Just as school holidays had been happier and more carefree when my father was away, so his death lifted a great brooding awareness not only from the house but from the whole of existence.' He was actually grateful to his father for going when he did. 'It is the duty of all good parents to die young,' he used to tell us. 'Nobody is completely grown up until both his parents are gone.' Samuel Butler believed that every son is given a new lease of life on the

death of his father.[5] This might well be true. In my own case, the
new lease took a peculiar form: a search for identity or, to put it
in other words, a disconcerting inflation of the egocentric element
in my nature. 'What am I now that I wasn't then?' 'Where am I
expected to stand in relation to his memory, to his work, to our
family, to our surname?' 'Am I duty-bound to carry something on?
If so, what is it?' From the mists of all these fatuous, unintelligible
questions, a few bleary conclusions eventually showed themselves.
Perhaps I had at least found a starting point.

It is a natural function of the evolutionary process (is it not?) that
a man should desire a son in order to duplicate his own finest male
qualities, to make a replica of himself that will take up his ideas,
his prejudices, his humour, his attractive nose and his neatly curved
bottom and pass them on, like a baton in a relay race, to generations of his descendants, as yet unborn. It is also a natural function of the evolutionary process (is it not?) that a boy should inherit
(whether by mimicry or by the transfer of genes) many of the traits
that are strongest and most useful to the continued fitness of his line.

As a small girl, my youngest daughter used to lean her head back
and flicker her eyelids as she laughed, a distinctive gesture that I
had only ever seen before in two people: her great-grandmother
and her great-uncle. The great-uncle she had never met, the great-
grandmother died before she was born. If she thought she was
expressing her individuality by laughing in this unusual way, she
was wrong. It made me wonder what evolutionary purpose this
quaint mannerism could possibly serve but also if there is any such
thing as a genuine expression of individuality.

I do not wish to diminish the role of mothers, sisters, great-
aunts, school-teachers or anyone else with claims to influence the
individuals around them, but this book is not about them. It is only
about fathers and sons. It is also my specific intention to allow the

[5] Of his own father Butler wrote: 'He never liked me, nor I him; from my earliest
recollections I can recall no time when I did not fear and dislike him. Over and
over again I relented towards him and said to myself that he was a good fellow after
all; but I had hardly done so when he would go for me in some way or other which
soured me again.'

principal characters to tell the story as much as possible in their own words. As professional writers, they were all gifted with great powers of expression. I can assure you they will not let us down.

If any other family has preserved such a diverse, comprehensive and intimate archive of material relating to fathers and sons I would be amazed to hear of it, but at present I believe the Waughs to be, in this respect, unique. My story starts in the late 1860s with my great-great-grandfather, a disagreeable Dr Waugh, with a sadistic attitude to his sons. It ends – or, should I say, it is abandoned with a short open letter to my son in the sixth generation: a modest smidgen of fatherly advice.

Papa surprised me once by describing people who do not wish to know anything about their ancestors as 'evil', a strong word for him: 'incurious', a little 'stupid', perhaps? I have often wondered what he meant by this and why he used such an uncharacteristically violent word.

When he caught me meditating once on the frailties and strengths of my own personality, Papa shook his fist through the door of my bedroom and accused me from without of 'wafting odious clouds of self-think'. The opprobrium was well deserved. Both my parents railed often against the dangers of self-think. We were taught, all of us, to despise it. The Delphic oracle that once proclaimed, 'O Man, know thyself,' must have been an idiot, for there is no difference between this ancient 'wisdom' and the abominable teenage egotism of 'I need to discover the real me.' Perhaps 'O Man, know thine ancestors' would be a more useful motto for the modern egotist to pin on his puffed lapel. For the key to his identity, if such a thing even exists, will be found to lie not where he instinctively looks for it in the mirror-glass in front, but furtively concealed all about the hedgerows and borders of the long, twisting, dusty road behind.

II

Midsomer Norton

I am now going to have to introduce a character whose acquaintance you may not wish to make. He was neither as famous as Evelyn Waugh nor as prolific as Alec Waugh; he did not have the dash of Auberon Waugh nor, dare I suggest it?, the wit of one. But if you skip this chapter your understanding of what follows will be diminished, for he was the progenitor, the patriarch who singlehandedly carried his family into the bright world of literature and who was the spur from which all the father-son relationships in this book are derived. His name was Arthur Waugh, my great-grandfather. His sons were Alec and Evelyn.

To understand how a man behaves as a father it is useful to know how he was treated as a son, but since every father is, or was, himself a son, the process, thoroughly undertaken, would require an investigation right back to the formative origins of fatherhood, all the way to the greedy apple-scoffer of Genesis, or, as Darwinians prefer, to the first protoplasmal, primordial, atomic globule of the paternal line. Vain hope! My male line is not even traceable beyond the seventeenth century. In those days Waughs were farmers at East Gordon on the Scottish Borders. I suspect they ate their porridge with their fingers. I suspect also that they were ponderous about their religion, badly educated (except in Bible matters), shabbily dressed, dirty-faced and bereft of humour. I have no idea how they got on together in their father and son relationships and there is no way of finding out. So I shall begin where the writing Waughs begin: with the story of Arthur.

Until I went to university Arthur Waugh was little more than a name to me, one of the nondescripts in a long list that my father had inspired me to con by heart:

Thomas begat Adam; and Adam begat Thomas; and Thomas begat Alexander, famed as the 'Great and Good'; Alexander begat James and all his brethren; and James begat Alex, the 'Brute'; the 'Brute' begat Arthur; and Arthur begat Evelyn; and Evelyn begat Auberon who (besides better begettings) begat me.[1]

Papa used to groan at the mention of his grandfather's name. When I showed him, in draft form, the entry I had written on Arthur Waugh for *The New Dictionary of National Biography* he pushed it to one side. 'He doesn't deserve it,' he said. When my elder sister was pregnant, wanting to call her baby Arthur, he protested: 'But all Arthurs are rubbish – Arthur Waugh, Arthur Onslow . . .'[2]

'What about King Arthur and the Duke of Wellington?' I asked.

'All rubbish,' he said.

At Manchester University, where I read music, I had chosen as the subject for my final-year thesis the symphonic procedure of an obscure English composer called Arnold Bax. When I told this to Papa he said he thought Bax might have been a friend of the Waughs in Hampstead. Together we set off for the library to find a copy of Arthur Waugh's autobiography, *One Man's Road*, to see if there were any references in it to Arnold Bax. There weren't, but his brother, the poet Clifford Bax, was mentioned, as a passing reference only, in a long passage devoted to Arthur's eldest son's prep-school

[1] Papa disqualified the first Thomas Waugh (1632–93) from this list on the grounds that 'all good pedigrees must begin with Adam'.

[2] His father-in-law (my maternal grandfather) of whom he was extremely fond.

cricketing record. How unfortunate for Arthur that his great-grandson, on the first occasion of his seeking to know anything about him, should have stumbled at the outset on what must be the feeblest, the most inane and the most irredeemably second-rate paragraph that any man has yet committed to the pages of an autobiography. From that moment Arthur Waugh was marked in my mind as a twerp and I was ashamed to be his descendant.

The passage in question was of no use to my musical researches but I shall reproduce it here as a helpful illustration to that aspect of Arthur's character which his younger son, Evelyn, had previously described in his diary as 'ineffably silly', and to give you, my reader, a useful foretaste of two of Arthur's burning obsessions: the game of cricket and his eldest son, Alec:

> Alec's four years at Fernden brought us some pleasant reunions, more especially at the Annual Paters' Match. At the first of those encounters there were still not enough boys to make up an eleven, and the two masters very notably strengthened the side. But Alec opened the bowling, and caught and bowled a sturdy Major off the first ball of the match. One of the fathers, Mr Gainsford, who had played for the Yorkshire second eleven, came over to me at tea-time and said, 'That boy of yours is a born bowler. He has a natural break from the off. If he is carefully nursed he should do well.' I went home that night very happy; but Alec's achievements were to come with the bat rather than with the ball. After he left Fernden his bowling seemed innocuous, except in house matches, until the years after the War gave him a new chance in the cheery, sporting tours of Mr Clifford Bax. Perhaps the trend of modern coaching had something to do with it. The batsmen get most of the attention at the nets; bowling is commonly regarded as a skill that needs 'heaven-sent moments'. Perhaps that is the reason why there are so few fast bowlers in England today.

It is hard to understand how the author of this passage could have fathered one of the greatest prose writers of the English language, but there it is. After that, and by popular request, Papa used to declaim his grandfather's 'Bax Passage' (as we came to call it) in a fluty, ecclesiastical tone for family and friends round the dinner-table. My mother, who disliked this form of showing off intensely, barracked him with loud protestations to desist, but at each interruption he would look up to the ceiling, stick out his tummy and say, 'Right, I shall begin again.' And begin he did, from the very top, with his voice pitched a semitone higher and the volume defiantly turned up: 'Alec's four years at Fernden, brought us some pleasant reunions . . .'

In fairness *One Man's Road* is not all as wasted as this short gobbet from it implies. When I read the whole thing, many years later, I was entranced, particularly by the first half with its intimate picture of a timorous boyhood spent in the rarefied atmosphere of Victorian rural England. The book's most obvious defect is its sentimentality – a glaring error of judgement that stretches far beyond the fashion of its age. I have always believed sentimentality to be a gross self-indulgence and was brought up to treat sentimentalists, especially those among my relations, with unreserved suspicion. 'Sentimentality,' as Papa used to say, 'is the exact measure of a person's inability to experience genuine feeling.' Arthur was cripplingly sentimental. Cricket and his elder son were, as I have said, dominant triggers, but so were his home, his school, women on bicycles, his mother – ah, yes, his mother:

Home meant Mother alone; it was she who lit the light, fanned it with tender hands, and kept it glowing in her children's imagination, by day and night. For four years I had the kingdom to myself and did not undervalue it. Morning after morning in the sunny sitting room, mother and son nestled together, the mother only too often lying full length upon the sofa (for in those days she was very delicate), the boy on a footstool at her knee. She taught lessons, she cut out, in paper, birds, beasts and fishes; she sang; she told tales of her own childhood; she filled the day with enchantment. It was her first real home and she found happiness in making it happy for others.

And, Arthur, tell them about that nursery poem you could never hear without the 'washed eyes of Cordelia shaming your boyhood':

> I love it! I love it! And who shall dare
> To chide me for loving that old armchair?
> 'Tis bound by a thousand bands to my heart,
> Not a band will break, not a link will start:
> Would you learn the spell? A mother sat there;
> And a sacred thing is that old armchair.

The saccharine sentiments expressed in *One Man's Road* are not of themselves especially moving, but no alert reader could fail to be stirred by the image of Arthur Waugh luxuriating among them. This inadvertent exposure of all that was most soft, frail and fat in the author's personality is what elevates this book, in my opinion, from the level of a fatuous piece of fluff-candy to that of an absorbing and often poignant psychological study. It would have been even more poignant, though, if instead of sentimentalising about his mother, Arthur had had the gumption to write more about his relationship with his father, but he flunked that task, fearing his sisters' recriminations.

Dr Alexander Waugh, the father in question, has been labelled by his descendants 'The Brute' partly to distinguish him from an earlier Dr Alexander Waugh nicknamed 'The Great and Good', and partly in fair recognition of his most repulsive attributes. Evelyn's children, seeking to be amused, often asked their father to draw pictures of the Brute for them. He was a deft caricaturist and the arresting images he produced – snorting nostrils, flaming devil's eyes, lascivious mouth and snapping black-dog teeth – never failed to set their imaginations aflame. In youth the Brute was not unattractive; some might even have thought him handsome. He had jet-black hair and clever, piercing eyes set flat in a round and well-proportioned face. Perhaps he seemed dashing to the blushing young ladies of the 1860s and 1870s, but a long life of cruel, selfish behaviour gradually showed itself upon his face.

Victorians never said 'cheese' to the camera. That is a modern conceit. Instead they donned maudlin expressions of philosophic thoughtfulness, proud eminence or family piety in which to pose for the new-fangled machine. I have photographs of the Brute striking all three of these attitudes but none of them credibly, for he had no facial expression winning enough to obscure the core loutishness of his nature. He was a small man – barely five foot in his socks. Towards the end of his life he was portly. All his jackets and hats smelt of pipe and cigar smoke, and the exhalations of his mouth filled the air around him with a rank, second-hand savour of whisky. By 1870 a rich thicket of grey hair sprouted from either side of his face, providing his contemporaries with a vision of patriarchal gravitas, but concealing from them, no doubt, a heinous host of suppressed sexio-socio emotional inadequacies. To the modern eye, the Brute's Dundreary whiskers might look ridiculous, but, as a means of concealing the flaws in his nature, they were, in their day, perhaps no sillier than any of the hairstyle tricks devised and paraded by the social inadequates of our own age.

At Radley College the Brute was a tough little child of solid achievement, not only in the classroom (where he came top in every subject) but on the games field and in the school theatre also. As third prefect he developed a taste for flagellation that never deserted him. He represented the school at football, captained the rowing team, and was champion in both the mile and the two-hundred-yard running races. In 1858 he left Radley for the Bristol Medical School, completing his studies at Guy's Hospital in London, from which institution he walked away with all the major prizes, including the Senior Prize for Practical Anatomy, as well as gold medals in medicine and surgery. At about this time he invented an obstetric apparatus called 'Waugh's Long Fine Dissecting Forceps', which continued to be used by generations of surgeons after his death. I shudder to think how they worked. When the word 'sadist' was first explained to Arthur he is reported to have nodded in recognition: 'Ah, that is what my father must have been.'

But you won't find many examples of the Brute's sadism recorded in Arthur's memoirs. There are passing references only to the 'dolorous' hours spent learning Latin verbs in his study and to his father's pointless and exacting discipline: 'The great lesson of my childhood was undoubtedly discipline: the discipline under which I began, continued and ended every day. I was bred to obedience and I believed what I was told. Hands folded for grace; chair straight to the table; to bed without demur when the clock struck:

— day after day, week after week, discipline, discipline and discipline . . .' The only evidence of the Brute's sadism in *One Man's Road* is a small matter concerning a dog. As a boy, Arthur was frequently taken shooting by his father and it was his unfortunate duty on these occasions to carry the old man's ivory-tipped whip. Whenever their Irish setter, Grouse, misbehaved by barking or chasing birds, Arthur had to convey the weapon to his father and look on as the yelping pet was thrashed to within an inch of its life. These floggings made a deep impression on the boy. In a juvenile poem entitled 'The Power of the Dog', composed in memory of one of these unpleasant experiences, Arthur sides with the beaten animal, who avenges his master's cruelty by leaving home with a cocky sneer on his face.

> Well, we beat him, oh, we beat him! But he lay upon the
>   ground;
> He never writhed, he never snarled, he never made a sound!
> And when our arms were weary, and the walloping was done,
> We felt there'd been a battle, and we knew that *he* had won!
> With an air of tired repose, full of dignity he rose,
> Stalked across the lawn before us, as some shining vanguard
>   goes!
> 'Twas the progress of a monarch who had never known defeat,
> For the dog had proved his power; and revenge is passing
>   sweet!

But Grouse was not the only one to suffer from the Brute's lashes, for his master carried his ivory whip wherever he went. When a wasp settled on his wife's forehead during a carriage ride, he squashed it with the tip of this cane to ensure that it stung her face. In a temper he used to smash ornaments about the house or strike out against his children and servants. These acts were usually preceded by great beakers of Scotch whisky, gulped down in a hurry on his return from work.

Arthur, who was born in August 1866, was the Brute's eldest child by four years. He had three sisters, Connie, Beatrice, or Trissie, and Elsie. Alick, his younger brother, was plucky and rebellious, and for that was the one most frequently whipped.

Arthur, by comparison, was a lily-white boy, 'pale and peaky', as he described himself, besotted with his mother, scared of the organ in church, scared of twigs in the garden, scared of ghosts, scared of scissors, scared of lemonade. He suffered from asthma and was consequently no good at sport. The Brute's solution to his elder son's *faiblesses* was to enrol him on a toughen-you-up induction course based on the old-fashioned wisdom: "'Tis fear as makes 'em brave.' To this end he forced his son to cling for his life to farm gates as he swung them violently back and forth, shouting, 'Hold on, m'boy.' He perched him on high branches, deserting him there for hours on end, and then would creep up behind him, blasting off both barrels of his gun just inches from his ear – all this to fortify Arthur's character and to teach him about surprises.

Shooting and fishing were the Brute's keenest pleasures. Every year he shot partridge and pheasant near his home in Somerset and grouse in Scotland; he fished for trout on the Thames near Hungerford and for salmon at Lough Leane near Killarney in Ireland. These things he did with a relish that perennially lightened his outlook. 'Those who knew him best,' wrote Arthur, 'will always remember him as most completely himself when the first of September had dawned with a cloudless sky, when the guns, cartridge bags and gamesticks were in the front of the dog-cart, bound to make merry with the coveys on Gallants Hill.' They say he could have made a considerable fortune had he chosen advancement in the City instead of the fees of a country doctor, but his passions for shooting and fishing prevailed over his ambitions and, immediately after qualifying in London, he set up a practice in the mining village of Midsomer Norton, near Bath, close to his own West Country childhood home at Corsley. After he had inherited from his father – a strict and pointlessly patriarchal clergy-man – the Brute took a lease of land from a local grandee on which to run his own shoot. The cupboards at Combe Florey are cluttered to this day with engraved plates, horn trophies and silver cups that testify to the Dead-eye Dickery of his aim.

Arthur was good at shooting, too, but he disliked it, and this was a sore disappointment to his father. Dog-whipping and sudden explosions by the earhole had done nothing to sharpen his boy's enthusiasm for the sport, so the Brute tried another ploy to arouse his interest. Every night for a week he dragged Arthur out of bed and pushed him into the damp gloom of a downstairs cupboard where, shivering in his pyjamas and doubtless crying like a baby, he was ordered to kiss his father's gun-case. This didn't seem to work either.

Of the Brute's three daughters Trissie was his favourite. She knew how to please her father by taking a lively interest in all of his hobbies. She was a plainish but intelligent girl, well informed about hunting, fishing and horticulture, on which matters she regaled the whiskery one in false, cute tones that found favour with him but aggravated her siblings. When Arthur was sixteen, he composed a little ode to Trissie, illumined by a pen-and-ink drawing of a small book, ironically entitled *The Wise Sayings of My Pet Daughter* by Alexander Waugh. Arthur's doggerel runs thus:

> Her voice is like the sound of silver bells
> And endless comfort to her father tells
> The rest are all despised, rejected quite,
> The gentle Beatrice puts them out of sight.
> No music half so sweetly to him sounds,
> As her 'Yoicks' 'Tally Ho!' that casts the hounds,
> For he has found in one of tender age
> The sportsman, gardener, expert and sage!

Neither Trissie (the plain one), Connie (the bitchy one), nor Elsie (the hysteric) ever made it to the altar. After their parents' deaths all three continued to occupy the old house at Midsomer Norton, surviving off small dividends of a stake in a Welsh colliery that had belonged to their mother. For fifty years they gave Bible instruction classes to the villagers. 'So far as there can be any certainty in a question which so often reveals surprising anomalies,' Evelyn wrote in 1963, 'I can assert that my aunts were maidens.' When he saw Connie, shortly after his twenty-first birthday, he supposed that a life of chastity had rendered her insane: 'I was surprised on seeing her again to find she is every bit as crazy as my Raban relatives. I think that perhaps it is virginity which makes elderly women mad when they suddenly realise that it is too late to hope for beastly pleasures.'

I suspect some, if not all, of these maiden aunts to have been put off men for life by the indecent interferences of their brutish father, but since I cannot lay my hands on a single shred of testimony to support this theory, I suppose I had better not elaborate upon it here.

When Elsie, the last remaining, died in 1952, Evelyn plotted to buy the house and convert its elegant reception rooms into an Evelyn Waugh museum exhibiting souvenirs of his life and literary achievement. He wrote to his wife (my grandmother) suggesting the scheme, but she ignored it, and continued to ignore it until his enthusiasm fizzled out.

The house at Midsomer Norton was small but its elegant, symmetrical front concealed a tangle of unsuspected corridors and incongruous levels behind. The gardens were extensive. An impressive array of stables and outbuildings enclosed a courtyard at the back, which captivated Evelyn's imagination during the long summer holidays of his childhood. He remembered especially the library, full of arresting specimens in glass jars that the Brute had collected during his student days. (What happened to these? I wonder.) He particularly coveted a phial containing the 'White Blood' of a patient who had died from an exalted form of anaemia in the late 1860s. As a small boy he noticed that the blood had already turned a brownish yellow and congealed. 'When, after the death of the last of my aunts, I came to superintend the disposal of their property,' he wrote in his autobiography, 'I sought vainly for this delight of my childhood.'

There was also a monkey, brought from Africa by a great-uncle, that collapsed from sunstroke while being exhibited to a party of schoolchildren in the rectory garden at Corsley and was immortalised with a hideous desiccated grimace by a taxidermist from Frome. For many years it was suspended in a glass box above the bath, whence it glowered through a steamy glaze at Evelyn and Alec as they washed their bottoms in the tub below. (I wonder what became of that too.) Elsie, Evelyn's favourite aunt, made a point of identifying those objects in the house that her relations wanted and spitefully offering them (even though they were not legally hers) to third parties, who neither cared for, nor wanted them.

Much of the contents of the house was disposed of in this way. Elsie, a sharp, selfish *soi-disante* invalid, used, as an old lady, to spend her days decked in heavy Victorian jewellery, counting her possessions in languid recline on a *chaise-longue*. There she awaited her eldest sister's deliveries of tea, sandwiches and cake, nicely laid out on a silver tray. 'I try not to feel bitter when I see Connie, much older than me and able to go everywhere and do everything,' she said.

The house at Midsomer Norton is now an office, surrounded by Tarmac, full of people at desks pulling important faces with computers. Within twenty feet of the front porch, where once there was a rose garden, now stands a colossal telecommunications centre in brown-stained concrete with Vitrolite windows, surrounded on three sides by a parking area for two hundred cars. The orchard, where Arthur, Connie, Trissie, Elsie and Alick used to play cricket in their quaint Victorian clothes, is now the site of an orange-roofed bungalow development, each house with flat plate windows and a meanly individuated front lawn. The Brute's conservatory has been pulled down; the apricot tree that poisoned the donkey with a surfeit of its unripe fruit is no longer in evidence. The stables, where every holiday Evelyn carved his name on the rafters, have been split into three modern, American-style condos. The traffic roar is incessant and deafening. In the cemetery, across the way, the Brute's high stone-carved Celtic memorial has not weathered well. The script on the plinth beneath is now barely decipherable and a few yards away, where Connie and Elsie are interred together, the stone cross that once marked their spot has long since smashed on to the grave beneath and buried itself in a thick mound of ivy. At the town's best pub I was served a rotten lunch. Midsomer Norton is a horrid place now — *tout passe, tout lasse, tout casse.*

Arthur Waugh's wife, my great-grandmother, detested her father-in-law. Years after his death she would shudder at the memory of his bad and his good moods alike. 'A very common little man', she called him — and, if it had not been she who coined the sobriquet 'Brute', it was certainly through her that most of the evil stories about him circulated. She remembered sourly how, during her long engagement to Arthur, he exploded with rage when he found them playing piquet with a pack of cards that he had especially reserved for whist. 'They will not work for whist now you have used them for piquet!' he yelled. 'You have disempowered them.' She also took mortal offence when, on the only occasion that the Brute came to stay with her and Arthur in London, he left prematurely, complaining that 'a week of your son and your dog would render me insane'.

Arthur, on the other hand, juggled a mixture of emotions towards his father. He felt loyalty and admiration at some times, and resentment, bitterness and fear at others. From his tenderest years he had been brainwashed by the culture of the Victorian paterfamilias. That his father was important and to be respected, whether he liked him or not, was an intrinsic creed that Arthur could never shake off. Like so many sons, he spent too much of his time in search of paternal approval. He knew that the best way to the Brute's heart would be to follow Trissie's example – to take a pleasure in, or to show enthusiasm for, those things that excited his father, but this was not easy. In politics, the Brute was boorish and verbose: as chairman of the Taunton Conservatives' Association his bullish Tory opinions were not to be gainsaid. In 1889 he threatened to withdraw his medical services from anyone at Midsomer Norton who failed to vote for his preferred candidate in the local council elections, and when the scandal was gaining circulation around the village he threatened to sue anyone who repeated it. A case of slander was eventually brought against a Mr George Carter and dramatically lost. Arthur worked for his father, liaising with solicitors during the case. It was a bad time for their relationship.

Because of Arthur's asthma, his mother, a natural panicker, had extracted a promise from his school that he would not be made to take strenuous exercise. He was banned from the school football and running teams because of this. He was bored by fishing, hated shooting and had no stomach whatever for the medical profession. Indeed, Arthur and the Brute shared very few passions, but there were at least two: cricket and amateur theatricals.

Cricket is a good outdoor game for asthmatics as it requires little by way of physical commitment at the amateur level. Even so, Arthur was never much good at it. He played for a club at Midsomer Norton that was founded and presided over by his father. Typically he was kept out at twelfth man or put in as umpire. Only occasionally was he allowed to bat. On none of the surviving score sheets is he registered as notching any more than ten runs.[3] His sisters, all keen players for the women's team, were better at batting than he was, but in spite of this minor humiliation Arthur remained a fanatical enthusiast of the game all his life.

Trips with the Brute to see England play at Lord's or at the Oval in London ranked high among the happy memories of his childhood. Most thrilling of all was his first sighting of W. G. Grace, by far the greatest batsman of his age, in a match between Gloucestershire and Australia at Clifton College one sweltering day in August 1882. W. G. was at the height of his fame. Forty-five years later, in an introduction to a book of cricketing stories, Arthur recalled the happy moment: 'He is coming! He is coming! And he is seeing the ball as big as a balloon. Oh, that first sight of W.G. in his red and yellow cap, his big beard flowing over his chest, his foot cocked upwards like a signal! Fortunate boy, to see him make 77, the very first time.' On the train home Arthur and the Brute shared their indignation at the way W.G. had been given out: 'Of course he wasn't out!' W.G.'s remarkable career continued for another twenty-six years, ending in 1908 with 126 centuries, 54,896 runs and 2876 wickets.

Throughout his adult life Arthur used to say: 'With a thorough knowledge of the Bible, Shakespeare and *Wisden's Cricketing Almanac* you cannot go far wrong.' Even in contemplation of death he was able to console himself with the hope that some of his body's atoms might eventually find their way, wafted by a favouring gale, on to the playing-field at Lord's. This idea he expressed in a staggeringly fatuous article in 1927:

Why should we fear the gentle arms of Mother Earth, with her comfortable bed beneath the greensward of our game? She is very tender with her children, and folds them closely to her

---

[3] For those who do not understand cricket this means that Arthur had a bad eye for the ball.

heart. The wind, too, blows whither it listeth; and who knows where it may waft our own poor dust in the days that are to be? It may even carry some of it across the field at Lord's, scattering its particles by the well-worn wicket, in the very thick of the fight. Then in the sunlight we shall surely wake to remember many things; and in the darkness we shall not forget.

The Brute's obsession with amateur dramatics was, I believe, inextricably connected with his personal need to show off. His egocentricity was a phenomenal force. Although he was regarded as a jovial cove — indeed, as a rounded and popular pillar of local society — his returns home after work were awaited in a mood of apprehension by his servants and family. As he entered the hall he would stamp his feet on the marble floor. If concerned faces did not instantly pop up from all around to greet him, he clamoured and bellowed some more until everyone in the house had dropped what he or she was doing and rushed to ask him how his day had passed.

His good moods were no less oppressive. When happy the Brute was facetious, sentimental, patronising, demonstrative and overbearing. He liked to be at the centre of attention and believed (because people were too afraid to signal to him otherwise) that he was a great wit. By today's honed standards, his humour would be thought clumsy: it relied heavily on exaggeration — mock-wailing, false, rollicking laughter, theatrical rages, lofty musings with eyes closed and hands outstretched to the heavens. All his life he made an art out of hamming. The Brute performed so often that he eventually lost touch with whatever real self was originally within him. He was only ever able to act. Like Mrs Cheveley in Wilde's *An Ideal Husband*, he found being natural 'such a very difficult pose to keep up'. And, indeed, it is, but neither the Brute nor Arthur (who was similarly inclined) was able to sustain a natural pose for a single minute. To both of them 'fatherhood' was synonymous with 'theatrical opportunity' — a go-ahead to strut and fret, to spout quotations, and fill the air with noisome and ridiculous voices. 'Be'ave, Geaarge, be'ave!' the Brute used to bellow in an assumed Somerset accent to each and any of his children at table.

Mealtimes were ritualistic. The Brute sat always at the head on a carved oak armchair that nobody else was allowed to use, even when he was not in the room. Before supper, when his blood-sugar levels were at their lowest, he would bellow to the servants to speed things up and, as he sat down, regardless of what food was being served, could be heard to holler:

> Puddin'! Puddin'! Puddin'!
> Gi' me plenty o'puddin',
> So pass me plate,
> And don't be late,
> And *pile* it up wi'puddin'.

Polite laughter was expected.

Children were permitted to dine with their parents from the age of ten. At the end of dinner, those who had not left the room in tears were expected to rise, tuck their chair under the table and bob to each of their parents in turn: 'Love to Mother, compliments to Father,' then leave the room quietly.

Theatricality has proved itself the besetting sin of the fathers in my family for at least six generations. The Reverend James Waugh, rector of Corsley (the Brute's father), always acted the part of a trembling old prophet even when he was young and fit. 'Of course every man has a touch of the actor about him,' said Arthur. 'We all like to imagine ourselves in heroic attitudes. Even if we are too sensitive to set our fancies free when we are awake, what devils of fellows some of us are, to be sure, in our dreams.'

Evelyn likewise looked upon the duties and responsibilities of fatherhood as an actor might look upon his craft. As he revealed in the excoriating self-portrait *The Ordeal of Gilbert Pinfold*:

[Pinfold a.k.a. Evelyn Waugh] without design, gradually assumed the character of burlesque. He was neither a scholar nor a regular soldier but the part for which he cast himself was a combination of eccentric don and testy colonel and he acted it strenuously, until it came to dominate his whole outward personality. When he ceased to be alone, when he swung into his club or stumped up the nursery stairs, he left half of himself behind and the other half swelled to take its place. He offered the world a front of pomposity mitigated by indiscretion that was as hard, bright and antiquated as a cuirass.

Evelyn was more self-critical than his father and grandfather, neither of whom appeared to notice the masks they were wearing or to register the effect of them on others. Under such circumstances it is hardly surprising that Arthur and the Brute should have been most at their ease together when indulging in their passion for amateur dramatics. As a boy Arthur wrote hundreds of short plays, many in verse and many with a principal part for a tyrannical ogre that suited the Brute. These were performed at home or in the nearby community hall. Together, father and son joined a local society for amateur thespians and continued to act until the year of the Brute's death when they starred alongside one another in Sydney Grundy's *A Pair of Spectacles*, the Brute as Uncle Gregory, a shady con from Sheffield, and Arthur as his soft-hearted, easily deceived younger brother, Benjamin Goldfinch.

It was through such amateur endeavours as these, and the occasional trip to see a Shakespeare play performed by the boys at Downside School (where the Brute was school doctor) that Arthur first came to love the written word. His teenage enthusiasm for literature was given no encouragement from his father, but it ripened under the tutelage of inspired teachers at his boarding school in Sherborne. Although the Brute quoted often from Shakespeare and the best-known poets of his day, Wordsworth and Tennyson in particular, he was not a literary man. As far as he was concerned, literature afforded no career for his son, and was not a serious topic for conversation. For the Brute, literature offered little more than a convenient vehicle for his showing off. When his son first mooted the possibility of a literary career it was in the face of his father's violent antipathy. At first the Brute refused to allow it, but in time realised that Arthur's heart, for once, was dogged and set. 'Why can't you write slashing political pamphlets or bullish leaders for *The Times*?' he roared. That was the only form of 'literary' career that made sense to him and the only one that would have made him a proud father.

For twenty years the Brute cherished a dream that one of his sons might study medicine and, in time, take over the practice at Midsomer Norton, but it was not to be. Alick, the rebel, quick to tears and sick to death of his father's domineering presence, had resolved to leave home at the earliest opportunity and, in 1883, aged only twelve, he enrolled as a naval cadet aboard HMS *Britannia*. Arthur saw him off, with an admonition to control his blubbing:

> If thou would sail o'er seas in future years
> Take my advice – abstain from tears.
> Most unseasonable is the grief
> In which your wounded feelings find relief.

For two years Alick scrubbed the decks until he was made a midshipman aboard the *Iron Duke*. He was in the Channel Squadron and later sailed the Pacific with the Surveying Service, painting exquisite watercolours of all that he saw. For years at a stretch he stayed away from home. On a rare and flying visit to Midsomer Norton in 1893 Alick found his father in a rage because he had not received the usual invitation from Sir John Horner to shoot at nearby Mells Park. Eventually it arrived and the Brute calmed down, but Alick recorded the affair in 'The Legend of Mells Park Shoot'. It is a terrible piece of writing – unworthy of the name of Waugh – but it was not for this reason that Arthur disclaimed it. He was terrified that if the Brute saw it he might get the blame. On the back of the manuscript is written in Arthur's hand: 'I certify that I have this evening read this poem for the first time and that I have not assisted in thought or act in its composition. Signed Arthur Waugh.' It should not be difficult to understand why Arthur was worried:

> What makes the Doctor look so mad?
> What makes him look so worn?
> Why do you see his pallid cheek
> On such a nice fine morn?
> With all his bedside invalids
> He may be very cute
> But Mr Horner of Mells Park

Won't invite him to shoot.

He watches every post come in
And messengers ride by.
He thinks of the old shooting times
And prays that he may die.
Never has such a season
Been so very slow
He used to shoot four days a week
About two years ago.

The evenings go by very slow
With no shoot for the morrow
And Adam Thatcher says he can't let him Scotch Whisky borrow
He cries – 'This room is very dire –
The hall of wash-boy smells.'
But all of this he'd soon forget
If he got asked to Mells.

One morning not so long ago
When his poor wife came down
She saw her precious husband
A-grovelling on the ground.
He cried out, 'Please forgive me all,
I know I've been a brute,
For Mr Horner of Mells Park
Has invited me to shoot.'

His children on their knees then go
And say a silent prayer.
Their father is convulsed in tears
It's more than they can bear.
Then Budge comes in and prays there too,
And Jolly tries to bark,
They're all so pleased that Father has
Been asked to shoot Mells Park.

The poem goes on for many verses. The Brute gets to Mells and shoots well, has a big lunch and boasts to his friends of his sons' fine achievements.

> He tells them of his sailor son
> Only just nineteen
> Who from the navy was picked out
> To converse with his Queen.
> Of his son Arthur too they hear,
> Mr Poet of this land,
> Who last week walked with Tennyson
> And held him by the hand.

But even after the Brute's successful day at Mells he remained unpleasant to his younger son. Alick left and did not return for six years. In 1899, he met Florence Webster, a Tasmanian eccentric from Hobart, married her and brought her back to Midsomer Norton, where she was treated as a simpleton by the whole Waugh family (including Arthur) and where, in the early months of 1900, she gave birth to a son called Eric.

At sea Alick had put on an enormous amount of weight and was hardly recognisable when he returned. Like all the men of his family he was unable to resist stuffing his face with bread:

> The boy stood on the burnished deck,
> His waistcoat buttons far undone,
> He stuffed himself with bread.
> 'This is my 50th crust!' he cried
> In accents clear and wild.
> 'Just one more crust before I bust!'
>   – He was a vulgar child!

Many nights the Brute was out on call. He owned a small cottage in the town where, I suspect, he lodged a mistress – I am informed that several of his descendants in bastardy live, to this day, at Oxford. In an untypical flash of generosity, spurred perhaps by guilt, he vacated the cottage for Alick and Florence so that she could look after her baby there while her husband was at sea. Within three months of their arrival Alick, who had been bitten by an Anopheles mosquito in the Solomon Islands, was struck down with a malarial ague. Throughout the summer of 1900 he was bedridden; by late August, he was a pathetic wreck, jactating in a lake of his own sweat. After that he was comatose. His kidneys and spleen swelled each to the size of a party balloon and his blood turned to a sticky jelly – too glutinous to pass through the vessels intended for it. A few weeks after his twenty-ninth birthday, the fever overcame him and on 2 September he died. Alick was the first of his family to go and one of the first of the town's inhabitants to be buried in the new cemetery, four hundred yards over the road from the church.

Arthur was overcome with grief at the loss of his younger brother and poured out his heart in touching funereal verse. Thirty years later he was still mourning: 'The first loss that a family has to face,' he wrote, 'the first vacant chair at the Christmas gathering – these are among the ineradicable testimonies to the passage of time. They leave those upon whom they fall older in heart and more uncertain of their bearings. Other losses that follow may bring greater changes, but it is the first loss that makes the deepest scar. Death has come up into our own stronghold, and the childish sense of security is gone.'

Immediately after the funeral, the Brute evicted Florence and her baby from the cottage and sent them back to Tasmania. But before she could leave he ordered her to pay the undertakers' expenses and to settle Alick's tailor's bill for suits and cravats that he had acquired long before she had met him.

Arthur, ashamed of his father's behaviour, kept in touch with Florence and Eric through the years, looking on them with a mixture of warmth and genial derision. In 1921 they came to visit their English relations. The Brute was, by then, long gone. Evelyn, aged seventeen, noted in his diary: 'I do not dislike my Aunt but Eric is terrible. How Uncle Alick, who appears to have been one of the stoutest Waughs for some time, could have produced him defies eugenics. I am quite miserable in his company. He is fat, uncouth, self-complacent, good-hearted and vulgar.' Evelyn's mother clearly felt the same. Just after the Tasmanians had moved on to Midsomer Norton, she wrote to her elder son: 'It was somewhat of a relief to see the last of our relatives. (Our house is still full of their luggage) . . . Eric's appearance was against him – big clumsy and uncouth with an impediment in his speech . . . he has no judgement or criticism. I wonder what the Aunts make of him. I expect they'll soon love him.'

At Sherborne, Arthur maintained his determination to pursue a literary career against all paternal counsel. He won the Senior Poetry Prize, edited the *Shirbirnian*, the school magazine, founded another called the *Fifth Form Magazine*, wrote plays that were performed and others – including a daring skit entitled *The Headmaster* – that were not. But it was only when he had left school in 1885 that the Brute finally reconciled himself to the fact that neither of his sons would inherit the practice and that he needed to find himself a partner from outside the family.

Arthur was nineteen when he went up to New College, Oxford, in January 1886 – not an especially handsome man, but better-looking, I suppose, than either of his sons at a similar age. He had large grey eyes that might be described as 'owl-like', but the rest of his face, his weak chin and flat pale cheeks, betrayed a timidity more typical of sheep than of owls. His nose had something of the puffin's bill about it. Timidity, the bane of his schooldays, proved the bane of his university years too: 'My own Oxford days,' he wrote, 'resulted in discouraging inaction. Partly from shyness and partly from sheer inability, I joined the vast army of those who look on at what others are doing, instead of doing anything themselves.' He regretted not having joined the OUDS, Oxford's dramatic society, or involving himself in the editorship of student magazines as he had at Sherborne. In attempting to get a few of his poems and plays published, he was politely rejected.

Despite these minor setbacks Arthur's Oxford years were not without success. He wrote the libretto to a burlesque tragedy, which he directed, produced and acted in at the Holywell Music Room. It was a fringe effort that mocked the OUDS and gained him notoriety. Shortly after that, and much to his surprise, he won the coveted Newdigate Prize for poetry with a long, flowery epic about General Gordon, the empire hero decapitated at Khartoum three years earlier. Winning this prize was no small feat. The roster of previous winners included John Ruskin, Matthew Arnold, Oscar Wilde and Lawrence Binyon. The publication of Arthur's winning poem, 'Gordon in Africa', by Thomas Shrimpton & Son of Oxford in May 1888 was not, it has to be admitted, a major literary happening. Shrimpton's paid the author ten pounds for the rights and probably made a loss on the deal, but looking back on that event, more than a hundred and fifteen years later, we can see that the publication of 'Gordon in Africa' marked the birth of a remarkable literary dynasty. Works by Waughs have been in continuous print ever since: nine of Arthur's descendants have produced 180 books between them. Novels, plays, poems, essays, histories, travelogues, philosophies and biographies have gushed from our pens in cataracts ever since. In 1888 Arthur had no idea of the torrent he was unleashing but he was, at least, sure of one thing: the Newdigate Prize had vindicated his decision to go to Oxford, and his father would have to look again at the feasibility of a literary career for his son.

In a mood of overweening pride Arthur telegraphed details of his victory to Midsomer Norton. The Brute was away fishing all that week but his ecstatic reaction to the news when it caught up with him at the Bear Hotel in Hungerford, survives:

My Darling Boy,

I cannot describe to you my feelings when I read mother's telegram. Yesterday I nearly cried with joy. You have made us very very happy and it is such a good thing for you in connection with any literary career you may take up & I am so glad also because you have had disappointments and have borne them so nobly and now you have gained this great distinction — & one I know you will prize.

You will want some sherry and fine men to drink your health so I will direct Mansford to send you a little case from Frome.

I will write again when I get home. I leave this place tonight. God bless you my own darling son & make your career worthy of your best endeavours & then I know it will be a glorious one.

Ever your loving hopeful father, Al. Waugh.

True to his word, he wrote again, two days later, standing on his feet:

My Darling Boy,

I have read, reread, your poem over and over & the more I read it the more I like it not only for its beauty but for the high tone throughout. I am very proud & thankful my dear dear son. Everyone fixes on those lines of the Voyage out, the final scene is so excellent and the imagery so strong there & the lines on page 7 & the description of the hero on the watch tower impress me most. I shall try all I know to run up for the Commemoration. I MUST manage it – Mother is in Bristol which is very sad but she wants to be all right before going to Oxford.

We have had some tennis. Connie is playing up very well, Hooper is a very nice man & plays a good game as does Tisdale.

Now I must stop. I have not sat down all day.

With fondest love
Your loving hopeful father
Alexander Waugh

But the Brute's excitement was short-lived. When next they met he was irritated by the 'self-satisfied atmosphere of puffed success' that Arthur was generating. He had always found it easier to be kinder to his son under the shadow of failure than in the gloat and glare of triumph. Later, when Arthur told him of the poor third-class degree he had been awarded, the Brute was memorably forgiving. 'My dear boy,' he said, 'do you imagine that I look upon my sons as machines for the gratification of my self-esteem? You did your best and that is more than enough.'

Arthur's timidity was either inherited or copied from his mother, for she, like him, was terrified of everything. As an example of Annie Waugh's paranoia, I can offer a letter she wrote to Arthur in 1907 about his nine-year-old son who had made himself sick eating blackberries on a train: 'I have a theory (I know you will laugh at an old mother's fads) that Alec's spine is not over strong and that kicking a football is felt by the weak part and goes to his brain – for his sickness never seems so much like stomach sickness as brain sickness because he does not feel it coming on long before. Well I am likely wrong, but a rest will show if it is football.'

When Arthur was about to be born in August 1866, she was petrified lest her labour should interrupt the Brute's first day of partridge-shooting. Later she would cower in anxiety if Arthur went for a swim, or walked under a tree in the rain. She was not dissimilar to the nanny who looked after me in the late 1960s: when I asked her for a pair of scissors to cut a cardboard lavatory roll into the shape of a steamship funnel, she screamed in the shrill ululations of a Halifax lunatic: 'If yer ask for scissors, yer'll be asking for pins, an' if yer ask for pins they'll spill ont' floor, an' TRAVEL OOP YER BODAY!'

And so it took a great deal of alien courage for Arthur's petri-fied mother to write to her second cousin on his behalf. The cousin in question was Sir Edmund Gosse – not, perhaps, so famous now but, in his day, one of England's foremost men of letters. At the time he received Annie Waugh's letter he was a well-known poet, translator of Ibsen, biographer and editor of Thomas Gray's works, a regular contributor to the *Spectator* and other periodicals, as well as a personal friend to many of the most illustrious writers of his day. Annie remembered him as a small, pasty-faced lad whose mother had died when he was eight. After that he came frequently to stay with her and her sisters, treating their home as a sanctuary from the puritanical *froideurs* of his loathsome father. Gosse *Père*, Philip Henry Gosse, was a religious maniac, a member of the Plymouth

Brethren, once famed for his zoological insights but now best remembered as the inventor of the creationist counter-argument to Darwin. 'God deliberately planted fossils into our soil to make it look as though the earth is much older than it really is – a divine ploy, deliberately done to test our faith.' The story of Edmund Gosse's childhood, his stays with Arthur's mother's family and his eventual escape from the paternal yoke to the brighter, happier world of English letters, is recorded in his little masterpiece, *Father and Son*, first published under a *nom de plume* in 1907. It is the only book by Sir Edmund Gosse that is still in print.

For all Gosse's faults – and they were legion – he received Annie's letter warmly and invited Arthur to tea. Henry James was in the house at the time and young Arthur had never felt so nervous. After an edgy, testing consultation, Sir Edmund agreed that he would write to the Brute on Arthur's behalf suggesting either that he give his son an annuity of a hundred pounds a year while he found his feet in literary circles, or set him up as a wine merchant in the West Country. Looking at the costs of each, the Brute reluctantly agreed to the cheapest, which was the former. His payments to Arthur lasted three years and, for the rest of his life, he never allowed Arthur to forget the extent of his generosity.

With his father's annuity Arthur rented himself a small flat in London's Gray's Inn Road. He had enough money left over for food, clothes and occasional cheap seats at the theatre. Within a year he had met, mainly at Sir Edmund's literary *soirées*, not only Henry James but W. S. Gilbert, Thomas Hardy, Arthur Conan Doyle, Robert Louis Stevenson, Rudyard Kipling, Henrik Ibsen, Aubrey Beardsley, and a host of lesser lions. Arthur, a quaking West Country bumpkin, sat at the far end of Sir Edmund's polished table, drooling on these idols with his eyes popping and his weak chin wavering in excitement. Gosse noticed Arthur's bedazzlement and was quick to exploit it. For nearly thirty years he used his wide-eyed young cousin as a punching bag, a useful target for his obloquy, someone who would serve to keep his own wit flowing when conversation with those he sought to impress was in danger of drying up. Arthur accepted his pilloried position and maintained it with a quiet, humorous dignity until Gosse's death in 1928.

Through Gosse's patronage Arthur soon found ways to turn an honest penny on the London literary scene. He started off as a humble publisher's reader, with a few magazine short stories and poems to his name, but by the time of the Brute's death in December 1906, he was a plumping, reasonably well-off married man with two sons, living in a modest terraced house in North London. He had written one bestseller – the first biography of Tennyson – and had contributed an important article to the inaugural edition of that scandalous organ the *Yellow Book*. He was an established critic and literary editor, a poet of small repute, the London correspondent to an influential New York newspaper and managing director of Chapman and Hall, a respected London publisher whose principal revenue derived from its exclusive copyright tenure on the works of Charles Dickens. If Arthur was not exactly famous he was known to all in the highest literary circles of his day.

I am sure the Brute, in his own way, was proud of all this but, alas, I have no record to substantiate the claim. Shortly after his sixty-sixth birthday he came down with a nasty flu, but continued to shoot pheasants and to minister to his patients in spite of it. Sneezing filth all over them was no doubt recognised as sloppy doctoring even in those far-off days, but somehow this particular show of obstinacy has since been interpreted by generations of Waughs as a singular example of the Brute's integrity and dedication to duty. History does not record if he spread the infection among his patients, only that he got worse and worse until his flu had turned into full-blown pneumonia. It was some time before his wife and daughters realised the danger he was in. Arthur was telegraphed in the middle of the night and on the next morning took a train from London to Bath, whence he was driven by horse-drawn cart at breakneck pace through a blizzard across the snow- and ice-covered Mendip Hills. By the time he reached Midsomer Norton the Brute was already dead.

The funeral was well attended. The Brute's coffin was borne on the shoulders of six of his old retainers – those who, no doubt, hated him – to a waiting cart. From there it was pulled a quarter of a mile to the new cemetery and laid to rest above the coffin of his sailor son – the flogger, *in perpetuum*, on top of the flogged.

In his autobiography Arthur recorded the death of his father without emotion: he hadn't particularly liked him. The will wasn't signed and the Brute's finances were all of a mess. Fifteen months later, Arthur's mother died: 'As I stood by her open grave I knew that I was burying with her the last associations of my childhood: that the light of the old home was extinguished for ever, and that I must look elsewhere, during the rest of my life, for the inspiration and the hope that keep the heart young in the midst of change and decay.'

III

Golden Boy

In 1908, at the time of his mother's death, Arthur was middle-aged. His waist had started to spread – due, in the main, to his uncontrolled passion for bread and butter; he was partially deaf in one ear and his hair was turning grey. His publishing and writing careers were moderately successful but static. Although he had succeeded, by prudent management, in pulling Chapman and Hall from a financial slump, he remained terrified of shareholders' meetings and regarded the recruitment of authors as a passive occupation. Manuscripts were sent to him: he read them and decided yea or nay at his office desk; he was not active in creating a list and, in consequence, many of the best writers of his day fell into the hands of his rivals. After work he returned home, where he would not discuss business matters.

He did not enjoy parties, nor did he invite many of the famous authors of his acquaintance to his home. He continued to attend Edmund Gosse's grand literary dinners, leaving his house under duress but invariably returning in good cheer. 'A capital evening!' he would say. When he was tipsy and in high spirits everything was 'capital' – 'capital fellow, capital lunch'. Despite his shyness in company he was lively, trusted and popular.

At home his verbosity was inclined to run away with him and, like his father, Arthur could not resist spouting quotations from literature, the Bible or hymnody to embellish the finer points of his conversation. Despite his recurrent asthma, for which he bought himself Himrods Mentholated Cure, he continued to smoke pipes until the end of his life so that the smell of his home and office comprised a distinctive mixture of these two ingredients. He had a large collection of pipes, which he cleaned ceremoniously at the kitchen table.

In 1907, from his share of the Brute's estate, Arthur had built himself a plain suburban villa in the deco style in Hampstead, North London, and named it 'Underhill' after a lane at Midsomer Norton where he had walked with his mother and first kissed his future wife. It was erected on a green site just outside what was then Hampstead village. In the years that followed, the Underground arrived and every spare patch of grass was built upon. Then the house was officiously numbered by the postman, 145 North End Road, and the area lost its rural charm as it merged with the new developments of Golders Green, to become a typical suburb of the bustling metropolis. The house was architecturally plain but to Arthur — who had followed its progress from the foundations upwards and who, as the years went by, had added to and extended the building and its gardens — Underhill remained a magical hearth that replaced in his imagination the obstinate fantasy of Mother and Midsomer Norton. 'No doubt it was never anything more than an ordinary suburban villa,' he wrote, 'but it was a great deal more to me.' He loved it with a passion and he loved it all the more because he had supervised its creation. He wrote, in the *Quarterly*: 'As the home rises, brick upon brick, from its broad concrete and trenches to its comely rough-cast chimney stacks, every stick and stone of it has its own association. You even remember upon what day, and under what complexion of sky, each pleasant finishing touch was given. Here is the real sense of possession. However small the tenement, it is at least all yours.' When he was away from Underhill he would wail in mock lamentation:

> *'Hame, hame, hame, O hame fain would I be —*
> *O hame, hame, hame, to my ain countree . . .'*

Built on three floors and set in large gardens, Underhill was designed to be light and airy. Instead of a conventional drawing room, Arthur had insisted on an oak library, which he called the 'book-room', with french windows leading into the garden. It was here that he read to his family after dinner. The great fault of the house was that it had only one bathroom, on the first floor. Who was to use it first each evening became a frequent cause of family friction. I am told that most middle-class families had only one bathroom in those days. Can this be true?

Arthur described the house as 'old' even though it was new — for he attached this epithet to things that he loved without discrimination for their age. By 'old' he meant 'cosy and endearing'. He referred to Underhill's 'stout old timbers' as though it were a ship. Following an unseemly battle with his sisters over the ownership of some family portraits at Midsomer Norton, which he lost, Underhill was decorated mainly with prints and signed photographs of famous authors. The furniture was solid English oak — 'not disreputable', as Evelyn used to say.

Underhill today is divided into three flats. Arthur's extensive gardens have long since been redeveloped — to the left a brand new house; to the right and behind, a 'drive-thru' car wash proclaims with a gaudy sign: 'Woodstock Motors Handwashing and Valet Centre. While-u-wait service.'

In 1893 Arthur married my great-grandmother Catherine Raban (whom he always called K[1]) after a long engagement attenuated by unnecessary insecurities over money and a reluctance on her part (I think) to commit to him. Their first son, Alexander Raban Waugh (Alec) was born five years later and their second, Arthur Evelyn St John (Evelyn), five and a half years after that. I do not know why these events were so spread out. Sexual, medical, or psychological inconveniences doubtless played their part. Evelyn complained to his friends at university that he was an unwanted child, which might have been true, though I cannot imagine how he would have known it.

In any case, by the time of his mother's death in 1908, Arthur was forty-two, his eldest son was ten and Evelyn was five years old. As he stood beside his mother's open grave in the cemetery at Midsomer Norton dewy-eyed, reflecting on the past and

---

[1]Although she was christened Catherine with a C, she was known throughout her childhood as Katie — K was extrapolated from this.

wondering how to keep himself young at heart, Alec, sitting on his own at a harsh boarding school a hundred miles away, took out a pen to write him a letter:

Dear Father,

I was very sorry to hear Gaggie was dead. We shall never forget her, not if we live to be a hundred. The Headmaster told me after lunch, he was very, very nice about it. I am not with the others but in the big classroom. Only this morning I was looking forward to the summer when I should see her dear old face again, but now I shall never see it. Mother told me in her letter that you had gone down to Midsomer Norton, but I did not think for an instant she would die. How sad for Mother, you and the Aunties. She was the most loving and kind mother you could wish for. How long will you stay at Norton? How could we have thought that we would be parted from her forever and so soon? Now as I think of her, always kind, always gentle and loving, it makes me cry to think that I shall never see her again.

Love from your loving son, Alec

Arthur and K's first child was born in July 1898. They christened him Alexander, not in homage to the boorish flagellant of Midsomer Norton but to honour the Brute's grandfather, Dr Alexander Waugh DD, known to all his descendants as 'Alexander, The Great and Good'. This venerable Scottish minister was, in the early nineteenth century, one of the founders of Mill Hill Grammar School and the London Missionary Society. Although he talked with an impenetrable Lauderdale accent, he is revered by his descendants for one deed above all others — for anglicising the family. It was he who put an end to our scooping porridge with our fingers, to our strapping sporrans to pantless kilts, to blowing bagpipes, tossing cabers, kenting faithers and all those abominable habits that are still considered so quaint north of our border. These reckless ceremonies had bonded Waughs to their chill and puritanical obscurity for long enough. Now it was time for something better. In 1782 the Great and Good packed his bags and moved south with his large and growing brood. London was a revelation to the Waughs. For the first time they could experience for themselves the polished manners, the blithe humour, the dignity and the affluence of southern England from which none of us has ever looked back.

As a preacher, Alexander Waugh was widely admired; as a father of ten children and grandfather of sixty, he was unsparingly adored. In every surviving account, he is portrayed as amiable, modest, fair-minded, humorous and a good violinist to boot. When he died in 1827, in his seventy-second year, his coffin, horse-drawn from Trafalgar Square to the City of London, was trailed by a stream of mourners that stretched for over half a mile. His remains lie to this day with those of John Bunyan, Daniel Defoe and William Blake in the Bunhill Fields cemetery – but I digress . . . In any case, by September 1900, Arthur's little boy's name had been pruned from Alexander to Alec, in honour of his recently deceased uncle, the malarial mariner, and from 1909 onwards Arthur had a special name for Alec, which was 'Billy'.

From the outset Arthur had assumed that the only two passions he had successfully shared with the Brute – cricket and amateur theatricals – should form the basis of his relationship with his own son. By the time Alec was six Arthur had already taken him to see most of the famous Shakespeare plays. He had acted *Julius Caesar* in the nursery at Underhill and taken the title role in a production of *Hamlet* at his grandfather's house in Midsomer Norton. Every summer Arthur and Alec went to cricket matches at Lord's, at the Kennington Oval or on the Hampstead cricket ground. During the day, they played a single-stump version of the game in Underhill's garden. When it was too cold for that, Arthur regaled his little boy with tales of cricketing deeds or the scores of foreign test matches, gleaned from the pages of *Wisden*. At other times they walked together across Hampstead Heath holding animated discussions about literature and 'ideas'. Every night Arthur sat on Alec's bed, drawing pictures in his sketch book, usually of men being killed. Before meals he would read poetry aloud – so much and so often that by the time Alec was nine he was intimately acquainted with all the major works of Shakespeare, Kipling, Tennyson, Browning, Shelley and Swinburne. As the years passed, Arthur's absorption in everything that Alec did and said came to occupy most of his waking thought, and the boy was swept along in the tide of his father's affection. 'My father was a wonderful companion,' Alec wrote, many years later. 'When I look back on my first years I find that every memory I have is connected with him. My nurses are shadowy figures, my mother did not become distinct until a much later day. I remember my father reading to me, my father taking me for walks, my father playing cricket with me . . .'

Alec was small – diminutive beside his classmates – and he never grew above five foot five. At school he excelled in games and at English literature. His brightness could be credited to his father's assiduous grooming, and to the force of his own enthusiasm – not, perhaps, to the hereditary efficacy of his brain. He had perfect manners. I remember him when he was an old man, visiting my father at Combe Florey. Did he make strange clicking noises in his mouth? Did he look a bit like a monkey? These are my memories. Papa was very fond of him.

If the clicking mouth and simian posture were features also of Alec's youth, they probably passed unnoticed by his father, who was pressed to observe a single fault in his elder son. To Arthur, everything that Alec did or said was a glory and a holy miracle, and he was hurt when others thought differently. Alec's headmaster believed that he was a spoiled brat and told Arthur so; another school-master, S. P. B. Mais (later a well-known novelist) accused the boy of 'putting on side of a peculiarly unpleasant sort . . . unbearably rude and unbearably miserable, drifting he knows not whither. Probably he will end up by getting expelled.'

In defence against these accusations Arthur advanced the theory that Alec had two 'soul-sides' to his nature and that the side which he adored was rarely, if ever, visible to anyone but himself. 'There is no doubt that I get the best of it,' wrote Arthur. 'I wish the rest of the world got some more, however.' To an old friend who had recently come to stay at Underhill and had clearly missed the point of the golden youth, Arthur wrote: 'How I wish you could have stayed longer. You and Alec could have explored the world together in his mother's absence, and I know you would learn to like each other. For Alec improves immeasurably on acquaintance. His pearls are hidden in a rough casket: but he shows them shyly to those he loves.' The same point was frequently put to Alec with regular pleas from his father to 'open up your heart a little': 'You are much too ready to conceal your feelings; when you do show them, as you do to me, you are the nicest boy in all the world. But many people won't believe me when I say so because you hide your real self under a rough and rowdy exterior.'

Within a few years of the Brute's death Arthur's paternal devotions had inflated into something of an obsession. By 1911, when Alec was boarding at Sherborne, Arthur was writing to him every day and awaiting his responses in the palpitating manner of a teenage paramour. News of Alec's marks in class or his achievements on the games field was read with more urgency than news of the impending war: team scores and class marks were copied and telegraphed to Arthur's friends and relations up and down the country. In his pocket, wherever he went, Arthur carried about with him his treasured copy of the Sherborne school roll in which he kept a detailed record of all Alec's scores and marks, underlined the names of pupils and masters that Alec liked and carefully noted his weekly position in class. Every Friday after work Arthur left his office in Covent Garden with a small suitcase of clothes, took the train from London 150 miles to Sherborne and set up court at the Digby Hotel, where he invited Alec and his muckers for every meal, befriended their teachers, watched games on Saturday and attended services in the school chapel on Sunday morning.

I think that Arthur may have suffered from the same syndrome that is claimed of the pop star Michael Jackson. Those who are brutalised by their fathers often find themselves unable to grow up: they are consumed with a need to relive their childhood over and over again to get it right. This is what I have heard. Arthur's craven desire to relive his childhood found expression not just in his love for Sherborne and Alec but in a redrawn fantasy-idyll of childhood and home at Midsomer Norton. In 1914 he wrote an article entitled 'Lights of Home' for the now defunct Fortnightly Review:

The old homeward way always finds every one of us a child again. What is it but this longing to revive the heart of child-hood that leads our feet so often to the old, familiar hills? . . . It was here that we were young; here that we first hoped; here that we first loved. And when youth and hope and love are all at an end, it is here that we would choose to rest, returning, like a hunted stag, to the spot where we were roused, in the land which memory has always kept unspoiled and unspotted from the world.

By 1912 the relationship between Arthur and Alec had become so intense that it was not long before those who cared for Arthur began to worry for his sanity. Others were less kind: as he walked into his office at Chapman and Hall his staff would call to him sarcastically, 'And how is Master Alec this morning, sir?' Arthur did not seem to mind for he could barely bring himself to think or talk of anything else. In December 1913 he wrote about it to an Anglican priest who specialised in the confessions of fallen women:

What a poor wavering leaf in the wind am I. I know that I worry too much about Alec, and expect too much. But, you see, I have built my earthly hopes on him, and one must have something to keep one's ambition young and fresh. Once I had a certain amount of ambition for myself. Then I learned through bitter experience that I must give up 'running' myself as a spir-itual speculation and that the only possible way for my life was to forget myself in somebody else! There, that is a true confes-sion, and Alec's career has, no doubt, in consequence grown too large in my imagination. But I do want to see him doing some of the things I have had to give up hope of doing – not only on the cricket and football fields (where he romps to triumph weekly) but along the hard, beaten, stony path of life.

Despite the blatant attractions of Sherborne, with its golden ham-stone abbey and its winding streets of quaint shops and cottages, Arthur had hated his time at the school. He had been lonely and miserable, especially in the first two years, and the discipline was onerous. Sherborne was not his first choice for Alec: Charterhouse, Rugby, Shrewsbury and Winchester were all on his list, but when Alec failed the Winchester examinations and his attempt at a scholarship to Rugby, the idea of Sherborne suddenly presented itself. The school had changed since the brutal old days when Arthur was there, but K, who had heard all the stories, strongly disapproved of Alec going there. Arthur, however, was impulsive and could not abide discussions for fear they would evolve into acrimonious disagreements. As Evelyn recalled in his autobiography:

> He detested controversy and to him all deliberation smacked of it. When any discussion arose, however amicable, and however little directed against him, he was liable to cry, as though in agony:
>
> > 'Let the long contention cease!
> > Geese are swans and swans are geese.
> > Let them have it how they will!
> > Thou art tired; best be still;'
>
> And to leave the room declaiming behind him in the passage:
>
> > 'They out-talked thee, hiss'd thee, tore thee.
> > Better men fared thus thee . . .'
>
> His decisions, even on matters of some importance, were instantaneous.

So it was that Alec was sent to Sherborne.

Four years earlier Arthur had taken a similar snap decision concerning Alec's prep school. Sitting on a train he had struck up conversation with a thin, blue-eyed stranger, with gleaming white centrally parted hair and a curled moustache. He was the headmaster of a new prep school in Surrey called Fernden, and before the journey was ended Arthur had agreed to send Alec to him. What he did not know was that Norman Brownrigg was a perverted and pathological disciplinarian. On his first day Alec's fingers were dipped into sulphuric acid to stop him biting his nails. The food was filthy but Brownrigg insisted that the boys finish up whatever rubbish was plonked on their plates. Alec particularly detested semolina pudding and, on one occasion, just as he had rammed down the last dollop of this hateful substance, he was suddenly, quietly and unostentatiously, sick into his bowl. Brownrigg, who happened to be watching, barked across the room, 'Finish up your pudding, Wuffy', and stood over his eight-year-old charge until the last spoonful of vomit had been reintroduced to the poor boy's system. Because of this, Evelyn was not sent to Fernden.

Arthur had experienced similar cruelties when he was at Sherborne, but when he showed Alec round the school in November 1911 he had either forgotten or wilfully suppressed his negative memories of the place. Indeed, he was exhilarated by the sight of it. The school houses, the chapel, the vaulted dining-hall rejuvenated him instantly – 'I felt no more than 14 when I walked across the court' he told a friend. Alec and Arthur spent 'four days of sheer delight' meeting masters and looking at classrooms. When they left Alec had been offered a place and 'I,' wrote Arthur twenty years later, 'had learnt a little more of the secret of keeping young in a world that will never grow old.'

Soon, Arthur was deep in love with Sherborne in a way that he had never been as a child. The place became for him the symbol of an extraordinary spiritual bond between himself and his son, and on this precise theme he composed an ode and posted it to Alec.

'Tis thirty years since my Father said 'Goodbye' to the dear old school,
And laid his brief authority down in exchange for a harder rule,
But I know thro' the rugged ways of life he has held her precepts dear,
And has lighted his path in the shadowy world by the light that was lighted here.
For the years may come and the years may go, as clouds go over the hill,

But the love of Sherborne binds the son to the love of the father
   still!

'Tis thirty years since my Father sat in the seat where I sit
   today,
And it's hard to believe he was young as I, who is now so old
   and grey,
But I've seen his name on the study door, and the date below
   to tell
Of the days when he loved the dear old school that today we
   love so well.
For the years may come and the years may go, as clouds go
   over the hill,
But the love of Sherborne binds the son to the love of the
   father still!

Another thirty years may pass, another race may run,
Till the place I have filled, that I fill today, shall in turn be
   filled by my son.
He will walk on the slopes above the field and fight our fights
   again
While the Abbey chime, like an ageless rhyme, rings out its
   old refrain!
For the years may come and the years may go, as clouds go
   over the hill,
But the love of Sherborne binds the son to the love of the
   father still!

At the same time Arthur wrote a winding, amorous article about
the school for *Country Life* magazine in which he lost himself in
heady sentiment: 'Most fathers like to send their sons where they
know that they themselves are certain of a welcome. But when we
acknowledge that Sherborne is a dreamer, we would not for a
moment have it imagined that her energy is apt to lose the name
of action . . .' In 1915, he published, in book form, a collection of
his best literary essays, called *Reticence in Literature*. Not only did
he dedicate the book to Alec but went to great pains to ensure that

the cover was printed in precisely the same tint of blue and gold as the Sherborne School colours. 'As for the book itself,' he wrote to a friend, 'I only did it to please Alec.' When Alec won his colours for cricketing prowess Arthur wrote to him: 'The blue and gold of Sherborne have always been my Eldorado, and much as I would have given to see them on myself, I value them much more upon you.'

Arthur's new-found love for Sherborne invigorated him. But the excitement was transient for, as he knew only too well, Alec was growing up, he was boarding a hundred and fifty miles from home, and he was making new friends. Naturally Arthur was excluded from much of his son's life. Seven years after leaving Sherborne Alec (always one to generalise from personal experience) wrote a book entitled *Public School Life – Boys, Parents, Masters*. In it this problem is seen from the boy's angle:

> To a public school boy his parents' interest in his school life must appear superficial. When his father comes down he has to answer innumerable questions as to his prowess on the cricket field; and very often indeed the chief pleasure that his athletic successes brings him is the thought of the delight that his father will experience. But the intimate side of his school life, his thoughts, his friendships, his troubles, his ambitions, do not enter into his relationship with his parents . . . Home and school present to the average boy two water-tight compartments.[2] They are different lives, a different technique is required. And human nature has at least one property of the chameleon.

Arthur was desperate that Alec should treat him not as a parent but as an equal, as a friend, and tell him everything that was going on in his life:

> And, above all things remember, keep nothing from me, for I know all. I beg you always to trust me, and to tell me all your troubles and to be sure of my best help. For

[2] Please note this expression, 'watertight compartments'. It will feature later on.

I am not your 'governor', your critic, or your judge, but always in the darkness and in the light, your true friend, your real sympathiser, and your devotedly loving Father.

At first Alec was obliging, but as his behaviour at school led him into deeper and deeper water he began to withdraw confidences from his father and to polish up his performance as a chameleon instead. Naturally enough he tended to inform Arthur only of the good news. Although at school he was a rebel, and a bolshy one at that, his years there were crowned with enough solid achievement to make any modest parent proud. He won the school prize for English prose, he gave a precocious speech on Byron to 'The Duffers', the school literary society, in which he offended many masters by recommending marital infidelity. Initially Arthur had been involved in writing it, but stopped when his rebellious son refused to moderate its tone. When Alec delivered it Arthur, back at Underhill, was stewing himself into a frenzy of nervous anxiety on his boy's behalf: 'All yesterday afternoon when you were reading your paper I was as restless as a hyena before feeding time. I kept prowling from one room to another – picturing you and wondering how it went. That is 'one way of love' – it is mine – and like all true love it is full of pain.'

There were successes, too, for Alec on the sports field. Arthur was convinced that he would grow up to be a champion cricketer – either that or a famous poet: he did not seem to mind which but wallowed equally in both fantasies. For a time life for Arthur was sweet. As he recalled, a year after Alec had left Sherborne: 'I think your terms in 4a and 5b were the happiest in my life unless it was the weeks when you were getting into the cricket 11.'

The only black cloud seemed far off on a distant horizon. Every week brought news of Sherborne masters and old boys killed in the trenches of the war that was raging in Europe. In 1914 Arthur believed, like many others, that the conflict would be over by the time Alec left school. That autumn all the boys were keen to enlist and Alec was no exception, but he was still too young. For Arthur, the prospect was not then a pressing worry. What he failed to realise in his happy, dream-like state was that Alec's life at school was not all that his letters made it out to be. He had problems, most of which concerned sex.

On Alec's last day at Fernden School, Brownrigg had called him into his study to lecture him on the traps and pitfalls of senior school: 'How can you ask some pure woman to be your wife if you have been a filthy little beast at school?' he had asked. Alec had no idea what he was talking about. When he got home he begged his father to explain to him what his headmaster had meant but Arthur became flustered and ducked it. A year later Alec told him that one of the boys in his dormitory at Sherborne had been expelled for 'smut' and that when he had asked a master what 'smut' was he had been informed only that it was the same as 'immorality'. What? Arthur, guilty at having passed on the first round, gave his son an equivocal explanation as they marched, hand in hand, over Hampstead Heath one summer evening, telling him that 'immorality' concerned 'urges' and that these 'urges' would one day erupt within him, but he was not to concern himself with such things until he was older. Alec, who was only eleven, still could not understand.

It was not long, however, before he knew from personal experience exactly what those 'urges' were all about. One day he was caught misbehaving and, by way of punishment, was ordered to spend the night kneeling on the stone floor of the school chapel. It was there that he first worked out how to masturbate. He had been warned of the evils of this habit, but found the temptation nevertheless irresistible. Soon he found ways to fuel his imagination and magnify his pleasure. A corny novel published in 1912 called *Joseph in Jeopardy* fired him off – so to speak. I recently discovered a copy in a second-hand bookshop and read it with assiduous attention to every paragraph in the hope of understanding my great-uncle better. He must have been very innocent in those days: a few kisses, a whiff of scent, the possibility, but not the actuality, of an adulterous liaison – these were the things that had 'turned him on'. Marlowe's *Hero and Leander* was another inflammatory source, but for Alec, in those early days, the pleasure of his habit was far outweighed by the grief that it caused him. This I have extrapolated from another passage in *Public School Life*:

The boy who practises self-abuse suffers from the misery of an incommunicable grief. He is apart from his fellows. If he told them his secret he thinks they would despise him. He becomes morbidly introspective. He makes vows to break himself of the habit, fails and despises himself. He begins to search for symptoms of his approaching physical and intellectual collapse. If he makes a duck at cricket, misses a catch in a house game, or fails badly in his repetition, he tells himself that the process has begun. There are times when he wants to steal away by himself like an animal that is sick.

In despair he ripped the offending pages from *Joseph in Jeopardy* and threw them away. But even without them his habit continued unabated – until, that is, in May 1914, tormented by guilt and confusion, he confessed all to his housemaster who despatched an unclear letter to Arthur. Arthur wrote immediately to Alec. This last is a minor masterpiece of some sort (though I cannot say which) so I shall reproduce it in its entirety for you here. I have taken the trouble to include a few erudite footnotes in the hope that they might curb your levity and give your reading of it at least the *illusion* of sober scholarship:

My Own Dear Boy,

Stuart-Prince[3] will have told you that he has written to me. I found his letter waiting when I came back this evening; and at first I was rather dazed (as I thought all was going well), and I could not quite make out what he meant. I did not know whether you had got into trouble with a small boy, or what it was exactly. But now that I have been out alone on the Heath, and read his letter several times, I think I understand it all. I gather that you have been unable to break yourself of the habit of self-abuse, and have told him about it, and that you let him

[3] D. Stuart Prince, housemaster of School House, Sherborne, 1913–14; scholar of Corpus, Cambridge, he was deaf.

tell me. I know by experience that there is nothing that eats into and corrodes the soul more than a secret. Now that you know that *I* know, you can feel that there are two of us to fight this trouble – two of us absolutely as one. And I think that ought to be some help to you. At any rate I mean to try and make it so.

And, first, let me carry you back . . . back to your first term at Sherborne. Do you remember how you wrote and asked me what immorality was? And I told you that the time would come when these feelings would get hold of you, and that until then you would rest content, and be thankful to God for your innocence? Well you see, the days have come, as I foretold: and we must reckon with the situation together. And I have not the slightest doubt that you will come out the better and the stronger for having confided in your father.

It is quite natural that you should experience these temptations. Everyone does. As a boy emerges into a man, the sap (as it were) in his body rises, as with trees in spring: and these desires are the result. But nature affords a certain safety valve in what we used to call as boys 'wet dreams' – when you lose a certain amount of sap or seed in the night. Now, if you are old enough to have had one of these dreams, you will know that in the morning you feel slack and weak after it – perhaps with a slight headache. That is because the seed comes from near the backbone, and the backbone is the thread of life. Every time seed is lost from the body, the backbone is slightly affected. But if one feels weaker after a natural loss, it follows that a forced loss of seed, such as self-abuse entails, is much more mischievous. It is indeed a deadly danger because it undermines the very seat of life. The result of self-abuse, if carried on persistently, is first weakness both of body and mind, and finally paralysis and softening of the brain. This is absolutely true: and that is what makes it so perilous.

And something more. The man who is addicted to self-abuse generally becomes the father of feeble and rickety children, even if he is not incapable of being a parent at all. It is an awful thought that someday you might take to a pure girl's arms a body that will avenge its own indulgences upon children yet unborn. It is a deadly thought. It must be prevented at all costs.

So far I have spoken of the effect on the body only: but it is equally bad for the character. Any secret vice is poison to the character – secret drinking, secret drugging, self-abuse. The man who has a secret is never quite frank with you. You know there is something he is keeping back. But more, unless this thing is resisted, it grows. *Crescit indulgens sibi,*[4] and the end is damnation. For unless you learn to resist this temptation young, the power of resistance leaves you, and then, when you are independent in London, and women are at large upon the streets, you go the easy way, and before you know where you are, you are actually dying of the most awful of all diseases. For 75 per cent of the women who live by sin are infected with a disease, which they give to every man who lies with them. And then the body rots away in horrors which I will not dwell upon. It is only too true, Dear Boy, that the wages of sin is death.[5]

And now I will tell you something in return for what you have told me. When I became engaged to your mother, I was able to tell her that I had never had anything to do with any woman in the world. And the chief reason why I had that inestimable gift to give her (for a man's innocence is the finest of all marriage gifts) was largely the fact that, as a boy, I broke myself early of the habit which is worrying you, and so learned to make resistance a daily law of life.

But *how* to resist? You say. Well I will tell you. Say it is Saturday night and the idea attacks you. Put it from you

---

[4] Horace, Odes II, ii. 13, '*crescit indulgens sibi dirus hydrops*': 'His own indulgence makes the dreadful dropsy grow.'

[5] Masturbation was not considered unhealthy until 1710 when John Martens, a quack doctor and pornographer, proclaimed it as such in a book called *Onania*. Martens's fortune derived from the medicine sold in conjunction with his book. The Church did not consider masturbation a sin, or indeed link it to Onan's behaviour in Genesis, until after the publication of *Onania*.

at once. Think of cricket[6] or the day's game, of the probable team next week: and say I swear I won't do it till Wednesday at any rate. If you swear to yourself (and to me) you will keep it: and then Wednesday comes, you can say — 'Well: I managed to resist for one half of the week. Why not for the next? I swear I won't until Saturday.' So by degrees, as Hamlet said of a precisely similar temptation, resistance will bring its own reward.[7] The more you abstain, the easier it becomes.

And choose your reading carefully. Swinburne, who was a victim of self-abuse (as I once told you), is not a very wholesome companion. Nothing inflames the mind like a lascivious picture or a suggestive line of poetry. Try to concentrate on the more manly poets and give as much of your mind as you like to games, out of school. That is the proud boast of the English system that its games banish morbidity. You won't get your firsts unless your body is in subjection. Train the body, by this perpetual effort of putting off temptation, to be the handmaid of the soul, and not its cruel mistress.

I have told you all I know about the subject. A father can do no more. And what helped me to bear the bitterness of Stuart-Prince's letter was his assurance that you are trying, really trying hard, to live a clean and decent life. That in itself is the beginning of grace. What can we, any of us, do but try? And in all your efforts, your struggles, your failures, your beginnings again, in all that makes life one perpetual battlefield, you have at any rate one fellow soldier by your side; one who has fought all your battles before you and knows every inch of the way.

Well I know thy trouble,
O my servant true:

---

[6] Field game played with bats and balls.

[7] Hamlet says to his mother (Act 3, scene 4): 'Go not to my uncle's bed . . . Refrain tonight, and that shall lend a kind of easiness to the next abstinence.'

> Thou art very weary;
> I was weary too.[8]

But Billy darling, your father is by your side. Lift up your eyes unto the hills.[9] Fight the good fight.[10] Faint not nor fear.[11] We have gone all the way together. We shall rest together in the glory that shall be revealed.[12]

Ever your devoted friend, your true and loving father.

Alec had shown courage in revealing to his teacher that he was a masturbator, but what he did not admit, either to his father or to any of his masters at school, was that he had also fallen in love with a boy called Simonds. In the letter above, Arthur had intimated his relief that Alec's trouble did not involve younger boys – a far graver sin than masturbation – and it was not the first time that the subject had been broached between them. Eighteen months earlier he had written:

> As you know, my ambition for you is illimitable. There is nothing I could not hope to see you do. But I would rather that you were ploughed in every exam, and never even get your seconds or your house-cap, than that any boy should be able to say that he had injustice at the hands of Waugh, or any small boy that he regretted the day when Waugh had first spoken to him

History does not record if Simonds regretted the day that Waugh first spoke to him, but the relationship did not in any event last

---

[8] From the Lenten hymn 'Christian, Dost Thou See Them?' in which Jesus's words continue, 'But that toil shall make thee someday all Mine own. And the end of sorrow shall be near My Throne.' The same hymn contains the warning against snares set by the powers of darkness: 'Christian, dost thou feel them,/How they work within,/Striving, tempting, luring,/Goading into sin.'

[9] Psalm 121.

[10] 1 Timothy 6:12.

[11] Deuteronomy 20:3.

[12] Isaiah 40:5; Romans 8:18.

long. Soon Alec was in love with someone else, another 'small boy', this one called Davies Minor.[13] Alec wrote to a schoolfriend: 'I shall never get tired of kissing Davies *mi*, he is a darling. But he is leaving this term, *O lacrymarum fons*, it will be lonely without him.' And as his affair with Davies was still raging on, Alec wrote again to the same friend:

These loves are great passions while they last. They are mad and short and burn themselves with their own fire. I doubt that I shall ever feel again the same ecstasy that I knew three years ago when I discovered that I was in love with Simonds. You will probably smile at this but it is true . . . The love of boy for boy is in my mind one of the most beautiful things in life. The first time we love, we love a person, afterwards we only love love. The first is the greatest and whitest passion and it is usually one of boy for boy.

It is not known to what extent Arthur was aware of these goings-on. Davies was invited to stay with the Waughs in Hampstead in 1915 after he had left the school, but in the event he did not come, 'merely because his silly ass of a father thinks he might be hit by a Zeppelin'. Arthur opened his doors to a constant stream of Sherborne boys and masters during the school holidays, but neither Davies nor Simonds would have been invited, as friendships with younger boys were strictly forbidden. But Arthur wasn't blind. He suspected that secrets were being kept from him, and every Sunday in church prayed vigorously for the moral welfare of his elder son. 'This morning Mother and I went to the 8 o'clock service at St Augustine's (where you were baptised) and by some strange fitness we had the hymn you used to be so fond of as a little fellow. And all the time my thoughts and prayers were of you, and you, and only YOU.' On Alec's birthday, the following year, Arthur went to High Mass at Notre Dame cathedral, in Paris, 'and before the altar

---

[13] William Wookey Northam Davies, died in 1965. He is called Davies Minor, some-times abbreviated to 'mi', because he had an older brother at the school, Henry Davies (born 1896), who became a solicitor in Wales.

of so many historic memories I prayed with all my heart that a good year might be opening before you'.

No sooner had he sent Alec his strictures on self-abuse than Arthur was back with the old refrain. Billy must tell his father more:

> We have had some sorrows to share together this year: but the great thing is that we have *shared* them, and that you have dealt with me as a man. Last year there were some secrets in your life which you had not told me, and in a way I was happy in ignorance. But that is no real happiness. To know all is to forgive all. There may be secrets that you keep from me today: but I hope and believe that they are not many, nor serious. So long as you can confide in me, all must be well: for your very repugnance to have to tell me things will make you avoid doing them. And this has been a year I hope of real progress and advance in character for both of us. Because I learn all the time, side by side with you. I learn to understand and to discount. And *you* I trust learn to rely on my love, and (where experience is of any use) on my judgement. 'The Lord watch between me and thee, when we are absent one from another':[14] and may nothing ever disturb our sympathy, or ever cloud our mutual understanding!

But Alec's letters home still did not tell Arthur all he needed to know: they were factual accounts of cricket or rugby matches, his advances from house captain to school prefect, his marks in class and small items of parochial gossip concerning teachers and pupils.

At the beginning of 1915 Alec informed his father that he wished to leave school before his final year and to fight in France, like other boys, for his country. He was still too young to join the army without his father's permission, which, given the long lists of casualties published in every daily newspaper, was not unnaturally withheld; but Alec resented having to stay on at school and began

---

[14] Genesis 31:49.

to turn against the hallowed place. On one occasion his father was shocked to hear him describe Sherborne as 'a hole'. Alec was moody and adamant: 'It is a poor place bound down by fatuous pedagogues and their antiquated ideas. A rotten lot they are!' Many of his friends had left and so had several of the best young teachers.

By 1915 Sherborne was empty and forlorn and Alec wanted out. But Arthur needed him to stay on, not just to keep him out of the war for as long as possible but so that he, Arthur, might not lose those sensations of vicarious youth that had, over the last four years, made Sherborne so dear to him. Apart from anything else his ambitions for Alec's school career were not yet fulfilled. In February he wrote to him:

> The whole of my heart's ambition these last years has been centred in the hope of seeing you lead Sherborne to great things, your soul well knit and all your victories won. For that I have prayed and thought and wrought — trying to order my own life so that it should be a help to you in ordering yours. Your career has been a discipline to me. Without blasphemy I can truly say that I have nailed my own soul to your cross. I know your troubles, your difficulties, the intolerable loneliness that comes upon every man of spirit now and then. 'Who knows them, if not I?' But let us hold on to the last. We may yet see light before the summer, and you may yet go back in September to the golden year that I have dreamed of so often . . . May you leave Sherborne with a double-first and a history scholarship. Then there will be no more to ask, except and above all, that good name which I know you are really striving hard to leave behind you.

It was not to be. On top of his fond embraces with Davies *mi* Alec had also started experimenting with another young boy called Mervyn Renton.[15] What they did together, I am not sure. Alec

[15] 'Merv the Perv Rentboy', as he was known, left Sherborne in 1918. He became a major in the Royal Artillery and died of wounds at Fort Caput in 1941.

admitted to 'kissing' and to whipping other boys' bare bottoms with a wet towel. It might have been one of those simple pleasures or it may have been something more physically convoluted. Whatever they did, it was classed as 'smut' and they were caught at it, *in flagrante delicto*. The second master, George Morris, wrote to inform Arthur, who rushed immediately to Sherborne, sobbing with grief, to plead with the headmaster, known as the Chief, not to expel his son. By the end of their long and emotional meeting Arthur had won a small concession. The Chief agreed that Alec could finish the term but would not be allowed back for his final year. Renton, as the younger of the two boys and, by definition, the 'victim', was allowed to stay on. Meanwhile instructions went out to the school that no boy was to be seen in the company of that 'dirty little beast' Alec Waugh.

Arthur returned to London a broken reed. All of his dreams, his high ambitions, his soft romantic hopes, all brutally shattered. He also felt humiliated. For four years he had been boasting to his friends and relations about the glories of Sherborne and Alec's fine career there, telling them how much he was looking forward to Alec's final year, when, who knows?, he might be head of house, head of school, captain of cricket, captain of everything. Now he had to explain to them all why those carefully laid plans had suddenly changed – he would have to invent a lie. Arthur's letter to Alec of 5 June 1915 reveals the depth of his despair:

My Own Dear Boy,

The Chief has taken out of my hands all choice in the question which we have so often debated together. He has asked me to take you away at the end of this term; and that is an end of all the matter. But, when I tell you this, I beg you to keep it sacredly to yourself. It is the first time to my knowledge that such a thing has happened to a Waugh. I want no one to know of it, except the Chief, Mother, you and I. It is enough that we should have to bear it. So let us keep it to ourselves. It is enough.

Although Morris has written me a most kind letter, I do not know – and I do not think I want to know – the exact particulars. But at any rate I know that this boy Renton is one whom you have never mentioned to me; and I can tell you, Alec, that I tremble for fear of what other name may come up next. There are two months left of term. I pray you as you honour the peace of your home that this is the last blow that Sherborne is able to deal. I know you will see to that. We have had enough.

You will understand of course that I cannot put in any more appearances at Sherborne in the festal way; so I shall write to the Chaplain to tell him that I shall not be present at Commemoration. And as I know, knowing you better than all the Sherborne world, how sad you will be to have brought such sorrow to your home, I entreat you to do no wrong, nor think it, in the days that are left to you. The honour of the family depends upon your conduct.

I wish you had written to me yourself. Morris wrote the kindest of letters but you had no need of any intermediary. I feel for you and sorrow for you, and love you through all your troubles. And so does Mother. And I told Chief that my confidence in you is such that none of these disappointments shakes my faith in the real Alec, the true Alec, the son of my soul, who has walked so many miles, his arm in mine, and poured out to me a heart that the rest of the world will never know, but which I treasure as a golden gift from God. No failure can disturb my faith in that. And the true test of life still lies ahead of us.

> 'Faint not nor fear: his arms are near
> He changeth not, and thou art dear.'[16]

That is as true of earthly fathers as of the one supreme Father to whose care I commend you in my prayers tonight.

Ever in trust,
Your devoted Daddy

[16] Last verse of the hymn 'Fight the Good Fight'.

For the two remaining months of that term, Alec was shunned by all but a handful of his closest friends, while Arthur quivered in London, deep in a mire of his own despair: 'I cannot now say what I think of Sherborne as a whole. My heart is *really* nearly broken with bitterness and disillusionment.' But through the hazy sheen of his tears, through his hot suffering, Arthur sensed that the bond between himself and Alec had been intensified by the upheaval: 'Dear Boy, I am sure there is some spiritual relation between you and me which transcends the merely material world.' He now believed that he could reach out to his son by some form of mystic telepathy, that he could sense when Alec was in danger or in need of his love. On Sunday 20 June he went, as usual, to the service at St Augustine's Church in Kilburn where he knelt down and started to pray intensely for Alec. Then the choir struck up the very hymn – number 595 – that Arthur always used in his Alec prayers: 'When in sorrow, when in loneliness, in thy love look down and pity their distress.' The coincidence was too great, the sound too emotional for the father to bear. 'And as the choir sang that, I felt in sudden certainty that you were in trouble, so keen that the tears welled out of my eyes, and the people next to me couldn't help seeing that I was crying.'

Arthur was convinced that his relationship with Billy, the 'son of his soul', was a special gift from God. K found the idea incomprehensible, but Alec also believed that he and Arthur could communicate with each other by telepathy even when they were hundreds of miles apart. When the decree went out for Alec to be ignored by all the boys and masters of Sherborne, Arthur once again claimed to have sensed that Alec was in trouble before the news had reached him:

On Monday, when I got your letter, I felt certain you were keeping something back. That is why I wrote and entreated you not to withhold your confidence in me. There must be something super-natural in such a tie: and bitter as the thought of this boycott of my Boy is to me, and mad as I feel with the Sherborne I used to love, I am thankful that you have told me all about it, and that I can share

your grief and perhaps help you to bear it. The nails that
pierce the hands of the Son are still driven through the
hands of the Father also.

The concept of the father and son bound together by the nails that
pierce through them both was one that he had developed earlier.
In a frenzy of saturated religious emotion Arthur now saw himself
as God the Father and Alec as the Saviour Jesus Christ at the point
of death, with both of them, nailed, suffering, bleeding and entwined
on the cross at Golgotha:

> There is a rare sort of crucifix found in one or two Gothic
> cathedrals in France, in which behind the figure of the
> Son, as he hangs upon the cross, is vaguely to be discerned
> the figure of God the Father also. The nails that pierce
> the Son's hands pierce the Father's also: the thorn-crowned
> head of the Dying Saviour is seen to be lying upon the
> Father's bosom. And it is always so with you and me. Every
> wound that touches you pierces my own soul also: every
> thorn in your crown of life tears my tired head as well. Be
> sure of that, as you are also sure (for you *must* be that)
> that when your hour of redemption comes, the first to
> share it will be the father who has never doubted or given
> way. God bless you Billy. It is a bad time but I know you
> will bear it like a man . . .
>
> With deep love and unfaltering trust, still and always, your
> ever devoted and hopeful Daddy

It was Arthur's belief that he and Billy had somehow merged into
a single spiritual entity and, as such, he was willing to share in the
punishment of his son's disgrace. 'Though Sherborne has still the
power to banish her defenders, the fault is ours first and foremost.
And I take the blame with you, my son, and bow to the rod, and
lift up my heart in the hope for better things to come.'

And then, of course, the likelihood of war for Alec dawned. In
Arthur's last letter to his son at Sherborne, he hardly mentioned

the war but on the day he wrote it, he also composed a stirring poem in which the jubilant shouts of schoolboys on their last day are submerged by the din of the summoning guns of France. It was called 'Last Day of Term' and later, when Arthur discovered it crumpled in the pocket of an old suit, he sent it to the *Spectator*. Despite the defeat and despair evident in the last letter, Arthur tried his best to sound an optimistic note:

> I cannot resist a feeling almost of anguish, as Time drives in these last nails – the last half-holiday, the last Sunday, the last concert with its Valete of many memories.[17] A few hours more and the Sherborne where my heart has journeyed almost every hour of the day these last four years will be fading into the past. But I have learned that even if there had been no war and no trouble the hour had struck to go. There are many leaves turned down in the record of the last four years to which my memory will recur often and often in the days to come – golden hours we have spent together, some bright hopes realised and dreams fulfilled and many, very many evidences of your love and loyalty. Sherborne has done that much good for us. 'For the days that have been, we bless thee, Mother of Men.' And gratitude for what has been helps me to look forward with hope to what lies ahead. God bless you, son of my soul, and help us all along our way. And so good-night to Sherborne and a welcome to the world beyond.

> Ever, as you know,
> Your devotedly loving
> Daddy

---

[17] The 'Valete', the Sherborne farewell ode, was traditionally sung by the whole school to those who were leaving at the end of the summer term: *'We shall watch you here in our peaceful cloister / Faring onward, some to renown, to fortune; / Some to failure; none, if your hearts be loyal, / None to dishonour.'*

IV

Lacking in Love

The birth of Evelyn Waugh at ten thirty in the evening of 28 October 1903 was neither an emotional nor an obstetrical triumph, as far as Arthur and K were concerned. Both felt deflated at having had another boy. 'I always longed for a daughter,' Arthur wrote to Alec, thirty years later – it was another of his regular refrains. K consoled herself by giving the new baby an effeminate name, by fluffing up its hair and by dressing it, for longer than was usual even by the standards of those days, in the laces, bonnets, ribbons, smocks and frilly appurtenances of the dream-girl she had craved. Alec, at five and a quarter, tried to lighten the mood: 'Good. Now at least we shall have a wicket keeper,' he said, on hearing of his brother's birth.

But Arthur and K were not for cheering. Quite apart from the baby's sex, its delivery had gone badly wrong. The precise details of Evelyn's birth have not survived but I happen to know that it was a gory affair entailing heavy loss of blood before the doctor's arrival and a great deal of surgical stitching after. K told this to one of her daughters-in-law, who told her son, who told me, so it must be true. I do not know if her father-in-law's Long Fine Dissecting Forceps played any role in the proceedings.

Only one scribbled entry appears in K's diary between 28 October and 17 November that year. After that the entries were occasional and scratched in pencil, which implies that she was still laid up in bed – pots of ink were unwelcome in bedrooms; she did not resume in pen until 24 December. Her first attempt to venture downstairs was on 13 December, a month and a half after Evelyn's birth. Three days later a wheelchair was delivered to the house and on 18 December a fit maid pushed her up and down Hillfield Road for three-quarters of an hour in it. Although by late January 1904 Arthur described K to a friend as 'picking up strength' she was still too weak for social engagements and remained depressed. Postnatal traumas of one sort or another continued to dog her for the best part of that year.

I do not say that Arthur took against Evelyn because of these things, only that it was an inauspicious start to their relationship. I am sure there were other factors. The day after Evelyn was born K received a strange letter from her Tasmanian sister-in-law. It was found, many years later, tucked into her diary at the day of Evelyn's birth and reads: 'What a pig Edmund Gosse must be to tell such lies about you. People like that are a constant annoyance and irritation to one and are much better out of your lives and I know if I were in your place I would have no more to do with him. There are plenty of good people in the world without seeking out the unpleasant.' This is mystifying. What could these lies have been that Gosse was spreading about K during her pregnancy? In my fantasies Great-granny was having affairs with lots of men, Evelyn was a bastard, Arthur was not his father – I am not I, thou art not he or she: they are not they, such things as dreams are made on . . .

In the early days of Evelyn's youth he was a warm, bright, sweet-natured and affectionate child who worshipped his mother. For many years he did not notice K's minor limitations. Adored by all who met her, she was a stoic, the humble backbone of Underhill; aloof, quiet and undemonstrative, she acted as a sponge to Arthur's loquacious theatricality. She was shrewd and prudent, but not particularly bright. She read books uncritically, hated writing letters and was perplexed by poetry. Thrifty and furtive with money, she saved her small allowance over forty years into a substantial hoard at the post office, but told nobody about it. Her savings book was discovered under her bed only after her death. She was born to the Raban family, who may have been anciently Jewish but for five generations at least, were of sturdy Christian colonial stock. K was a teetotaller, who lived for her family, her country and for the Empire. Her brother Bassett, killed in the trenches of the Great War, was ADC to George V at the Delhi Durbar. Her father, grandfather and great-grandfather – judges, soldiers and colonial whatnots – all died in India.

Evelyn knew that Alec was his father's favourite son but, as a small boy, tended to regard this state of affairs as perfectly normal. As an adult he dismissed the problem with the traditional British stiff-upper lip, describing his childhood as 'blissfully happy'. 'I was not rejected or misprized,' he told a friend, 'but Alec was their firstling and their darling lamb.'

Evelyn's biographers have all asserted that, while Arthur preferred Alec of his sons, K's favourite was Evelyn. This was the version put about by Alec, who was made to believe it by Arthur – perhaps to assuage his guilt at the exclusivity of their own relationship. In later life Alec did much to rewrite the history of Evelyn's relationship with his parents, but there can be little doubt that Evelyn believed both of his parents – not just his father – loved Alec best: he was '*their* firstling and *their* darling lamb'. The evidence of surviving letters supports this, suggesting that Arthur and K were united in their unbounded fascination for Alec. It was a *folie à deux*. Although K was officially allotted Evelyn to entertain while Arthur and Alec went out for long walks on the Heath, to cricket matches or to the cinema, her heart was also with Alec and his amazing school career. In this she shared in all of Arthur's enthusiasms, breaking down in tears of emotion when Alec won prizes, gained his school colours or scored well in a cricket match. 'A thousand congratulations! It is almost too good to be true,' she wrote to him. 'How we have longed to see you wearing that blue and gold ribbon and now at last you will do so.' In the morning she would rush to Covent Garden if there had been a late-arriving letter from Alec, so that Arthur could read it in his office. 'You are always with us in spirit,' she told Alec, 'our lives and interests all centre in you.' Her demonstrative reaction to Alec's being on the winning side in a house match has also survived:

My dearest Alec,

Happy, HAPPY, HAPPY! Hurrah! HURRAH! HURRAH! I am so awfully pleased at your winning that cup. It has been my one wish all these days and now that it has been fulfilled it is almost too good to grasp. I nearly went mad with joy – and your 77! Some score that! It was a real fine performance. I am *so* happy, my joy is unspeakable. Thank you ever so much, Ally boy, for the pride and pleasure you have given me. May you always play the game wherever you are and come out strong in an emergency . . .

In her letters to her elder son K frequently complained about Evelyn: 'He was particularly patronising and bumptious these holidays'; 'Evelyn went about in a depressed manner with contemptuous looks.' Remarks like these are interspersed with extravagant praise for Alec, for his 'nobleness of character', for his 'championship of the oppressed and the misunderstood'. She calls him 'my precious Baba boy', 'my pretty fluffy one', 'my little Duckling'. There were no such epithets for Evelyn. K, unlike Arthur, never admitted to her favouritism. When Evelyn once asked her, 'Daddy loves Alec more than me. So do you love me more than Alec?' she replied artfully, 'No, I love you both the same.' 'In which case,' Evelyn retorted, 'I am lacking in love.'

If it were not true that K quietly preferred Alec of her sons, Evelyn nevertheless had cause to assume that she was not ultimately a player in his team. Her first allegiance was to Arthur. When he arrived home after a day's slog at Chapman and Hall, he would shout from the hall, 'K! K! Where's my wife?' and Evelyn would be deserted for enthusiastic, grown-up conversations about Alec. As Evelyn recalled in 1962 of his father: 'My earliest memories of him are of an interloper whose visits confined me to the nursery and deprived me of my mother's company. The latch-key which admitted him imprisoned me. He always made a visit to the nursery and always sought to be amusing there, but I would sooner have done without him.'

When Alec read this passage in a newspaper he wrote to its

author from Singapore: 'How different our lives were! Your day ended at the very point when mine began – with the click of our father's latchkey in the door.'

In the summer of 1912, when Evelyn was eight, he developed acute appendicitis. The doctor decreed he must have an operation. For a week before Evelyn was confined to bed where he composed a little rhyme:

> I hate so much to stay in bed,
>   They seem to think I am almost dead,
> I want to sing, and dance and leap
>   And not to have to go to sleep
> O glory to the time when I
>   May leap and shout mine own war cry.

The operation was conducted with chloroform on the kitchen table at Underhill. Evelyn committed a picture of this traumatic event to his diary. It shows a jubilant doctor waving scissors and a knife in the air as Evelyn is held down by his mother. Another figure (probably Arthur) bangs a chisel into his son's penis. For six days after the operation Evelyn was too ill to write and remained strapped to his bed for a week in order that he would not rip his stitches. When at last he was released his legs were too weak to stand. Arthur sent him to a vacated girls' school to recuperate where they forced him to undergo electric-shock and cold-water treatments. Of course Evelyn was miserable: 'For the first time in my life I felt abandoned.' Arthur sent him a typed letter describing K's supreme courage, her suffering and her anxiety at the time of the operation. Because Evelyn had not written home, he was scolded by Arthur for his ingratitude in an elaborate letter invoking the precedent of Jesus and the ungrateful lepers. At no point did Arthur seem concerned or interested in his younger son's suffering. In *A Little Learning* Evelyn wrote, 'I was moved not to penitence, but intense resentment by this missive.'

At home Arthur did little to disguise his preference for Alec. When Evelyn asked for a bicycle in April 1914 – a contraption for which, as we shall discover, Arthur indulged a peculiar fetishism –

he went off and bought a bigger and better one for Alec, and gave Evelyn a small box of theatrical facepaint instead. As future 'head of the family', Alec was always served first at table. He always got the best presents. Everything Evelyn was given came to him 'shop-soiled and second-hand', and he knew it. When Alec asked for a billiard table it was put into Evelyn's nursery where it blocked the room and was bitterly resented. On his return from Sherborne at the beginning of the school holidays he was greeted by a festoon banner draped across the grandfather clock in the hall which proclaimed, 'WELCOME HOME THE HEIR TO UNDERHILL'. This happened several times until Evelyn finally shamed his father by asking: 'And when Alec has the house and all that's in it what will be left for me?'

Alec and Arthur were a two-man gang from which Evelyn was excluded. No wonder he supposed that they were conspiring against him. From the age of eight Alec was given limited powers to discipline his younger brother and, for a while, contemptuously referred to him as 'It'. Evelyn told friends outside the home that he hated Alec, and believed that his father and brother hated him, too. In 1914, when Evelyn was eleven, Arthur wrote to Alec at Sherborne:

> Mrs Fleming cordially told me that I had never been a good father to Evelyn, who was afraid of me, and at his worst in my presence! Cheery news!! But she told one good story of his sharp tongue. He went round the other evening in a bowler hat. They exclaimed – 'Eve, fancy you in a bowler.' And he replied, 'Yes, it belonged to father first: then it descended to Alec: now to me. In fact it has come down to me from generation to generation of them that hate me.' So she added – 'You see, he is always at his best with me. Quite different from what he is with you.'

Evelyn was not sent to boarding school until he was fourteen because Arthur had decided that, with the imminent prospect of war, he was unlikely to be rich enough to put both of his boys through a good boarding school education so Evelyn was instead sent to a cheaper day school, near Underhill, called Heath Mount. Much of

Evelyn's youth was spent at home with his mother and father while Alec was away at school, and conversation was all of Alec. It was 'Alec this and Alec that', 'Sherborne this and Sherborne that'. Arthur's obsessive interest in his *alma mater* did not recede even after Alec had left the place. The 'goodnight to Sherborne and welcome to the world beyond' that he had predicted in his last letter to Alec at school never materialised. Even when Alec had joined the army a year later, his father wrote to him of Sherborne: 'I dreamed of Sherborne all last night – it was amazingly vivid – every stone of the place stood out – but I cannot remember now any incidents of the dream – only the glowing picture of the abbey and the chapel in the morning sun.' And when Alec wrote to Arthur to inform him that he, too, had had an interesting dream about Sherborne, Arthur was so overcome with emotion that he was 'reduced to tears at the breakfast table. I found it quite difficult to pull myself together and get off to the office.' As Evelyn revealed in his autobiography: 'Every night of his life, my father told me, he dreamed of being a new boy at Sherborne.'

Evelyn naturally longed to follow in his brother's footsteps and to experience at first hand all the excitements of that hallowed place that had so occupied his father's dreams and waking thoughts, but Arthur, as I say, was afraid that he would not be able to afford to send him there. His income had remained the same for several years and war offered no hope of improvement. 'Look here,' said Evelyn to his father, in October 1916, 'Hooper is going to Sherborne in the summer term. Can't you buck up and do some articles for the *Fortnightly* so as to be able to afford to send me also?' Arthur was injured and wrote immediately to Alec to complain: 'Seeing that I had had an assessment that morning for £142 income tax to be paid in January and had worked just on eight hours at my desk and was dead tired, I felt this insult was about the last straw!'[1]

In the end Evelyn was sent not to Sherborne but to Lancing College, a Woodard Foundation school on the Sussex Downs near the sea. He had been put down for Sherborne and taken by his

[1] Evelyn's friend Ernest Hooper entered Sherborne in the spring of 1917. For spying he was awarded an OBE. He ended his career as commissioner of Chinese Customs.

father to see it, but in the year that he was due to go there *The Loom of Youth*, Alec's hastily written, autobiographical novel about his schooldays at Sherborne, was to be published. Arthur arranged a lunch with the headmaster, explaining to him that Alec's book might shortly be in print and that it might be seen, in places, to take a highly critical view of the old school. 'Suppose it is published,' he asked the Chief, 'can I possibly send Evelyn to Sherborne?' In his autobiography Arthur says: 'We agreed that I could not.'

Evelyn was unforgiving that his father had been party to such an 'agreement'. In his eyes Lancing, about which he had heard nothing, was vastly inferior to Sherborne, about which he had heard so much. The decision to send him there was, as always with Arthur, made on the spur of the moment. Evelyn was admitted, before Arthur had even inspected the place, on the basis of a few photographs the headmaster had sent in the post. The reason for Arthur's choice was that Lancing's high Anglicanism might suit Evelyn's religiosity. But Evelyn's religious phase had come and gone three years earlier when he was eleven. Then he had shocked his father by announcing that he wanted to be a priest, but all that now remained of this old enthusiasm was a lingering fascination for Gothic architecture and illuminated manuscripts. He wondered if Arthur's decision to send him to Lancing was some kind of punishment – but for what?

Arthur and Evelyn saw Lancing College together for the first time when they travelled down from London on a cold damp morning in May 1917. They were both struck by the magnificence and vastness of the college chapel. Arthur, according to K's diary, was 'well satisfied with the place', though Evelyn remembered him comparing it unfavourably with Sherborne. They had tea with the headmaster, then Arthur took a taxi back to the station leaving his younger son to his fate. As Evelyn later recalled, 'I parted from him without a pang.'

Arthur was never cruel to Evelyn in the way that the sadistic Brute had been cruel to him, and Evelyn was never afraid of his father. Taken as a four-year-old to Hampstead fair, Evelyn enjoyed himself so much that when Arthur told him it was time to go home for lunch he lay on the ground beating his fists on the grass, yelling at the top of his voice, 'You brute, you beast, you hideous ass.' Arthur was amused. He only beat Evelyn twice and on each occasion it was for defacing Underhill – once for cutting the corners off a mantelpiece with a new knife and once for smashing a hole through the back of a downstairs cupboard in order to crawl into the foundations to play. Arthur needed always to be liked, and he liked to be praised: to this end he was lavish in his compliments to others. Evelyn, on the other hand, had an advanced talent for seeing through people and was blunt in his criticism. In an article for the *Sunday Telegraph* he later admitted, 'My father, though irritable, was constantly kind. I took this for granted in childhood with many other benefits which I have since learned are not universal. Taking good things for granted is the essence of a happy childhood and my nursery days were spent in unclouded joy and love; love of my mother and nanny; not, at that age, of my father.'

His criticisms of Arthur were that he was old, boring and slightly preposterous. Arthur was thirty-seven years old at Evelyn's birth and was grey-haired by the time that his son was old enough to form memorable opinions of him. He was also fat-bottomed, he wheezed due to his asthma and surrounded himself in ostentatious clouds of pipe smoke. His face was red and he talked too much. At school Evelyn boasted to his friends that his father was an officer in the Royal Navy, but the truth was written in his first diary, during September 1911, when he was only seven: 'Daddy is a Publisher he goes to Chapman and Hall office it looks a offely dull plase.' In his autobiography fifty years later, Evelyn elaborated:

Many little boys look on their fathers as heroically strong and skilful; mighty hunters, the masters of machines; not so I. Nor did I ever fear him. He was restless rather than active. His sedentary and cerebral occupations appeared ignominious to me in my early childhood. I should have better respected a soldier or a sailor like my uncles, or a man with some constructive hobby such as carpentry, a handyman; a man, even, who shaved with a cut-throat razor . . . I never saw him as anything but old, indeed, as decrepit.

It may be true that in his first ten years he saw his father as a decrepit old bore, 'a figure of minor importance and interest', but it is also the case that he tried hard to win his approval. It was never going to be easy: anything that Evelyn could do Alec necessarily did better. In the areas of Arthur's keenest interest, cricket, literature and amateur dramatics, Evelyn stood no chance. When he was old enough to pick up a bat Alec, with five years' advantage, could easily bowl him out and, more easily still, reduce him to tears by throwing the ball at his toys, at his rabbit hutch or at his head. In terms of literature and amateur dramatics Evelyn was again too far behind to impress. Alec had acted Hamlet before Evelyn had learned to walk. Arthur had taught his elder son to write poetry as soon as he could write prose. Night after night Arthur read aloud to Alec in his bedroom, praised his juvenile verses and pumped him full of enthusiasm for English literature.

One subject, dear to Arthur's heart, in which Alec took no interest whatsoever, was religion and it was here that Evelyn thought himself able to establish a rapport with his father that would not be eclipsed by his older brother. Every morning Arthur led the family and servants in paterfamilial prayers in the dining room, just as the Brute had done a generation earlier and every Sunday the Waughs went *en famille* to church. Arthur could scarcely open his mouth but to quote from the King James Bible or from Cranmer's Common Prayer, but what Evelyn did not realise – maybe never realised – was that he had no hope on this front either for Arthur had long ago allied himself spiritually to Alec. All of his religious feelings were inextricably linked in his mind with ties of sentiment to Midsomer Norton, to the memory of his grandfather, the Reverend James Waugh, at Corsley rectory, and to his special love for his elder son. When Evelyn was three years old Arthur was already busy writing religious poems to Alec. Here is an example:

'A Boy's Prayer'

Holy, blessed Jesu,
   Life is very wide;
Keep, oh keep a little boy

Always by your side.
In his work and playtime
Wheresoe'er he be
Teach him to do all things,
Lord as unto thee.

Written for dear Alec by his father (June xxix 1906)

When not engaged in the composition of religious verse for his
son, Arthur produced it by the yard for the local church. The vicar
of St Augustine's, Kilburn, let him read it out during the service.

To take the cross on our shoulders, to bear it with willing hand:
To stand at its foot in the darkness on the trampled, desolate
    sod:
To keep our twilight vigil as one of the little band,
And to join our voice to the witness that *this* is the Son of God!
For so, in the golden morning, we shall wind to the vacant
    tomb,
We shall hear the angelic tribute to the Lamb that was sacrificed,
And the stone of despair shall be rolled away from the sepulchre
    of doom,
And we who have suffered with Jesus, shall be risen again with
    Christ!

By 1913, when Alec was at Sherborne, Arthur, as we have seen,
had come to believe that his eldest son was a gift to him from
God and, every morning, he offered up prayers of thanksgiving
for him. His religion centred around Jesus and the concept of
love. 'Love of the world finds its utterance in religion alone,' he
wrote. 'The New Testament has the truest law of life. For it is
the Gospel of Love; and Love is the only thing that counts. "He
that hath Love, hath all," said St John, when he was a very old
man; and no man ever said a truer thing.' Arthur's love for Alec
and the imagined bonds of 'nails that pierce through father and
son' magnified and intensified his religious zeal. I believe that he
justified the intensity of his love for Alec by ascribing it to his

Christianity. It is ironic that Arthur's letters to Alec should be far more religious than those he wrote to Evelyn and yet it was his younger son, not Alec, who early on showed such a keen interest in this subject.

If Evelyn had hoped, as a youngster, to win his father's approval and to gain his attention by showing signs of religious fervour, he came, later on in life, to despise what he saw as Arthur's soppy, debased brand of Christianity. My own father felt the same about love-based Christianity: 'From St John's revelation that God is love,' he once wrote, 'it has been a very short step to identify "love" with a state of vacuous euphoria involving an infantile dependence on group stimulation.'

Whether wilfully, or subconsciously, Evelyn's early interest in religion helped him to feel a part of Arthur's world, not just an appendage to it. It also helped to ingratiate him with his Bible-bashing aunts at Midsomer Norton and enlivened Sunday mornings at home. Most of Arthur's male relations were priests. His grandfather and great-grandfather, two of his uncles and two of his first cousins were all Reverends Waugh. On K's side, too, his father-in-law and his brother-in-law were Reverends Raban. Many of Arthur's friends were priests as well (odd that Evelyn denied this in *A Little Learning*). One of them, the Reverend Kenneth McMaster, was his confidant and counsellor for forty years. Evelyn and Arthur shared their delight in the camp pulpit performances of another, the Reverend Basil Bourchier, who flashed an electric crucifix above the altar and threw salt at the congregation during his services at St Jude's, Hampstead Garden Suburb. K thought he was ridiculous.

When Evelyn was twelve he set up a shrine in his bedroom at Underhill so that he could play at being a priest. He bought some incense and enlisted his aunts to make a frontal for his altar. Instead of the toys that normal boys asked for at Christmas, Evelyn requested that Aunt Elsie send him a crucifix and Aunt Trissie two brass bowls to fill with flowers. He spent many hours at his shrine emulating priestly actions in the flamboyant manner of Mr Bourchier. At Midsomer Norton in the holidays he learned to serve Holy Communion. Alec showed no interest in any of it.

On 24 August 1916 Arthur celebrated his fiftieth birthday and Evelyn presented him with a very special present: a leatherbound volume, printed on hand-made paper, of a religious poem he had written. It was called 'The World to Come; a Poem in Three Cantos', modelled on Cardinal Newman's *Dream of Gerontius* and composed in unrhymed trochaic tetrameters. Like Dante's *Divine Comedy*, 'The World to Come' tells of a soul's guided tour through heaven to the spot where God resides. Although in later life Evelyn claimed that 'the existence of this work is shameful to me', he was justly proud of it at the time. It was a fine effort for a boy of only twelve, full of puff and religious portent, ending with all the pitiful bathos of *Paradiso*:

> Cyprian bade me farewell, saying
> In a voice most sweet and tender:
> 'Now my pleasant task is ended,
> We have travelled far together
> And have viewed all heaven's glory,
> But the time is now approaching
> When we pass on different missions,
> I to pilot wandering spirits,
> You to go before your Maker.
> Now farewell, your time approaches,'
> And I turned towards the entrance.
> *Finis*

Arthur wrote to the Reverend Kenneth McMaster to trumpet Alec's success in a recent Sherborne mathematics exam and mentioned Evelyn's 'most wonderful' present. It was the first time that he had alluded to his younger son in nearly twelve years of regular correspondence with McMaster. 'Not bad for a twelve year old,' he wrote. 'My poor wife sits in lonely sorrow at intervals wondering for what conceivable purpose she was made the instrument or vessel for bringing such creatures into the world. A turnip-faced clod-hopper she could have endured with pride. But these changelings of a distorted muse!'

Arthur often put his own ideas into his wife's head and I suspect that, in this case, it was he, and not K, who wondered at his purpose in bringing such creatures into the world. Whatever he thought of Evelyn's birthday poem he remained convinced that it was Alec among his sons, not Evelyn, who was destined for great things. In any case Alec's time for war was fast approaching and he might, within a year, be shot in the trenches. Arthur's eschatological concerns were not focused on Evelyn's Dante-esque picture of heaven, but on a posthumous rendezvous with the 'son of his soul'. Often he told Alec, 'You and I shall be able to communicate with one another in the afterlife.' Evelyn's intrusions into this exclusive fantasy were as unwelcome as they were irrelevant.

The idea to give Arthur such a glorious birthday present came to Evelyn after observing a similar gesture of Alec's only the year before. For Arthur's forty-ninth birthday Alec had given him a half-morocco bound volume containing the manuscripts of most of his best poems and inscribed it: 'TO MY FATHER *Where the heart lies, let the brain lie also.*' Evelyn could not have failed to notice Arthur's puckered, emotional reaction to Alec's present and doubtless hoped for a similar response as he handed out his own effort a year later. But, alas, the effect could never have been the same. After seeing Alec's present, Arthur wrote: 'My eyes were so full of tears when Alec gave it to me that I could not read a word. Whatever he has been in the world, Alec has at any rate been a devoted son to me.'[2]

At home or at social gatherings Arthur gently teased his friends or, as Evelyn put it, subjected them to 'genial ridicule', but he was never malicious or cruel. Perhaps it was in mistaken emulation of this trait that Evelyn developed his sharp tongue. From an early age he enjoyed the effortless sense of superiority that emanated from his father and, whenever possible, joined with him in ridiculing others. In his diary for August 1914, the ten-year-old described a trip with Arthur to Bath. Architecture and history are of minor importance in this account:

---

[2] Evelyn had his revenge fifty years later when he wrote to Alec to inform him that 'some lunatic' had offered sixty guineas for a copy of *The World to Come*. Did Alec still have a copy? If so, he could make money, too.

We would have had a nice journey down if it was not for the presence of a drunk man in our carriage who kept on making weird signs to his son who answered them with equally weird gesticulations. When we got out we went to the Roman Baths and had a grand time; there was an ass of a guide who showed the others round but Daddy and I did not, preferring our guide book to the repulsive look of that awful guide.

Treats like this were rare, but on the few occasions when Arthur took Evelyn out he invariably impressed his son with his lavish and enthusiastic sense of occasion. On excursions to the Tower of London and St Albans Abbey, Evelyn remembered how he 'gave lively explanations of all we saw, put himself on good terms with Beefeaters and vergers, tipped liberally, creating a little aura of importance about us that was lacking when my mother and I were out alone together'.

If Arthur created for himself an aura of importance it was because, in his own jocular, actorish way, he felt that he was indeed important. He was proud to be a Waugh and engendered in both of his sons a fierce loyalty to the clan. He would frequently invoke the name in reproaching them: 'No Waugh has ever done this before', or 'Your action is unworthy of the name of Waugh.' He told his friends that he expected Alec to be a great success in life and to 'give a new impulse to the family name'. And of course Alec did, though not as great an impulse as his younger brother gave it – but Alec was proud of Evelyn and, to his dying day, recognised him as a vastly superior writer. In 1951 he wrote to his mother: 'Do you quite realise mother dear (I wonder if any of us do quite) how considerable a contribution Evelyn has made to the culture of his day, and how much honour he has brought to the name of Waugh?'

I do not know if Arthur ever bothered to look up 'waugh' in the *Oxford English Dictionary* but if he had it did not seem to affect his passion for the name. As an adjective it is defined there as, 'tasteless, insipid; unpleasant to the smell or taste, sickly, faint, weak, etc.', and as a noun, 'an exclamation indicating grief, indignation or the like. Now chiefly as attributed to N. American Indians and other savages.' J. R. R. Tolkien, author of *Lord of the Rings* and one time professor of English Language at Oxford, told my father that 'waugh' was the singular of Wales and effectively meant a single (no doubt sickly, insipid, etc.) Welsh person. Papa gleefully told this story to Diana, Princess of Wales, but to his dismay she didn't appear to understand it.

In any event none of this was what 'Waugh' meant to Arthur. He looked upon the name with fierce and glowing pride, exhorting his sons to 'reverence the past' as they contemplated it. He spoke frequently to them of the 'sentiment of blood which is perennially thicker than water', 'the ties of family', 'the imperishable passion of home'. On his finger he wore a fat gold signet ring stamped with the Waugh family crest – a wheatsheaf standing on a cushion with an apple stuck on the front or, to put it in the arcane vernacular of the heralds, 'a garb or proper charged with a pomeis vert on a wreath of the liveries or and az'. Evelyn took an early interest in it, drawing and colouring the crest and escutcheon, complete with the Waugh family motto *industria ditat* ('work enriches'), on letters and the backs of envelopes when he was eleven years old. By his bed at Underhill, next to a picture of a Peter Pan–Captain Hook duel, he hung a portrait of Alexander Waugh, the Great and Good, founder of the English Waugh family. The picture is entitled *Dr Waugh and the Perverse Pupil*, a sketch pulled from a temperance magazine, framed in plain wood moulded with crucifixes at each corner. Ponderous and bespectacled, Dr Waugh sits on a throne remonstrating with a bolshy student who is sucking his scarf and turning away. The story of how he brought this recalcitrant boy to his senses is told on the back. Evelyn was so taken by it that he recounted the tale, almost verbatim, in his early school play, *Conversion*.

If Arthur Waugh was proud of his forebears I take my own pride in them for reasons that are unconnected with his. I have never liked the name Waugh, particularly in its anglicised pronunciation. It was originally a Celtic word meaning 'stranger' or 'outsider', but by the eleventh century the Scots had started to apply it as a term of abuse to any member of the retinue of Alan FitzFaald (founder of the noble houses of Stewart and Howard), who had lately barged his way to Scotland from Wales. These unprepossessing invaders were dismissed by the natives as 'walghs' and showered, no doubt, with gob loads of Scottish phlegm each time the word was uttered. Over the centuries the name in its varied forms – Welsh, Welch, Walsh, Wallace and Waugh – came simply to mean a disagreeable Welshman. I wonder if Evelyn was thinking of his distant Waugh ancestors when he described the Welsh silver band's arrival at the Llanabba Castle sports day in his first novel, *Decline and Fall*:

> Ten men of revolting appearance were approaching from the drive. They were low of brow, crafty of eye and crooked of limb. They advanced huddled together with the loping tread of wolves, peering about them furtively as they came, as though in constant terror of ambush; they slavered at their mouths, which hung loosely over their receding chins, while each clutched under his ape-like arm a burden of curious and unaccountable shape. On seeing the doctor they halted and edged back, those behind squinting and moulting over their companions' shoulders.
>
> 'Crikey!' said Philbrick. 'Loonies! This is where I shoot.'

Arthur's family pride did not extend to any connection with these moronic Celts, merely to his immediate forebears. But whereas Arthur was proud of his father for being a fine shot, a figure of note in Midsomer Norton and a trusted doctor, my own pride in the Brute rests solely in his invention of Waugh's Long Fine Dissecting Forceps. Nothing else about him appeals to me. Only in this single achievement do I take ghoulish delight.

Similarly Arthur was proud of his grandfather, James Hay Waugh, for being rector of Corsley for forty-four years. In his autobiography he praises James Waugh's pulpit eloquence, and salutes him for teaching 'all that is meant by family tradition and the love of a name'. But my own pride in James Hay Waugh has nothing to do with his rectorship at Corsley or his eloquence, or even his gifted viola-playing. After leaving Oxford he set up in business with a younger brother, George, at 177 Regent Street, a chemist shop with exclusive rights to import the mineral waters of Vichy, Seltzer, Marienbad and Kissingen. But his fortune was made from his medicinal experiments. These included Waugh's Curry Powder, which is still available today – and delicious – Waugh's Lavender Spike, an ointment for aches and bruises, and Waugh's Family Antibilious Pills. It was this last invention that excites my pride the most. Made from soluble cayenne pepper in crystals, this wonder drug was singlehandedly responsible for curing Queen Victoria's wind. A letter to Waugh & Co. from Windsor Castle survives:

Messrs Waugh,

I beg leave to congratulate you on the result of so valuable a discovery, having no doubt that ultimately it will be generally approved of and preferred to any others, more especially by those men who may, through their professional pursuits, feel the necessity of judging impartially of the discovery in question.

Please send me one dozen bottles for Her Majesty's Use. I sent today such as I generally send – BUT THEY PREFER YOURS.

I am, Gentlemen, your obedient servant, A. Vilmet (Her Majesty's Purveyor at Windsor) Oct 8, 1849

James Hay Waugh's success with Her Majesty's flatus was, alas, short-lived. After a few years he sold his share in the business to his brother and, in the fashion of his father (The Great and Good), entered upon a career in the Church. From his fart-pill profits he built himself a magnificent rectory at Cerne Abbas in Dorset, and when he left a few years later he generously donated it, with all its land, to the parish.

Under George Waugh's sole management, the chemist's in Regent Street earned a great fortune. George became a property developer and two of his daughters married, in succession, the pre-Raphaelite artist William Holman Hunt, while a third married the sculptor Thomas Woolner.

Arthur never mentioned his grandfather's experiments in chemistry. In general he looked down on science and on scientists. The higher intellect, he argued, is interested in literature and 'ideas'.

Scientists, in their mad scramble for facts, are spiritually inert, for 'science', he once said, 'has ridden roughshod over the word and is now found to have effected absolutely nothing in the service of the soul of man'. Evelyn inherited this opinion, which passed, in refined variants, down through three generations of Arthur's descendants. My father was more contemptuous of scientists even than Arthur, mainly because he did not believe any of their claims. He did not accept, for instance, that man had landed on the moon in 1969, or that light travelled: as far as he was concerned its movement was instantaneous. Computers, he argued, did not work:

> They spend a large part of the time frozen, crashed out or in remission, unusable in any way and liable to wipe out all the information they have been given. This misbehaviour is not the result of user-error, but simply a question of mood. One can live a happy and fulfilled life without having anything to do with these machines, which grow more unpleasant and threatening every day.

At Lancing Evelyn took a vehement dislike to his science master, carrying Arthur's science-versus-literature battle from the dining-table at Underhill into his classroom. A letter home, dated 29 February 1920, would, he hoped, win his father's favour:

> My chief activity at the moment is a guerrilla warfare with Treble, the science master. We simply hate each other and spend the whole time trying to score off each other. I am about three up still, although I got detention for impertinence yesterday. My latest piece of hubris is to write my science essay in blank verse. I don't think he will spot it as I have written it as prose and he is most illiterate. Here's a sample:
>
>> This figure shows the apparatus used
>> For making oxygen. The flask is held
>> Upon a tripod and on wire gauze
>> At B, and heated by the flame of C,

A Bunsen burner, and a long glass tube
Convey the gas down to the water trough,
Which, bubbling through the water, fills the jar
At E. The piece of rubber tube at F,
Is there to disconnect the tube and flask,
That when the air contracts as it grows cold,
It does not suck the water up the tube
Nor break the flask.

Please don't think that I am on the road to ruin. All other masters will give an excellent report of my conduct and hard work. This is really done more out of curiosity than anything to see if he can spot it. I doubt that he would notice it even if it were in rhyming hexameters.

Today I am opposing 'This house approves of the education of the masses' in the morning, reading a paper on 'Humour in Art' in the afternoon, and probably speaking in the school debate on 'This house considers that curiosity is the best trait in human character' in the evening. Quite busy.

Please don't get frightened about Treble. I know when to stop, and he is a very contemptible little man. I had another lesson in script from Crease on Thursday. I am really learning an awful lot from him.

Your prodigal son,
Evelyn

Evelyn's attempts to curry Arthur's support in his scraps with school-masters were never successful. Neither did he make any headway in his bold efforts to set those masters he did actually like against his father. 'Terrible man, my father,' he told a teacher at Heath Mount. 'He likes Kipling.' To his tutor at Lancing Evelyn frequently referred to his father and brother as 'the Philistines' until this got back to Arthur and greatly upset him. In general Arthur would not support either of his sons in their rebellion against authority. If he was disapproving of the insolent assault on Mr Treble he was even more distressed to discover that Evelyn had taken to slipping out of the school grounds late at night to walk by the sea with a friend from another house. At first Arthur panicked, fearing that Evelyn, like Alec before him, had taken to homosexualising with younger boys that would be the cause of another devastating Waugh scandal. Evelyn never knew of his brother's disgrace at Sherborne until he read of it in Alec's memoirs in 1962 for the secret had been closely guarded. His seaside escapades were entirely innocent, but Arthur wrote in desperate tones. Evelyn's nonchalant response was recorded in his diary:

> We were just going down to Shoreham to get some wine when I got a frenzied letter from Father who has heard about my going out. He was quite unconvincingly rhetorical about it and threatened to take me away if I didn't promise never to do it again. I think he is absurd, but I am rather glad he has taken a strong line about something at last.

Arthur's original letter is preserved in the British Library:

> My dearest Evelyn,
>
> Mother and I had a sickening shock when we learned this evening that you are making a practice of escaping from the house and going down to the seashore at night. It is years since we have heard anything that has so disturbed us. That you, a House Captain, in the confidence of your leaders, should play such a rotten and contemptible game. It is unworthy of the name of Waugh and doubly unworthy of yourself of whom we have always been so proud.
>
> I can't threaten my own sons. I never have. I can only appeal to them. When Alec told me this sort of thing was going on at Sherborne, I asked him for his word of honour that he would never do it. He gave me that word and he kept it. I appeal to you to send me by the first post your honourable assurance that never again will you break bounds, never go out at night, never do anything so fatuously

foolish to endanger your whole future. If you give me that word, I know you will keep it up. If you do not give it I shall take my own steps even if it be to the entire upsetting of your future career. I cannot have a son of mine betraying his trust and be privy to his conduct.

Evelyn, I did not think it of you. Mother did not think it of you. We are deeply hurt and humiliated. I beg you to write and give us your promise. I feel sure you will. It can only be thoughtlessness that has led you into such an entirely silly, vain and purposeless display.

Please write by return and restore yourself to the confidence of your loving Mother and Father.

It was typical of Arthur to invoke Alec's good example in reprimanding Evelyn, and, in this case, it was also dishonest. When Alec saw part of this letter reprinted in Evelyn's autobiography in 1964 he wrote to his brother: 'I was surprised by our father's outburst about your nocturnal excursions at Lancing. I never considered breaking out at night at Sherborne and I don't remember my father ever having discussed it with me, certainly not having extorted a promise from me.'

Evelyn's relationship with Arthur deteriorated sharply while he was at Lancing. The Treble letter was exceptionally detailed and jocose; maybe because he wanted something out of Arthur, it starts: 'I am out of money. Could you send me a few pennies, do you think? The cost of living is very high now that the grubber has started having cream buns and eclairs.' In general, when he was not appealing for funds, his weekly letters home were dutiful, uninformative, disengaged and often negative in tone: 'Work goes fairly well but running rather depressingly. I am afraid I have little hope of getting in the team. All the people who had flu last year will be running this time'; 'Is there any merit in these verses? They are a bit sentimental I am afraid. I don't think the first verse is bad, is it?' Perhaps fearing that his father would take less interest in his achievements than he had in Alec's at Sherborne Evelyn deliberately played everything down. Even when he won the Scarlyn Prize for Literature his tone was studiedly disinterested:

> Dear Father,
>
> I've got the Scarlyn, all right. It was put up yesterday. It hardly seemed worth writing as it wouldn't go before tomorrow. I am a little cheered. Of course it is no testimony to my brain – there was no serious competition.

Arthur was irritated by Evelyn's disaffected attitude. In *One Man's Road*, he recalled, 'Alec was up to his neck in the life of Sherborne. Evelyn, on the other hand, took the routine of his school in a sort of negligent stride. He did what was required of him but he did it without relish or genuine interest.' In response to one particularly aloof effort from his younger son, Arthur reprimanded him:

> Dear Evelyn,
>
> Many thanks for your letter which had been eagerly looked forward to. The art of correspondence will be found, upon a study of the examples left us by the greatest masters, to consist not so much of rigid communication of facts, as in the exchange of views and sentiments between those who are united by a mutual sympathy. Lovers do not communicate many facts, but their mutual interchange of notions and emotions, revealing the hidden springs of life and character, have undeniably afforded them infinite satisfaction and will continue to do so as long as ink and paper survive.

The excitement and intense involvement that Arthur had shown over Alec's school career did not exist for Evelyn at Lancing. Until his last year Evelyn never asked friends to stay in the holidays. With Alec there had been a continuous stream of masters and boys from Sherborne visiting Underhill in the holidays. Many years later, Evelyn felt guilty about this: 'Young friends were a necessary requirement of my father's well being, and I did not provide them.' He knew that Arthur lacked the sense of identity with himself that he had shared with Alec at school. His recollection for the *Sunday Telegraph* in 1962 is a little sad:

> My brother was a zestful schoolboy and my father shared all his enthusiasms. He would have liked to do the same with me, but my school was less conveniently placed for visiting [*sic*] and the hard times of the First World War made hospitality difficult. Moreover I was not a zestful schoolboy. After my first two years I was not unhappy but I had few enthusiasms to impart. I was reticent, wrote dutifully once a week but seldom sought sympathy or advice. It was a disappointment to him that he did not get from me the renewal of youth which my brother had injected.

In his late years Alec admitted that his father's favouritism had given him a superiority complex. 'I was confident that I was going to make a considerable mark in the world. Evelyn may well have felt himself relegated to second place.' In an unpublished manuscript, entitled 'My Childhood', he had written: 'For my first five and quarter years I was an only child, and I remained an only child to all practical purposes right through my childhood, my brother Evelyn being in those early days no more than an encumbrance in a corner. My childhood centred round my father.'

At the end of his life Alec went sombrely through his papers, sorting manuscripts and letters into batches. Those from his father he tied neatly together with string and appended to them in his tiny, spindly handwriting, a note of explanation:

> I feel that these are some of the most remarkable letters ever written from a father to a son. There are those who may feel that they are too personal to be read outside the family and that they should have been destroyed. After very careful thought I feel that my father would like them to have been preserved and I think that they will be of some interest to the student. I believe that my brother Evelyn will be an object

of public interest for many years, and the compiler of a thesis will surely be aided by an insight into his father's character. No equivalent relationship existed between my brother and my father, and the fact there was no such relationship may provide a clue to my brother's complex character. I do not see how any one could read these letters without realising what a wonderful father I had.

A.W. 1970

V

Out in the Cold

In August 1914 Alec, like most of the boys in his class at Sherborne, had been eager to leave school in order to fight the Germans, but within a year the war had emptied out the place, and the list of pupils and masters killed in the conflict was growing weekly. Arthur kept a weary eye on them and reported the latest in letters to his friend Kenneth McMaster:

> Do you remember Cornish — the Sherborne boy with a smile — whom you liked at the station? He is shot once through the left hand and three times through the right arm and has no sensation or movement in his right hand at all. And Jack Woodthorpe has lost an eye and a part of his jaw is shot away: and I know not how many friends are gone altogether beyond the reach of the enemy's hate. And this is the glorious war which was to end at Xmas 1914.

Two weeks later the son of another of Arthur's priestly friends, who was chaplain at Sherborne school, was shot dead leading a valiant charge from a trench in Northern France. Arthur sent his grieving father a poem, from which I quote the first verse:

> Bright be the morning sun, Dear Boy,
> Bright as your happy parents' joy,

> That sees you gathered and enrolled
> In the Good Shepherd's guarded fold,
> Where, freed from fear, and safe from harm,
> He holds his lambs within his arm.

By the end of his last term, in the summer of 1915, Alec was no longer convinced of the glories of war – in fact, he was dreading the prospect of an army career. He, too, looked at the lists in dismay, convinced that the name of Alec Waugh would soon be up there among those of the fallen. Little did he know then that, within twenty months, nineteen of the forty-one boys with whom he had enrolled at Sherborne in the third term of 1911 would have been killed in action.

When the headmaster refused to have Alec back for the winter term of 1915 he might as well have pronounced a death sentence on him for he had no other option than to join the army. On 8 September Alec went into training, first at Lincoln's Inn OTC for two weeks and from there to a camp at Berkhamsted in Hertfordshire. He hated the gruelling routine of long marches, meagre food and sleep deprivation. By August he had severed ties with Davies *mi*. 'He can never lie in my heart again,' he wrote to a friend, '"dead and forgotten as last year's flowers and all sweet things that have had their day". I have never risen to such heights as I did with him. He was my pilot star. But the passion is dead now.' Later he was to discover, to his great distress, that Davies had only canoodled with him in the first place because he was on the rebound from another boy: 'So he chucked Taylor[1] and thought that to make up he would let me kiss him and so that was the only reason of what I have considered so great a triumph. Afterwards, however, he said he actually got rather keen on me. Which only proves that he is a bigger ass than I thought him to be.'

Alec had never told Arthur of his love for Davies Minor. These things were kept secret, strictly concealed in the 'watertight compartments' that he had described in *Public School Life*. In 1919

---

[1] Frank Sherwood Taylor went on to become a popular science writer and was a director of the Science Museum at the time of his death in 1956.

he gave his brother instructions in the chameleon art of separating home and school life. Evelyn was impressed by the whole 'watertight' concept, confiding to his diary on 23 September: 'Alec once said that he kept his life in 'watertight compartments'. It is very true; here I am flung suddenly into an entirely different world, different friends, and a different mode of life. All the comforts of home are gone but one doesn't really miss them much.' In his fragment of an unfinished novel, written a year later, Evelyn included a character, Ralf, who was based on Alec: 'One of the awfully clever things that Ralf had said was that life should be divided into watertight compartments and that no group of friends or manner of living should be allowed to encroach upon any other.'

Evelyn tried to emulate Alec's 'awfully clever' example but his own watertight compartments were prone to leak. When he started at Lancing in 1917 he was proud of his family. He allowed his friends to send their English essays to Underhill for Arthur to mark, and invited his father and brother to address the Lancing College Literary Society, but after a while, as he started to integrate with the life of the school, he chose to keep family and friends apart. For one thing, Arthur was too interfering: he always wanted to be best friends with his sons' best friends. He would show off with them, woo them with his charm, stay up late talking to them, reading them poetry or extracts of Dickens after dinner, and hogging the conversation at table. In effect he stole them for himself.

Dudley Carew, a close Lancing friend of Evelyn's, came to stay at Underhill and noted in his diary: 'The books and rooms are in such perfect taste and I can truthfully say I've never enjoyed myself anywhere else half so much and I think I made one complete conquest – Arthur.' He was so impressed by the old man that he prayed Evelyn might one day 'grow into the comfortable image of his father'. Afterwards he started a private correspondence with Arthur and before long he was asked to Underhill at Arthur's invitation rather than Evelyn's. In some ways Arthur seems to have preferred him to Evelyn. In a twenty-first-birthday letter to Carew he made a pointed comparison with his younger son: 'With all my heart I wish you all good things; what is more I am confident that you will attain them. You are not afraid to work and you realise that without work there are no prizes. You do not despise the things that matter or speak cynically of character . . .' Many years later Carew wrote, 'I was so attached to Arthur that it is hard to be objective about him.' Evelyn, not unnaturally, dropped him as a friend. In a letter to a friend after Evelyn's death Carew wrote of the end of his friendship: 'I realised that it was inevitable. I had been too close to him, too close to Underhill and to his parents, Arthur especially.'

On the rare occasions when his friends came to Underhill, Evelyn did his best to steer them away from his father. Dudley Carew recalled how he loved listening to Arthur telling stories. As he sat in the book-room awestruck by Arthur's stream-of-consciousness monologue, Evelyn became restive:

> Sometimes he would content himself with sighing, sometimes he would say outright that he had heard the particular story his father was telling before – not once but many times. Then it was the turn of Arthur to assume an air of meek martyrdom, an air calculated to bring out the worst in Evelyn, and the atmosphere round the table would become sulphurous.

In the company of friends Evelyn yawned with boredom, clicked his tongue and rolled his eyes to the heavens whenever Arthur held forth. One of his schoolfriends recalled Arthur turning to him and asking, 'How is it, Evelyn, that you are so charming to your friends and so unkind to your father?'

'Because,' replied his son, 'I can choose my friends, but I cannot choose my father.'

Alec's school and army friends were also dragged into close relationships with Arthur. Often this was successful. When one came to stay at Underhill Arthur read aloud a second-rate poem by Austin Dobson, 'Molly Trefusis'. Two years later, the friend wrote to Arthur: '"Molly Trefusis" is not an especially good poem but it is almost sacred to me now. It means you and Alec, and the first time you read to us, as Alec and I sat on different halves of the old chintz armchair in front of the fire. I shan't ever forget that evening. I felt too happy to live. I was to have gone the next day; but I told Alec I couldn't. I must stay.'

Alec was not always pleased when Arthur moved in on his friends. When Claude Hamilton came to stay at Midsomer Norton in the summer of 1915 he was careful to ensure that his father did not dominate the proceedings. While he and Claude cavorted about the house spouting 'ideas' at each other, Arthur was left to talk with his maiden sisters. It nearly broke his heart. He complained that Alec's spirit had 'stiffened', that all of his 'old tenderness' had gone. 'I suffered a lot those weeks,' he afterwards recalled, in a letter to Alec, 'while you and Hamilton were thundering against one another: the couple of you seemed so arrogantly certain of yourselves, so contemptuous of the voice of experience.' This was Arthur's worst nightmare: youth spurning age.

In August 1915 Alec had a poem accepted for publication by the *Chronicle*. This was followed by more verses in *Poetry Review* and a controversial article on 'The Public School in Wartime' for the *Evening Standard*. By now he was convinced that he could make his mark as a writer or a man of letters in the manner of his father, but the army was a bleak impediment to his progress. The prospect of war made him moody and depressed. At Berkhamsted he was given leave for one weekend each fortnight. His fellow cadets spent a proportion of theirs in nightclubs and bars, but Alec never did: he and his father lived for each other. 'I doubt if father and son could have been closer than we were during those months,' he wrote. 'I never needed any company but his. All I wanted was to be alone with my father and talk of poetry and of writers he had known as a young man.' Arthur's memories of that time were similarly rose-tinted: 'The remembrance of those days is so poignant as to be almost intolerable,' he wrote, 'but, seeing that they were among the most significant in all the course of one man's road, their record cannot honestly be shirked or mitigated.'

The fear that Alec might be dead in a year's time made them even hungrier for each other's company. Arthur would meet Alec off the train at Euston station and together they would make their way to a cinema, usually to see a Charlie Chaplin film, then chatter excitedly all the way home. 'In the evening we read poetry together, as though we had made an unspoken alliance to share all the interests possible before it might be too late,' Arthur recalled, 'and every Sunday evening father and son went back to Euston, and talked at the barrier until the last moment before the train was off.'

Although in their autobiographies, both Arthur and Alec remembered discussing poetry and literature on these occasions, the surviving correspondence suggests that they also talked a great deal about Sherborne – a subject that Arthur simply could not drop. The other main topic was Alec's state of mind. He had declared that life was pointless, and this disturbed Arthur greatly. Having geared his whole life around his son's career, having created and afforded him opportunities that had never been available to himself at that age, Arthur despaired at his son's black moods.

For the first time it dawned on him that he might have spoiled his golden boy by allowing him to become too self-absorbed. Perhaps the headmaster at Sherborne had been right all along:

> Dear Boy, what you really must take to your soul is the truth that no man can live to himself alone. Your dreams of life have hitherto been too self-centred. I blame myself greatly. I have lived entirely in your career, feeding my fatherly pride. I should have been much wiser, no doubt, not to let all the world know – and you among them – how engrossed I am in you. But I can only love one way, and I have to pay for it. But the punishment will be too hard – harder surely than I deserve – if, at seventeen, with life before you (as we hope), you throw up the struggle and protest that you have lost confidence in life.
>
> All the world is in fetters now and you have at least for consolation the entire devotion of your father. But for all of us who are worthy of the name of man, the road must wind uphill all the way, the crown of roses must be thrown aside, and the crown of thorns must tear the brow. 'Is it nothing to you all ye that pass by? Behold and see, if there be any sorrow, like unto my sorrow.' . . . For the world can only be conquered by love, by submission, by discipline. Some of that discipline you are getting now, in bitter form enough, but it may be the golden time for you if only you

will not turn aside from the voice of Wisdom and close your ears to good advice. Be confident; be courageous; be steadfast. I see already a great change in you for the better . . . You seem to have softened again and, what is more, to have changed to a better man than you ever were before. You are once more the beloved son who walked the Sherborne slopes with me, before the coming of evil, happy, expectant, confident in life, filling me every morning with thanksgiving that I should be alive and the father of such a son. Here I believe is a proof that the discipline of life, however bitter, is what every nature needs: here I see the messenger of love, bringing its own in its hand.

Do not for a moment lose confidence in life. 'Though he slay me, yet will I trust in Him.' It is a pagan confession of faith, but I have often said it to myself in hours of suffering and doubt. 'Though he slay me . . .' but if he let me live, then after all these tribulations my life, my art, my everything I love shall be devoted to the cause of gratitude . . . 'Thank God for life! Thank God for you!'

Ever, Dearest Boy,
In hope infallible, Your devoted Father

But, despite Arthur's most fervent efforts Alec could not be easily bucked. His days remained dreary and miserable – for all he knew his whole life would be over in twelve months' time before he had had a chance to fulfil his dream of becoming a famous poet. Arthur tried every argument he could contrive to rally his son's flagging spirits. He begged him to stop worrying about things that *may* happen: 'You *may* not be hit. You *may* be hit slightly and come home like Lumley. Many many things *may* happen.' He pointed out that the chances of Alec earning his living as a poet were slim. Wordsworth had been a controller of stamps and Matthew Arnold toiled all his life in the Education Office. He urged him to reflect on the noble life of a soldier, on the value of dying for one's country and, above all, not to brood, not to be ungrateful for the life God had given him: 'I want you to be hopeful. Yes, I want that more than anything just now and I pray for it all the time.' He tried to paint a picture of the future that would contrast optimistically with Alec's doom-laden vision of death in the trenches. He imagined him married to a caring wife, who

> I am sure will be very proud of your poetry, and just a bit fond of talking it over with your old Daddy, when he drops in to tea on Saturday afternoons. At your age I had never thought at all of the future. Think not too much, beloved, however bitter the path today. I live in such dreams as these – the war over, your character strengthened by discipline, your way clear before your feet. And your old father, sitting by you and yours in the sunset happily murmuring his *Nunc Dimittis*.

In those far-off days the relationship between father and son was at the peak of its intensity. To the objective eye their behaviour might have resembled a pair of star-crossed teenage lovers. 'I simply go about thinking of your love for me all the time,' wrote Arthur, 'and I think the devotion is deeper since it no longer feeds itself with form-places, scores or achievements, but is just a matter of our own souls and their sweet companionship.' And all the time there was a brooding awareness that the war might snatch it all away: 'If you fall in this war, I have nothing more to do than creep into my narrow bed, and the sooner sleep comes, the sooner shall I be released from suffering.' Arthur's need for Alec's company was hot, clammy and compulsive. No sooner had he returned home from Euston station on Sunday night than he would sit down to write a letter full of sweet or hurt memories – 'I want to see you again badly, even if you do think all my ideas the lumber of the scrap heap, and all my gods the idols of a twilight day!' and again the following morning:

> Nothing will ever dim my memory of the happy hours of yesterday. It was a truly golden time and the happiest thought to me is that you are still the same old Billy, always glad to see me and full of interest and confidence.

I see other people sitting about with their sons and seeming to be happy: but nobody seems to have a son so thoroughly in sympathy and loyalty as I have. Surely if God still holds his own in heaven, he will not let so true a tie be broken. But even death could not do that. You will always live for me in every place we have visited together and every high thought and hope that we have shared. God bless you most dear Billy. There is no one like you to your ever devoted father.

Alec's letters to Arthur are far less passionate than the ones he received. They show a lively interest in Arthur's journalism, in books, cricket, Sherborne news and training-camp gossip, but where Arthur could happily fill his epistles with ruminations on the state of their extraordinary bond Alec always replied in sanguine, down-to-earth terms: 'I have left my sponge and toothpaste as well as my pen at home, love to all, Billy.' The letters he sent to friends at this same time are far more cheerful and robust. They seldom mention Arthur.

During his time in military training Alec thought romantically and often about Sherborne. His father frequently reminded him of how the events of June 1915 had left him feeling broken and old and this made him brood on the injustice of his departure from the school with increasing resentment. He honoured the promise to Arthur that he would keep the details of his disgrace from Evelyn and his friends, but he felt a burning need to explain and justify himself.

For several months he had been sending Arthur his poems, which Arthur would either return to him corrected or forward to friends in the press for publication, but now it was time for the precocious young soldier to turn his talents to something on a grander scale – to write a novel. By dragging himself out of bed at half past four in the morning and returning to the manuscript at night after his day's parades, the seventeen-year-old cadet succeeded, in just seven and a half weeks, in completing a novel of 115,000 words. In later years Alec was to describe *The Loom of Youth* as his 'love letter to Sherborne', but that was not how Sherborne saw it when it came to be published a year later.

In his autobiography Alec claimed of *The Loom of Youth*: 'I did not offer it to Chapman and Hall because I did not want the world to say that I had only got it published because I was my father's son. Nor did I ask my father to recommend it to his friends in the trade. I wanted to do this on my own.' This was not strictly true. Arthur was in fact asked by his son to publish it but refused to recommend it to the board. In *One Man's Road* he wrote, 'My own position in the matter was not an easy one. From the day when he sent me the first chapter I felt that I could not publish the book, seeing that I knew so many of the people involved.' This is nearer to the truth. What he had written to Alec on seeing the first draft of the first part in January 1916 was this:

Dear Billy,

I have now read the manuscript. It is absorbingly interesting to *me* but I do not see how it could be published. Neither you nor I could ever go to Sherborne again if this book appeared . . . The portraits of your contemporaries are too candid to be tolerated by them. So far there seems to me to be hardly any fiction in it at all. Only fact. As a spiritual diary of your life it is of the utmost interest and value . . . but if it were printed you would make enemies everywhere and that would be sheer folly. I can recognise nearly everyone. So I think the portraits must be very good, but that is just the damnation of the book. All the world would rise against you and Sherborne would be wronged . . .

I think you will agree with me about the prudence of publicity; but I hope you will preserve the record and go on with it. Perhaps in years to come it might be touched up and brought out when these old feuds are forgotten and the heart is colder in remembrance. So do go on with it. It helps me to understand you a little better, if that is possible, than I did before.

Years later Alec stuck this letter into a scrapbook of items concerning *The Loom of Youth* and next to it wrote, 'I must confess I smiled to myself when I read this letter. Does he really imagine that I am going to write an entire novel so that he can understand me better?'

Arthur must have been relieved as publisher after publisher rejected *The Loom of Youth* — Secker, Constable, Hutchinson, Methuen, and Chatto and Windus all turned it down. 'I must confess that I was surprised to read some of the letters which accompanied the refusals of one after another of my colleagues and rivals to have anything to say to my son's first novel,' he wrote in *One Man's Road*, 'Once or twice I was sorely tempted to change my mind, and recommend the book to my own board . . . but without a little editing, my conscience could not shoulder the burden.'

As Arthur stubbornly continued in his refusal to help, Alec grew bitter trying every ruse he could think up to make his father relent: 'The thing is clearly unmarketable,' he expostulated, 'it had better be put away and forgotten.' But still Arthur would not budge. Twelve years later Alec wrote another novel called *Three Score and Ten* about an intimate relationship between a father and son closely based on his own with Arthur. In this book the fictional father and son are both lawyers. The father 'lived in and for his son . . . His life was lit by a purpose — his absorption in his son gave a meaning to the most commonplace incidents of his day', but when it comes to helping his son in his legal career, the father is too afraid of accusations of nepotism to act:

> Not only would he not help his son to work through his own offices, but he would not make use of the quite considerable influence he possessed. Hilary had the sudden feeling of being rudderless in life.
>
> 'He's done nothing for me; he never will do anything for me,' he thought. 'I've got to run my own show. Well, and I will, since he insists on it.' In a belligerent mood he came to that decision and set himself to its fulfilment.

Alec tried to win his father's support by despatching the manuscript to him in sections, chapter by chapter. Arthur returned each batch with suggestions and corrections, all the while praying that the book would get no further than Alec's bottom drawer, but a year later, as Alec was admitting to his friends that he was desperate and would 'gladly accept any contract', he received an offer from an enterprising new publishing house, Grant Richards. On 31 January 1917 Alec, knowing how much his father was opposed to publication. wrote to him: 'Grant Richards has accepted *The Loom*, offering terms which seem to me as good as I could expect . . . I doubt if this will cause unqualified satisfaction at Underhill but I am afraid I am too much of an egoist to feel anything but an enormous elation.'

Arthur was petrified when he heard the news and tried helplessly to hide his emotions in his reply of 1 February:

> Of course, dear Boy, I am very proud that *The Loom* over which we spent so many happy hours last year is to see the light of day and I congratulate you with all my heart. You know that no one has been from the first more deeply concerned in its fortunes than your dear old Daddy.
>
> . . . Of course this means the end of your brother as a Shirburnian, but I have always been very uncertain about the advisability of sending Evelyn there . . .
>
> Dear Billy, I hope you quite understand how pleased I am for your sake but just for the moment the situation bewilders me a little: but I will not 'panic' and I feel sure that things will turn out all right. But I know you will go through it finally from the point of view of taste and judgement. Remember: before it appears you may be in the thick of it in France: you may even be − God knows where − let it remain as a worthy memorial to your time at Sherborne, stripped of any petty reprisal, clear eyed and eager hearted, as you used to look as you came down the Digby Road to meet me in the morning sunlight in the days which I grow surer every month were the happiest my life is ever going to see.

And God bless you dear, dear boy in everything you do.

Your devoted old Daddy

If there was any bitterness between father and son over the publication of *The Loom* it was soon buried with Alec's tender-hearted
dedication of the book to his father. Composed in the same effusive
open-letter style that Arthur had used in dedicating his own book,
Reticence in Literature, to Alec two years earlier, it was a very public
declaration of filial love. In *Reticence* Arthur had indulged his passion
for Alec over two meandering pages, ending:

> The Sherborne days are drawing to a close now . . . But what-
> ever lies ahead of us the past will always be our own. 'The
> gods themselves cannot recall their gifts'; and among the best
> gifts which life has brought me have been the comradeship,
> the sympathy, and the unclouded devotion, which you have
> given with such full hands to your equally devoted Father,
> ARTHUR WAUGH.

Now it was Alec's turn to repay the compliment. Arthur later
recalled: 'When I read, in my son's crabbed handwriting, the letter
of dedication addressed to myself, I should have been a poor sort
of father indeed if I had not felt that the harvest of parentage had
come home in golden sheaves.'

As it appears in all printed editions of *The Loom of Youth* Alec's
dedication is by far the most emotional letter that has survived
from son to father and is written in the ripe, intimate language of
his father's most florid epistolic style:

My Dear Father,

This book, which I am bringing you, is a very small return
for all you have given me. In every mood, in every phase of
my shifting pilgrimage, I have found you ever the same – loving,
sympathetic, wise. You have been with me in my success, and
in my happiness, in my failures and in my disappointments,

in the hours when I have followed wandering fires. There has never yet come to me a moment when I did not know that I had but to stretch out my hand to find you at my side. In return for so much, this first book of mine is a very small offering.

But yet I bring it to you, simply because it is my first. For whatever altars I may have raised by the wayside, whatever ephemeral loyalties may have swayed me, my one real lodestar has always been your love, and sympathy, and guidance. And as in life it has always been to you first that I have brought my troubles, my aims, my hopes, so in the world of ideas it is to you that I would bring this, the first-born of my dreams.

Accept it. For it carries with it the very real and very deep love of a most grateful son.

A.W.

Immediately Alec began work on a second novel to be called *Iphigenia in London* or *Mastered Circumstance* or *Elusive Ardours* or *Ungainly Wise* – the title was never settled – but he finished writing it (seventy thousand words) with breathtaking speed. *The Loom of Youth* had been posted chapter by chapter to Arthur for his comments and amendments, but that system had caused tension. This time he made sure that Arthur saw the book only when it was finished, reminding him: 'There's no need to revise this time, I did it myself.' The manuscript arrived at Underhill with the morning post on 15 January 1917. It was read that day and Alec received a response by the first post of the following morning.

Arthur was distraught. He hated it. Nothing had ever made him so unhappy: 'The hope of my life is almost hidden in the mist.' His chief objection was the plot's immorality: it was about a pleasure-seeking artist who married in boredom, had an adulterous affair, then left his wife for a mistress. 'I don't object to immoral figures in a novel,' Arthur wrote, 'but I shiver when I find them proclaiming that evil is their good.' As managing director of Chapman and Hall he had published many authors of whose morals he did not approve, believing their work of commercial value to the firm. The problem this time was that the author in question was his own son, a guardian of the family name.

> Suppose you were sent to the front this year and were killed. My life as you know would be over. That is one thing. Life can still be 'fastened and fed without the aid of joy'. But behind you you would have left this book recording to those who wanted to know the sort of man you were the impression that you were intensely interested in the vicious side of life . . . I am bitterly anxious that you should not give the world a false impression of your own character, which I shall always believe to be much nobler, and clearer and purer than you let the world see.

Alec's response was sincere and contrite:

> My dear Father, I am really sorry that my book has made you unhappy. Heaven knows that that is the last thing I wanted to do and if my writing is only going to make those I love wretched, then I had better go and buy a barrel organ . . . I hope you will be all right in a day or two . . . your loving son, Billy.

The manuscript was put away and never offered to a publisher. Alec decided to collect up some of his best poems and send those to Grant Richards instead.

At Berkhamsted Alec had made friends with the family of W. W. Jacobs, who lived in a comfortable house called Beechcroft not far from his training camp. No longer famous (except perhaps for a much anthologised, ghoulish and atypical horror story called *The Monkey's Paw*), Jacobs had been England's most successful writer of comic short fiction. Only Kipling could command fees as high as his for a short story in the *Strand Magazine*. Jacobs and Arthur knew each other but Jacobs, by nature anti-social, found Arthur's garrulous bonhomie unappealing.

In October 1915 Alec thought he might be falling in love again – for the first time with a member of the opposite sex. Barbara was Jacobs's eldest daughter, 'a soft, drooping girl', as Evelyn later described her, 'lethargic but capable of being roused both to strenuous activity and to gaiety'. She had a boyish look, which may have attracted Alec to her: she bobbed her hair and eschewed conventional ladies' apparel such as high-heeled shoes, hats and gloves. The photograph which Alec took with him in his haversack to the trenches shows a dumpy muskrat of a girl in a white cotton dress hunched apprehensively under a tree. Her mouth is downturned and her eyes narrow. But in these same eyes Alec believed he could see 'cool waters' and in her hair 'plunging cataracts'. He talked of her dark, brooding beauty, admired the cadence of her voice and was seduced by her 'charming habit' of shaking hands whenever she agreed with him on any subject. Her aloofness, though, was a challenge. So was her father, who protected his favourite daughter keenly.

Alec decided that the best way to advance his courtship was to conduct it through letters to her deaf mother. She, being an eccentric – who had been to prison for throwing bricks with the Suffragette Movement and eventually committed suicide – responded with twenty-four siders about socialism and modern problems. To some extent the plan may have backfired as Barbara, to her dying day, believed that Alec had fallen in love with her mother. This was not the case. For months Alec kept his infatuation with Barbara a secret from his father, pleading in July 1916 with a friend: 'Not a word about Barbara. If my small brother knew it would be all around Hampstead in a week.'

Eight months passed before Barbara and Alec were unofficially engaged. Still they had not kissed – they hardly knew each other. Their few unchaperoned conversations had consisted of stilted, showing-off one-liners about art and poetry. Alec had expounded to her his aesthetic 'ideas' – that a search for 'Beauty' is the purpose of all intelligent life, that a poet's duty is to find this Beauty and to reveal it for the benefit of mankind. Despite his efforts Alec had no experience of heterosexual love and his rare meetings with Barbara were excruciatingly painful: he was not in the least bit sure that she liked him.

Arthur should have been pleased by the Alec–Barbara romance. She was, after all, the daughter of a friend who was a famous writer and, on the face of it, an ideal partner for his son, but she threatened his own relationship with Alec. Of course, when challenged, he strenuously denied it. During a walk after lunch at Beechcroft Barbara told him that she felt 'a beast' being the recipient of all Alec's best thoughts and letters. 'I vehemently begged her to believe (what is perfectly true) that not a shade of jealousy crosses my thoughts of you two and so long as you are happy, I could desire nothing better.' But at heart Arthur was not sure that he liked Barbara. Their tastes were not the same. She was excited by all things new and faddish, by Cubism and jarring new poetry; she was a feminist, a believer in co-education; she lauded none of Arthur's Victorian idols, and was not especially won over by his twinkly charm and theatrical manner. She, like her father, found him silly. Arthur thought *her* silly too, but in spite of that and of their extreme youth (Alec was eighteen, she was sixteen) he saw no point in quarrelling with his beloved son in the last weeks or months before he set off to war. Instead he patiently tried to suggest that Alec bide his time, wait until he was sure, till the war was over, and he had found his footing on the professional wheel. But Alec was ready for all those arguments. He did not have much time, he replied. Within months he might be 'plugged full of lead'. He asked his mother whose side she was on and Arthur, who hated arguing in teams, was hurt and dropped the subject.

Arthur's early dislike for Barbara may also have been motivated by another issue. He was quietly hoping that Alec might marry another girl, a neighbour from Hampstead, originally Evelyn's close friend called Jean Fleming. Jean was perhaps the first of Arthur's many surrogate daughters, young women, usually in their teens, with whom he enjoyed close, intimate but, according to Evelyn, 'in no way libidinous' associations – I hope Grandpapa was right about this. Arthur had a tendency in any gathering to make a beeline for girls of the teen age or younger. Persuading them to call him 'Uncle' or 'Poppa', he bought them sweets and joked and frolicked with them in a way that nowadays, in our heightened hysteria over paedophilia, might be deemed 'inappropriate'. With Barbara Jacobs's youngest sister, Olwen, Arthur played 'tickling games' in the garden – 'a form of recreation,' as he described it, 'which only her tender age excused from indiscretion'. He sent his surrogate daughters letters, took them to theatres and cinemas, for walks across Hampstead Heath, and showered them with flowers and presents. He gave Jean Fleming a green ostrich fan for Christmas, a slave bangle for her birthday and, throughout the year, generously pressed books upon her. During the Great War he wrote a play called *Feed the Brute*, in which Jean and her younger sister Philla played wife and mother to the pampered brute – who, of course, was Arthur. This bizarre exhibition was hauled around the convalescent homes of North London during the spring of 1917.

Arthur was highly sexed. During his engagement to K he alarmed her easily by his immodest and demonstrative gropings. In July 1893 he had written to her: 'I long for you so much, but after being away from you for so long, I can't promise I should be good. So for the sake of your peace of mind, Old Chum, it's just as well we can't meet . . . don't long for me to come to you for you know I am a brute and that it's better for you that I stay away.' K was young then. In 1937, when Arthur was over seventy, he employed a 'dark-eyed, curly-headed, dainty, smiling little fairy of about 23 *fair springs*' called Mollie Udale-Smith to massage his bottom. She was supposed to be curing his rheumatism. Arthur described her first visit in a letter to McMaster:

> 'Will you take off your trousers, please' she whispered. Trembling all over, I obeyed and buried my face in the pillow. For twenty minutes she directed infra-red rays to my hinder parts and put me to a perpetual shame. Then I thought she had finished. Not at all. She waved her delicate fingers mystically, and began taking the most reprehensible liberties with my body. For another twenty minutes she persisted in her caresses; and when at last she rested,

I was ashamed to look my wife in the face. Next morning she reappeared and the same saturnalia was repeated. Then she said 'I think you'll do now,' smiled a benediction and presented me with a slip of paper announcing that Mr Arthur Waugh owed Miss Mollie Udale-Smith a guinea. It was the cheapest enchantment I have ever undergone, but my conscience has tortured me ever since.

People like Mollie Udale-Smith and her mystical fingers are appealing to many types of men, but in other respects Arthur Waugh was not so typical. I think he indulged in an unusual fetishism concerning young ladies and bicycles. He courted K in the 1890s on long rides through the Somerset lanes. Later he taught his young lady-friends to ride bicycles in a London cul-de-sac, remembering fondly in his autobiography their 'wild gyrations' as they attempted to keep their balance. He believed the bicycle to be responsible for exciting improvements in women's clothing, applauding the change it brought from dreary billowing sleeves and long skirts to swishing apron-skirts, gym-knickers and tight-fitting hose. 'The bicycle,' he claimed, 'was the real beginning of woman's emancipation.' In 1898 he published an anthology of verse called *Legends of the Wheel* in which concepts of love and bicycling are sensually intertwined. In one of these poems Arthur teaches Lady Godiva how to ride; in another he imagines himself as the bicycle with a 'deftly-shod' woman riding atop him:

> Swift as the Swift.
> Winger of Woman,
> Banishing petticoats,
> Bringing the female
> (Long since irrational)
> Rational dress.
> Ho! Then, the Park,
> And the pleasaunce of Battersea.
> Ho! Then, the hose
> Of my deftly-shod womankind.
> I, the ubiquitous

Angel of Exercise,
I am the 'Bike'.

During the First World War Arthur took Jean and other young women out on long bicycle rides to the suburbs, which vexed K greatly – especially when Arthur and Jean got caught in the rain. When she was very old Jean was asked by one of my more brazen cousins if Arthur had ever – well, you know. She was indignant at the suggestion, but remembered him always as her 'particular friend'. He described her as 'delicious' – 'You know, I have always got on better with women than men,' he once confided to her.

Arthur made no secret of the fact that he wished for Alec to marry Jean and tried subtly to arouse his son's passions for her. His powers of suggestion were contagious. In October 1916, while Alec, unknown to his father, was courting Barbara, Arthur wrote to him: 'This morning I met Jean looking like a Magdalen lily in the dew.' A week later Alec wrote to his friend Hugh Mackintosh: 'Jean Fleming is going to be something, an angel, I think. She is really rather attractive in a way, pale and tall like a Magdalen lily.' Three months later at a party at the Flemings' house in Hampstead Alec checked himself on the brink of kissing her. 'I suppose the warmth and colours of the evening and the scent she was wearing got on my brain, but I never felt so attracted to her before. If we had been alone I feel certain I should have kissed her . . . God the last thing I want to do is make love to Jean. I should feel bound to her, she is so sensitive, so fragile, so tender and with such depth of feeling. And I must be free, I want Barbara not her.'

Alec was suffering because Barbara was too aloof to show him any affection. He was not at all sure how she felt about him. Her letters were coolly signed 'yours Barbara'. He read them over and over but still could find no clue as to what was on her mind. Did she care for him at all? Was she simply too shy to express herself? Was she cold, frigid, gauche? In the early part of January 1917 Alec wrote 'The Poet's Grave', which reveals not only his turmoil over Barbara but his perception that his ambitions to become a great

English poet might be cut short by death in the trenches. The first verse describes a group of people assembled at a poet's grave in praise of his artistic legacy and the poem continues:

> 'The body dies, the soul lives on,' they said.
> 'We lay upon his grave not grief but praise.
> The magic of his music has been shed
> Over the years unto the end of days.'
>
> Beneath the clay the poet heard and smiled
> The cynic smile of one who long has mused
> On broken things, and had not reconciled
> God with the bitterness that was diffused
> Throughout his Life . . .
>   And the worms heard him say,
> 'I sang to find one woman's heart but she
> Was cold and heeded not and went her way.
> I do not care what these men think of me.'

Unlike Barbara, Jean Fleming might easily have kissed Alec on the lips had he presented her with such an opportunity – at least, that was what Alec believed. Some seventy summers on, as Mrs Guy Crowden, she remembered, 'Alec was very sweet. I thought he was wonderful. I must have been keen on him, but we never got beyond holding hands under the tarpaulin on the tops of buses.'

On first hearing of Alec's passion for Barbara, Arthur fretted about Jean being left out, as it were, to dry. To a friend Alec wrote in June 1917:

Father has made himself miserable about it because of Jean. Damn it, I've never encouraged her, not since that Xmas years ago before the war. My father talks a lot of rot about her. She wouldn't suit me. I want someone to help me in life. She's too soft. She wants a good honest fellow who would make her happy. She is an ideal wife, but I am an impossible husband. If I don't get Barbara, I don't intend to marry, but just drift, seeing life, learning it, if possible interpreting it in books.

Within a year Alec was writing to his father from the war-zone: 'I dreamed about Miss Fleming last night. She drove me so mad that I flung my gas mask at her and fled – a very suitable missile.'

Arthur had many reservations about Barbara, not least that she interfered with his plans concerning Jean, but he was not a man to stand against his son. At Alec's insistence Arthur even agreed that Barbara could lodge at Underhill from September 1917 while she attended an art course in London. Barbara was not noticeably artistic. She had a handful of artistic opinions, radical by Arthur's standards, which had all been gleaned from her mother. Above all, she desired to be free of her baleful parents in Berkhamsted. During her time at Underhill, in Alec's absence, she became a close friend of Evelyn. For obvious reasons she was never popular with the Fleming girls. Late in her life Philla remembered Barbara as 'a horror'. By October Arthur, in typically generous spirit, had told Alec untruthfully what he wanted to hear: that he was fond of Barbara; but still he pushed his point about Jean. Alec tried hard to convince him that Jean was a non-starter, claiming in a letter to his friend Hugh Mackintosh, 'Father is at last realising that Jean is rather childish after all these days! Not too good a psychologist. The fact is he does not care for people who don't care for him, at first he was beastly about Barbara. Now of course he loves her, but then he couldn't very well help it. She is wonderful.'

Alec was deluded: Arthur never took to Barbara – and she knew it. She also knew that Arthur was obsessed with Jean. At the same time as he was reassuring Alec about Barbara, Arthur wrote a poem for and about Jean inscribing it to her 'with true love, Arthur Waugh'. He gave a copy to Alec, perhaps in the hope that it might awaken his ardour for the Magdalen lily:

> And oh, the mystery of her eyes,
> So tremulous with shy surprise,
> Rapt in a dream half-understood,

The mystic dream of maidenhood.
They falter, hesitate and glow;
Nor tell me half I long to know.
What do they see? What do they dream?
Shy goddess of the secret stream.

At the beginning of 1916 the government had raised the minimum age for soldiers going to the front from seventeen to eighteen, which left Alec, who was still seventeen, temporarily in no man's land as far as his immediate future was concerned. He had finished his training but had nowhere to go and so he was despatched to Southwold to hold the coast in the event of a German invasion. Thirty men slept in a barrack cottage the size of a shoebox. They were given straw beds and straw pillows, and held in abject conditions behind barbed wire, eating filth and freezing to death. One night Alec witnessed from a distance a German gunboat raid on Lowestoft as it was intercepted by the British fleet. Convinced that his demise was imminent he wrote to his father describing a lucky escape: 'If our fleet had not come up they would have bombarded Southwold in which case there would now be no more Billy.'

Arthur wrote immediately to Major Sir Frederick Kenyon (a tutor from his Oxford days, who, by chance, was now the officer in command of Alec's company at Berkhamsted) pleading with him to have Alec recalled. Kenyon took immediate action, and Alec and the rest of the cadet troops at Lowestoft were removed to a more comfortable billet. But Alec could not for ever be so easily saved. Arthur was aware of that. Time was running out and soon he would be sent abroad to face the German guns.

On 28 July 1917 Arthur, K and Evelyn were looking forward to welcoming Alec home on leave from the Harrowby camp in Grantham where he was perfecting his machine-gun skills. Alec, too, was looking forward to the weekend as Barbara and her mother had been invited to stay at Underhill. His relationship with Barbara was heating up: there had been one day of bliss, in which he and she had held hands for a whole afternoon in the garden at Beechcroft. He had put his arm round her neck, touched her cheek with his fingers and afterwards they had stood in the 'green room' locked in each other's arms: 'She yielded herself utterly to the demand of love,' he wrote – but this is not, as we shall soon discover, to be construed as meaning that they had full sexual intercourse. Whatever they had done together, he couldn't wait to see Barbara again at Underhill and eagerly counted down the days to his departure. His mood was buoyant. Only the day before Arthur had telegraphed him with the first review of *The Loom of Youth*. It was a good one in the *Times Literary Supplement* that flattered both father and son: 'As an example of precocious literary talent, for which heredity must be allowed in part to account, the book is indeed remarkable.' But just as Alec's leave had been granted so it was suddenly and unexpectedly withdrawn. There was no telephone at Underhill in those days so he was unable to warn his family.

At Underhill the day dragged on as they waited for his arrival. By the evening there was still no news and the Waughs retired anxiously to bed, not knowing what had happened. Alec's orders were to leave from Victoria station at seven the next morning. He arrived in London late and caught the last train to Golders Green heavy at heart that his parents, expecting a happy weekend, would instead only have a few hours in which to say their goodbyes. Some time after midnight K was awoken by the sound of mud hitting her bedroom window. She looked out to see Alec laden with bags: 'I cross to France first thing tomorrow,' he shouted up to her. According to Arthur, 'There was no sleep in Underhill that night.'

Early next morning Arthur, K and Evelyn went with Alec to the station. Their parting was as vivid to Arthur fourteen years later as it had been on the very day:

Those blear twilights at Victoria Station; the half dumb journey in the underground, with its pitiful, loving pretence of anecdote and jest; the clanking staircases; the sobbing women; the snatches of song; the guard's determinate whistle; the last desperate glance of courage and hope – will our generation

Dr Alexander Waugh, the 'Great and Good' founder of the English Waughs, remonstrating with a 'perverse pupil' in a picture that once hung in Evelyn's bedroom at Underhill.

Arthur with his toy shotgun, 1871.

Dr Alexander Waugh, the 'Brute,' after a good day's shooting, c. 1890.

The family on the steps at Midsomer Norton, 1879. Back row: Mrs. Waugh holding Elsie, Arthur in straw boater. Front row: Connie looking wistful, the Brute with his favourite child, Trissie, on his knee and Alick, far right.

rthur's sketch of his father salmon fishing,
1880.

Together on stage: Arthur as Benjamin Goldfinch and
the Brute as Uncle Gregory in an amateur production
of *A Pair of Spectacles*.

Courting days: Arthur and K about to set off for an exciting day on their bicycles, c. 1892.

Arthur clasps baby Alec in his arms at a friend's house, Chalfont St Giles, Buckinghamshire, 1898.

Evelyn on the steps of 11 Hillfield Road, the house where he was born, with his nanny, Lucy Hodges.

Arthur teaches Alec to walk on Bournemouth beach in the summer of 1899. In the background, Marquis cools his paws.

K, Arthur, Evelyn and Alec on holiday at Midsomer Norton, 1904.

School prefect—
'son of my soul'.
Alec at Sherborne, 1914.

Arthur, Alec and K relax in the garden of
their newly built Hampstead home,
Underhill, 1909.

Arthur with cricket bat
aged six, 1872.

Alec with cricket bat
aged six, 1904.

The Annual Paters' Match at Fernden
embarrassingly described in *One Man's Roa*
Alec bowls a 'sturdy Major'; Arthur holds
his bat at the bowler's end.

The Chapman and Hall staff cricket team. Captain, Arthur Waugh, sits in the front row with Alec
scowling between his legs.

Arthur, outside the Aeolian Hall, London, congratulates Evelyn on winning the Hawthornden Prize for his biography of Edmund Campion, 24 June 1936.

Happy times: Arthur and Alec at a cricket match in Corsham, 1939.

Piers Court, Stinchcombe, at the time Evelyn and Laura bought it in 1937.

Edrington, Joan's house near Silchester set in eighteen acres of garden, which made Alec feel inadequate.

ever forget the things which it endured in those hours of morning sacrifice? They seemed to collect and embody into one all the partings of a lifetime; as one stood there and watched the train gather pace and round the vanishing corner, one felt that all one's life had been spent in saying good-bye to some fond hope or vision, amid the roaring, regardless clamour of an inexorable traffic.

The Waughs returned without Alec to Underhill and polished the silver around the kitchen table in nervous silence. Barbara and her mother arrived, as arranged, in time for lunch. 'I have wondered sometimes whether there would have been a different outcome to it all if my posting had come three days later and I had had that leave,' Alec later mused. 'Things were never the same between Barbara and myself again. A current had been switched off.'

As soon as Alec reached the shores of France he started to feel isolated and scared. In camp he wrote a nostalgic, elegiac poem about Sherborne: 'Beautiful, sad and calm . . . It will dwell in me all my length of days . . . For half of my wayward heart is buried there.' He wrote to Barbara asking her to send him photographs of his parents. 'I haven't got a photo of them at all. It would make a lot of difference to have one to look at when I am lonely.' Though not immediately ordered to the front line, he, like all his fellow soldiers, was passing the dead and wounded every day. How long would it be before his turn came? Within a month some of Alec's closest friends had been shot or blown to pieces. He wrote frequently to his father, always careful to reassure him of his own safety but unable to hide his disgust at what he was seeing all around him:

It's pretty awful. Both Jackson and Knight have been killed — the same shell and there are several casualties among the men . . . what I have seen in the last few days has banished my illusions about the glories of war. What is there fine and noble in young men carrying boxes up the line, suddenly hearing a shell and dropping everything and falling flat in a ditch? One is frightened. But I must say the artillery drivers are magnificent, they go on bringing up shells all day and night and don't seem to care a damn. But it's a filthy show. Knight and Jackson were two of the best fellows you could meet — blown to bits. Oh well, by the time you get this I shall be in a rest camp.

Arthur's agitation at these letters was predictable and after a while his old-maidish fretting began, even at such a distance, to fray Alec's nerves. 'Is my father panicking?' he wrote to Hugh Mackintosh in London. 'I hope not. He takes things far too seriously. He won't realise that I am only an individual. I am a *mons marinorum* to him. It's depressing.'

Like all the young fighting men in Flanders, Alec had been induced by his parents to believe that a soldier's death was noble. This was the only way that the older generation could justify the deplorable mass sacrifice of their sons. Alec compared his parents' philosophy of the 'noble death' to the sight of the rotting corpses lying around him on the battlefield and forged the idea into a powerfully morbid threnody. Originally entitled 'Carrion' the poem — one of the most devastating to come out of the Great War — was addressed to K, whose brother Bassett had been shot a few months before Alec had left for France. In sentiment, it was equally addressed to Arthur. When they read it both Arthur and K were horrified, not least by the tasteless title. Alec agreed to change it to 'Cannon-Fodder' and, in a semi-legible scrawl that revealed his pitiful state of mind, wrote to explain himself:

The idea of the poem was that to the people at home death has a certain nobility. They cannot see, as we see, the roads littered with corpses, bits of corpses, a stray foot or head. We shall always look on the death of a soldier as something like that. It was an idea nobody seems to have thought out yet. But no applause and I thank you.

Cannon-Fodder
by Alec Waugh

Is it seven days you've been lying there
   Out in the cold,
Feeling the damp, chill circlet of flesh
   Loosen its hold
On muscles and sinews and bones,
   Feeling them slip
One from the other to hang limp on the stones?
Seven days. The lice must be busy in your hair,
And by now the worms will have had their share
   Of eyelid and lip.
Poor, lonely thing: is death really a sleep?
Or can you somehow feel the vermin creep
   Across your face
As you lie, rotting, uncared for in the unowned place,
That you fought so hard to keep
   Blow after weakening blow?
Well. You've got what you wanted, that spot is yours.
No one can take it from you now.

But at home by the fire, their faces aglow
   With talking of you,
They'll be sitting, the folk that you loved,
   And they will not know.

O girl at the window combing your hair,
   Get back to your bed.
   Your bright-limbed lover is lying out there
   Dead.

O mother, sewing by candlelight,
   Put away that stuff.
The clammy fingers of earth are about his neck.
   He is warm enough.

Soon like a snake in your honest home
   The word will come.
And light will suddenly go from it.
   Day will be dumb.
And the heart in each aching breast
   Will be cold and numb.

O men, who had known his manhood and truth,
   I had found him true.
O you, who had loved his laughter and youth,
   I had loved it too.
O girl, who has lost the meaning of life,
   I am lost as you.

And yet there is one worse thing,
For all the pain at the heart and the eye blurred and dim,
   This you are spared,
You have not seen what death has made of him.
You have not seen the proud limbs mangled and broken,
The face of the lover sightless, raw and red,
You have not seen the flock of vermin swarming
   Over the newly dead.

Slowly he will rot in the place where no man dare go,
Silently over the right the stench of his carcass will flow,
Proudly the worms will be banqueting . . .
   This you will never know.

He will live in your dreams for ever as last you saw him.
Proud-eyed and clean, a man whom shame never knew.
Laughing, erect, with the strength of the wind in his
   manhood —
   O broken-hearted mother, I envy you.

Flanders, September 1917

Alec found himself manning a machine-gun emplacement in the front-line at Passchendaele – the muddiest and bloodiest battle in military history. A quarter of a million British soldiers were lost for the gain of five miles of desolate squelching terrain. But he was extraordinarily lucky. On the night before the battle he was commanded to move right up to the front with two men and take a German pillbox, with orders to hold it until reinforcements arrived. The three of them pushed the dead Germans out. They found apples, pears and whisky in the pillbox and although relief did not arrive for four agonising days and nights, neither Alec nor his men were required to fire a single shot. Outside, within spitting distance of where Alec sat, three thousand British guns released four million rounds of ammunition. During the battle Alec wrote a long letter to 'My own darling Barbara', a stream of consciousness that, owing to his trapped condition, rolled on for page after page before it could be sent. It was too dangerous to ask the stretcher bearers to carry letters out. Alec asked Barbara (when and if she received the letter) to read it aloud to Arthur:

> The shell holes are so close together that you can't find a way across, they are about 4 ft across and full of water. Last night I fell into one full length and in consequence felt fairly miserable this morning with my clothes wet and clinging. When will all this end? Never again shall I fret about being in a cushy bit of line and clamour for war. I've seen it and know how utterly horrible it is. But the relief should be here soon. When I was being shelled on Thursday night I felt if I come through this alive I'll prove my life was worth saving. I'll try to think less of myself and more of others, make life fit in with the lives of those I love, instead of trying to make theirs fit into mine. That may sound sentimental and dramatic but it is what I felt and still feel when shells are falling round. One hasn't time to put a veneer over what one feels. One can actually hear one's heart speaking . . .
>
> War is not a big thing but squalor on a large scale.

Death is noble usually, here it is pitiable. There is something tragic and splendid in the idea of young lives laid down willingly, but war does not get to the idea; it is utterly loathsome, it is not tragic, it is miles below tragedy, just horror on a massive scale . . .

It is hard to realise that while I am in this land of corruption you and father are sitting in the loggia watching the sunlight fall across the garden, the same sun that is shining in the dust thrown up by the shells. Oh well I shall be back to it soon . . . perhaps.

Some pretty awful news has just come through. My section officer and my servant have just been killed; if I hadn't come up here I would probably have been in the same box. Oh my God this is hell. The men who were bringing up our mail and rations have been laid out; it seems there's no trace of them. I am in command of the section now; it is awful, my Lord it is. My word it is awful. My section officer had not been married a year. They were fond of each other, every day they wrote each other huge long letters. It really knocks the life out of one. I have had luck, my word I have. If I had stayed with him, I should probably be done for by now. What a filthy business it is. I've done with warfare!

After Passchendaele Alec was moved south to the desolate landscape of the Somme. He and Arthur exchanged letters every day. Arthur sent him the flood of reviews and letters concerning The Loom of Youth. H. G. Wells had written to him, 'Your son is an astounding young man, and I've rarely read a first novel with so much interest.' Arnold Bennett had hailed it a 'staggering performance', praising the 'very remarkable gift of this man', and the eminent poet and critic J. C. Squire had written:

To what prodigy have you given birth? (if the phrase may be used of a male parent?) It is very pleasing to see you as the dedicatee. In this straw infested age the too common doctrine is that there is something shameful, almost disreputable in the relationship of father and son – that the younger generation should not only knock at the door but lift it off its hinges and knock the old man over the head with it. I shall be proud indeed if one of my offspring treats me as yours has treated you.

Not everybody was as delighted with Alec's literary accomplishment as J. C. Squire. As predicted, the headmaster of Sherborne was outraged. He saw the book as a vile slur on his great institution. Although in the novel the school is called Fernhurst, no one who had had anything to do with Sherborne could have failed to recognise the setting. It contained portraits of masters who were still employed at the school, was critical of Sherborne's ethos of athleticism, suggested that all boys were routinely dishonest, and that homosexual affairs were rife throughout the school – that such things went on all the time, that everybody knew it, but 'the one unforgivable sin is to be found out'.

By modern standards of defamation many of these connections are oblique. You could easily read the whole book without noticing the homosexual passage that so scandalised society at the time: 'Morecombe [Davies *mi*] came up to Gordon's [Alec's] study nearly every evening and usually Foster left them alone together. During the long morning hours when Gordon was supposed to be reading history, more than once there came over him a wish to plunge himself into the feverish waters of pleasure.' That is about as far as it goes – far tamer than the equivalent passage from Thomas Hughes's *Tom Brown's Schooldays*, written sixty years earlier. Hughes, who was writing about Rugby, described 'miserable little pretty white-handed curly headed boys, petted and pampered by some of the big fellows who did all they could to spoil them for everything in this world and the next' and added in a footnote: 'There were many noble friendships between big and little boys, but I can't strike out the passage: many boys will know why it has been left in.'

That Alec's book should have caused such outrage was a sign of the times. At a shaky moment in the nation's history it brought into question the whole ethos of the public-school system. It was brazenly frank. Correspondence about *The Loom* ran for ten weeks in the *Spectator* and for six in the *Nation*. The book was described as 'disgusting', 'unpleasant', 'wholly untrue' and 'pernicious stuff' in letters from bishops, pupils, politicians and the ex-headmaster of Eton. Schoolboys up and down the country were caned when they were caught reading it. Sales boomed. While Alec was on active service, *The Loom* went into a fifth impression. Despite all this success he was disturbed to hear that it had gone down badly at Sherborne and wrote a letter, of self-justification rather than apology, to the *Shirburnian*, which refused to print it; in a separate letter, the Chief wrote to Alec asking him to resign from the Old Shirburnians. To those people to whom these sorts of things matter, they matter very much indeed. Principles are called into play. On principle Alec refused to resign; on principle the old boys' society (whose president was the headmaster) removed him from the roll; on principle Arthur entered the fray in support of his son; on principle the games master, Mr Godfrey Carey, who recognised a barely disguised portrait of himself as the Bull in the book, wrote a stinker to Arthur, accusing him of having aided and abetted his son in the creation of this evil novel: 'A poisoned dagger,' he fumed, 'largely forged and guided by you has been aimed at the heart of the old school.' On principle Arthur himself resigned from the Old Shirburnians: For him to do so was a devastating blow – time for a second farewell to Sherborne:

> I felt that my own devotion to the school had been strained to the breaking point. I could not choose but stand by my son, and follow him into exile. But when I said 'Good-bye' to Sherborne, I broke irrevocably and for ever the magic wand of Prospero, which had kept the spirit of youth still living in a heart that was now beginning to grow heavy under the hand of time and change.

But for Arthur worse was yet to come. In late April Alec and a few of his men were given orders to hold a gun emplacement to slow down a German advance near the village of Neuville-Vitasse in

Northern France. They were asked specifically to guard the valley beneath them but could not help noticing a sea of German soldiers assembling round them on the opposite side from that which they had been commanded to defend. They were confused by these troop movements and unsure how to proceed. Many of their comrades-in-arms seemed to be in retreat. One infantryman, attempting to relay a message to the British troops behind, returned with the news that the road back to camp was blocked. They were cut off. Suddenly Alec and his small band came in for heavy shelling, first by the German light artillery and then by pernicious high-velocity whizzbangs. Alec turned in time to see several of his finest men and closest friends blown to pieces. By noon it was clear to those who had survived that they were deep in sticky jam, surrounded on all four sides by German forces, who were closing in fast.

At Underhill Arthur was starting to feel extremely anxious. A few days had passed and not a line from Alec. He couldn't sit down. K too was shaking. She had lost a great deal of weight during the war and her ribs were starting to protrude. Whenever she heard the guns over London she shook or burst into tears. A few days became a week – and still no news. Arthur was pacing up and down, quoting poems, praying, sighing, pressing Jean Fleming's father at the War Office for regular bulletins.

Evelyn, who was fourteen, and Barbara, who was seventeen, were unperturbed by all the commotion in the house – or, at least, chose to counter it with a lighter mood of their own. Barbara's art lessons were 'great fun' and she had made a close friend of Evelyn whose humour and intelligence she greatly admired, introducing him to the delights of Cubism, which he found a refreshing antithesis to the fey Victorian tastes that had been foisted upon him by his father. While Arthur was pacing anxiously for news from the Front, Evelyn and Barbara occupied themselves upstairs with painting the walls of the 'day nursery' (renamed 'the studio') with a large 'Cubist' fresco of their own design. The tension was more than Arthur could bear, as he explained in a letter to his 'if-only' daughter Jean:

Barbara and Evelyn have been busy for two days defiling the studio with the most awful paint. They have painted the fireplace and walls all over cubes of colour, yellow, red, blue, in irregular splotches. You never saw anything so awful. And as they do it, their loud laughter rings through the house. I sit alone and think of the other boy — lonely, cold, hungry, even if he is alive; and I wonder *what* their hearts are made of. Truly it is a strange world; and love is chiefly made up of suffering. But those who have really loved, would rather suffer than not have known.

Ever, dear, your loving friend, Arthur

As far as Arthur was concerned, the painting, splotching, giggling and flirting had to stop. He sent Barbara back to Beechcroft and despatched Evelyn to his maiden aunts at Midsomer Norton.

At the same time as all this was going on at Underhill, Captain Jack De Vieux, of the British Expeditionary Force, encamped somewhere in a muddy corpse-strewn field to the east of Arras, was sitting down to type a letter. It was addressed to Mr Arthur Waugh:

Dear Sir,

It is with the deepest regret that I inform you that your son, 2.Lt. Alec Waugh, is missing.

On the 28 March he was with his section together with Lt. Sime when the enemy attacked. Nothing more was seen or heard of them after they had dispatched their first report, so I can give you no idea of what might have happened to him.

As his Company Commander for 8 months I knew him both as a soldier on parade and off. I could never wish for a better officer and he is a great loss to the Coy, and to all officers as a true friend. He was exceedingly popular with all ranks, especially with his section. He would always join his men in any sport that they were having when out of the line and was always thinking of what he could do to amuse them. When in the line he was always to be found working hard and doing his duty in a manner that was a credit to the Coy.

Please accept from all officers, N.C.O.'s and men of the 233rd M.G.C. our deepest sympathy in your great loss,

Yours sincerely,
Capt. J. H. De Vieux

VI

Spirit of Change

Arthur and K learned that Alec was missing in action before Captain De Vieux's letter had arrived at Underhill. Jean Fleming's father, who worked at the War Office and was in charge of casualty reports, had been scanning despatches on Arthur's behalf. When he saw Alec's name he sent his daughter round with the grim news. She arrived with a pale face and whispered into Arthur's ear 'the worst news that had ever tried my strength to the uttermost'.

English newspapers soon got hold of the story: 'Author of *The Loom of Youth* is Missing'. Arthur was inundated with correspondence. Ten days later he had replied to over two hundred letters of sympathy, but there was still no news of his son. On the eleventh day he spotted a telegram buried among his letters and tore it open in haste. It was from the Red Cross in Geneva, announcing that Lieut. A. R. Waugh was among those officers being held prisoner who had arrived safe and well at Karlsruhe. Arthur had a card printed with the good news on it, which he sent to all his friends.

Shortly afterwards he received a line from Alec: 'It must have been miserable, the waiting after you got the "missing" message from the War Office. But it's all right now – *fini la guerre*.' He explained that his capture had been 'a foolish affair – No order came through and we found ourselves mysteriously surrounded. Our ammunition ran out, our guns got hit – *voilà*.' One senses the lie in that final verbal flourish, or at least a certain economy of truth. In his book *Prisoners of Mainz* published just after the end of the war he was even more elusive about what had happened: 'At seven o'clock the Germans came over, and by twelve we were being escorted to Berlin. Our actual engagement resembles so closely that of every other unfortunate during those sorry days that it deserves no detailed description.'

Rumours soon spread that he was a coward, a deserter, a traitor, even. At Lancing Evelyn gave a black eye to a boy called Dungy for impugning his brother's honour. It was not until the publication of his autobiography some twenty years after Arthur's death that Alec was willing to give a slightly fuller account:

> The incoming tide was stealing closer. We were cut off and we were defenceless. My section commander and I looked at each other. 'I don't see that there's anything we can do,' he said.
> I nodded.
> 'We'd best destroy the guns,' he said.
> By noon it was all over and we were the wrong side of the line.

In different circumstances, home life without Alec might have strengthened the relationship between Arthur and his younger son, but Evelyn found his school holidays joyless, especially during the war. His mother, whose companionship he craved, was employed in the Voluntary Aid Detachment with the Ambulance Corps and was mostly out of the house. When Arthur returned from work his principal conversation was of Alec. Even after the news had reached him that he was safe in a prisoner-of-war camp in Germany he continued to worry, terrified that the Germans would execute all their prisoners rather than send them home once hostilities had ceased. Armistice Day on 11 November 1918 was thus a nervous day for Arthur. He was not happy again until six thirty p.m. on 5 December when Alec arrived at Underhill 'shining eyed and looking splendid'. During Alec's incarceration at Mainz, Evelyn's presence at home had become an irritant to his father, who was vexed by his younger son's seeming indifference to Alec's fate. Both he and K detested Evelyn's 'sharp tongue', and K told him that this was his besetting sin. 'And do you know what is your besetting sin?' Evelyn asked her – of course she did not.

To keep Evelyn out of his way Arthur sent him again to Midsomer Norton, where the 'virgin' aunts were supposed to check his 'sharp tongue' and send weekly reports. 'We are all struck by the great improvement in Evelyn,' Aunt Connie wrote to Arthur in August 1918. 'He couldn't be nicer – so pleasant and ready to do anything we want him to do and pleased with any little joy we try to arrange. I don't think he is nearly so satirical as he used to be. We are all very happy together.'

While Alec was languishing at the Kaiser's pleasure, Arthur sent Jean Fleming a present of Compton Mackenzie's sad, semi-autobiographical novel *Sinister Street* with a letter outlining his state of mind:

> I hope I do right in sending you *Sinister Street* and that I did not dull the edge of your zest for life. After all, not all young men go through such tragic and distracting experiences, I did not for one. But it is well to know what life *can* be like. To know all is to forgive all. And one cannot really sympathise with one's fellow creatures until one knows how terribly the human heart can suffer . . . One by one all Alec's friends are taken from me, and their going is a great wrench. A part of *him* seems to vanish into the valley of the shadow, as each new one goes over into the fight. I wander what has happened to his company and to Capt De Vieux who wrote to me so kindly. There has been heavy fighting where they are. I am afraid some of them will have fallen. The war seems very near us again just now and I feel very lonely.
>
> Evelyn has been invited to paint some of the carved angels in Clandown Church about two miles from Midsomer Norton. He wrote today for endless paints and brushes. He has also been serving at the altar and going to picnics – a weird mixture of faith and frivolity . . .

It is bitterly cold today and I rather hope you are not
bathing. I think it is too cold for you. Take care of yourself. You are of great value to many people – not least you
may be sure, to your loving friend, Arthur

Briefly, in the summer holidays of 1915, Evelyn had worked as a
despatch boy, running files up and down corridors for Jean Fleming's
father at the War Office. In August 1918 he spent several days as
an errand boy at Chapman and Hall. In the holidays he went often
to the cinema, to museums or out for walks with K, but for all
these distractions the hours at Underhill dragged slowly by. On
Saturday mornings Arthur required the house to be silent while he
wrote his weekly book review for the *Daily Telegraph*. At luncheon
he held forth. His subjects were Alec, youth, age, and the younger
generation. In the afternoon he went for a walk. Everyone changed
for dinner. On Sunday mornings the family went to church and
after lunch Arthur had a rest and the house had to be quiet again.
In the evenings he attempted to lure everyone into the book-room
so that he could read to them.

Holidays were made more bearable for Evelyn by Barbara's presence. In his autobiography he claimed that he was never physically
drawn to his brother's fiancée: 'She had many admirers but I never
thought her particularly beautiful or attractive,' he wrote. 'With
Barbara there was never a hint of physical contact.' Perhaps this was
true. Perhaps also they were a little in love. Certainly Barbara enjoyed
a closer friendship with Evelyn than with Alec before his return from
Germany and even for a while after it. Evelyn called her Bobbie. She
remembered him years later as 'a darling, a perfectly darling boy. He
was the nicest boy you could possibly imagine.' She was two and a
half years older but treated him as an equal, laughing at all his jokes,
repeating his wise words and encouraging him to look at the world
outside the narrow confines of Underhill. Together they explored
London on foot, or on the tops of double-decker buses. They visited
galleries, cinemas and theatres; they rowed on the lake in Regent's
Park. She accompanied him to the station on his return to school.
Evelyn and Barbara found in each other a little streak of anarchy that
bonded their friendship, at times to the exclusion of all else.

After dinner Barbara and Evelyn – if they could not get away in time – would be trapped into listening to Arthur's stagy readings in the book-room. He recited them large chunks of Dickens, poems by Symonds, plays by W. S. Gilbert and Sir Arthur Pinero, in which he took all the roles, revelling in exaggerated changes of accent to indicate which character was speaking. When he acted or read aloud he pinned his gaze on one member of his audience. It was excruciatingly embarrassing. Although Evelyn sometimes enjoyed listening to him reading poetry when they were alone or with Alec, he felt ashamed when people from outside the family were present. One of his diary entries reads: 'This afternoon I went with father to hear him lecture on Dickens' women to the St Augustine's Guild. A good lecture but incorrigibly theatrical as usual.'

We would have known a great deal more about Evelyn's home life during these years if he had not been afraid that someone might snoop in his diaries. Only hints remain:

Friday 10 October 1919
This morning I tore out and destroyed all the first part of this diary about the holidays. There was little worth preserving and a very great deal that could not possibly be read and was really too dangerous without being funny . . . I shall have to be wiser next holidays in what I record.

A year later he touched again on the same problem:

What a futile thing this diary really is. I hardly record anything worth the trouble. Everything important I think had better be stored in my memory as it consists chiefly of 'shops in morning; cinema in afternoon'. I ought to try and make it more profound but it becomes so dangerous.

If home life fatigued Evelyn, school was even more depressing. Lancing was painful and he was bitterly unhappy there. He started a society of disaffected depressives called the Corpse Club. Not unnaturally, it failed to cheer him. Tossed between Scylla and Charybdis – home and school – he wrote, 'I think a lot about suicide. I really think that if I were without parents I should kill myself; as it is I owe them a certain obligation.' In his first published piece of fiction, a short story called *The Balance*, written five years later, the young Adam Doure imagines his own suicide and looks on in disgust as his parents discover his body: 'A scene of unspeakable vulgarity involving tears, hysteria, the telephone, the police.'

At school and at home, Evelyn believed that his best policy was to maintain Alec's ethos of 'watertight compartments'. Arthur did not often visit Evelyn at Lancing; nor was he encouraged to do so. On one of the rare occasions when he came down to take Evelyn out to lunch, his son remarked sullenly in his diary: 'I did not enjoy it much.' Later he wrote to Arthur requesting him to stop writing so often as he was embarrassed at receiving more letters than any of the other boys. Schoolfriends were not invited home for the holidays. It was a self-imposed rule to which Evelyn adhered rigidly until his last year at Lancing when he broke it for his most unusual friend, Francis Crease.

At the height of this friendship Evelyn wrote: 'I am feeling very depressed and unhappy. Crease will be away a month and he is the only real friend I have here.' Evelyn was then sixteen and a half. Whether or not he was handsome seems to have been a matter for dispute. He was small for his age with thick ginger hair, big ears and bright, staring eyes. His most remarkable feature was his razor sharp wit: he could be painfully and absurdly funny. Whether people were prepared to describe him as 'handsome' or 'ugly' seemed to depend on their reaction to this wit. Evelyn thought of himself as 'quite pretty in a cherubic way'; Barbara's sister, Luned, thought he was 'very funny' and consequently 'very handsome' – they frolicked with each other at parties. Harold Acton, who thought Evelyn one of the wittiest men alive, remembered him with aesthetic lust at Oxford: 'I still see Evelyn as a prancing faun, thinly disguised by conventional apparel. His wide apart eyes, always ready to be startled under raised eyebrows, the curved sensual lips, the hyacinthine locks of hair I had seen in marble and bronze at Naples . . .' And then there were those who did not find his jokes funny at all, those who were too stupid to understand them, or who felt inadequate or diminished by his ready repartee. Harold Nicolson described Evelyn in 1930 as 'a bright eyed, pink faced, reddish haired, stocky jawed, coarse lipped youth'; and Alec's friend Marjorie Watts, who was terrified of Evelyn and remembered him as a schoolboy, wrote, 'He was hideous. He had two pink eyes, he was most unattractive. Just the kind I detest. Pale face and pink-rimmed eyes because he was fair.'

Evelyn's close buddy Francis Crease was one of those who happened to enjoy his wit and who found him attractive. But Crease was no ordinary friend. He was middle-aged. A plump and effeminate dandy, with a pink and white face, prone to hysteria over small things – someone who might have been described in the mid-1970s as 'a mincing fairy' or, in the more cautious terminology of our times, as 'a mannered homosexualist'. Evelyn believed that Crease was entirely without sexual interests. Their relationship was never physical, though in temperament – on Crease's side at least – it seems to have blown hot and cold in the petulant manner of adolescent love. Crease was both a shady and a secretive figure. Nothing was known about his past; nor would he ever speak of it. He lived by private means in rented rooms at a farm called Lychpole, a long walk across the fields from Lancing. He was an amateur scribe. All his interests were artistic. The friendship between these two began in January 1920 when Evelyn arranged to take weekly lessons in calligraphy from him. After the first on 29 January, Evelyn wrote:

Dear Father,

The lettering lesson was great fun. Crease is the truest dilettante I have ever seen. He lives the life of a recluse in a suite of rooms he has taken and furnished beautifully in old oak and old china in a farm miles from anywhere. He is very comfortably off, rather effeminate, rather affected, very refined and artistic, well bred and charming. Apparently his career has been spoiled by ill-health. He had some rather distinguished job at Corpus, Oxford. He is a great admirer of Alec, particularly of his poem, 'Sherborne

Abbey', which he gave me to letter out as being the 'most worthy of beautiful treatment of any modern poem'. I don't admire his lettering awfully – it is rather affected but he says that I have the makings of a really fine scribe. I think he is going to be a really good friend.

At first glance this letter appears to be a deliberate attempt to make Arthur worried; but it was not. It mirrors (sometimes word for word) his diary entry of the same day. All of the points mentioned to his father in the letter are also included in the diary, but the latter contains more – details that Evelyn wisely decided not to pass on to Arthur. According to this version, on the day of that first lesson, he had walked through the rain to get to Crease's house:

He met me at the door and led me to his bedroom where he lent me dry socks, trousers and shoes . . . he was most flattering . . . at half-past four we had tea. It was then that I saw most of his character. He strikes me as being a man who may have a big influence over my Lancing life . . . He is a great student of character and claims to be able to sum anyone up by intuition at first sight. He has taken a great interest in Roberts . . . He was most kind to me and I think rather likes me. I could gather practically nothing of his life. He learns all he can without giving anything out. His secretiveness is his only bad quality as far as I can see . . . He has asked me to bring Fulford over sometime . . . he has impressed me a lot.

Memories of Alec's homosexual entanglements at Sherborne five years earlier should have sounded alarm bells for Arthur but he did not seem unduly concerned by Crease's influence over his younger son. He was unwilling to get involved but others proved less afraid. One master at Lancing, J. F. Roxburgh, was every bit as interested in Evelyn as Crease. He, too, was a homosexualist, a theatrical dandy – perhaps not unlike Arthur in some respects – whom Evelyn admired greatly. Early in his school career Evelyn had been invited to tea in Roxburgh's sanctuary and plied with cream buns and sensitive observations about poetry. Roxburgh's rivalry with Crease, whom he sarcastically termed 'the Sage of Lychpole', was obvious to all the boys. One day it was decreed that no boy was permitted to visit Lychpole as Crease was not known to the boys' parents: Evelyn thought he could put this to rights by inviting Crease to Underhill during the school holidays.

At Evelyn's suggestion, K sent a letter of invitation to Lychpole that Crease was at first reluctant to accept. He had read an article by Arthur Waugh describing the treatment of the young poet, Ian Mackenzie, who had come to stay as a guest at Underhill: 'He used to start the morning singing; and we made him roar with laughter at the breakfast table as we imitated the strains that accompanied the process of his dressing.' Crease was pathologically shy: the idea of a household of ear-flapping Waughs listening in on his morning ablutions did not appeal to him at all. Evelyn was furious that his father could have written anything so fatuous. He hated the 'hail-fellow-well-met' tone of the piece and resented being dragged into Arthur's 'we' of jovial Underhillers. In particular, he was enraged by another passage from the same piece: 'He loved good acting and was never tired of the theatre. Like ourselves he would rather have a bad show than no show at all.' This might have been true of Arthur and Alec, perhaps even of K, but it was certainly not so for Evelyn, and Arthur's sweeping statement rankled with him for many years. In 1926 he wrote a short story about a sane man who lives with his lunatic family. The family falsely claims that it is he who is the lunatic. The sane man is taken out by his tutor:

The first time he went to a revue he was agog with excitement, the theatre, the orchestra, the audience all enthralled him. He insisted on being there ten minutes before time; he insisted on leaving ten minutes before the end of the first act. He thought it vulgar and dull and ugly and there was so much else that he was eager to see. The dreary 'might-as-well-stay-here-now-we've-paid' attitude was unintelligible to him.

When he read this story, Arthur was pained by Evelyn's little dig at him and complained bitterly to Alec.

Evelyn might not have believed that he was the only sane member of a lunatic family but he told Crease that his people were Philistines and that Arthur had grossly exaggerated the *bonhomie* of life at Underhill. From that moment he continued to describe his family as 'the Philistines', once telling Arthur, 'Until I met Crease I lived among the Philistines', which, needless to say, upset the old man greatly. 'You will regret you ever said that when I am dead and gone and pushing up the daisies.'

In the end, by special pleading, Evelyn succeeded in persuading Crease to stay at Underhill. Arthur thought Crease was a big joke and subjected him to 'genial ridicule'. After dinner when Arthur read poetry aloud in the book-room Crease was too shy, or too embarrassed, to remove his hands from his eyes, peeping out only occasionally from the cracks between his fingers. Only K was moved by Crease's fragile pansy qualities and felt an urge to mother him. When, some years later, he was arrested on charges of sexual indecency she allowed him to dry his tears on her lap. Although Crease spent most of the weekend hiding in his bedroom, he told Evelyn afterwards that he had enjoyed himself and had found Arthur 'charming, entirely charming, and acting all the time'. For Evelyn this was a revelation. 'My eyes were opened,' he wrote, 'and I saw my father, whom I had grown up to accept in complete simplicity, as he always must have appeared to others.' From that moment (Evelyn was sixteen years old) he could not look at his father without noticing the ham actor within and regarded him as something of a fraud. In his diary Evelyn wrote:

This has been a wretched week. Father has been ineffably silly the whole holidays. The extraordinary thing is that the more I see through my Father the more I appreciate Mother. She has been like Candida and went to Father, whom she must have despised, because he needed her most. I always think I am discovering some new trait in his character and find that she knew it all along. She is a very wonderful woman.[1]

---

[1]This passage does not appear in the published diaries. In 1973 Alec sought out the editor of Evelyn Waugh's Diaries, Michael Davie, and bade him excise it at proof stage.

Evelyn had read Bernard Shaw's *Candida* a few weeks before in his school reading group. If he recognised in the eponymous heroine the finer qualities of his mother he could not have failed equally to have noticed in the role of Morrell (Candida's flaccid windbag of a husband) many of his father's traits. In the play, a young poet, in love with Candida, asks Morrell how it is possible for her to love him: 'Is it like this for her here always? A woman, with a great soul, craving for reality, truth, freedom; and being fed on metaphors, sermons, stale perorations, mere rhetoric. Do you think a woman's soul can live on your talent for preaching? . . . It's the gift of the gab, nothing more, nothing less. What has your knack for talking to do with the truth? Oh, it's an old story: you'll find it in the Bible. I imagine King David in his fits of enthusiasm was very like you, "But his wife despised him in her heart".'

Before long Evelyn's sharp critical gaze would fall upon his friend Crease who, to his intense irritation, was falling for Arthur's charm and the bogus magic of Underhill. The point of his going there in the first place was so that Evelyn would not be disbarred from visiting Lychpole, but this no longer mattered to Evelyn. Soon Crease, like the others, had become more of a friend to Arthur and K than to Evelyn. Several months after that first visit Evelyn wrote in his diary: 'Crease is back at Lychpole. The spell is broken. His influence is quite gone. I just see a rather silly, perhaps casually interesting little man.' Evelyn had fallen under a new spell, another middle-aged man, another father-figure, perhaps: J. F. Roxburgh.[2]

When Alec returned from Germany after the 1918 armistice he was treated by his family as a hero. Evelyn, who had previously thought him aloof and priggish, especially during his time as house captain at Sherborne, now viewed his brother in a more glorious light. He was proud of Alec's smart, mature appearance and his handsome face. From that moment Alec, who had not previously bothered much with Evelyn, became his brother's mentor. Not

[2] In May 1954 Roxburgh fell headlong into his bath while attempting to undo his cravat and drowned, but long before that Evelyn had lost all enthusiasm for him as well. By 1922 he had 'come to the conclusion that he is thoroughly second rate'.

only did Evelyn regard him as the genius behind that 'awfully clever' watertight-compartments idea but he accepted him as tutor and guide in sexual matters. Once in France and once in Mainz, just after his release from the citadel, Alec had visited a brothel. He was no longer a virgin (at least in the heterosexual sense of the term), which gave him the confidence to instruct his younger brother in these matters. He persuaded Evelyn to buy himself a copy of Marlowe's *Hero and Leander* in the Everyman edition — which had given him such a masturbatory thrill at Sherborne. If that did not work Alec's four volumes of Havelock Ellis's *Psychology of Sex* were made available for Evelyn's perusal. 'I am reading all the case studies in Havelock Ellis and frigging too much,' Evelyn wrote to a friend. In 1927 Alec introduced him to the red-light district of Marseille, an episode Evelyn recalled in his first novel *Decline and Fall*. Alec was not precisely a father-figure to his younger brother but cast himself more in the role of a lubricious uncle. The uncle-nephew relationship between them was jocularly and openly maintained until Evelyn's death in 1966.

After his return from Germany, Alec found his passion for Barbara had waned. He was still an officer in the regular army but wanted to resign or, at very least, be offered a staff job that would allow him to resume his writing career. Since *The Loom of Youth* he had published only one slim volume of poetry, which had been badly received. The reviews, which Arthur had posted to him at the prison camp in Mainz, had made both Alec and his father sick. He had also written two novels. Arthur had objected to both of them on moral grounds, so neither was submitted for publication.

Increasingly Alec believed that *The Loom* had been a one-off *succès de scandale* never to be repeated. His star had shone brightly two years earlier; now it was all but extinguished. Supposing that he must do something — no matter what — he forged impetuously ahead with plans for his marriage to Barbara. Like many of the young men returning from the great upheavals of war, Alec craved stability, and Barbara, he believed, was the quickest way to attain it. Arthur, however, remained convinced that Alec's marriage plans were ill-fated and, in the most tactful words he could muster, wrote to 'My dearest Billy' urging him to hold off:

As to the marriage I am sure you know that your happiness is the very first consideration of my life. To that I postpone every other interest and nothing would delight me more than to see you happily settled at the earliest possible date. My only anxiety is to be sure that the foundations are laid for a really happy state of things. Marriage is a great deal more than a Romeo and Juliet consummation of love's rites, it is inextricably intermingled with all sorts of exasperating material considerations.

There are some girls who have the independence and devil-may-caredom to go anywhere with a man; into digs, into camp almost and to rough it through chop and change . . . Barbara of course is not like that. She has been brought up in great comfort: she has been used to have everything done for her: and though she may believe now that she would be quite happy roughing it in a wild Welsh cottage, I very much doubt how she would feel about things when she had to leave her warm bed to light a kitchen fire.

Barbara, as I understand her, is in no great haste herself. That is generally the woman's view and quite naturally so. She has a lot to give up and things lie ahead of her of which she has only the most shadowy premonition. So, if you feel things can be left till the prospect is clearer I am absolutely certain in my own mind that you will be doing what is wisest and surest for the future. I see you growing in strength and wisdom every week. That is my one comfort and inspiration. I live in it and for it all my days.

Ever most dear Billy, Your devoted Daddy.

If by 'things lie ahead of her of which she has only the most shadowy premonition' Arthur meant sexual intercourse, events were to prove him wrong. Alec was unwilling to heed his father's counsel and four months after that letter was written, in July 1919, he and Barbara were married. But the marriage was never consummated. I do not

entirely understand how this problem manifested itself in their particular case and suppose it would be indelicate to guess — out aloud
as it were — here. Trying to get to the bottom of this old family
mystery in 1981, my father explained to readers of the *Spectator* that
Alec 'couldn't get into her, achieve penetration or whatever' — a
coarse phraseology that resulted in the sternest of rebukes from the
descendants of Barbara's third marriage. Still, it left a mystery. Why
could Alec, whose motto on the sports field was 'Hard, High and
Often', not translate this simple dictat to his bed? In his autobiography he put it blithely: 'I had no idea of the amount of tact and
skilful patience that is required to initiate an inexperienced girl into
the intimacies of sex . . . I had been nicknamed Tank at Sandhurst,
yet I could not make my wife a woman. I was too ashamed of myself
to consult a doctor. By the time we did in the following summer it
was too late. Mental inhibitions had been created.'

Barbara and Alec kept a dog in their bedroom, which may have
accounted for a proportion of the problem. I have often heard of
dogs objecting (sometimes violently) to the copulation of their
masters or mistresses and happen to know that this particular
animal was possessed of an evil nature. When W. W. Jacobs came
to stay he awoke Alec and Barbara in the middle of the night to
complain that the dog had been trying to turn on the gas to
asphyxiate them in their sleep. Alec got out of bed and put a
tumbler over the gas tap to prevent the murderous mutt having
its wicked way.

So should we blame the dog for the young couple's difficulties
and leave it at that? Or shall I go on? Well, Papa always suspected
that the failure was Alec's — a malfunction of erectile tissue due
to invisible emanations from a silver cup inscribed from W. W.
Jacobs, which was kept, for some unclear reason, next to the
newly-weds' bed. Another possibility is that Alec had not entirely
rid himself of his homosexual interests. Perhaps he never did.
One of his sons told me that he remembered Alec in his old age
sitting outside a café in Tangier watching a handsome Arab stroll
by: 'Just think of the firm dusky limbs quivering beneath that
fella's djellaba,' he sighed.

During his marriage to Barbara Alec wrote two books that painted homosexuality in finer brushstrokes than those he had used for the gayest moments of *The Loom of Youth*. *Public School Life* might, in places, be read as a handbook on the art of homosexual seduction. 'If a senior boy is casually attracted by the appearance of a smaller boy, he asks a friend lower down in the house to make enquiries as to the morals of the small boy. If the "go-between" discovers that the small boy is "straight" the elder boy lets the matter fall from his mind.' In *Pleasure*, published in 1921, a soldier cadet meets up with a homosexual flame from his old school and reminisces wistfully on their previous encounters:

> There was no need for words between them, who had shared so many things.
> 'I say, what's the time, Geoffrey, we mustn't miss the train.'
> 'Oh that's alright, another minute or two.'
> Tenderly Geoffrey gazed at the features that during the last months had stamped themselves so indelibly upon his heart. How well he knew each shadow of that loved face, the long, slow line of the throat, the weak almost girlish chin.

Arthur was uneasy at his son's continual harping on this theme and accused him of being 'coarse and risky'. But Alec, though desperate not to upset his father, believed himself in the right. 'It seems absurd,' he wrote to him from Mainz, 'that one may not deal with a natural and often beautiful emotion that was felt by Socrates himself: but that anyone can deal with the most perverted forms of sexual bestiality – as long as there is a woman in it. For in our delightful country Sapphism may be practised if not discussed with perfect freedom, and then women talk of inequality of the sex laws.' A third book written in the period of Alec's marriage to Barbara reveals some of his thoughts about women – thoughts guaranteed to raise Barbara's feminist ire: 'The best seller is written for women, usually by women,' he remarked in *Myself When Young*. 'And it is by a masculine intelligence that the masterpieces of prose literature have been produced . . . Art is the fine raiment in which the civilised man arrays himself before a woman. And it is, perhaps, because women have need of no such artifice that their contributions to the museum of the world's art have been so casual and so imponderable.'

Barbara was not a fan of Alec's writing at the best of times. 'That silly book' is how she described *The Loom of Youth*. Before he went to France he had bound a copy in expensive calf and presented it to her with a loving inscription:

> Four years of wandering more or less,
>   Of struggling ignorant why I strove,
> The odyssey of selfishness,
>   And yet the prelude to our love.

Barbara was as unimpressed by this as she was by his disappearance in the Ludendorff offensive, but when Arthur saw this inscription he burst into tears.

Alec and Barbara's marriage broke down quickly. It was all over within thirty fretful months. Arthur was appalled and blamed Barbara entirely for the fiasco. She, he insisted, had impugned his son's honour by denying him 'love's rites'. He talked openly with the young Fleming girls about the failure of consummation: 'How could it happen? How could it happen?' he gasped, twixt asthmatic wheezes. K was more forgiving. She became the repository for many of Alec and Evelyn's discarded friends, and although the brothers never saw Barbara after the break-up of that marriage in January 1922, K kept in touch for the rest of her life.

At the time of their wedding in July 1919 Alec had already succeeded in extricating himself from the army and had taken a job as a reader at his father's firm in Covent Garden. At first he and Barbara lived at Underhill. They converted the day nursery into a library-sitting room to give them a modicum of privacy but they dined always with Arthur and K. Soon the burden of working and living with his parents, added to the harrowing failures of the bedroom, started to weigh heavily on Alec. At the time Evelyn's friend Dudley Carew wrote in his diary:

> Got to the Waughs about 7 o'clock . . . they were all very
> kind but Alec has an extraordinarily chilling and repressing
> influence. Directly he comes in Arthur stops making jokes,
> Evelyn stops being clever and only Mrs W is left undisturbed.
> He has gimlety eyes, a baleful glare which, unlike Evelyn's,
> is quite unconscious and a big dome-like forehead and a rather
> quick almost nervous way of speaking. A personality.

Carew did not realise that Alec was miserable, but Evelyn saw him wandering around the house with a gaunt expression, muttering of suicide.

After a year of this torture, Alec decided to reduce the time he spent at Chapman and Hall from five to two days a week and, in the summer of 1920, he and Barbara moved out of Underhill to a pink-roofed prefab bungalow at Ditchling in Sussex of which they were both sorely ashamed. Arthur came to stay with them most weekends, and Alec started writing again, but the move did nothing to inspire his sex life. When Barbara was at Ditchling, Alec stayed at Underhill; and when he was in the bungalow writing his books, Barbara would visit Evelyn at nearby Lancing or, in the holidays, move back to Underhill without her husband, to be with his younger brother. Before long Barbara and Alec were leading separate lives. Alec stayed from Friday to Monday at Underhill and, mid-week, booked himself into a quiet pub, the White Horse at Shenley, to write his books. By July 1922 he was 'deeply committed to a sultry tempestuous romance' with an older woman who taught him hetero-sexual confidence. Barbara wrote to him requesting an audience. She came to his office and they went for a walk in St James's Park. 'It's a funny thing to ask one's husband,' she said, 'but I want to be married again.'

'Do you think it would work?' Alec asked, assuming she wanted to 'give it another go'.

'That's my problem, isn't it?' She smirked coldly.

Her second marriage was equally unsuccessful.

Alec's job at Chapman and Hall was a mistake from the start. Arthur had offered it to him mainly because he wished to be near his son – he still could not let him go. To the board he justified hiring Alec on the grounds that the firm needed a young person who understood the youth book market and would introduce young modern authors to the list. For the first year Alec sat, lugubriously reading manuscripts, in a small shared office three floors above his father. He felt out of it, wanting to be downstairs with Arthur, talking about literature, telling him how to run the company. But his father was always busy – 'driven', as he used to call it – and, as we know, he hated discussions. Despite all the time they had spent together yackety-yacking along the Sherborne slopes or across Hampstead Heath, allowing one subject to roll freely into another, Arthur required a different order of communication at work. Alec, who resented having to share his father's time with the office staff, stored up ideas to discuss with Arthur when they got home, but Arthur always made a point of refusing to talk shop at Underhill. Consequently their glorious relationship became fraught and disharmonious – at least as far as Alec was concerned. It must have been the same for Arthur, but I cannot find the evidence to show it. Arthur was a loyal clam. In 1929 he published a centennial history of Chapman and Hall called *A Hundred Years of Publishing* in which he wrote glowingly of Alec's contribution to the firm: 'It is said to be a difficult thing for father and son to work together in business; but if there was any difficulty in this particular alliance, it was certainly not felt upon the father's side. Those were years of the happiest association and the firm's programme expanded rapidly under the influence of youth.' This compares interestingly to the equivalent passage from Alec's *Early Years*:

It is perhaps never easy for father and son to work together in business, and the very fact that in all other things we were so close made it the more difficult for us. It placed our relationship on a new basis. My father and I were very different; I was more like my mother. The attraction of opposites brought us the closer, emotionally, but in the conduct of business it made special difficulties. My father's mind worked fast. He liked to make quick decisions. He disliked discussions. Discussions seemed to him a brother to argument and cousin to quarrel. I, on the other hand, like talking round a subject.

Business discussions between father and son were not the only cause of tension between them. Alec's first major book after *The Loom of Youth*, a record of his German captivity called *Prisoners of Mainz*, was published by Chapman and Hall in 1919, but he felt that publication by his father's firm restricted his freedom as an author and sought, wherever possible, to place his books elsewhere. This led to dissent among the ranks of Chapman and Hall, who accused Alec of disloyalty. In the office at Henrietta Street Arthur was on his guard against showing favouritism, and when a young man who worked beneath Alec in the firm's hierarchy demanded a place on the board, Arthur would not offer his son a promotion unless Alec presented a written application stating his reasons why he also deserved to sit on the board. For Alec this was both a humiliation and a betrayal. However, he wrote his application and the young men eventually joined the board together.

During his time at Chapman and Hall Alec persuaded Arthur to employ Evelyn as an illustrator of book jackets. Evelyn's drawings were, if not brilliant, at least lively and arresting – likely, in Alec's professional view, to appeal to young readers. It was a scheme that put money into Evelyn's pockets and brought him kudos among his schoolfriends.

At Lancing Evelyn was of the loose opinion that he was a 'genius'. The school was dim and depressing and he was certainly brighter than most of the people in it. He knew that he was funnier than all of his contemporaries, he was better read, better at drawing, better at writing both poetry and prose; he was wittier than his father, more critical than his brother – he had no doubt that he would make his mark on the world. But how? 'It's rotten when you've got a touch of genius and you don't know how it's going to turn out,' he complained to a friend.

Like many people of outstanding talent Evelyn hovered between the opposing forces of arrogance and self-loathing. Dudley Carew had decided early that Evelyn was a genius and collected, during the course of their school friendship, every scrap of paper on which he had jotted. He turned out to be right and many years later, after Evelyn had died, he sold his schoolboy hoard for a considerable sum to the University of Texas.

For a time Carew attempted to persuade everyone he met of Evelyn's potential greatness. At home he was disbelieved. At Underhill he was listened to with interest. Arthur knew that Evelyn was different, unlovable perhaps, not the sweet daughter he had always wanted, but a distant and brilliant boy. He did not like Evelyn's manner; he detested his sharp tongue, his cynical wit and satirical humour. He felt more comfortable with the flirtatious, confidence-boosting Alec than he did with brittle, complex Evelyn, in whose presence he felt uneasy. But, for all this, he was not blind to his younger son's potential. In response to a notion of Carew's that Evelyn would turn out to be the Max Beerbohm of his age, Arthur is reported to have said, 'No, he will be greater, for Evelyn is a creator.' When Arthur was being harried for a debt incurred by Evelyn at a restaurant, Alec apparently said to him: 'You know, Father, if Evelyn turns out to be a genius, you and I might be made to look very foolish by making a fuss over ten pounds, seventeen and ninepence.' Arthur's response, according to Alec's recollection, was 'Would I, would we, that's not much consolation now.'

At the end of his school career Evelyn wrote a play and sent the script to Underhill for his father's approval. The last such submission, an essay on the subject of Romance, had been dismissed by Arthur as 'too satirical'. He did not like the play much either. It satirised school life, lampooned *The Loom of Youth*, and sniggered at the backward opinions of Evelyn's maiden aunts, but Arthur was a keen enough critic to spot that his son had literary talent, even though it was of a type he could never instinctively admire. He wrote to Evelyn at school:

Dear Dramatist,

Congratulations on your wit and cynicism. I read your play yesterday with admiring amusement. The glorious nonchalance of your bloods – entirely unlike anything that existed in my generation – seems to me most cleverly portrayed, and the turn of the situation at the end – a little Shavian, perhaps – is wonderfully witty. You certainly have a most ingenious brain. You could do much. I do indeed congratulate you on a most excellent piece of work. With such promise I feel you are bound to come off at Oxford. That is precisely the Oxford wit. You have at 17 what we laboured to get, and couldn't, at 23. Go on and prosper and my heart goes with you.

After the show, which Arthur did not attend, he received a letter of congratulation from J. F. Roxburgh, lauding Evelyn for his 'touch of genius'. In his last school report, at Christmas 1921, Roxburgh had written: 'His work has great merit and is sometimes really brilliant. I think he has quite unusual ability and a real gift for writing. We shall hear of him again.'

When Evelyn was in his third year at Lancing, Arthur produced a second volume of his collected literary criticism. The first, it may be remembered – *Reticence in Literature* – had been bound in the blue and gold of the Sherborne colours and dedicated to Alec. *Tradition and Change* was grudgingly dedicated to Evelyn. Arthur told Alec that he wished he could write another book for him but, all things being fair, this one had to be for his brother. To appear even-handed he wrote an equivalent letter of dedication to Evelyn. It is shorter than the one to Alec and far less amatory, very sentimental and yet, between the lines, it reveals the deep unease that characterised Arthur's fragile relationship with his younger son at this time.

To
Evelyn Arthur St John Waugh

My dear Evelyn,

I do not go into the old nursery now so often as I used; it is too full of memories to be altogether comfortable. But I found myself there last night, looking for one of the many pictures you painted there last holidays; and as my eye wandered around the familiar walls, I felt that the room might well serve as a sort of treasure-house of our happy home life. I remembered days when it rang with the sound of battle, and all the tea things were broken by a flying dart. I remembered its transformation into a theatre. I saw it decorated with Alec's cricket and football groups upon one wall; and then I turned to the other, which you and Barbara have frescoed with strange Cubist pictures; and I do not forget that it had been renamed the 'Studio' – your private temple of the most modern school of art. The room has changed many times since the summer when we built Underhill; but the good sound walls and timbers are still the same, and sometimes, when the house is silent in sleep, they may whisper to one another of many cheerful hours, enshrining the same spirit as of old, although we ourselves have all grown so much older.

In memory of that room and of all that it has seen, I should like to offer you this book, which is, in its way, only another tribute to the passage of Time, the certainty of Change and the imperishable influence of Tradition. You are born into an era of many changes; and, if I know you at all, you will be swayed and troubled by many of them. But you are not yet so wedded to what is new that you seem likely to despise what is old. You may copy the Cubist in your living room, but an Old Master hangs above your bed. You may accept the new social order of tomorrow, but your hope is still rooted (and long may it remain so!) in the old Faith that is the same yesterday, to-day and for ever. I wish you nothing better than to change gently, like the old room where we have spent so many happy hours, reflecting the wiser fashions of the passing day, but still looking out, through sunlit casements, upon green grass, a garden of flowers and God's blue sky above you. If that is not the happy life, I do not know where happiness is to be found.

Your loving Father
ARTHUR WAUGH

Evelyn could not have failed to notice the difference in tone between Arthur's dedication to Alec and this one to himself. The feeble skirting, the 'if I know you at all', the 'in memory of that room', the piffle about growing older and looking through sunlit casements was a million miles from the heartfelt gush of his brother's dedication four years earlier. Gone are the references to the mutual 'comradeship', 'sympathy', 'unclouded devotion' and the 'joys that have made our life so pleasant and our companionship so sweet' that Arthur offered Alec. If he hadn't spotted it already, Evelyn could now easily see, by flitting his eye from one published page to the other, how his relationship with his father compared with that of his brother. Nor could he have failed to notice within that book Arthur's pointed references to youth and age, his attack on wise young men, on literary Cubists and, in particular, on a poem by Orrick Johns which Arthur despised:

> This is the song of youth,
> This the cause of myself;
> I knew my father well and he was a fool,
> Therefore will I have my own foot in the path before I take
>   a step.

'Here surely,' steamed Arthur, 'is the reduction to absurdity of that school of literary licence which, beginning with the declaration 'I knew my father well and he was a fool,' naturally proceeds to the convenient assumption that everything which seemed wise and true to the father must inevitably be false and foolish to the son.'

A few months later, during the winter of 1920, Evelyn set to work on his own book, a novel. He was seventeen years old. It was to be 'a study of a man with two characters by his brother' and was clearly based on Alec. At first his family showed no interest in the project, but Evelyn was persistent. Eventually Arthur admitted, without much enthusiasm, that he liked it. K worried that Evelyn would be ruined by becoming a public figure before his time, and Alec – if Evelyn's diary account is to be believed – showed apprehension at having a rival. That Evelyn was nettled by a comparison

of his father's two book dedications is apparent from his own
dedication of his novel, which should be read as a direct attack on
Arthur, on Alec, on Arthur's dedicatory letter to Evelyn and on
the whole precious, bookish atmosphere of Underhill:

To myself,
Evelyn Arthur St John Waugh
to whose sympathy and appreciation alone it owes its
being, this book is dedicated.

Dedicatory letter.

My dear Evelyn,

Much has been spoken and written about the lot of the
boy with literary aspirations in a philistine family; little
can adequately convey his difficulties, when the surroundings, which he has known from childhood, have been entirely
literary. It is a sign of victory over these difficulties that
this book is chiefly, if at all, worthy of attention.

Many of your relatives and most of your father's friends
are more or less directly interested in paper and print. Ever
since you first left the nursery for meals with your parents
downstairs, the conversation, to which you were an insatiable
listener, has been of books, their writers and producers; ever
since as a sleepy but triumphantly emancipate school boy,
you were allowed to sit up with your elders in the 'book-
room' after dinner, you have heard little but discussion about
books. Your home has always been full of them; all new
books of any merit, and most of none, seem by one way or
another to find their place in the files which have long over-
flowed the shelves. Among books your whole life has been
layed [*sic*] and you are now rising up in your turn to add one
more to the everlasting bonfire of the ephemeral.

And all this will be brought up against you. 'Another of
these precocious Waughs,' they will say. So be it. There is
always a certain romance, to the author at least, about a

first novel which no reviewer can quite shatter. Good luck! You have still high hopes and big ambitions and have not yet been crushed in the mill of professionalism. Soon perhaps you will join the 'wordsmiths' jostling one another for royalties and contracts, meanwhile you are still very young.

Yourself,
Evelyn

Through lack of confidence and positive encouragement, Evelyn abandoned the novel after only a few thousand words in January 1921. The new year was to prove a bad one for him. For most of it he was listless, hating his school, bored and lonely at home. It did not seem to matter that he had won both the school poetry and literature prizes, that he was head of his house, president of the debating society, that he had written a play, which had been performed with great success to the whole school, or that he was editor of the school magazine. He believed that his aloofness had made him unpopular with masters and boys, and his headmaster's report confirms this: 'Last term he had begun to grate against his surroundings and the friction was bad for him. He threw out sparks which made little fires in some of the characters about him, partly, no doubt kindling, but partly destructive. For all his brilliance he is curiously young and out of touch with reality.'

He planned to run away. He also thought about killing himself. Even the frustrations of Underhill were preferable to the stale atmosphere of school and he wrote to Arthur begging to be removed. He would, he assured his father, find himself a decent job in London and contribute towards the costs at Underhill.

When he received his son's letter, Arthur panicked. Remembering Alec's Sherborne disgrace, he jumped immediately to the conclusion that Evelyn had been caught in a brothel and was being blackmailed into finding an honourable excuse for leaving. Once he had been assured that this was not the case he reluctantly agreed to his leaving at the end of the winter term.

Despite the embarrassment and *ennui* that Evelyn sometimes felt in his father's company he was not past wishing to please him. Like

Alec, Evelyn's principal pleasure at his own successes was intensified by the happiness that they brought to Arthur. He remembered
the joyful day in September 1920 when Arthur had taken him on
a tour of Oxford, telling him about the student adventures of past
Waughs and their colleges, of his own time at New College, showing
off the architecture, the podium from which he had recited his
Newdigate prize poem, steeping his son in the history of that beautiful city. Evelyn must have believed that if he won a place at
Oxford he might enjoy with his father the same intimacy Alec had
enjoyed with him at Sherborne. Alec had decided against university – as an established author and veteran of Passchendaele, Oxford
had seemed a backward step to him. Evelyn worked hard for his
exams. Arthur wanted him to apply to New College where he had
spent his own student years, but Evelyn, noticing that scholarships
were worth more elsewhere, put himself down for the less illustrious Hertford College instead. He did this to save his father money.

When news of Evelyn's scholarship came through Arthur was
overjoyed. No doubt he, too, felt that their relationship might
improve once they had the Oxford experience to share. Perhaps
he might now enjoy a second shot at staying young, living through
the life and career of one of his sons. He wrote to Evelyn quoting
from Psalm xxxv:

> 'Heaviness may endure for a night: but joy cometh in the
> morning.' I cannot express to you the grateful happiness
> that fills my heart today. Next to New College, I would
> have chosen Hertford. It is a small but thoroughly good
> college and the emoluments are the best on the list. Strangely
> enough it was of Hertford that Young made the famous
> remark to Coy-Dixon: 'It is most satisfactory; and a blame-
> less career is crowned by a first class success.' That word I
> can repeat to you with a grateful heart. Thank you, my
> dear Boy, for the honour and happiness you have brought
> to your home. May the future be worthy of this beginning.

If Arthur was hoping to fish a few vicarious thrills from Evelyn's
Oxford career he was to be sorely disappointed. At Oxford Evelyn

did not join the OUDS or act in *Hamlet*; he did not tour with his college cricket team, nor did he bother to finish his submission for the Newdigate Prize. In fact, he did nothing to excite his father's pride and much to incur his resentment. But before embarking on this sorry part of my tale let me backtrack a month or so to examine a curious item published in the *Lancing College Magazine* in December 1921. Entitled 'The Younger Generation', it was Evelyn's last editorial for the school rag. I shall clip it to the gist:

> During the last few years, a new generation has grown up. What will the young men of 1922 be? What will they stand for and what are they going to do? They will be above all things clear sighted. The youngest generation are going to be very hard and analytical and unsympathetic.
>
> The young men of the nineties subsisted upon emotion. They poured out their souls like water and their tears with pride; middle-aged observers will find it hard to see the soul in the youngest generation.
>
> But they will have – and this is their justification – a very full sense of humour. They will watch themselves with probably a greater egotism than did the young men of the nineties, but it will be with a cynical smile and often with a laugh. It is a queer world which the old men have left them and they will have few ideals and illusions to console them when they 'get to feeling old'. They will not be a happy generation.

On first inspection what we seem to be reading is Evelyn's declaration of war against his father or, at the very least, a rebellious setting up of barriers between them. Evelyn later dismissed the piece as a 'preposterous manifesto of disillusionment', but the references to the older generation 'subsisting on emotion' and to the man who 'pours out his tears with pride' imply something else. They seem to point an accusing finger not at any non-specific model of that generation but directly through those 'sunlit casements' of Underhill at Mr Arthur Waugh. But closer inspection shows that none of the ideas expressed here is especially new. In his Lancing diaries Evelyn made repeated references to the generations. 'What a ridiculous generation we are. In the last generation people never began to think until they were about nineteen. Time can only show if we are going to be any better for it . . . We certainly are precocious if that is at all a good sign.' His school play, subtitled *The Tragedy of Youth*, demonstrated in three burlesques Alec's point from *The Loom of Youth*, that the older generation is out of touch with the realities of school life. In making these points Evelyn was being neither observant nor original, for these were the very same views expressed many, many times by his own father.

To any reader who has kept even half an eye to the whiles of this unfolding saga, Arthur must appear as a man obsessed with generations, with the passing of time and with the matching of youth and age. His empty relationship with his own brutish father, his stifling love for Alec, his ambition to live vicariously through his elder son's school career — all these are signs of a man for whom the subject of generations is uppermost in the mind. The book he dedicated to Evelyn, *Tradition and Change*, deals at great length with the issue. It was the leitmotif of his conversation. If Arthur and Evelyn's relationship was bad it could be explained — justified, even — by the differences between one generation and another. Alec, too, had caught something of his father's passion for the subject. *The Loom of Youth* is, after all, chiefly concerned with the difference between school as pupils see it and as it is viewed by an older generation. In his late teens Alec wrote a poem entitled 'Song', which might well be read as a conversation between himself and Arthur:

> Saith the sage: youth flieth by,
>   As the dawn before the day:
> Soon the flagon must run dry,
>   Soon the rainbow fade away.
> Store your treasures for old age:
>   Saith the sage.

> Saith the rose: one thing is sure,
>   Nothing is more sweet than laughter.

Who can tell what may endure,
　　What man knows what follows after?
Rake what's certain ere it goes:
　　Saith the rose.

Saith my heart: life's secret lies
　　Not alone in age nor youth,
But to both the same voice cries,
　　Colours change but not the truth.
Only love and never part:
　　Saith my heart.

When Evelyn or Arthur wrote about the generations, as they often did, it is always as though they were writing, first and foremost, about each other. Of course, the Great War divided the generations to some extent. Those, like Evelyn, who were too young to fight felt a greater estrangement from the previous generation than those who had seen action. But that does not alter the fact that the Waughs at Underhill were obsessed with youth and age, and that this obsession was entirely driven by Arthur. After the success of his early novels, Evelyn became the British media's 'voice of youth' and the key to his early fame was his self-identification with the younger generation and his repudiation of much for which his father stood. In 1930 he wrote a witty piece for the *Daily Herald* entitled 'What I Think of My Elders':

I admire their lack of scruple. It takes a great deal to rouse them, but when some feature of their comfort is really threatened they will suddenly plunge into conflict with every artifice their long lives have taught them. I admire their lack of ambition. I admire the resolution with which they hold to their own opinions; their indifference to the traps and pitfalls of logical proof. I admire their sense of humour, those curious jokes which seem to gain lustre and pungency with each repetition . . . Old people only make themselves ridiculous by pretending to be young.

Arthur had tried hard to join in with the spirit of the young in a way that his own father would never have contemplated, yet it was painful for him to admit to himself that the experiment was not working; he could not change his own nature, it was cast in immutable form. Inevitably the time would come when the overweight Victorian sentimentalist could no longer keep up with his boys, when he would be left puffing and panting in the ditch as they both sprinted on ahead. He calculated this coming but noticed it far too late. In the closing pages of his autobiography (composed at the same time as Evelyn's piece for the *Daily Herald*) he wrote, in a mood of deflated self-pity:

There is no denying that our children have the advantage of our generation in many ways. They will not make our mistakes of impulse and emotion; they are saved from sentimentality, without doing wrong to their hearts; and where we were eager to keep young, they are content to be mature before their time. Perhaps indeed, when the final reckoning is cast, it will be found that the greatest mistake our own generation made lay in its effort to keep on equal terms with its successor, to be brothers and sisters to its boys and girls. We meant so well in the beginning but it was an impossible undertaking. We saw the limitation of the Victorian home; the autocracy of the arm-chair; the lack of confidence between father and son; the insincere covering up of the facts of life; the secret whispers, shrugs and lifted eyebrows. We distrusted it all and we protested that our children should live their lives out after their own fashion and that we would share every yard of the way with them, knowing exactly what they wanted and recognising their right to their own personalities, their own ambitions and goals. We would be young with the young. Alas, vain boast. It cannot be done. It never has been done and never will. Avoiding one pitfall, we stumble into another. Youth and age can never keep on terms together.

Fading age deludes itself with the dream that youth enjoys its company, but the young do not really want us. Why should they? They have their own experience to make and must make it their own way. Every man has his own road to follow; his own companions to choose; the hardest lesson that age must learn is the knowledge that the time has come to look on at the race, while others run it. That is the great ordeal by change, the final test of character.

What a curious irony that Evelyn managed to found his early success as Fleet Street's 'voice of youth' on his father's wistful waffle, while Arthur's lifelong obsession with youth and age led only to his own crushing defeat. 'The Great War marked the end of my generation,' he wrote in *One Man's Road*. 'We did not realise it at the time, but it was the end all the same. There was no sudden revolution, no public holocaust of the old standards; but the spirit of change was pervading every side of life, and the traditions for which our age had stood began, slowly, one after another, to wilt and wither.'

Oh dear, oh dear – how sad this story waxes.

VII

In Arcadia

Waughs do not do well at university. Arthur got a third-class degree, so did Evelyn (a poor one at that) and so did I. My father fared even worse by failing his first-year exams and flopping out after only three terms. We all have, or had, our own excuses. There is no common theme. In Evelyn's case it was a cocktail of drunkenness, lassitude, and raw, adolescent rebellion that did it.

University started off on the wrong foot for Evelyn. Originally it had been agreed that he would spend some time in France, learn the language, then go up to university at the same time as most freshers join, in the autumn term; but Arthur, as ever anxious about money, wanted his son's education to be over and done with as quickly as possible. With minimal reflection, he sent Evelyn to Oxford in January 1922. History was repeating itself. Because Evelyn had entered Lancing in the spring term of 1917 he had found it hard to make friends among those who had already teamed up – another misfortune occasioned by Arthur's impetuosity and his fear of arguments.

In *One Man's Road* Arthur complained: 'I was a week late at my dame-school; at Sherborne I began my time in the summer, instead of in the autumn, when the new generation commonly arrives; and now, at Oxford, I was in the least lucky case of all, for the freshmen of 1885 were already well established in work and friendship before I made my belated appearance and it took me all the length of my first year to recover lost ground.' For his late entry to Oxford Arthur had blamed his father, who had failed to sign and return the registration papers on time. This irony did not pass Evelyn unnoticed: 'It is curious,' he wrote in *A Little Learning* 'that, alive as my father was to the disadvantages of his own experience, he should have set me on precisely the same road.'

Evelyn's three years at Oxford have been amply chronicled in countless biographies and in the lewd memoirs of several of his raffish friends, so I do not intend to examine all the gory details here. I shall not delve into what he did, or did not do, with his tongue at the Hypocrites Club, nor shall I be pokin' m'nose into his intimate friendships with Richard Pares, Alastair Graham and Hugh Lygon. Academics, scholars and dusty experts from the English faculties of important universities around the world have, for the past forty years, sifted and evaluated the evidence and continue to do so today: 'Was it Platonic?' 'Did they kiss?' 'Did they touch below the Mason-Dixon?' 'Did the one squirt the other with the fluids of his epididymis?' These are very, very clever questions for very, very clever people. I do not propose to tackle them here.

Alec's homosexuality at Sherborne affected his relationship with Arthur. Afterwards, as I have said, he continued to publish his opinions on homosexual love to his father's acute discomfort. I do not know if Arthur suspected Evelyn and his university friends of sexual congress, but I think he probably did. When Alec visited Oxford he sensed a 'strong homosexual undertone' among Evelyn's set and Arthur must have noticed it also when Evelyn brought his friends to stay. These things, especially when they develop into love affairs, cannot be easily hidden. Arthur found most of Evelyn's university friends undesirable and the more flamboyant homosexuals among them were not welcome at Underhill. One of these, Terence Greenidge, a dirty and eccentric boy, was sneaked into the house in the middle of the night and remained upstairs until Arthur had left for work. Evelyn once tried to conceal Greenidge in this way for five days at Underhill, but Arthur recognised his smell: 'Has that dreadful boy been in my house again?' he asked.

Many years later Greenidge had most, if not all, of his brain removed in a surgical operation that seemed to have altered his memory of events. Sitting next to my father at dinner on board an express train in November 1963, he claimed that Arthur had particularly admired him from the start. Papa reported back to Evelyn:

> I enjoyed the evening with railway enthusiasts most tremendously, although the motion of the train and the excitement of the conversation had the most deleterious effect on me the next morning, and I felt very ill indeed. Greenidge said: 'The most extraordinary thing about Arthur Waugh was the way I could tell he took to me immediately. I was most flattered because he did not take to all of Evelyn's friends.' I thought his talk of having a leucotomy was a delusion as he constantly pointed to his forehead like a warrior showing his wounds but there was no mark there. On the other hand he did seem exceptionally placid.

Evelyn was intensely irritated whenever Arthur 'took to his friends immediately' and made sure that the case was straightened in the autobiography he was then writing.

It may be that Greenidge was more obviously homosexual in his demeanour than some of Evelyn's other friends, but camp behaviour would not in itself have been sufficient to alarm Arthur. Both Dudley Carew and Francis Crease, from Evelyn's Lancing years, were homosexual – Crease particularly and ostentatiously so – yet both were frequent guests at Underhill at Arthur's invitation and in Evelyn's absence. I suspect that he made no link in his mind between camp mannerisms and homosexual activity and, like Evelyn, supposed Crease to be epicene. Had he suspected Crease, or anyone else, of homosexual behaviour I think that Arthur would have disapproved. He flatly refused to shake Oscar Wilde's hand or even to rise from his chair when they last met at a café in Paris in the late 1890s.

Fathers have always felt uneasy about their sons' homosexualising.

Even the ancient Greeks abhorred any form of sodomy that did not conform to the paederastic rite of passage between *erastes* and *eromenos* condoned by Athenian convention. Outside it, sons who continued as homosexuals were derided as 'soft', radishes were stuffed up their bottoms and they were disinherited. The present-day emotion concerning sons and homosexuality is by no means as straightforward as homophobia, but perhaps it is related – a discrete and less noxious cousin, shall we say? In this regard my family is no exception. When homosexuality was illegal, fathers had to bear – along with the usual anxieties of morality, lifestyle and patri-lineage – the added fear that their sons' careers would be ruined by exposure to scandal.

When Alec became a father of two strapping sons he worried himself sick lest they turned out to be er, you know? Andrew, the eldest, did not marry until he was thirty-four: 'I had begun to worry about him "in that way",' wrote Alec, in one of his late remi-niscences. 'In these days it is impossible for parents not to worry about whether their son is going to turn out gay.' Andrew's marriage was a relief to his father, and his concerns for his younger son dissolved when Peter was at home on leave from the army. Alec's wife thought she might have heard a girl giggling in Peter's bedroom. Phew! 'Nothing queer about Carruthers,' Alec gloated.[1]

Evelyn, who labelled his children indiscriminately, decided that his youngest son, Septimus, was going to be the 'pansy' of the family. He was not worried by this, only slightly disappointed.[2] My own father, who, as I have said, never had a serious conversation with me in all his life, had been told (I suspect by my mother) that a streak of misogyny had developed in me. She was right. I had recently been chucked by a girlfriend at school and was strutting about the house, vowing to have nothing to do with women for as long as I lived. I was invited into the library (a rare occurrence) to discuss the situation with my father. I knocked and entered apprehensively. He was writing, and looked pained to be reminded of the duty he had elected himself to fulfil. I stood awkwardly in

[1] Peter Waugh tells me this story is entirely untrue. So what could those giggling noises have been?

[2] Septimus married young. He has three children. Ever gay? I doubt it.

front of his desk and waited for him to speak. 'My dear boy,' he pronounced, 'the anus was designed for the retention and expulsion of faecal matter, not for the reception of foreign organs, however lovingly placed there.' I left the room in tears of laughter.

In later life Evelyn told a friend he was anxious that his son – my father – should not discover about his homosexual past. But there are clues to it in many of his books and also in his diaries, which he must have known my father would one day read. In 1954 he wrote to his friend Nancy Mitford: 'I went to Oxford and visited my first homosexual love, Richard Pares, a don at All Souls.' He was not secretive about his homosexual youth with others; it only seemed to matter that his son should not find out. Perhaps men with sons will understand this.

Of greater concern than homosexuality to Arthur during Evelyn's time at Oxford were his drinking, his inability to work hard and his constant overspending. Arthur was not a rich man. He earned about £1000 a year, and it was a sacrifice for him, even with Evelyn's £100 annual Hertford scholarship, to keep him there. He agreed to the minimum £220 grant. Arthur was not mean, nor was he extravagant, but he worried excessively. On top of the £220, Evelyn reckoned, with birthdays and impromptu demands, to screw another fifty pounds out of him during the year and to earn a little extra designing bookplates for friends and dustjackets for Chapman and Hall. Even this was not enough. He mixed with people richer than himself and he was lavish in his generosity to them. He liked giving presents and developed an unquenchable thirst for antiquarian books, smart suits, hats, gold watches, walking-sticks, champagne and restaurants. When his bank refused permission for him to withdraw cash, he borrowed recklessly. He sold his books, pawned his watch, his ring and his decorative skull. The only way to stop his tailors and book-dealers foreclosing was by placing more orders with them on account. Several times he furtively approached his mother, who emptied her savings account to bail him out.

Alec was continuously loyal during this period. He came down to Oxford every term to recruit young authors to the Chapman and Hall list and to check on his younger brother's progress. He lent Evelyn fivers, took him and his friends to dine at the George, commissioned him to draw the dustjackets of his latest novels and to design for him a personalised bookplate. Evelyn duly produced a charming ink-drawing of a cricketer in a top-hat peering round the Waugh coat of arms. In the bottom right-hand corner a plump Cupid sits, concealing its genitals, on a pile of books. The allusions to cricket and books are obvious. Perhaps only the cupid needs explaining. Although Alec was small, not especially handsome due to his overlarge lower jaw and, by 1923, completely bald on top, he had developed a range of remarkably successful seduction techniques[3]. He was not especially choosy about his girls for he had arrived early at the conclusion that quantity was preferable to quality – some, even he would admit, were hideous.[4] From the last months of 1922 until the day he died, Alec led the life of an eager and adroit womaniser. I think he was an erotomaniac. In 'periods of chastity' he paid for sex or would find a blue movie. In 1930 Evelyn wrote to his agent: 'Alec goes to an indecent cinema every day.' In old age, living in New York, he ventured out each morning in his outsized sable-lined, high collar coat, heading for the old Hudson Theater on West 44th Street to enjoy an hour or two of American hardcore pornography after breakfast.

When Evelyn was at Oxford he and his friends nicknamed Alec 'the bald-headed lecher', and during the holidays they stalked him around London. As soon as he had ingratiated himself with a young woman they jumped from their place of concealment, screaming, 'Boo to Alec, the bald-headed lecher!' Once they hid outside the window of his flat and, as the lady he was entertaining leaned back

[3] He operated on the simple assumption that if he was attracted to a girl, she would also be attracted to him.

[4] I have only come across one example of Alec's turning down a sexual opportunity. In September 1926 he wrote to a friend from Siam: 'I couldn't think how anyone would have consented to a coupling with the Malayan object with which a Chinese pimp presented me. I could not think of it as a human creature. It woke in me no more ardour – rather less, in fact, than Winifred's nice grey cat. For a moment or two I gazed sorrowfully upon it. Then shook my head, patted its dusky rump, and transferring two dollars to its henna-ed fingers dismissed it to its waiting mother.'

on the sofa and Alec dimmed the lights, they rapped on the window shouting once more: 'Boo to Alec, the bald-headed lecher!' When Evelyn missed his train back to Oxford, he invariably headed to Alec's flat. On one occasion, forgetting the number of Alec's apartment, he opened every door in the block shouting at the top of his voice: 'Is the bald-headed lecher sleeping in here?' Next day the neighbours joined forces to demand that Alec find himself another home.

The flat, I should explain, was at 22 Earls Terrace. Had it not been for Alec's lust, I dare say he would have stayed on at Underhill, but he needed a discrete base for his seductions and, in January 1924, he moved all his clobber from his father's house and set himself up as a sexy Kensington bachelor. By this stage his relationship with Arthur had relaxed since the early days of his working at Chapman and Hall and his marriage to Barbara, but no sooner had he pitched his tent in Kensington than he began to realise once again how much his father meant to him and how greatly he missed his company. Even though he was still seeing Arthur on his two days a week at the Chapman and Hall office he made a point of staying every Saturday night at Underhill. Arthur and K were his first guests for dinner at Earls Terrace.

To Arthur, Alec's removal from Underhill was a bitter blow, another doleful reminder of the passing of generations and the inexorable approach of the Grim Reaper:

My dear Billy,

Your departure from Underhill is a real wrench. Hitherto when you have made other homes, one anchor at any rate has always been made fast here. We have had your things about us, hostages for your return. This parting is different; and though I am sure it was inevitable, it means the breaking up of a tradition.

But whenever you will come to us, everything will be just the same. And I know in years to come, you will often remember the happy little dinner party of last night and your own kindness in counting us to be your first guests.

It will be written in all our hearts forever.

If the future is half as good as the past, there are many good days to come. In that hope . . .

> 'On to the bound of the waste,
> On to the City of God.'

Ever, as of old, your loving 'Daddy'

At Oxford Evelyn's relationship with his father deteriorated rapidly: university presented him with a bright new life. Now his father, Underhill and suburbia were 'quite indescribably dreary'. In the holidays he spent as little time as possible at home, preferring to stay at friends' houses or to wile away his days and evenings cavorting with them around London, using Underhill only as an occasional place to sleep. Evelyn and his friends referred to Arthur as 'Chapman and Hall', sometimes just as 'Chapman', always with a sneer. At first Arthur thought this was funny, but after a while he came to hate it.

Although Evelyn admired, teased, confided in and borrowed from his older brother, Alec's close bond with Arthur cast him, to some extent, into the enemy camp. At Oxford Evelyn had joined the Aesthetes, a self-conscious band of students whose central philosophy was to laud 'Art' and deride money. To these attitudinising young men the worst a fellow could do was earn his living from 'Art'. This, of course, was the sin that both Chapman and the baldheaded lecher had committed. To Evelyn, with all his young idealism, his family was therefore guilty of a gross betrayal of artistic principle. 'Bald Head makes *money* out of writing,' he complained to his friends.

Nor could he be certain how much of his dissolute life at Oxford Alec might be reporting back to Arthur. He swore Alec to secrecy but knew that, even if he kept his counsel, Arthur had other friends at Oxford who would doubtless relish the opportunity of bringing scandalous news to Underhill. Alec's last Oxford visit, in the summer of 1924, was particularly suspicious – perhaps he *had* come as Arthur's spying envoy. He stood for a moment in Evelyn's rooms,

lecturing him on his profligacy, his drunkenness and the unsatisfactory quality of his friends. Evelyn was irritated by Alec's
'gamecock maturity' but not offended and twenty years later
satirised the meeting in *Brideshead Revisited*, in a scene that cast Alec
as Charles Ryder's priggish cousin Jasper:

> Towards the end of that summer term I received the last visit
> and Grand Remonstrance of my cousin Jasper . . . Duty alone
> had brought him to my rooms that afternoon at great incon-
> venience to himself . . . Jasper would not sit down: this was
> to be no cosy chat; he stood with his back to the fireplace
> and, in his own phrase, talked to me 'like an uncle'.

Jasper criticises Ryder for idling his time, associating with
undesirable people and for grossly overspending on clothes, wine
and pointless decorative artifacts for his room, but Ryder remains
unrepentant:

> 'I am sorry, Jasper,' I said. 'I know it must be embarrassing
> for you but I happen to *like* this bad set. I *like* getting drunk
> at luncheon, and though I haven't yet quite spent double my
> allowance, I undoubtedly shall before the end of term. I
> usually have a glass of champagne about this time. Will you
> join me?'
>   So my cousin Jasper despaired and, I learned later, wrote
> to his father on the subject of my excesses who, in his turn,
> wrote to *my* father . . .

In 1948 Alec sportingly picked this passage for inclusion in *These
Would I Choose*, a 'personal anthology' of the poetry and prose most
connected with his life.

The 'Jasper' meeting was not without effect. Evelyn's words had
evidently sunk deep into Bald Head's bald head. They resulted in
a curious letter that was written by Alec as though it came from
Evelyn's hand. He took Evelyn's points and forged them into a
coherent argument for Arthur. There is no record of Arthur's reaction to it. He must have wondered why his younger son had become

so detached as to be unable tell him these things in person. Whatever Arthur thought, Alec was pleased enough with the letter to have it published in the *Sunday Times* under the title 'Youth's Protest – The Right to Satisfy Oneself – A Letter to a Father' by Alec Waugh. As well as being a defence of Evelyn's Oxford behaviour, the letter also contains a hint that Alec may have been dissatisfied with the special brand of paternal relationship that had hemmed him in at Sherborne:

> I am very sorry, my dear father, that my career in Oxford is making you unhappy. I have done, you say, extremely little work during the last three terms, and unless I put in at least ten hours' work a day my chances of getting even a second are most unpromising. Well father I have never attempted to deceive you. I have never pretended that I was working when I was not. I worked extremely hard to get my scholarship because I knew that probably I would not be able to come up without it. I worked fairly hard to pass my history previous because, had I not passed, I should have lost my scholarship. If I had worked harder I would have probably, you say, have got 'distinction'. I am vain enough to agree with you. I think I should. But I did not want distinction. I only wanted not to lose my scholarship. That was a year ago. Since then I have done practically no work at all. It is most unlikely that I shall get a second, though I shall be surprised if I do not get a third.
>
> Thirty years ago I would have been told that my behaviour was unfilial, that the least I could do in return for all you had done for me was to get a first. That was the old attitude and perhaps, father, that is the difference between our generations. 'For twenty years,' you said, 'my father has given me a home and worked extremely hard to pay for my education. He has denied himself a great deal so that I might go to a great school. He has the right to ask something of me in return. It would give him immense pleasure if I get a first.'
>
> That is the way we are told to feel towards our parents,

but is it a compliment to them if we feel like that? Is it not as good as saying that our career is nothing more than a focus for parental pride; that our parents are asking us to succeed not for our sakes but for theirs, so that they shall be able to say in their clubs: 'My boy made eighty yesterday against Shrewsbury' or 'My boy has got a scholarship'? Is it not as good as saying that our parents send us to schools and colleges so that we may provide them with opportunities of self-laudation? That we are, in fact, to live, not our life there, but theirs; that school and Oxford are not to be the foundation to our careers but the coping-stone of theirs?

I am not going to be a schoolmaster or a barrister or a civil servant. And I cannot help feeling that outside the learning professions the distinction between first and third is not going to matter much. Not enough, at any rate, for me to think that the gaining of it would compensate for the number of things I would have to lose by working for it. But father, I am throwing my energies into other things. Into the things that appear to me to be more important. I may be wrong of course, but if I am, I shall pay for it. I am prepared for that. It is after all my career and if I fail it will be myself that will have to suffer.

That, at any rate, father, is the way in which I and my friends look upon things. We are prepared to pay for our mistakes, but we have, we consider, the right to satisfy ourselves that they are indeed mistakes and not, as we think them now, the ways of wisdom.

At university Evelyn's bumptious behaviour earned him many enemies. The most prominent of these was his history tutor, later the Dean of Hertford, C. R. M. F. Cruttwell. Evelyn's description of him in *A Little Learning* is memorable:

He was tall almost loutish, with the face of a petulant baby. He smoked a pipe which was usually attached to his blubber-lips by a thread of slime. As he removed the stem, waving it to emphasis his indistinct speech, this glittering connection, extended until finally it broke leaving a dribble on his chin. When he spoke to me I found myself so distracted by the speculation of how far this line could be attenuated that I was often inattentive to his words.

Cruttwell loathed Evelyn as much as Evelyn loathed Cruttwell. But the student was brighter, sharper and funnier than the tutor and in the long battle that raged between the two it was Evelyn who would eventually emerge as victor. Cruttwell took Evelyn's scholarship away; later he blocked his attempts to get a job, and did his level best to throw a spanner into the works of his first marriage. In retaliation Evelyn outed Cruttwell as a dog sodomist, prancing under his windows with a stuffed whippet in the middle of the night singing at the top of his voice:

> Cruttwell dog, Cruttwell dog, where have you been?
> I've been to Hertford to lie with the Dean.
> Cruttwell dog, Cruttwell dog what did you there?
> I bit off his penis and pubic hair.

Freudian scholars of Waugh have reached the unanimous conclusion that Cruttwell was innocent of these charges, concurring, to a man, that Evelyn invented the slander in order to deflect attention from his own sexual embarrassments. I cannot agree. Evelyn's rooms were directly beneath the filthy dean's and he heard, with his own ears, night after night, the helpless yelps, snaps and growls of Cruttwell's canine victims as, one after another, they were pinned to his seedy office floor as he forced them down with urgent, lascivious strokes, ramming at them with his fat merciless trunk. Furthermore my father was told by a geography professor from Hertford whom he met years later on Paddington station that the carpet in Cruttwell's room, which had not been changed since the twenties, still carried the irradicable proof of his crime – STAINS! I believe this implicitly. My father was so shaken by these stories in his youth, that he developed a lifelong attachment to Pekineses and a desire to protect all canine species from the baleful effects of human injustice. In the 1979 general election he stood for Parliament in the interests of the Dog Lovers Party, polling nearly eighty votes from like-minded enthusiasts in North Devon.

Cruttwell died in ignominy and despair at a lunatic asylum in Bristol in 1941. Until that date Evelyn had littered his fiction with twerps called Cruttwell. As each book was published the real Mr Cruttwell shuddered in apprehension of what new character Evelyn might have devised to taunt him. One of his novels has a 'fluffy-haired' girl called Gladys Cruttwell; then there is Toby Cruttwell, 'a very silly' criminal who pops up in another. General Cruttwell, a conceited ass, makes his appearance in *Scoop*. They are everywhere these Cruttwells. Evelyn's books are full of them: Cruttwells with fake tans, Cruttwells who are junior shop assistants, Cruttwell the bone-setter, Cruttwell the scoutmaster and even Cruttwell the raving lunatic. And his passion did not die with the real Cruttwell's demise in '41. After his death the game enriched itself and continued to be passed, like a relay baton, down through the generations. In much the same way as a son of the Italian Mafia class finds himself honour-bound to treat his father's enemies and all their descendants as his own bitterest foes, so the Waughs have soldiered on with their vilification of this horrible man's memory. My father, who was only two years old when Cruttwell died, never missed a chance to harass it: 'It was from this unfortunate man that the word *Cruttwellism* was coined to describe the abominable vice of sodomy with a dog,' he wrote in the *Spectator*, 'but if he is remembered at all today, it is usually with pity. Nobody spares a thought for his dogs.'

Papa took up the theme again in a long review of *The Dictionary of National Biography* for the specialist magazine *Books and Bookmen*. On browsing the volume that covered 1941–50, he was disconcerted to find that the dean, whose only possible claim to fame was an inaccurate and outdated history of the First World War, should be honoured with an entry in those hallowed pages. Most of all he objected to one sentence: 'Perhaps the warmth of Cruttwell's nature appeared most attractively in his passion for flowers and for country life: he was never happier than at his country home with a friend and a gun.'

Loyalty, filial piety, family honour – what was it that bade him expose this sinister whitewash?

> The idle reader might, I suppose, think it curious that no affection for animals is mentioned, or that in place of the usual cliché of a dog and a gun, with which so many people are never happier in the country, Mr Cruttwell would seem to have preferred a friend and a gun. Nor is much clue to the mystery afforded by the one criticism which the *DNB* does allow: 'He had his prejudices (although misogyny, of which some suspected him, was not among them)' – so I suppose I had better blurt out my piece in simple English. Some may have suspected this repulsive man of misogyny – I do not know – but the peculiarity for which he was much more widely suspected was sexual congress with dogs. Whether he was innocent or guilty of this crime it is for this that he is fabled in song and story and now that his history of the Great War has been superseded by newer and better books on the same subject, it is probably the only thing for which he will be remembered at all.
>
> If we only have the *DNB* as our guide his evil memory will have receded into this new image of a flower-sniffing country lover, so far removed from any improper relationship with dogs that he even refused to take one out shooting with him, despite the obvious temptation: his passions were reserved for flowers, which are unprotected by law.

As part of the Evelyn Waugh centenary celebrations in 2003 I was invited to give an after-dinner speech in the dining hall of Hertford College to an audience of two hundred international Waugh scholars. Together they made a glorious spectacle: a Chinese, next to an Indonesian, next to Spaniard, next to an American, next to an Australian, next to a Russian – each a learned professor whose life had been devoted to the study of my grandfather's work. As I stood addressing these good people from a spot directly beneath a pompous boardroom portrait of Cruttwell (cack-handedly executed by his cousin Grace), great waves of family pride engulfed me. That ancient wound needed once more to be reopened. 'Let us now raise our glasses and drink to C. R. M. F. Cruttwell, that he may for ever be remembered as a dog sodomist and a total shit.' With V signs to the portrait, our glasses clinked and the two hundred clever professors drank deep.

I do not know how many of them represented the Freudian branch of scholarship or if any had yet 'discovered' a link between Evelyn's detestation of Cruttwell and his half-suppressed, bitter exasperation with his father. Perhaps there is none, but in these days of lean pickings, scholars must at least appear to be shining their torches into every dark hole. Without prejudice – or should I say without much enthusiasm for the psychoanalytic? – I offer a few pointers in that direction.

In November 1923 Evelyn wrote a short story for one of the Oxford University magazines entitled 'Edward of Unique Achievement' in which a history scholar who has recently had his scholarship revoked (Edward) forms a violent dislike for his tutor, Mr Curtis. 'Edward hated him with an absorbing and immeasurable hatred, so that at last he became convinced that Mr Curtis' existence was not compatible with his own.' One day Edward walks coolly up to Mr Curtis's study and kills him mid-sentence, as he sits, looking pompous, in his chair. Shortly after Evelyn had written this story he made a woodcut for a series called *Seven Deadly Sins*, not *the* seven deadly sins but seven new ideas of his own choosing. They included 'The Intolerable Wickedness of Him who Drinks Alone', 'The Horrid Sacrilege of Those that Ill-Treat Books', and 'That Grim Act of Patricide' in which a young, dissolute, bruised and probably drunken son points a revolver at the head of his father as the old man stares up at him from an armchair.

In Evelyn's famous short story 'Mr Loveday's Little Outing', written in the 1930s, a young girl campaigns to free an inmate from her local lunatic asylum, whom she believes to be entirely sane. The inmate, Mr Loveday, convinces the asylum governors that all he desires is 'just one little outing' after which he will return to minister to the other inmates. Originally the story was entitled 'Mr Cruttwell's Little Outing', but the publishers got windy and Evelyn changed it. How much he was thinking of

C. R. M. F. Cruttwell when he wrote it is impossible to say: Loveday is perhaps too mild-mannered a man to pass for an accurate portrait of Cruttwell. But what is interesting is the act for which the Loveday/Cruttwell character is committed to the asylum – an act which he slyly recommits on his little outing: it is a violent crime resulting from a kinky obsession with women on bicycles. Now, Arthur was never violent, least of all to women, but it is odd (is it not?) that he and Mr Loveday/Cruttwell should both express a fetishism for innocent young women on their bicycles?

During his three years at university Evelyn, to add to his sins, may well have 'dabbled' (as they say) in the 'dark arts'. He wrote several short stories and most of a novel about black magic. Raoul Loveday, a contemporary and fellow member of the Hypocrites (after whom 'Mr Cruttwell's Little Outing', was eventually named) went with a group of Oxford undergraduates – including possibly Evelyn's close friend Harold Acton – to study black magic with a sinister menace in Cefalu, Sicily.

Evelyn, whose great enemy in life was boredom, was easily drawn to danger. He craved heady experience. If it is true that he had 'dabbled' in this way it did not make him happy. Homosexuality, drunkenness, idleness – all these things contributed to periodic fits of melancholy. 'I am highly depressed,' he wrote to Dudley Carew from Oxford. 'A worthless fellow and quite broke and rather stupid and quite incredibly depraved morally . . . for the last fortnight I have been nearly insane . . . I may perhaps one day in a later time tell you some of the things that have happened . . . I do not yet know how things are going to end . . . I want to go down for good but I cannot explain and my parents are obdurate.'

At the beginning of his last year Evelyn had written to his father seeking permission to leave university and be sent to Paris. Arthur, not unnaturally, had refused, telling him that the previous two years would be wasted if he did not get his degree. In the end Evelyn decided to put in a spurt of work but it was not enough: he had left it far too late. In his heart he hoped he might scrape a second but after turning the first paper and finding the questions on it to be wholly inconvenient, he convinced himself that he was in for a third and telegraphed Arthur with his gloomy prognostications. Arthur, who was prone more to anxiety and despair than to anger, could hardly protest as he himself had come away with the same result, from the same university. In those days Oxford operated a rigid policy that no one could receive a degree, whatever their exam results, if they had not attended for a minimum of nine terms. Because Evelyn had arrived in January 1922 he was obliged to sit out a further term after his exams with nothing to do. Naturally he looked forward to this period of summer idleness and booked himself rooms, but since his scholarship had been withdrawn, Arthur had no intention of paying him to twiddle his thumbs in Oxford for three months. Instead he told Evelyn that his third-class degree was not worth having and enlisted him at an art school in London for the coming term.

Perhaps Arthur's attitude enraged Evelyn at the time, but by 1962, with his own experiences of fatherhood to reflect upon, his sympathies were with his father. For the *Sunday Telegraph* he wrote:

At university I disappointed my father gravely. He hoped that I would win the Newdigate and succeed where he had failed in taking a good degree and, perhaps, getting elected president of the Union . . . I regarded my scholarship as the reward for a brief period of intense effort at school, not as did the college authorities as the earnest for further effort, nor, as my father did, as a relief to his own legitimate expenses. I believed myself entitled to some self-indulgence. I realise now that I was exorbitant in this claim. It was the source of disagreement. Not only was my father not rich; he was, in the rising cost of living, rather worse off than he had been ten years earlier and he was reaching the age when his work, never excessive, was becoming irksome. He saw himself, with some exaggeration, as toiling in order that I might enjoy luxuries which he denied himself. He would have submitted happily enough, I think, if I had interests with which he sympathised but I was a pure waster and I cannot now feel that his resentment was unjustified.

There was, however, one student escapade with which Arthur sympathised enormously. In July 1924 Evelyn and a group of friends each put up five pounds to make a silent film. It was called *The Scarlet Woman* and Terence Greenidge was the producer. Evelyn wrote the scenario and, sporting a blond wig, acted as the chief baddie; Alec played an old mother in another wig and various cronies took peripheral roles including (in her first film part) the ginger-headed, shrill-voiced Elsa Lanchester. Evelyn and Alec had befriended her in a drinking-club that she part-ran with the actor Harold Scott in Charlotte Street. Later she married Charles Laughton and became famous for her role as Mary Shelley in the zany Boris Karloff movie *The Bride of Frankenstein* of 1935. Evelyn, who went to see all her films after that, prided himself on having 'invented' her.

Arthur lent Underhill to the young film-makers and much of the action was shot in the garden there. As president of the local amateur dramatic society and an irrepressible thespian, Arthur would have dearly loved, if not the starring role, at least a little cameo. Some of Evelyn's friends regretted afterwards that they had not offered him one, but Evelyn did not repine. Undaunted, Arthur took a chair into the garden and watched with glee as each scene was rehearsed, re-rehearsed and shot amid gales of young people's laughter. He was in ecstasy when the cast broke for luncheon, filling their glasses with red wine and babbling extravagantly to them about the theatre of his youth. When the film was eventually shown to him he could not sit still for excitement, interrupting whenever he recognised one of his own possessions on screen: 'Look, that's my chair . . . Take care you don't break that decanter!'

But Arthur's joy on this occasion did not signal the start of a happier relationship during Evelyn's remaining time at Oxford. Nor did matters improve after Evelyn had come down, skiving off his art lessons and abandoning the course after only a few months. Much time was spent traipsing around with Alastair Graham, the boyfriend from whom he was inseparable. First they went to Ireland, ostensibly to learn magic spells, and afterwards drifted aimlessly between London, a leaking caravan near Oxford and Graham's mother's house in Warwickshire. Evelyn, Graham and their effete circle praised the modern movement in poetry and painting that Arthur so abhorred, but their enthusiasm was neither intellectual nor aesthetic: it was an expression of delayed adolescence, a rebellion against parental authority. They spoke to one another in an affected code-language that grated on their parents' nerves, much of it was sexual by innuendo. Students were 'studenda', secret places were 'pudenda', brothers were 'bastards' and women were 'natural women' (to distinguish, I presume, from male transvestites); holding, fiddling or mending became 'masturbating'; to talk to someone was 'to lie with' them. It was in this vein that one of Evelyn's closest friends, Christopher Hollis (later an MP and Catholic apologist), wrote to him in 1925: 'Yesterday we lay with the monks at Downside. On the way we saw a man masturbating a traction engine. His name was Padfield. Young Graham made the older bastard drunk the other night and lay with him.'[5] On the rare occasions that Evelyn and Alastair were apart they wrote to each other in this casual manner. Alastair's letters include a great many references to bestiality – the crime for which Cruttwell was obviously and singularly guilty. During a brief stay with the son of a canon at Wells Cathedral in April 1924, he wrote to Evelyn to tell him that:

1. The Dean of Wells (Joseph Robinson) had the 'kinderlust' and seduced children in a 'pudenda' hidden behind a panel in the cathedral library.
2. The authorities at Downside School kept an ark of female birds and beasts for their sexual delectation.
3. Mrs Graham (Alastair's mother) performed the 'Rites of Astarte' on her dog, Seorus, and would be sexually aroused if she saw Alastair's picture (enclosed) of a hound with short front legs and a sticking-up bottom.

[5] 'The older bastard' refers to Christopher's brother, Roger Hollis, afterwards Sir Roger Hollis, head of MI5.

4. The Dean's wife, having discovered her husband's predilection for children, 'has lain aside all moral restraint and is Sapphistically lying with her own bitch'.
5. 'How interesting it would be to dress as a dog and sit in the Cathedral.'
6. 'We saw a horse masturbating in a field' . . . 'Just seen four dogs copulating on cathedral green on the way to buy this envelope.'

In his childlike love for Alastair, Evelyn bound these incoming letters into a single volume and entitled it *Litterae Wellensis*. A few moments ago, as I was browsing through it, the spine detached from the back revealing a slogan in Evelyn's hand. '*Rien est vrai que le beau.*'

Alastair and Evelyn disguised their handwriting on the envelopes of the letters they sent to each other so that their parents (particularly Mrs Graham, who was unreliable with the post) would not pry into their affairs. Evelyn got himself into trouble with his father by spreading word that Sir Edmund Gosse had 'lain' with a certain lady. When Gosse learned about it, he wrote a furious letter to Arthur, indicating that he would remain Arthur's friend but never wished to see Evelyn again.

Alastair and Evelyn encouraged each other in their heavy drinking but even without Alastair, Evelyn found ways to get stupendously drunk at any hour of every day. Both the teetotal K and Arthur (whose favourite tipple was Emu burgundy, much derided by Evelyn) were exasperated by the stream of inebriates that their younger son introduced to their peaceful Hampstead home – 'drunken beasts', K called them. And drunk they were, but Evelyn was the lion among them. Many of his friends noticed a manic, even suicidal quality in his drinking bouts. Dudley Carew later recalled, 'Evelyn went at the bottle as though he was engaged in a desperate murderous struggle with one who was at the same time deadly enemy and devoted comrade. It was almost a combat on the physical level.' He would arrange to meet friends in a pub, arrive early and, in the few minutes before they came, paralyse himself with a speed and deadly determination that, on one occasion, astonished even the hardened pub landlord: 'Never seen anything like it; not in all my life.' Take a typical episode from his diaries:

8 December 1924

Then I went to Oxford. Drove to 31 St Aldates where I found an enormous orgy in progress. Billy and I unearthed a strap and whipped Tony. Everyone was hideously drunk except, strangely enough, myself. After a quiet day in cinemas, I had a dinner party of Claude, Elmley, Terence, Roger Hollis and a poor drunk called MacGregor. I arrived quite blind after a great number of cocktails at the George with Claude. Eventually the dinner broke up and Claude, Roger Hollis and I went off for a pub crawl which after sundry indecorous adventures ended up at the Hypocrites where another blind was going on. Poor Mr MacGregor turned up after having lain with a woman but almost immediately fell backwards downstairs. I think he was killed. Next day I drank all morning from pub to pub and invited to lunch with me at the New Reform John Sutro, Roger Hollis, Claude and Alfred Duggan. I ate no lunch but drank solidly and was soon in the middle of a bitter quarrel with the President – a preposterous person called Cotts – who expelled me from the club. Alfred and I then drank double brandies until I could not walk. He carried me to Worcester where I fell out of the window then relapsed into unconsciousness punctuated with severe but well directed vomitings. On Wednesday I lunched with Robert Byron at the New Reform and the man Cotts tried to throw me out again. Next day I lunched with Hugh and drank with him all the afternoon and sallied out with him fighting drunk at tea time when we drank at the New Reform till dinner . . . Next day, feeling deathly ill, I returned to London having spent two months' wages. I had to dine with Alec, Richard Greene, Julia Strachey . . . and then back to Richard's home for a drink. Home at two.

Evelyn was not proud of himself – in fact, he was bitterly ashamed.

I do not doubt that he would have liked to please his father but he did not know how to set about it, and although he remained dependent on Arthur for financial support and for the roof over his head, he sought wherever possible to avoid him. He would arrive at Underhill when his father was asleep and surface only after he had left for work. It was best to keep out of his way. As he later wrote: 'The intermittent but frequent presence of a dissipated and not always respectful spendthrift disturbed the tranquillity of the home to which my father always looked for refuge. My coming of age was not celebrated.'

In April 1925 Evelyn went on a drinking binge with four of his friends. It involved several pubs, a party, a beer-swigging episode at Underhill and a car journey that took them spinning the wrong way round a central London roundabout and ended, after an entanglement with the police, in a prison cell at Bow Street. Because the driver of the car was the son of a former secretary of state the affair reached the papers. Evelyn was not mentioned by name but Arthur was ashamed to read in the *Evening Standard*: 'With him was another man in the car who was incapably drunk. A quantity of liquor found in the car was afterwards claimed by this man.' Arthur knew precisely who 'this man' was, but did not have the stomach to confront his son. All he could do was beg for sympathy with martyrish whines and appeals to heaven. One childhood friend of Evelyn claimed that Arthur had indulged him as a boy out of guilt for not loving him as much as Alec. This may be true. It may also be the case that Arthur was consciously reacting against the heavy discipline of his own youth. I have noticed that people who have been raised by a querulous, dominant or volatile parent are often afraid of conflict in later life.

Only a week before the drunken car episode described above, Evelyn had turned up at a friend's house wobbling with inebriation at four o'clock in the afternoon. He carried under his arm three bottles of champagne, whose contents they drank out of teacups. In the evening he took his friends to dinner at his club and generously settled the bill with a cheque. When it bounced, the club secretary telephoned Arthur at Underhill and asked what he proposed to do about it. Arthur protested that Evelyn must be held responsible for his own debts. The secretary had his answer ready: 'Do you realise,' he said, 'that this matter will have to come before the committee, which includes many prominent literary figures? Arnold Bennett is among them. Did Mr Arthur Waugh want the matter of his son's cheque to be brought before Mr Arnold Bennett?' Arthur agreed to settle the bill, but not without a great performance of heavy-weather histrionics.

It was a bad time all round for Arthur. Profits at Chapman and Hall had tumbled to their lowest since he had taken control of the firm in 1903. The valuable Dickens copyrights had expired and a host of eager new publishers had been quick to exploit the situation with cheap rival editions of their own. At Chapman and Hall what meagre profits there were came from scientific books in which Arthur took neither pride nor interest. The company (owned in Dickensian times by Messrs Frederic Chapman and William Hall and afterwards by their descendants) had been recently floated on the stock exchange and Arthur, unable to pay dividends on shares and, as ever, hypersensitive to criticism, dreaded the aggressive atmosphere of shareholders' meetings. As a small economy during the war he had taken to lunching at home. This meant three hours every day travelling back and forth between Underhill and his office, a double endurance of the long walk uphill from Hampstead station, and a luncheon gobbled at an unhealthy speed. His left ear was, by this time, completely deaf, he was obese, his wife was withdrawn and showing signs of depression, and his asthma attacks had grown steadily worse. In winter Underhill was cold and draughty. As he walked to and from the station, he was forced to stop every few yards to catch his breath, and after dinner, as he rose from the table, he propped himself against the mantelpiece wheezing for air. Any movement from a warm to a cold room brought on a devastating attack. Evelyn remembered his father at these times 'crying to heaven for release in a wide variety of quotation'.

Meanwhile, unknown to his father, Alec had been hoping to escape from his duties at Chapman and Hall. None of his books had been successful since The Loom of Youth. His original publishers,

Grant Richards, had gone bust and, much to his regret, all of his books were now being published in small quantities under his father's imprint. Then, in 1925, his scintillating novel about a kept woman — its elegant dustjacket designed by Evelyn — unexpectedly sold six thousand copies. *Kept* was not strictly a 'bestseller' but its comparative success was enough to draw Alec to wider attention. One thing led to another. Soon he was in popular demand for magazine short stories and articles. An American magazine bought the rights to another of his romances, *Love In These Days*, and Alec sensed he might be able to cut free and set himself up as freelance writer. But his spirits were low and his professional successes were not enough to buck him. He felt that his life was a succession of meaningless events that needed to be jolted into focus.

With this in mind, at the beginning of June 1925, he sold the contents of his flat in Kensington and bought himself a year-long round-the-world cruise ticket from the Messageries Maritimes. Of course, Arthur did everything in his power to dissuade him from leaving but his imprecations fell on deaf ears. By the middle of June Alec was gaily drifting around the Mediterranean. He had resigned his salaried position at Chapman and Hall but, in deference to Arthur's interferences, agreed to remain on the company's board.

Alec's journey took him through the Suez Canal to Ceylon, Malaya, Thailand, Laos, Singapore and Tahiti, where he had an affair with a 'comely Tahitian damsel' who 'bounded about the place like a Newfoundland puppy'. After a while he found her company tedious — she seemed more interested in securing work as a cleaner at the hotel than in her relationship with him — but, at the start, her sexual techniques made Alec very happy. 'It was the greatest fun making love to her,' he wrote, many years later. 'Polynesians, as hula dancers, acquire an astonishing mobility between the knees and navel.'

Back in England, Arthur was missing his eldest son terribly but he was also irritated and disappointed with him for having left. When Alec telegraphed Chapman and Hall from Singapore, in desperate need of thirty pounds, Arthur ungraciously refused to send it. Perhaps he hoped that if Alec ran out of money he would have no choice but to return to England and to his job at Henrietta Street. But if that was Arthur's plan it backfired sorely. When Alec was forced to borrow the money from a friend he resolved to announce his resignation from the board as soon as he returned to England.

When poverty didn't bring Alec home, Arthur resorted to another scheme – telegraphing his son in Tahiti to announce that K was desperately ill and needed him by her side at once. Her condition was not pleasant, but neither was it serious. Alec made arrangements to return to London.

On the journey, he met and fell in love with a wild, bad-tempered, red-headed married woman called Ruth Morris. She had had an interesting life: one of the first Americans to fly an aeroplane and, during the First World War, one of only a handful of American women to be given an army commission. As Ruth Wightman, she had written scripts for Hollywood films and trained as a bullfighter in Spain. In her youth she had been raped by the American novelist Jack London. Her husband, Gouverneur Morris, was a well-known novelist and short-story writer from the immensely rich Morris family that for generations had owned vast tracts of real estate in New York City and, I believe, the Philip Morris tobacco company. Gouverneur was twenty-five years older than his wife and an amiable drunk. Charlie Chaplin had begged her to sort him out. After a short series of illicit shipboard meetings which do not need itemising here, Alec had fallen head over heels in love.

By the time he arrived in London, Alec knew that his mother was better. He did not announce his return in order to savour his father's dramatic surprise. Instead he sent a telegram purporting to be from the sleazy Terence Greenidge: 'Dear, dear Mrs Waugh please can I spend the night at Underhill.' When he appeared at the house, he was greeted with pomp and cheer by Arthur, who had spent all day in a tedious board meeting:

> My dear boy I cannot tell you how glad I am to have you back. At the board meeting today I was wondering how I could go on. It will all be so different now. Some of the board members are good loyal fellows, I know that, but

we do not speak the same language. It will make all the difference now that you are here.

But Alec was far from happy. He was still bitter that his father had refused him thirty pounds and had drawn up plans for another Tahitian *rendezvous* with Ruth in a few months' time. He had come to tell his father that he wished to resign his directorship at Chapman and Hall. In a bowl by the door, a cable awaited him from Ruth: 'San Francisco is desolate without you.' He telegraphed back immediately: 'Arrived tonight in a London that might as well be empty.'

Alec found it painful explaining to his father that he did not wish to return to Chapman and Hall and Arthur's heartbreak saddened him. 'But my dear boy, you can't. Leaving me all alone.'

But the son was determined. So, too, was the father. All that night conversation turned in circles over Alec's future. 'It can't come to anything,' Arthur kept repeating. 'How can it? She's married. She's an American. She won't want to be transplanted, nor will you. Her husband is rich and prominent. She won't want to break that up. In a year's time you will both have realised that.' He told Alec that, with a bit of persuasion, the board might give him further leave, but that he must not, on any account, resign.

Alec's resolve was adamantine. As he revealed to Evelyn, many years later, 'I was never happy at No. 11 Henrietta Street.' Within a month he was sailing, once again, away from England, waving sweetly from the taff-rail of the good ship *Louqsor*, headed for Tahiti and for Ruth.

Alec's departure left Arthur feeling miserable, deserted and betrayed. He was growing to hate his work at Chapman and Hall and resented Alec for leaving him to fight the board and the shareholders alone. Before each meeting he imagined himself standing up at the end and saying in a clear actorish voice to the men before him, 'And now, gentlemen, there is one final thing. I must ask you to accept my resignation.' But he was not rich enough to do that. He had never saved any money, nor did he own any shares in the company. He was chained to the business for as long as they would employ him.

Alec's escape from London was felicitous. He adored travelling, sunshine, the sea, making new friends, casual sexual relationships. For the rest of his life he would never have a permanent base again. He was a sojourner and that was how he liked it. But despite the sense of liberation that attended his movements abroad, Alec's happiness was partially marred by feelings of guilt at having abandoned his father:

> I did feel sad on my father's count . . . My heart often bled for him during those years, and he looked reproachfully at me sometimes when he talked over his troubles. He felt that he should not be facing them alone. But if I had been on the board, my own anxiety about the firm's future would have increased the tension for him . . . My only regret was that my own books were still published by Chapman and Hall. I wished that I had no occasion to discuss business with my father.

Back in England Arthur's second son's fortunes were tumbling ever deeper into the depths. Evelyn had a few friends who were prepared to swear that he was a 'genius' but he had nothing to show for it and lacked the confidence to produce. He started work on a novel about black magic called *The Temple of Thatch* but was not sure if it was any good. He completed another called *Noah*, about nakedness and drunkenness, and sent it to several of the publishers with whom Arthur had connections – it was rejected by all. A long short story about a man wishing to commit suicide also elicited rejections. Meanwhile many of his less talented acquaintances were forging careers and moving on in the world. Having flunked out of Heatherley's Art School in December 1924, after four months of idling and truancy, Evelyn found himself a job at the *Daily Express*, but after only three months in Fleet Street he had contributed nothing publishable and was sacked. Reluctantly he took a teaching post at a Welsh private school. The job depressed him. During his second term *The Temple of Thatch* was returned to him in the post by a trusted friend, with a letter stating that he had not in the least enjoyed it. Evelyn consigned the manuscript to the flames of the school boiler.

The burning of his novel was a depressing moment but within weeks Evelyn saw a ray of hope. Alec told him to expect the offer of a job in Italy as secretary to a famous translator of Proust. Delighted at the chance to escape teaching, Evelyn handed in his notice. 'I even approached kindly feeling towards my father and contracted with him to surrender my allowance in exchange for my debts.' But within days news came that the job was off. It was at about this time that he tried to commit suicide. In *A Little Learning* he described a desultory attempt to drown himself, thwarted by a swarm of stinging jellyfish, somewhere off the Welsh coast. The book ends with him paddling back to shore, cold and humiliated; 'Then I climbed the sharp hill that led to all the years ahead.'

I suspect this to have been a literary contrivance, a comic and dramatic dénouement to the memoir of his early years: the jellyfish incident is not recorded in his diaries; neither did he mention it to any of his intimate friends. More likely, I think, is that his 'suicide attempt' took a different form. In his first novel, *Decline and Fall*, Evelyn describes an eccentric school teacher, Captain Grimes, who fakes his suicide by pretending to drown. Earlier Grimes discusses another attempt with a pistol: 'Well, I sat there for some time looking at that revolver. I put it to my head twice, but each time I brought it down again. "Public-school men don't end like this," I said to myself.' Two months before Evelyn lost the Italian job he had confided to his diary: 'I debate the simple paradoxes of suicide and achievement, work out the scheme for a new book, and negotiate with the man Young to buy a revolver from him.' When term ended and Evelyn was back at Underhill K discovered the revolver while unpacking his suitcase. He told her that he had bought it from Dick Young with the intention of killing himself because he was worried about his debts. She had a small capital of about two hundred pounds: she sold it and gave Evelyn the proceeds on the condition that the gun be thrown away.

Unfortunately no record has survived of Arthur's reaction to these events, but I don't doubt that they added to his exasperation. At this time Evelyn was bitter. He complained frequently to his friends of his empty life and railed against his parents, insisting that he was 'an unwanted child'. I do not know if Evelyn ever called his father an 'arsehole', or shoved him physically across a room, but I very much doubt it. Their mutual disregard manifested itself not in physical violence or even in words so much as a pernicious, simmering atmosphere – although Evelyn once jokingly wrote to a friend: 'I am staying with my father. At present it is all dignity and peace but I expect we shall soon have a quarrel & black each other's eyes & tear our hair and flog each other with hunting crops.' I have no doubt that, with his friends, Evelyn accused Arthur of the foulest deeds in his imagination, just as Alastair had accused his mother of every kind of sexual depravity. The saintly Christopher Hollis (who is quoted in the tractor masturbating episode above) wrote about this time in Evelyn's life fifty years later: 'As a matter of fact, as between him and his admirable father Evelyn was much more sinning than sinned against. Unpardonable things were all too often on his lips in the period as he afterwards most fully recognised.'

After the disappearance of the Italian opportunity, Evelyn dragged himself back into teaching, this time to a school at Aston Clinton in Buckinghamshire. After only five terms there he was sacked for trying to seduce the matron but told his father that it was for inebriation. Next he took a part-time job at a school in Golders Green but that, too, was a failure, and soon he decided that what he most desired was to lead the life of a simple country craftsman. Arthur paid a deposit for him to join a printing school, but no sooner had the cheque been cashed than Evelyn changed his mind and enlisted at a training workshop for cabinet-makers in Southampton Row.

As if all this was not enough for the long-suffering Arthur, towards the end of 1924 Evelyn had fallen in love with a girl of whom his father deeply disapproved. She was intellectual, but she was also argumentative, a social snob, a sex maniac, a sado-masochist, a depressive and a drunk. Although she had slept with many men – Paul Robeson and the painter Stephen Toulmin among them – she would not indulge Evelyn on the grounds that she did not find him physically attractive, yet was angry with him if he turned his attentions to anyone else. Arthur made her the scapegoat for Evelyn's failures. She had been, after all, involved in both the bouncing cheque and the Bow Street police incidents and, as far as he was concerned, was the primary cause of his son's depression, drunkenness and apparent lack of ambition.

Arthur's tolerance of all these things was nothing short of miraculous – but tolerance was not, of itself, enough to repair the damaged relationship. Evelyn wanted, maybe needed, his father to kick him in the pants. I have already shown how encouraged he was by Arthur's robust stand over his late-night promenades at Lancing, but his father's behaviour on that occasion had been uncharacteristic. For the most part Evelyn despised his father's tolerance and the uncertain atmosphere it created.

A sterner father would have packed me off to the colonies. Mine was not stern, but he could not conceal the despair with which he regarded me as a permanent encumbrance to his declining years.

All emotions of pleasure and pain found immediate and vivid expression in him. It was apparent that I came home only when destitute. That did not make my appearances at Underhill more welcome. I had the grace to feel a certain shame; it certainly never occurred to me, as it does to many unsatisfactory sons, to blame my shortcomings on him; but that did not make my company more agreeable. Our meetings became almost entirely melancholy.

That Evelyn could envisage no means of escaping from home was a piercing problem for him. He had no money, no wife, nowhere to live but Underhill, and the place with all its associations looked set to be his base indefinitely. How he must have envied Alec's freedom to roam the world, paying for hotels, women and adventure from the royalties of his books. For four years this sense of entrapment brewed into harsh feelings of hatred and resentment:

How I detest Underhill and how ill I feel in it. The whole place volleys and thunders with traffic. I can't sleep or work. Mother is away at Midsomer Norton where Aunt Trissie is dying. The telephone bell is continually ringing, my father scampering up and down stairs, dog barking, the gardener rolling the gravel under the window and all the time traffic. Another week of this will drive me mad.

When asked by a television interviewer in middle age what he thought to be his greatest fault Evelyn answered, without hesitation, 'Irritability.' At home during the years of his dissipation he found his father oppressively irritating. He was irritated by Arthur's heavy theatrical sighs, loud enough to 'carry to the back of the gallery at Drury Lane', by his showing off, by his pipe smoking. He hated Arthur's gobbling at table, his hurry to have a second helping before anyone else had finished their first plate. He confided to his diary his irritation with Arthur's ostentatious asthma attacks: 'This morning I received communion with my parents at St Albans Church; there was much flustering and retching by my father before the ceremony'; with his quaint and affected use of language: 'Chapman and Hall has a "quinsy"'; and with his anecdotal wit: 'Chapman and Hall had friends to dinner last night including a woman called Ruth with whom he is in love. He entertained them by making jokes which hardly amused me at all. Indeed they made me most uncomfortable.' In August 1924 Evelyn was intensely irritated by Arthur's 'tiresome toy', 'father's new electrical machine', 'a horrible wireless apparatus'. He particularly resented the suggestion that they should all huddle round it and 'listen in' after dinner en famille. 'Every evening I return wishing to do nothing except eat a prodigious dinner and go to bed early after an evening of desultory conversation or, less profitably still, in "listening in" to Chapman and Hall's horrible wireless.'

By February 1927 Evelyn was well aware that he had to pull himself together. It was nearly three years since he had left university and he had achieved little. It was time to stop frittering his talent and prove to his friends that he really was as brilliant as they thought. 'Today I have been trying to do something about getting a job and am tired and discouraged,' he wrote in his diary. 'It is all an infernal nuisance. It seems to me the time has arrived to set about being a man of letters.'

Alastair Graham had privately printed an essay by Evelyn about the Pre-Raphaelite Brotherhood. It was intelligently written but Graham's production was incompetent – full of typographical errors. In writing about the Pre-Raphaelites Evelyn was entering into the world of Arthur's enthusiasm. Two of Arthur's Waugh cousins had, in succession, married William Holman Hunt; he owned a high-backed oak armchair that had once belonged to Dante Gabriel Rossetti and held pride of place in the book-room. Arthur read Evelyn's essay and 'approved it'. At the same time Alec, in a gesture of goodwill before leaving for Tahiti, published one of Evelyn's short stories in an anthology he was editing for Chapman and Hall. It was not a brilliant piece of work, and only one reviewer noticed it. Neither the story nor the essay was recognisably a work of genius but each led to other things: the story to a commission for another from the *New Decameron;* and the essay to a commission for a biography of Rossetti from the publishing firm Duckworth, whose offices were situated three doors along Henrietta Street from the offices of Chapman and Hall. The man at Duckworth gave Evelyn a fifty-pound advance – twenty pounds on signature of the contract, the rest on delivery of the manuscript. The twenty pounds was spent within a week.

Arthur should have been overjoyed by the news that his reprobate son was at last falling into line and joining the family business: he, too, had started his career by writing a biography of an eminent man. His *Alfred, Lord Tennyson*, published within weeks of the poet's death in 1892, had brought him to prominence in London's literary circles, and he had followed it with biographies of Robert Browning and William Wordsworth. They were old-fashioned books, written in the old-fashioned style that flattered their subjects, hid their defects, and trumpeted their 'serene and unblemished' lives. For all their arcane ways, Arthur's biographies had launched him on a steady career; but with Evelyn's chance to follow in his father's footsteps, Arthur felt unable to celebrate. By 1927 all faith in his younger son had evaporated, perhaps not without reason. He continued to suppose that Evelyn's best hope was not as a writer but as an artist and, on hearing the news, he shook his head gloomily and sighed a deep, theatrical sigh: 'Duckworth will never see that book and I suppose I shall have to make good and pay them back their advance.'

But Arthur was wrong – very wrong, as it turned out. Evelyn finished *Rossetti* within the time agreed. It was published at the beginning of 1928 and not only was it a success – a brilliant achievement for a twenty-three-year-old – but, more importantly, it gave him the confidence to write more. In the end, *Rossetti* proved to be the first in a long line of startling successes and the launch of a scintillating career that would, to quote Alec, 'confer high honour upon the name of Waugh'.

Evelyn made his stand on the very first page as a representative of a bright new generation unafraid to pillory his elders. Some literary critics have suggested that the opening passage of *Rossetti* was intended to mock the arcane biographical style of Lytton Strachey, but I wonder what Arthur must have thought when he read it:

No doubt the old-fashioned biography will return, and, with the years, we shall once more learn to assist with our fathers' decorum at the lying in state of our great men; we shall see their catafalques heaped with the wreaths of august mourners, their limbs embalmed, robed, uniformed and emblazoned with orders, their faces serenely composed and cleansed of all the stains of humanity. Meanwhile we must keep our tongue in our cheek, must we not, for fear it should loll out and reveal the idiot? We have discovered a jollier way of honouring our dead. The corpse has become the marionette. With bells on its fingers and wires on its toes it is jigged about to a 'period dance' of our own piping; and who is not amused?

If this was, as I suspect, a subtle dig at his father it would prove to be by no means the last. From *Rossetti* onwards Evelyn pursued Arthur Waugh through each of his books with the same zeal and unbending dedication as that which he used to humiliate his former tutor, the wicked dog sodomist of Hertford, C. R. M. F. Cruttwell.

VIII

No Uplifting Twist

At the end of June 1928, two months after the publication of *Rossetti*, Arthur and K were staying at an inexpensive hotel in Bruges. For twenty years they had holidayed abroad, usually in the north of France — St Malo, Avranches, Caudebec-en-Caux — or in Flanders, taking all their meals *en pension* in the same hotel. In the early years they had deposited their boys with the aunts at Midsomer Norton but later left them to fend for themselves at Underhill. The previous summer they had taken Evelyn with them to Nîmes. It was a happy holiday, although Evelyn had been maddened by flies. A photograph of him sitting with Arthur at a café table dates from that trip. In 1931 the whole family stayed at the Comb d'Or hotel in Villefranche where Evelyn soon became bored and, after several excursions without Arthur and K to see William Somerset Maugham at his nearby villa, he and Alec left their parents to 'go wenching' down the coast. Arthur always wore a tweed suit even in the hottest sunshine. 'I like to feel wool on my skin,' he said. Underneath he wore a vest and long-legged woollen underpants, no doubt drenched with sweat.

Now, in 1928, as Arthur and K toured the local churches, parks and galleries, as they sipped coffee — Arthur cramming his mouth with croissant and *confiture*, talking volubly, smoking his pipe, K aloof, maybe bored — interesting things were going on at home of which they were only dimly aware. The directors of Chapman and Hall had convened in Arthur's absence to decide the fate of Evelyn's first novel

Decline and Fall. Narrowly they voted to accept it, and when Evelyn heard the good news, he rushed straight round to his girlfriend's flat, near Sloane Square, and agreed with her to an expeditious and secret wedding. All of this was signed and sealed by the time Arthur and K returned to London in the second week of July.

The young couple were not earnestly or romantically in love; they enjoyed each other's company and were happy together, but their affair had been short and they viewed marriage with a nonchalant, perhaps frivolous detachment. She was not unintelligent. Her sweet, indulgent nature might have hidden a tough core, but on the outside she was warm, and her warmth made Evelyn beam whenever they were together. She (who was also called Evelyn – the Honourable Evelyn Gardner) had a round, prettyish face, short bobbed hair and a boyish sort of body that may, or may not, have reminded Evelyn of Alastair Graham. Her father, who had died when she was young, was Lord Burghclere, a friend of Gladstone, and her mother, with whom she lived, was the elder sister of Lord Carnarvon who, six years earlier, had sponsored Howard Carter's famous excavations of Tutankhamen's tomb at Luxor. For three years She-Evelyn had been trying to escape the overweening influence of her mother. He-Evelyn was similarly keen to break from the bonds of Underhill, and although neither he nor she had much money, marriage for both of them seemed an amusing and convenient means of escape from the menace of parental opprobrium. They were engaged on 13 September 1927.

Evelyn Gardner had spent Christmas at Underhill. She was polite, helpful in the kitchen and generally eager to please, but Arthur was concerned by the apparent frivolity of the Evelyns' relationship. Both showed off about how lightly they took the obligations of marriage. She had an affected sweetie-pie voice, and used the faddish language of 1920s youth that Arthur deplored. To She-Evelyn things were always 'divine' or 'bogus' or 'too shy-making'; she talked of reading 'Proustie-Woustie', and wrote to a friend in India after her first visit to Underhill, 'I went and dined with the Waugh family on Monday. Old Mr Waugh is a complete Pinkle-Wonk. He wears a blue velvet coat at dinner, just like Papa did, and talks about the actresses who were the toasts of his young days. I like that kind of thing.'

Arthur accepted his younger son's engagement with tolerance but he was not enthusiastic; nor did he seriously expect a marriage to take place. He may have counselled delay, as he had with Alec and Barbara Jacobs, but he did not need to push the point for that battle was being waged with striking determination by the formidable and fierce Lady Burghclere – She-Evelyn's mother. This tireless old bat may have enjoyed many friendships in her day but she was not particularly liked by Evelyn, her youngest daughter, and was detested by Evelyn, her soon-to-be-son-in-law, who called her 'The Baroness' with a sneer. Although by a twist of fate this shrill panto dame turns out to be a great-great-aunt of mine on both my father and mother's sides of the family, I have no compassion or loyalty to her memory. Her main weakness was snobbery. She prided herself on being born into the aristocratic family of Herbert of Hampshire. When I was at school to call a boy a 'herbert' was to insult him, but for Lady Burghclere, fifty years earlier, a Herbert was something very special indeed. Since the death of her husband she had spent her time writing biographies of dukes, which had entailed much rummaging through papers at their stately mansions. The last thing she wanted for her daughter was an impoverished, suburban trainee carpenter.

Her efforts to prevent the marriage were relentless. She told Evelyn that he could not marry her daughter as she would not agree to it. He fearlessly replied that he would marry Evelyn right away if she carried on like that. In the end a bargain was struck. She would permit the engagement to be officially announced once He-Evelyn had a proper job and renounced his ambition to be a carpenter. In this way the crafty Baroness hoped the relationship would peter out naturally; but she did not leave it to chance. When Evelyn tried to get a job as a radio presenter at the BBC, she found out and, through her connections, blocked it. She used all her researching skills to uncover unsavoury facts about Evelyn's past in order to persuade her daughter to go for someone better. In May She-Evelyn wrote to her friend John Maxse in India:

Thinking all was going smoothly and our engagement would be announced this week, I was greeted by Mama who said

that she had interviewed the authorities at Oxford about E's
past career. A Mr Cruttwell and the Dean of Hertford. They
said that he used to live off vodka and absinthe (presumably mixed) & went about with disreputable people (there
followed a string of French remarks about 'ces vices' something or other, all beautifully pronounced but unintelligible).
    She then added that Evelyn:

(1) lived off his parents
(2) ill-treated his father
(3) had no moral backbone or character
(4) would soon cease to love me
(5) would drag me down into the abysmal depths of Sodom
     and Gomorrah and finally
(6) we are not to be engaged for 2 years

    To all of which we said fiddlesticks and flummery and
brow-beat her into agreeing that our engagement should
be announced in September and before that if E. had been
in a job for two months. Victory to the Evelyns!

How strange that one of Lady Burghclere's charges against He-
Evelyn was that he 'ill-treated his father'. Where could she have
got this from? I think Arthur must have inadvertently let it slip. As
soon as she heard of the Evelyns' engagement she had summoned
him to a meeting at her house in Mayfair. What was said we shall
never know, but according to Alec, there was 'a frank exchange of
views'. Afterwards Evelyn remarked how useful it was to have, at
such a time, a father with an unblemished reputation. Of all the
whispered meetings or furtive conclaves to which my family has
been privy in the last hundred years this one between Arthur Waugh
and Lady Burghclere is the one above all others at which I wish I
had been a fly on the lampstand.[1] I imagine that Arthur aimed for

---

[1] As a youth I put it around that I wished I had been a fly on the lampstand at my
own conception. This information somehow reached my parents and disgusted
them. When confronted I refused to recant: 'No, honestly, it's good to be open
about these things. If you fail to understand this you fail to understand ME!'

appeasement while Lady Burghclere pulled rank as she had with Evelyn: 'The late Lord Burghclere would never have wanted his daughter to marry a man who wants to be carpenter'; 'The late Lord Burghclere would not have thought your son a gentleman'; 'The late Lord Burghclere would have been appalled by the disreputable company he keeps . . .' It was a meeting to which Lady Burghclere had come armed. She had done her homework, and C. R. M. F. Cruttwell had proved a useful ally.

If only Arthur had done a little research of his own he could have put the ball squarely into Lady Burghclere's court: 'Madam, you have no right to be snooty,' he might have said. 'Frankly I am appalled that my genius of a son should be marrying into such a shoddy pack as yours. I understand, madam, that your husband was a bastard, that his mother was a lowly actress and that her mother was a semi-literate thespian whose maiden name cannot even be traced. I am also informed that your brother, the Earl of Carnarvon, is not genetically responsible for all of his issue. News reaches me, too, that your eldest daughter is a cat-obsessed hermit who deserted her husband; that your second daughter is a hypochondriac lunatic who spends all her day lying on the floor in a darkened room; that your third daughter also deserted her husband, a Y-fronts salesman from Kent, in order to set up shop with a rough and ready sailor. As to your little Evelyn, madam, I gather she has already been engaged to *nine* other men, that she dreams she is being raped by German princes, and that she holds you, Lady Burghclere, with your sarcasm, teasing jokes and snubs, to be responsible for her instability and failure . . .'

Of course Arthur did not say anything of the sort. The last part of my imagined diatribe (the bit about Lady Burghclere's sarcasm and cruel jokes) is taken from an article She-Evelyn wrote about mothers two years later. Arthur noted in his diary: 'Unpleasing article by Evelyn Gardner in the *Evening Standard*.'

The Evelyns' engagement was left dangling when Arthur and K went off on their foreign jaunts and so, too, was the fate of Evelyn's novel. He was convinced that his father would not like *Decline and Fall* and on at least two occasions waited until he had gone to bed before reading sections of it out aloud to his friends in the bookroom. Arthur, for all his joviality and lively mind, did not share

Evelyn's sharp wit, or his dry sense of humour.[2] By contemporary standards, *Decline and Fall* was also a little obscene. Arthur must have been worried what the aunts of Midsomer Norton would make of it. How would Connie, Trissie and Elsie react to scenes of prostitution, lavatories, and Welshmen with a predilection for the back end of sheep?

Evelyn knew it was risky but sent it, nevertheless, in a mood of eager anticipation to Duckworth in May 1928. They told him that they could not publish it without first making extensive cuts in the interests of good taste. Evelyn was horrified and refused, brazenly threatening to take it elsewhere. 'I've looked through the book again and come to the inevitable conclusion,' wrote the man at Duckworth. 'As it now stands it is unpublishable. I'm sure no other publisher will have the courage or the folly to issue it without at least as much revision as I suggested. But I realise that you are determined to make the attempt, and have no doubt that I shall hear of its publication later, *after* you have altered it.'

In dismay Evelyn resolved to show the manuscript, with all Duckworth's deletions scribbled across it, to his father with a view to having it published by Chapman and Hall. He would have preferred any other firm, but he was desperate. He wanted to marry, he needed money and he had no job. He was convinced that his book was good but could not afford to hang about waiting for rejections.

Arthur found himself in an awkward position. He could see that *Decline and Fall* was a brilliant piece of work, but he could not take to it. He was anxious about nepotism and his image for fairness within the firm. On the other hand he had let *The Loom of Youth* slip to a rival firm and that had been a bestseller. Could he afford to pass on *Decline and Fall* as well? In the end it was agreed that the board should make the decision in his absence. He would play no part in it.

But the man from Duckworth had been right about those changes.

---

[2] When Arthur's cousin Sir Telford Waugh, a diplomat at Constantinople, published a book called *Turkey Yesterday, Today and Tomorrow*, Arthur remarked: 'It should have been called *Boxing Day*.' This, according to Evelyn, was his father's only memorable joke.

When Arthur returned to his office a week after the wedding[3] he insisted on most, if not all, of the alterations that Duckworth had required. By this stage Evelyn was in no position to argue and he reluctantly consented to all of Arthur's prudish bowdlerisations. It was not until 1962, after his father had died and Chapman and Hall was printing a new uniform edition of Evelyn's works, that most of the original jokes were restored to the text.

But for all his trifling victories over words like 'lavatory' and 'sex' Arthur was still not happy with the book. Neither were many others. Eddie Gathorn-Hardy, Paddy Brodie and Gavin Henderson, who recognised themselves portrayed as two characters in the novel, threatened to sue – they were all homosexuals. For the third imprint Evelyn agreed to change the names of his queer characters 'Martin Gaythorn-Brodie' and 'Kevin Saunderson' to 'Hon. Miles Malpractice' and 'Lord Parakeet'. Alec pleaded with his brother to remove the name of his current girlfriend, Zena Nayler, from a brothel sign in one of his illustrations. The notice was duly changed from 'Chez Zena' to 'Chez Ottoline', which must have enraged the Oxfordshire hostess Lady Ottoline Morrell. Before Alec, Zena had had an affair with the popular black singer Hutch, who appears in the novel as Chokey, a jazz minstrel lover of Margot Beste-Chetwynde, a character who wears an 'almost unprocurable scent' and is in turn based on Alastair Graham's mother. In *Decline and Fall* everybody is somebody. Evelyn rarely invented his characters. He took the world as he saw it and the people he knew, bust them up, mixed them about a bit and stuck them back together in a dreamlike and often freakish capriccio. That was the key to his creativity. Between people he knew and his fictional characters he swapped names, personalities, sexes, sometimes mirrored or reversed the truth, but it was never enough to prevent his contemporaries spotting the refracted parts of themselves and their friends in the kaleidoscope. In *Decline and Fall*, the central character, Paul Pennyfeather, provides the innocent eyes through which a zany world is seen. At the beginning of the book he is sent down from Oxford

---

[3] Only four people attended the Evelyns' wedding service at St Paul's, Portman Square. Alec was one of them. Someone was typing on the altar.

through no fault of his own. He takes a job as a school-teacher in Wales and, after a series of fantastic semi-autobiographical *Alice in Wonderland* calamities, ends up, in the final chapter, in more or less the same position as he started out.

She-Evelyn knew that her mother would detest *Decline and Fall*, not just because she loathed her future son-in-law and everything he stood for, or because it was full of risqué jokes about sex and lavatories, but because she was in it, mercilessly ridiculed in the character of Dr Fagan, a racist headmaster 'disturbed and grieved' to learn that one of his daughters is engaged to an unsuitable man:

> The Doctor drew from his pocket a handkerchief of *crêpe de Chine*, blew his nose with every accent of emotion, and resumed:
>
> 'He is *not* the son-in-law I should readily have chosen. I could have forgiven him his slavish poverty, his moral turpitude, and his abominable features: I could even have forgiven him his incredible vocabulary, if only he had been a *gentleman*. I hope you do not think me a snob. You may have discerned in me a certain prejudice against the lower orders. It is quite true. I do feel deeply on the subject . . . I do not think that any daughter of mine could fall so low. But she is, for some reason, uncontrollably eager to be married to somebody fairly soon.'

No one who has been reading this book with half an eye to detail could fail to recognise in the character of *Decline and Fall*'s Mr Prendergast certain resemblances to the author's father, Mr Arthur Waugh. Prendergast is an ex-clergyman who has lost his faith and become a school-master. Paul Pennyfeather's first meeting with him re-creates the recurring problem at Underhill: whose turn is it to use the bathroom?

> After breakfast Paul went up to the Common Room. Mr Prendergast was there polishing his pipes, one by one, with a chamois leather. He looked reproachfully at Paul.
>
> 'We must come to some arrangement about the bathroom,'

he said. 'Grimes, very rarely, has a bath. I have one before breakfast.'

'So do I,' said Paul defiantly.

'Then I suppose I shall have to find some other time,' said Mr Prendergast and he gave a deep sigh as he returned to his pipes. 'After ten years too,' he added. 'But everything's like that. I might have known you'd want a bath.'

Later on, Pennyfeather invites Prendergast to dinner at a local hotel; his emotional reaction is reminiscent of Arthur's response to Alec's birthday present of August 1915:

'Really, Pennyfeather,' he said, 'I think that's uncommonly kind of you. I hardly know what to say. Of course, I should love it. I can't remember when I dined at an hotel last. Certainly not since the war. It *will* be a treat. My dear boy, I'm overcome.'

And, much to Paul's embarrassment, a tear welled up in each of Mr Prendergast's eyes and coursed down his cheeks.

When at last Pennyfeather and Prendergast are seated at the restaurant table of the Hotel Metropole Evelyn cannot resist poking fun at his father's table habits:

Mr Prendergast ate a grape-fruit with some difficulty. 'What a big orange!' he said when he had finished it. 'They do things on a large scale here.' . . . More food was brought them. Mr Prendergast ate with a hearty appetite . . . 'I wonder,' said Mr Prendergast, 'I wonder if I could have just a little more of this very excellent pheasant.' . . . Mr Prendergast ate two *pêches Melba* undisturbed.

In a twist that reversed Arthur's long chastisement of Evelyn for drinking, Evelyn allows Mr Prendergast to inebriate himself at the school sports where he accidentally shoots a boy in the foot with a starting pistol. The spectacle of Mr Prendergast drunk moves one of the characters to say, 'I hope he's none the worse for this. You know I feel quite fatherly towards old Prendy.' During the event itself Prendergast, deliriously intoxicated, repeats over and over one of Arthur's favourite phrases:

'Well run, sir!' shouted Colonel Sidebotham. 'Jolly good race.'

'Capital,' said Mr Prendergast, and dropping his end of the tape, he sauntered over to the Colonel. 'I can see you are a fine judge of race, sir. So was I once. So's Grimes. A capital fellow, Grimes; a bounder you know, but a capital fellow. Bounders can be capital fellows; don't you agree, Colonel Slidebottom? In fact, I'd go further and say that capital fellows are bounders. What do you say? I wish you'd stop pulling my arm, Pennyfeather. Colonel Shybotham and I were just having a most interesting conversation about bounders.'

The silver band struck up again, and Mr Prendergast began a little jig, saying: 'Capital fellow! Capital fellow!' and snapping his fingers. Paul led him to the refreshment tent.

'Dingy wants you to help her in there,' he said firmly, 'and, for God's sake, don't come out until you feel better.'

'I never felt better in my life,' said Mr Prendergast indignantly. 'Capital fellow! Capital fellow!'

Arthur was as offended by these small teases as he was appalled by Prendergast's demise. Throughout his life, Evelyn advised aspiring young novelists never to kill their characters. With a few exceptions he stuck to the rule himself, keeping his own alive, often moving them from book to book. It is odd, I think, that of the small handful of Evelyn Waugh characters that are murdered, two should have been recognisably based upon his father.[4] The manner of Mr Prendergast's death must have been especially galling to Arthur: his head is sawn off by a madman who wants to be a carpenter.

Needless to say, Evelyn Waugh's marriage to Evelyn Gardner was a failure. Perhaps the only joy in it for either of them had been

---

[4] Prendergast, in *Decline and Fall*, is murdered as above; Mr Plant in *Work Suspended* is murdered by a mysterious character whose name enigmatically resembles Arthur Waugh – Arthur Atwater.

the escape from their parents to a small, neat, rented flat in Islington. Lady Burghclere was not informed of the marriage until three weeks after the ceremony had taken place. Of course she was furious, but little did she know as she stamped her bossy foot on her drawing-room floor that the marriage had only thirteen months left in it. For most of the time either She-Evelyn was ill in bed, or He-Evelyn was absenting himself to write books.

By June 1929, She-Evelyn had fallen in love with, and become the lover of, a 'ramshackle oaf' from the BBC. At the beginning of July Evelyn was working on his second novel at a quiet pub in Beckley when he received a short letter from his wife informing him that she was having an affair with John Heygate[5] and wished to end their marriage. He returned immediately to London but she was already gone. Deeply humiliated, he wrote to a close friend: 'I did not know it was possible to be so miserable and live.' The Islington flat was in She-Evelyn's name and he had to leave it, but there was nowhere for him to go except back to ruddy Underhill. He asked Alec to break the sorry news to his parents and six days later, on 11 August 1929, followed up with a letter.

Dear Mother and Father,

I asked Alec to tell you the sad, and to me radically shocking news that Evelyn has gone to live with a man called Heygate.[6] I am accordingly filing a petition for divorce.

[5] Heygate was sacked by the BBC for eloping with Mrs Waugh. They married in August 1930 and were divorced six years later without progeny. He admired Hitler before the War. He married three times, suffered depression and syphilitic madness and shot himself in 1976. Shortly before his suicide Heygate wrote to my father: 'I have been thinking of the whole sad episode which brought such unhappiness into your father's life, and for which I suppose I was mainly responsible. Several people have asked me to write what little I knew about him, but I never have nor ever will. I merely wish you to know, Auberon, that whatever happened – and it was not good – I still retain now exactly the same feelings of love and admiration. Your father was a great man and one of the great writers and I feel proud to have known him.
[6] Heygate had lunched with Arthur, K and the Evelyns at Underhill two months earlier.

I am afraid that this will be a blow to you but I assure you not nearly as severe a blow as it is to me . . . May I come and live with you sometimes? ·

Love Evelyn

P.S. Evelyn's defection was preceded by no kind of quarrel or estrangement. So far as I knew we were both serenely happy. It must be some hereditary tic. Poor Baroness.

All of Evelyn's possessions arrived back at Underhill on 4 September. Arthur told his son that he never wished to speak to She-Evelyn again. K, however, blamed Evelyn for having left She-Evelyn alone for so much of the time. Most people sided with him, but the support of his friends was cold comfort as he was back where he longed not to be, in his father's house. He and Arthur were locked together once more and, in the words of a friend, 'sniffing at one another other like dogs'.

At the same time, as Arthur had forewarned, Alec's passion for the flame-haired American temptress Ruth Morris was headed nowhere; but still she dragged her hapless lover over mountain, sea and desert storm for illicit meetings that usually ended in tears. Besides her husband and Alec she had other lovers; one of them was a sailor to whom she always referred as 'the lad'. When Alec found out about him, Ruth was far from contrite: 'Don't you see?' she told him. 'I love my husband, I'm in love with you, and I'm fascinated by "the lad".' Alec, heartbroken as he was, pursued her for three wretched years until he finally had to admit to himself that it was time to let go. I do not think that he was ever, before or afterwards, so in love with anyone else as he had been with Ruth. In 1931 he wrote a poignant novel about their affair (*So Lovers Dream*), and when his library was sold in the 1960s it was the only one of his manuscripts that he kept back.

During his three years of travel in pursuit of the elusive Ruth, Alec never forgot about his father. They corresponded regularly and, unlike Evelyn, he was proud to consider Underhill a base of sorts. Although he was innately selfish he felt remorse at having abandoned his father to the baying dogs of the board room at Chapman and Hall. His apology, so to speak, was a 280-page love letter to Arthur in the form of a novel about fathers and sons, entitled *Three Score and Ten*. As novels go it is pretty feeble, and in later life he struck it off his bibliography. Alec's main weakness as a novelist was his incapacity to see beyond his own experience so that any father-son relationship in his fiction (and there are several) could do little more than mirror his own with Arthur. *Three Score and Ten* covers three generations but the relationship between the grandfather and the father is precisely the same as that between the father and the son, both drawn from Alec's own bizarre experience of Arthur. In the book the grandfather is Christopher Cardew, his son Hilary and his grandson Geoffrey but, for the sake of clarity, let us call these fictitious characters respectively 'Fake-Brute', 'Fake-Arthur' and 'Fake-Alec'.

In the first part of the book we are treated to a long description of Fake-Brute's relationship with his son Fake-Arthur. We learn that Fake-Brute recites his son's letters by heart and that he 'simply and unaffectedly lives in and for his son'. Just like Arthur and Alec. 'Fake-Brute's life was lit by a purpose. His absorption in Fake-Arthur gave a meaning to the most commonplace incidents of his day.' This goes on for 130 pages until Fake-Arthur is himself grown up, following in his father's profession (they are all lawyers), and with a son of his own (Fake-Alec) with whom (surprise, surprise) he is inordinately obsessed. All the incidents of real Alec's life are there: Fake-Alec is forced to swallow his own vomit at prep school, learns to play toy cricket with his father in the nursery and is read aloud to in the book-room. Fake-Arthur rejuvenates himself by watching his son play cricket, and when the boy gets into the first eleven, his father cries for joy: 'That is the best news we've had this century!' Their relationship is spiritual; mother doesn't geddit. Then Fake-Alec goes to war, comes back, gets married and (yes, you've guessed it) has a son and (yes, you've guessed it again) absorbs himself in him. Fake-Alec wonders aloud about how the little critter – still in his pram – will turn out in twenty years' time:

In silence Fake-Arthur listened. There it was, the old talk again. The father losing interest in himself, centring his ambitions in his son . . . And whatever happened the outcome would be the same. There would be the first years of happy intimacy; then there would be the drifting apart, the misunderstandings, the bitterness, and ultimately consolingly, indifference.

The closing pages go way beyond the sentimental to something that is, in my opinion, almost sinister in its saccharine tartiness:

The old talk, the old belief; Fake-Arthur wished he could feel ironical and bitter. He could not though. The subject did not seem fitted to irony or bitterness. And he would have turned away but at that moment he felt Fake-Alec's hand upon his arm, just as he had in the old days, when they had walked round the slopes at Fernhurst. And in his son's eyes was that old look of confiding friendliness; and in his voice the warm note he had not heard for seven years.

'Well, if I'm half the father to him that you have been to me, he won't have much to grumble over.'

Those words, coming suddenly after those frozen months, were more than Fake-Arthur could stand.

'My dear boy,' he said, but his voice choked he could not speak. If Fake-Alec really did feel that – if he had meant what he had said; and there had been that look in the eyes, that warmth in the voice. Surely he had meant them; anyhow they had been said. But he could not speak. He turned away, and the garden was misty before his eyes. The sounds of the garden were blurred upon his ears, so that he could not hear the harsh rhythm of the fox-trot, so unlike the dream-waltzes of his youth; so that he could not see the green grass and the flowered borders, and the young people, their faces bright with an unreasoning faith and courage, and the sunlight shining down on them.

Three Score and Ten, which was published by Chapman and Hall in 1929, may have healed the rift between father and son caused by

Alec's desertion, but it did nothing for the reputation of its author. The novel was eviscerated by the critics, who discarded it as a shoddy, sub-sentimental piece of unrealistic nonsense. 'It is surprising how much of an air of immaturity seems to cling to everything that Mr Alec Waugh writes.' Little did they realise that the novel was in fact based upon a real relationship, but how could they? It all seemed so improbable. One sharp critic, for the *New Statesman*, derided any father who would be so feeble as to sublimate his own career in the interests of his son. Arthur must have been wounded when he read this:

> Fake-Arthur, in Mr Waugh's book, ends as a failure, as a second rate barrister who has never dared to take silk, with no achievements of any sort to his name, simply because he was not strong enough and had not a broad enough view of life to take the bringing up of his son in his stride. A man of full intelligence and of full appetite for living would regard this duty as only one, even if the main one, in a career which should have many interests. It would have been better for both Fake-Arthur and Fake-Alec if Fake-Arthur could have done this. It is no great fun for a son to be the apple of his father's eye, nor a very good preparation for his own individual existence. If Mr Waugh had shown Fake-Arthur's career as the tragedy created by unavoidable surrender to a weakness of character, he might have written a more interesting novel than he has done.

Worse was to come. *Three Score and Ten* had, like so many of Alec's previous books (*The Loom of Youth*, 1917; *Pleasure*, 1921; *The Lonely Unicorn*, 1922; and *Public School Life*, 1922), dealt with the issue of public school and homosexuality. The writer Wyndham Lewis noticed this obsession and in his book *The Doom of Youth* devoted a whole chapter to 'the strange case' of Mr Alec Waugh: 'I do not believe that anyone dipping into *Three Score and Ten* would fail to detect something rather odd at once. The characters Mr Waugh creates are feminized, as it were, to an obsessional extent.'

Wyndham Lewis was on to something. He developed the theory

that Alec's relentless interest in little boys, with their 'clean ties and collars, pockets bulging out of shape with letters, knives, chestnuts, compasses', revealed that the author had the instincts of a woman and that the fathers' attitudes towards their sons in *Three Score and Ten*, were not *fatherly*, in the normal sense, but *motherly*.

> Mr Waugh must have the soul of a nannie more or less for he can go on like this for pages. Indeed if I had to say what I thought of the strange case of Mr Waugh, I should say that all the feminine, maternal attributes were excessively developed in him, and of course (Mr Waugh being a man) were thwarted. They relieve themselves, no doubt, by means of these incessant literary compositions about small boys with sooty faces and bulging pockets. One feels that the outlet is critically necessary . . . I do not wish to be offensive to Mr Waugh, but I think it is fair to say that there is something of an obsessional nature at work; and I do think that psycho-analysis would reveal the fact that motherhood in its most opulent form was what Mr Waugh had been destined for by nature, and that a cruel fate had in some way interfered, and so unhappily he became a man.

Alec was stung by Lewis's attack and avoided the public-school theme in his novels thereafter. When *The Doom of Youth* first appeared Arthur encouraged him to join with another author in suing Lewis for libel. The charge – not that Lewis had accused Alec of being a mummy-*manqué* but that he had implied that he was homosexual. The inference of homosexuality was drawn by comparing Lewis's comments on Alec being a woman with remarks about homosexuals elsewhere in the book: 'The homosexual is, of course, an imitation woman'; and, 'The traditional feminine obsession with youthfulness is not amongst the least of the female characteristics taken over, and exaggerated, by the homosexual.' Lewis hotly denied that he had accused Alec of being a homosexual and refused to give an inch to Alec's lawyers. As the case came closer to court Alec started to lose his nerve, imagining a tough cross-examination: 'Why exactly did you leave Sherborne, Mr Waugh? Why do so many of your books appear to condone homosexuality? Are you a *poof*, Mr Waugh?' What Alec did not know was that Wyndham Lewis was skint and burdened by four other cases of litigation against him. He, too, was edgy.

After a protracted show of brinkmanship, Lewis eventually capitulated, agreeing to have all unsold copies of his book pulped on the condition that Alec withdrew the charge.

Evelyn was less pleased that so many copies of *The Doom of Youth* had been destroyed: in it Lewis had described him as 'very intelligent and a great wit. He has written two or three books that are far funnier than those of anybody in England . . . his posthumous fame is assured.'

Shortly after the publications of *Three Score and Ten* and *Decline and Fall* Arthur decided that he had had enough of Chapman and Hall. He was sixty-four and had been trudging to and from that office every day for twenty-six years. Unfortunately he had failed to save for a pension. Perhaps it is a reflection of his usefulness to the company and his popularity with the staff and shareholders that he resigned as managing director, yet continued as a reader, consultant and company chairman from home on almost full salary. He started his retirement working harder than ever. Besides his duties for the 'old firm' he continued as chief book reviewer to the *Daily Telegraph*, president of the local amateur dramatic association, president of the Dickens Fellowship, and chairman of the Publishers' Circle. On top of that he wrote two books in quick succession: a history of Chapman and Hall and his autobiography, *One Man's Road*.

In 1930 both of Arthur's sons had their big successes. Alec published *The Coloured Countries* about his travels to Tahiti which, under the title of *Hot Countries*, sold eighty thousand copies in America and was chosen as the Literary Guild's Book of the Month. Evelyn published a travel memoir, *Labels*, with Duckworth and a novel, *Vile Bodies*, with Chapman and Hall. For the rest of his life Evelyn's novels went to 'the old firm' and his travel books to Duckworth.

Vile Bodies was an instant hit with the public and its success quickly established *Decline and Fall* as a bestseller too. From here on Evelyn never looked back. He was a famous writer in great demand, standing at the forefront of modern English letters, and remained so to the end of his life. Meanwhile Alec was realising, without a hint of jealousy, that he should sow his future career as a writer in the fertile soil of America. After a few years, the Algonquin Hotel in New York, where he kept in the basement a few pictures, cocktail glasses and a framed picture of Arthur, had established itself in his heart as his second home.

In England, Evelyn became, almost overnight, the kind of literary celebrity over whom, thirty years earlier, Arthur had drooled at the polished, Sunday afternoon tables of his cousin, Sir Edmund Gosse. In the early thirties Evelyn had achieved heights of fame and literary recognition that, in his youth, Arthur could only have dreamed about. The tight-knit bond between Alec and Arthur, which had controlled Underhill with its mutual admiration, telepathetic love and high-falutin' praise of poetry and literature, now found itself sidelined by the little boy who Alec used to call 'It', the unimportant figure, the quiet onlooker, the younger brother who had never been invited to join the team.

But there is another irony to Evelyn's success at this time that is sharper than the rest. For most of his working life Arthur had worried about the future of Chapman and Hall after the lapse of its most precious asset – the Charles Dickens copyrights. There were times when he had been seriously afraid that the company would have to cease publishing fiction altogether. Reprieve came in the form of his second, less favoured son. In twenty-six months Evelyn achieved at Chapman and Hall what his father had been struggling to achieve for over twenty-six years: he made the fiction list secure and profitable. Yet he did not wish to be published by Chapman and Hall and his father did not admire his novels. By February 1930 Evelyn's *Vile Bodies* and *Decline and Fall* were each selling more copies by the week than Alec's novels sold in a lifetime. 'O cruel Fate! What hurly-burly throw'st thou at me?'

But if 1930 was a year of success in the careers of Arthur's two sons it was also a year of bitter failure where his relationship with Evelyn was concerned. The day-nursery at Underhill, the peaceful first-floor room with a balcony looking out over the garden that had once been Evelyn and Barbara's Cubist 'studio', then Alec and Barbara's 'sitting-room', was now used by Arthur as his study and it was here that he finished writing *One Man's Road*. It was here, also, that Evelyn kept the books he had recently removed from Islington, including, neatly arranged on the shelf above Arthur's desk, two unguarded, morocco-bound volumes of his diary.

Naturally Arthur's curiosity got the better of him — and the effect upon him was shattering. Most of all, he was wounded by negative references to himself, 'immensely humiliated and distressed', as Alec, many years later, put it in a letter: 'My mother [K] told me that he never really got over it, that he kept harking back to it.' At the time he complained to Alec that Evelyn had criticised his style of reading aloud — one of his favourite pastimes — and referred in particular to Evelyn's sneer, 'a good lecture but incorrigibly theatrical as usual'. In 1914 Arthur had given a speech to the Sherborne School Literary Society in which he had read extracts from Dickens 'very dramatically', according to Alec, and afterwards a sixth-former had asked him if he had ever been an actor. Arthur had been as delighted by the compliment as he was now diminished by Evelyn's criticism. After that he hesitated to read aloud to anyone except his closest friends.

What hurt him most, though, was the passage in which Evelyn described him as 'ineffably silly' and despised by K, who must have married him only because 'he needed her most'. And we can only imagine how any father would feel after reading his son's lurid confessions to sadism, sexual incontinence and drunken debauch. Evelyn's description of his visit to a homosexual brothel in Paris between Christmas and New Year 1925 will suffice as a single example of the sort of diary incident to which Arthur must have taken the gravest exception:

They howled and squealed and danced and pointed to their genitalia. A boy dressed as an Egyptian woman sat himself beside me and pretended to understand my French. He admired my check trousers and made that an opportunity to squeeze my legs and then without more ado he put his arms round me and started to kiss me. I thought him attractive but had better uses for the 300 francs which the patron demanded for his enjoyment . . . I arranged a tableau by which my boy should be enjoyed by a large negro who was there but at the last minute, after we had ascended to a squalid divan at the top of the house and he was lying waiting for the negro's advances, the price proved prohibitive . . . I took a taxi home and to bed in chastity. I think I do not regret it.

Within a few short months of reading this filth, Arthur was in for another shock, perhaps a greater one even than the first. On 29 September 1930 Evelyn was received into the Roman Catholic Church. It is hard to imagine how much an old-fashioned Englishman detested the Church of Rome. To Arthur, whose whole family was steeped in the traditions of the Church of England, Evelyn's pugnacious Catholicism must have been far more offensive than Alec's agnosticism. Contemptuously he referred to Evelyn's conversion as his '*perversion* to Rome'. Arthur's worst nightmare had come true. Years earlier, when Evelyn was nine, he had given him a copy of Mary Macgregor's classical history *The Story of Rome*, inscribed with a warning against the lures of Catholicism:

> All roads, they tell us, lead to Rome;
> Yet, Evelyn, stay a while at home!
> Or, if the Roman road invites
> To doughty deeds and fearful fights,
> Remember England still is best –
> Her heart, her soul, her Faith, her Rest!

How prophetic Arthur's inscription turned out to have been. In *A Little Learning* Evelyn, by then a dyed-in-the-wool Catholic, wrote dismissively of Arthur's attitude to religion:

My father liked church-going with a preference for colourful and ceremonious services, usually attending whatever place was nearest, irrespective of its theological complexion . . . In my childhood my father read family prayers every morning. In August 1914 he abandoned this practice on the very curious

grounds that it was 'no longer any good'. His complaint
against Catholics was their clarity of dogma and I doubt
whether he had a genuine intellectual conviction about any
element of his creed. He would muse in vaguely platonic
terms about the possibilities of immortality.

This flip picture of his father's spiritual outlook is far from accurate.
I do not suppose that Arthur would have agreed with a word of it.
Behind this passage lies, of course, Evelyn's conviction of the superiority of Catholicism over his father's Anglicanism. But Evelyn knew
that Arthur was a deeply religious man. When he designed a bookplate for him in the 1920s he drew, in a position of prominence
just above Arthur Waugh's name, a large crucifix, signifying the
importance that religion played in his father's life.

We do not need to go into all the reasons for Evelyn's secession
here. As I have already suggested, his childhood enthusiasm for playing
priests was spurred by the need to gain his father's love and admiration. After that and until 1930 he was not especially religious. Twice
he suggested to Arthur that he wished to become a clergyman, then
considered a respectable gentleman's job for the younger sons of a
certain class. He went for a single interview that came to nothing.

Arthur did not take any of this seriously but in 1930 he took
Evelyn's 'perversion' very seriously indeed: he saw it as an act of
treachery against the tried and trusted traditions of his family, and,
in a typical act of 'transference' (I think that is what psychologists
call it), he wrote in his diary for 27 September 1930: 'K very, very
sad over news of Evelyn's conversion to Rome.' But on the same
day K wrote dispassionately: 'Evelyn to Lambs for weekend. He
told me he was being received into Roman Church next week.
Shopped with Janet.' When Arthur told Alec about Evelyn's conversion all he could say was 'Your poor mother, your poor, poor mother.'
But K was not especially religious: all she cared about was that the
move was right for Evelyn. Later Arthur wrote to a friend that
Evelyn was travelling in Africa 'fortified with the blessing of the
Pope. He is welcome to any comfort he can derive from such bene-
dictions. I prithee have me excused.'

* * *

The main effect of Evelyn's religious conversion on his relationship with Arthur was to create an alienating and irreparable chasm between the two. That he was still based at Underhill did not help. Father and son went to great efforts to avoid one another around the house. Many entries in Arthur's diary make clear the extent to which Evelyn, with the help of his mother, kept away from him during the day: 'Evelyn and K went to Hampstead shopping, so I went out alone'; 'Evelyn came back to dinner and sat with K in the book-room so I spent the evening alone upstairs'; 'K and Evelyn went to the cinema leaving me alone'; 'K and Evelyn again went out together – this time to the Hippodrome – and left me all alone.'

In April 1931 Evelyn came home with a temperature of 101°F and a mouthful of ulcers, having swallowed some offensive watercress at a nearby hotel. Soon afterwards Arthur fell ill of an unrelated complaint which Evelyn explained, much to his father's horror, was an attack of jealousy brought on by his own illness and K's tender nursing of her younger son. As Alec wrote in one of his many memoirs, 'My father wanted to have all the attention, always: particularly from his wife, particularly when he was ill.' When they had both recovered Evelyn apologised to Arthur with a dozen quarter bottles of champagne but Arthur complained that the champagne made him liverish.

It was during these years that Evelyn, in his eagerness to stay away from home as much as possible, discovered the delights of the large country house. Several critics have accused him of snobbery in this regard. I shall deal with this charge later but for the moment restrict myself only to the observation that no one except a fool or a Philistine would have preferred the drear, draughty lifestyle at Underhill to the glories of Madresfield, Mells, Biddesdon or any of the other great country houses to which he was a regular and welcome guest during the 1930s.

I do not believe that Arthur's relationship with Evelyn was confrontational at this time, yet the pair had never been so distant and communications between them had never seemed so hollow. Evelyn had always been allowed to do as he liked. He was a spoiled boy, and yet he was unloved by his father – a strange combination.

Without ever having the satisfaction of a blazing row Evelyn continued to tease and insult his father through his books. *Labels*, his Mediterranean travel journal, was written at the same time as Arthur was working on his autobiography and takes a swipe at him in the opening four lines: 'I did not really know where I was going, so, when anyone asked me I said to Russia. Thus my trip started, like an autobiography, upon a rather nicely qualified basis of false-hood and self-glorification.' Soon afterwards *Vile Bodies* was published. Here Arthur again saw, paraded before the public in the character of the eccentric Colonel Blount, many of his own worst characteristics and affectations. Like Arthur, who in 1924 had lent Underhill as the setting of Evelyn's student film, wishing desper-ately that he might be given a role in it, so in *Vile Bodies*, Colonel Blount lends his house, Doubting Hall, to a Hollywood producer, Mr Isaacs, on the condition that he may appear as an extra. During the filming Colonel Blount has 'never been so happy in his life':

'All right,' said one of the men with megaphones. 'You can beat it. We'll shoot the duel now. I shall want two supers to carry the body. The rest of you are through for the afternoon.'

A man in leather apron, worsted stockings and flaxen wig emerged from the retreating worshippers.

'Oh please, Mr Isaacs,' he said, 'please may *I* carry the body?'

'All right, Colonel, if you want to. Run in and tell them in the wardrobe to give you a smock and a pitchfork.'

'Thank you so much,' said Colonel Blount, trotting off towards his house. Then he stopped. 'I suppose,' he said, 'I suppose it wouldn't be better for me to carry a sword?'

'No, pitchfork, and hurry up about it or I shan't let you carry the body at all; someone go and find Miss La Touche.'

Vile Bodies also resurrects Arthur's banner for Alec 'Welcome home the heir to Underhill' and introduces the readers to Mr Rampole. This 'benign old gentleman', who reappears ten years later in Evelyn's novel *Put Out More Flags*, is a director of the small publishing firm, Rampole and Bentley, based (like Chapman and Hall) in Henrietta Street, Covent Garden. He lives in a 'small but substantial' house in Hampstead, goes to board meetings once a week and his 'chief interest in the business was confined to the progress of a little book of his own about bee-keeping, which they had published twenty years ago and, though he did not know it, allowed long ago to drop out of print'. Rampole has 'an ingenious way of explaining over advances and over-head charges and stock in hand in such a way that seemed to prove that obvious failures had indeed succeeded'. His attitude to authors is parsimonious. He does not like giving them advances, and issues as 'standard' a miserly contract: 'No royalty on the first two thousand, then a royalty of two and half per cent, rising to five on the tenth thousand. We retain serial, cinema, dramatic, American, colonial, and translation rights, of course. And, of course, an option on your next twelve books on the same terms.'

Arthur hit back, in a submissive sort of way, in his own book, *One Hundred Years in Publishing*, a history of Chapman and Hall. In this portentous tome the author devotes two pages to Alec Waugh who 'lived in the world of youth', and praises 'that honest and revealing story' *The Loom of Youth* (not published by Chapman and Hall), which set the 'world ablaze', and that 'equally honest record' *The Prisoners of Mainz*:

> A son's success is naturally a father's pride; but, better than all the tales of swelling loyalty, even in a publisher's office, is the steady advance of a sincere and self-respecting talent, widening as experience widens, and ripening as judgement matures. That first critic on the hearth, to whom were confided the earliest manuscripts of an eager schoolboy, has surely his peculiar right to hail the firm and confident workmanship of a novel such as *Three Score and Ten*, with its intimate study of the relationship of father and son, or the swift observation and comprehensive sympathy which render *The Coloured Countries* so acutely personal in its appeal. To see one's dreams come true in the achievement of the younger generation, is always a more satisfying recompense than to have realised them for oneself.

To Arthur 'the steady advance of a sincere and self-respecting talent' was preferable in every respect to the meteoric rise of his publicity-hungry younger son, who is mentioned only once, *en passant*, in a short sub-clause to a long sentence about other authors:

> Sir Denison Ross, that most learned and genial Orientalist, has been responsible for a library of ancient fiction, called the *Treasure House of Eastern Story*, and among the long regiment of novelists is yet another Waugh (Evelyn) – whose *Decline and Fall* and *Vile Bodies* have developed an original and highly entertaining vein of half-cynical, half-appreciative satire which has so thoroughly caught the public taste that both books have been reckoned with the best-sellers of consecutive years – while names as diverse in appeal as Gertrude Atherton, Rosemary Rees, Countess Barcynska, Ianthe Jerrold, Barbara Goolden, Constance Holme, Winifred James, Ruth Brockington, Mrs A. M. Williamson, Karen Bramson, etc., etc. . . .

Alec claimed this as a warm tribute but Evelyn disagreed, viewing as a snub his inclusion on a literary list that looked more like a roll-call of runners-up in the Hampstead and Highgate annual flower-arranging competition. He retaliated with a short story, 'Too Much Tolerance', about a man, remarkably like Arthur, who believes that most people are 'jolly good fellows', who rejects his own stiff Victorian upbringing to encourage everyone to do exactly what they want and is consequently shafted by all. The story ends:

> As I watched, he finished his business and strode off towards the town – a jaunty, tragic little figure, cheated out of his patrimony by his partner, battened on by an obviously worthless son, deserted by his wife, an irrepressible, bewildered figure, striding off under his bobbing hat, cheerfully butting his way into a whole continent of rapacious and ruthless jolly good fellows.

Arthur detested Evelyn's manipulation of the press and what he saw as his vulgar hunger for publicity – 'Publicity breeds an irresistible itch for vulgar display,' he used to say. In 1930, at the time of Evelyn's phenomenal success with *Vile Bodies*, he wrote:

Nobody seems content to do his work nowadays without blowing a horn to call attention to his proficiency. Nor is it his work alone, nor even his work principally, that is proclaimed to the world. The orgy of publicity follows him into the restaurants and parties, which now take the place of home; the social-gossiper hangs at the tail-coat of the public character, reporting next afternoon, the food which he ate over night, the eyes into which he smiled, and the degree of sobriety which enabled him to find his way home.

When Evelyn was sent to Abyssinia to report on the Italian war Arthur wrote to his friend McMaster: 'If any of you see that abominable rag the *Daily Mail*, you will know that Evelyn has gone to Abyssinia as its War Correspondent to the great discomfort of his parents. To-day's *Mail* is all over him. I never saw such flaming publicity.' It is true that Evelyn was an adroit self-publicist – he calculatedly set himself up as Fleet Street's 'voice of youth' and, after the success of *Vile Bodies*, ensured that as many as possible of his witty, iconoclastic opinions were quoted every week in the gossip columns of the British press. Arthur retaliated by starving Evelyn of the oxygen of publicity in his own small way: he omitted any mention of his career in *One Man's Road*. His last allusion to Evelyn concerns the play he wrote at Lancing in 1917, called *Conversion*. He praises Evelyn's teachers for 'allowing its reproduction in the Big School' and at the end of the same paragraph extols a Lancing teacher who had been pleased that 'success as a dramatist had not prevented the young man from carrying off the senior History Scholarship at Oxford'. After that, nothing. No mention of *Decline and Fall*, *Vile Bodies*, *Labels* or the extraordinary fame and success his younger son had achieved in the two years before the final proofs of *One Man's Road* were sent to the printers. Alec, desperate in later years to portray Arthur and

Evelyn's relationship as continuously blissful, excused the omission on the grounds that Evelyn's collapsed marriage and conversion to the Roman Catholic faith had somehow made reference to his successful career impossible. 'The whole story in the spring of 1931 when my father was at work on *One Man's Road* was too close for its emotion to be recollected in tranquillity. Better not attempt it.' Odd.

In the summer of 1932 – I have heard it said, on the rebound from Ruth – Alec became engaged to Joan Chirnside, a thirty-year-old adopted daughter of a sporting millionaire from Melbourne, Australia. He proposed on Arthur's birthday, 24 August, so that as soon as Joan had accepted him he could telegraph the news to Arthur as a special gift. No doubt there was much welling up of watery eyes that day at Underhill. Arthur adored Joan from the start. She was to him the daughter he had always wanted, charming, polite, generous, warm and a great *appréciatrice* of all that was most delightful in himself. 'You are a member of the family now, you must call me Poppa,' he announced, on hearing of the engagement. She was happy to oblige. K, who was uncomfortable with Joan calling her 'Momma', settled instead for the more comfortable but silly 'Mrs Wugs'.

The novelist Anthony Powell once claimed of Alec that he was curiously attracted to boredom and boring people and it was for this reason that he was such a popular dinner guest: he could be seated next to anyone, however dreary, and get along fine. Alec was, it is true, an excellent listener, which made him popular with egomaniacs and saloon-bar moralists. Recently I chanced on a collection of his essays, *On Doing What One Likes*, privately printed in 1926, the year he escaped from Chapman and Hall, and was surprised to find in it a passage extolling the virtues of boredom in literature, which seemed to support Powell's thesis:

> We cannot deny, if we are honest with ourselves, that we have rarely read a classic without being for quite long intervals considerably bored by it. And yet it is the reading of those

books that we recall with the most enjoyment; precisely, I sometimes think, because of those tedious interludes; those long accounts of trivial people and uninteresting conversations which provided so admirable a contrast for such sensations as the novelist had subsequently to offer. They were the breathing space. They bored him so that he should be able to relish more keenly the excitement when it came.

So much for literary criticism. But what Powell had been trying to say was that Alec was attracted to Joan Chirnside, not because she was rich or pretty or charming, but because she was boring. A far-fetched notion, but there it is. In any case, if it were true, Joan was clearly not boring enough, for Alec soon became restless in married life and longed to escape their Hampshire home and return to the Tahitian palm-tree and beach romances of the last six years.

Once married, Alec no longer needed a base at Underhill. The traffic, roaring up and down North End Road had increased exponentially since Arthur had built the house in 1907 and the long walk from the tube was increasingly tiresome to him. So, in the summer of 1933, Arthur decided to sell Underhill and move to a two-floor flat in a quiet street in Highgate. Departure from Underhill gave Arthur an excuse to wax and moan and to pour out his feelings on old associations and past times. Evelyn did not seem to care much, one way or the other. If anything, he was pleased to leave a place that had bored and irritated him. He liked the new flat, in which he was given a room to himself and, as a present to his parents, he paid to have the whole place repapered.

Only Alec was shocked and saddened by the sale of Underhill: he remembered wistfully how Arthur had described him as its heir. Arthur quickly established himself in his new environment, a few yards above the Highgate School cricket ground. All summer long he watched the boys play cricket and soon became a familiar sight to them in his Homburg hat, with his white hair, short round figure, red face, slow, shuffling walk and jet black poodle by his side.

I have not so far mentioned the black poodle scenario as it seems to have little to do with fathers and sons – but throughout their married lives K and Arthur had a succession of them. There was one called Marquis, one called Wooley (after the cricketer), one called Gaspard, one called Beau, who, according to Barbara Jacobs, 'lurked under the table and would rush out suddenly with red eyes flashing', and heaven knows how many others. Needless to say Arthur was hopelessly emotional about them all. When Gaspard died in November 1933 he wrote in his diary: 'Dear darling Gappy. No more walks together on the Heath. No more welcoming barks as I open the gate. Goodbye, dear little companion of so many happy hours,' but once again, I digress . . .

Three years after the tragic death of Gaspard, Evelyn was busy writing travel books, novels, journalism and short stories. Arthur must have shuddered when he saw, for the first time, the title of Evelyn's short story 'The Man Who Liked Dickens'. 'What new onslaught – what new patricidal biffing am I in for now?' The title alone was enough for him to know that he was in line for another of Evelyn's cruel, satirical wallops. As a man who described himself as 'a Dickensian', and was known to Ellen Terry as 'that dear little Mr Pickwick', who liked to dress in the old-fashioned frock coats and shirts of the Victorian era; as president of the Dickens Fellowship, a renowned expert who lectured on Dickens, who had edited two complete sets of Dickens's works, who, for thirty years, had been managing director of Dickens's publisher and who, throughout Evelyn's childhood, had read aloud the works of Dickens night after night to his sons, Arthur was not simply 'the man who liked Dickens', he was the maniac who was *obsessed* by Dickens. 'All the more likeable Dickens characters,' according to Evelyn, 'provided him with roles which, from time to time, he undesignedly assumed.'

In Evelyn's 'The Man Who Liked Dickens' Henty, an amateur explorer escaping a heartless wife in London, finds himself lost, alone and with a fever somewhere in the middle of an uncharted South American forest. He is revived by an English-speaking, half-caste, illiterate chief called Mr McMaster (also the name of Arthur's close friend) who implores Henty, once he is returned to health, to read to him from his treasured insect-chewed collection of

Dickens. At first Henty enjoys reading; but soon realises that he is trapped, that McMaster has no intention of helping him return to civilisation, but intends to hold him there for ever, reading Dickens. After a couple of years, when Henty has finished the whole of Dickens's *oeuvre*, McMaster makes him start again with *Bleak House*. Henty learns that before he came to the forest there was a black man who had also read Dickens aloud to Mr McMaster and that he, too, had been desperate to escape.

A clear parallel can be drawn between Evelyn's enforced return to Underhill following his wife's betrayal and Henty's situation in the Brazilian forest with Mr McMaster, but the story cleverly reverses, mirrors and refracts the events of Evelyn's life. McMaster, who inherited his love of Dickens from his father, uses his children to prevent Henty escaping. By reading Dickens aloud, night after night, Henty becomes a substitute father to the deranged McMaster: 'You read beautifully, with a far better accent than the black man. And you explain better. It is almost as though my father were here again.'

When a rescue team from England finally arrives, McMaster puts Henty to sleep with a native drug, gives them Henty's watch, shows them a grave and they leave. When Henty wakes, McMaster tells him of the Englishmen's visit in a chilling monotone:

'I thought you would not mind – as you could not greet them yourself I gave them a souvenir, your watch. They wanted something to take home to your wife who is offering a great reward for news of you. They were very pleased with it. And they took some photographs of the little cross I put up to commemorate you coming. They were pleased with that, too. They were very easily pleased. But I do not suppose they will visit us again, our life here is so retired – no pleasures except reading . . . I do not suppose we shall ever have visitors again . . . well, well, I will get you some medicine to make you feel better. Your head aches, does it not . . . We will not have any Dickens today . . . but to-morrow, and the day after that, and the day after that. Let us read *Little Dorrit* again. There are passages in that book

I can never hear without the temptation to weep.'

McMaster is not, of course, a precise character portrait of Arthur, but Arthur must have recognised Henty's entrapment in the house of a Dickens fanatic as a criticism of himself and a clear message from his son that he was desperate to escape his father's house. The story was reused the following year as the bitter dénouement to Evelyn's fourth novel and some say his greatest masterpiece, *A Handful of Dust*.

Arthur's exasperation with Evelyn reached a new peak at the time of the publication of 'The Man Who Liked Dickens'. In September 1933 when Alec and Joan had their first child, Arthur wrote a letter to his mewling grandson to be cherished when he was older. In it Arthur reveals, by a deliberate act of omission, that he has, by this time, more or less disowned his younger son:

My dear Andrew,

I send you my love and every fondest wish for Sunday. I am sorry I shall not be there; and I hope your father and mother are not vexed with me for not coming. But I should not see anything of you three in the crush; and my thoughts and hopes can be ever closer to you all here in the quiet. I shall be thinking of you all, all the time, and sending you every wish of love and hope.

If your parents put this letter away for you, so that you can read it when you are older, I should like to tell you that your father has been one of the three great things in my life. If you are half as good a son to him, as he has been to me, you will bring untold happiness into his life, and into your Mother's. The three great things in my life have been my mother, my wife, and my son – your father. Nothing else has mattered much to me but their love. You have a splendid mother. May you have as good a wife and may you and your father understand each other as well as he and I have done, all the days of our life together.

Your Grannie and I are sending you a Bible, which I
hope you may like to read in the years to come . . . May
you have love beside you all your days, my dear Grandson,
and it will lead you into peace. God bless you.

Your loving grandfather
Arthur Waugh

In the six years following the dissolution of his marriage Evelyn
travelled continuously abroad – to central Africa, British Guiana,
Brazil, Italy, Egypt, Norway and three times to Abyssinia. With Alec
he carved up the world into two territories so that their travel
books would not overlap. Alec took the far East, the Middle East,
the Caribbean and North America, Evelyn the rest. In London
Evelyn's meetings with Arthur were kept to a minimum. He stayed
as often as possible at his club or with friends, rather than at the
flat in Highgate, but he was still forced to keep the bulk of his
belongings at his parents' home. At the end of January 1935, on a
rare visit to his father, Evelyn destroyed many of Arthur's most
precious possessions. Arthur's diary of 29 January records:

Woke at 4 am to a strong smell of burning. On opening the
bookroom door found the room ablaze. Called K. Evelyn called
the firemen. The Whites were most kind; took us in and gave
us brandy. Firemen did not arrive for nearly twenty minutes
and soon got the fire under control, the armchair, Rossetti
chair, carpet, curtains all scorched. Firemen had gone by 5.
Evelyn went to bed again.

In an article for Nash's *Pall Mall Magazine* two years later Evelyn
wrote:

My father is a literary critic and publisher. I think he can
claim to have more books dedicated to him than any living
man. They used to stand together on his shelves, among
hundreds of inscribed copies from almost every English
writer of eminence, until on one of my rather rare recent

visits to my home, I inadvertently set the house on fire, destroying the carefully garnered fruits of a lifetime of literary friendships.

I have a few of Arthur's books, with charred spines, from this fire and my cousin has a mirror that was blackened in the blaze. The Rossetti chair did not survive. Papa told me that Evelyn had fallen asleep with a lit cigar, though in those days he may still have been smoking a pipe in emulation of his father.

I keep suggesting with each new father–son atrocity that it marked the apex of Arthur and Evelyn's poor relationship. Of course I am only guessing but, if I had been Arthur, the one deed that would have upset me most would have been the publication in 1936 of Evelyn's short-story anthology *Mr Loveday's Little Outing*. I have already mentioned the first story in which Evelyn pokes fun at a lunatic with a fetishism for women on bicycles, but the last one of this collection is by far the most poisoned dart Evelyn ever shot at his father. It is called 'Winner Takes All' and concerns two brothers: Gervase, the favourite, and Tom, who is ignored and deprived. There is no resemblance between the single mother of the story, Mrs Kent-Cumberland, and Arthur Waugh, but her attitude to her sons is identical to his.

Mrs Kent-Cumberland gives her elder son names that are 'illustrious in the family's history': Gervase Peregrine Mountjoy St Eustace. The younger is whimsically named Tom. Evelyn hated his name and envied Alec – Alexander Raban Waugh – for having names that were 'illustrious in the family's history'. In the story both boys are brought up to accept the elder's superiority and that he will one day inherit everything. When Tom is given a model car for Christmas by a generous uncle, Mrs Kent-Cumberland assumes there has been a mistake and swaps the labels so that Gervase receives the car. Later Gervase is sent to Eton, Tom to a 'less famous, cheaper school'. When Tom writes a book, Mrs Kent-Cumberland ensures that Gervase gets all the credit. When Tom walks out with a young girl of whom Mrs Kent-Cumberland disapproves he is sent to Australia to cool off and when he returns a few years later engaged to an attractive

Australian heiress, his mother sees to it that the girl marries Gervase instead.

'Winner Takes All' is a deadly story of favouritism, with no happy end and no uplifting twist. The younger brother is trodden underfoot from start to finish. Sadly no record has survived of Arthur's reaction to it. Had I been he, I should have been thoroughly ashamed.

IX

Happy Dying

Alec's marriage to Joan was not faring well. He was restless and when, after a short year, she was summoned to Australia to comfort her ailing mother, he seized the opportunity to organise himself a one-room bachelor flat in Abbey Road, book his son into a hotel with a nanny and set off on his own for America. Alec saw neither Joan nor his son for four months. By the time she left for Australia, Joan was pregnant again. Their second child, Veronica, was born on her return in July 1934. Arthur was thrilled and sent Alec his congratulations: 'I have always longed for a daughter. She will make a great difference to you when you are fifty.' Shortly after Joan's return, her father died, leaving her in possession of a large fortune and, as soon as her inheritance was fixed, she bought an attractive Queen Anne house near Silchester on the Hampshire–Berkshire border and called it Edrington after her father's estate in Melbourne. The famous *decoratrice*, Sybil Colefax, was hired to offer her fashionable opinions on carpets, curtains, wallpaper and kitchen fittings. A large retinue of domestic servants was hastily assembled – cooks, maids, cleaners, two gardeners, an unconventional butler, who wore a jersey and served Coca-Cola, and a uniformed chauffeur to sweep them all around in their spanking new 20 Speed Alvis motor-car.

But for all the creature comforts that Joan brought to her marriage, nothing would induce Alec to settle down. He felt discomforted and emasculated by her wealth, refusing to draw on it or to allow himself to feel at home at Edrington. Self-consciously he chose a tiny attic room for his study, but hardly ever worked there. He told his wife that he would pay for wine and proudly insisted on giving her four pounds per week as a contribution towards his upkeep.

'Isn't that rather ridiculous?' she said.

'I must be self-supporting. I must keep my self-respect,' he replied.

For thirty years Alec used Edrington in the same way he had used Underhill: as a handy place to store his clobber. It was never 'home' in the fullest, most sentimental sense of the word.

A few months after Joan had acquired Edrington, Alec was back in New York, this time pursuing a 'very pretty' twenty-year-old American. Her name was Donita. He had first met her as a school-girl and, I think, had previously kissed her mother, Donna. Though bald, small and something of a *roué*, Alec always scored well with American women. He spoke in a beautiful pure English accent embellished with a gentlemanly stutter for emphasis. The cricket blazers and club ties that he wore – regarded in England as slightly suspect – were, in America, admired as the stamp of the English gentleman. I do not suggest that Uncle Alec was a fraud – he never wore his MCC blazer in England – but his driving ambition was to seduce women, and if that meant dressing and behaving differently in different parts of the world, then so be it. Anyway, Donita fell hook, line and sinker for whatever part he was playing and before anything had advanced beyond the flirtation stage she had agreed to fly with him to a luxury hotel in Miami. That evening Alec knocked priapic on her bedroom door and walked in to see her sitting up in bed wearing a pink-striped dressing-gown. 'Sorry,' she explained. 'I'm having my period.' Poor Alec had to wait three days before he could consummate the passion.

How do I know such things? Well, my 'disgusting Uncle Alec', as Evelyn used to refer to him, was a candid man.

While Alec was abroad, Arthur regularly took the train to visit Joan, often without K, who stayed in London to look after the poodle, which was not welcome at Edrington. Joan and Arthur were very close. 'My darling old Poppa', she called him. 'All my life,' he wrote to her, 'I have always wished I had a daughter; but I am sure now that I could never have had a daughter of my body who would have been so kind, so understanding, so companionable as you have been.' Joan was the ultimate joy among all his 'surrogate' daughters, and for that reason Alec was too afraid to admit to his father that what he really wanted was to escape from the marriage.

Back at Midsomer Norton the virgin aunts were either dying off or getting too old and batty to be any fun. Aunt Elsie offered Evelyn and Alec all the family portraits, which, since his mother's death, Arthur had keenly coveted. Now that he knew he would never possess them he wrote to Alec in an effort to swing their distribution favourably:

My dear Billy,

Yes, I believe Aunt Elsie means what she says. Aunt Connie made the same suggestion to me about a fortnight ago. The facts are as follows: —

My father, who had his full share in the Waugh relish in talking about his death and post-mortem arrangements, used to say at frequent intervals, 'Arthur, you must have the family portraits and the cabinet.' But, he said nothing about it in his will, and left everything in the house to my mother. She died 15 months later, leaving everything of which she died possessed to her three daughters. There was a slip of paper in her writing saying that I was to have certain things, but it was neither dated nor signed. So it had no legal authority whatever.

Immediately after the death of her parents, Aunt Elsie developed a vindictive and bloodthirsty clutch upon all of the family possessions. She was unpardonably rude to Mother about it; and, in fact, burst out into hysterical fits, whenever anything was said about plate, glass, pictures, furniture, or any property in the house or grounds. The situation was so revolting that I vowed that never under any condition would I claim anything at Norton, or regard myself as having any stake in the place again. Believe me, it was the only possible thing to do.

Now that the portraits are peeling and some money has to be spent on them, Elsie changes front . . . But Elsie had better think carefully before making you the offer; for I feel sure that, when once the walls are bare, she will miss them very much. In fact I don't think she has counted the cost to her virulent possessiveness.

However, that is not your concern, or Evelyn's or mine. They have made you the offer; and, if you and Joan care for the portraits (and if I were in your place, I should care for them very much), I should certainly accept it. But I hope you won't give Evelyn first pick. I should like you to have first pick of one picture, then Evelyn the next and so on . . .

Alec was the opposite of Aunt Elsie: possessions meant little to him. He liked travelling and he liked girls. His brother, however, liked *things*. In the end Evelyn got more than his fair share of the Norton booty.

As Alec travelled round the world he knew that in every port a letter would await him from Arthur – affectionate messages of goodwill, with family gossip, review cuttings, compliments on his last book, encouragement for his next. Contrary to popular opinion, Arthur believed that his elder son was as important a writer as Evelyn, and he never wavered from this opinion. Alec, however, was under no illusion. He was well aware, long before he married Joan, that he was never going to be the 'great' writer and he knew, from the moment Evelyn published *Decline and Fall*, that his younger brother was in a different class but, like all true Waughs, he never repined. 'I have no illusions about the quality of my work,' he once wrote. 'I know myself to be a very minor writer.' He took pride in the workmanship of some of his novels and was aware that others among them were painfully second-rate. After publication of *Going Their Own Ways*, one of his sloppiest literary efforts, he snapped at Arthur's friendly encouragement. Instantly he regretted it: his father was still his lodestone and his most valued critic. Evelyn was patronising, Joan was uninterested, K found his books 'too sexual'. In the trough of professional despair, he started to believe that his novels were of interest to no one except his father. In writing to Arthur aboard the Canadian Steamship *Lady Nelson* as it sailed past Bermuda, Alec revealed the early stages of an unease that led him later to the brink of suicide:

My dear Father,

No sooner had I posted that last letter to you than I thought 'How ungrateful that must sound for the nice things you said about *Going Their Own Ways*' – and I hadn't meant to be: for I was so pleased by them and did appreciate them, and it means a great deal to me that you should still be able to take pleasure in the work that all those years ago you started upon its course. I hadn't meant to be casual. Your letter – and your having gone out on that Sunday morning to see if the *Observer* had reviewed it – touched me deeply. It's just that I'm despondent about it all – and I guess that will pass.

As always
Billy

By January 1938 he and Joan had physically and emotionally drifted apart from one another, but she wanted another child. That month, she and Alec set off on holiday to Morocco with the specific intention of conceiving it and nine months later their second son, Peter, was born.

On 17 April 1937 Evelyn married my grandmother. She was upper-class, a niece of Lady Burghclere who had died three years earlier, and the daughter of a dashing soldier and Balkan explorer whose father was Lord Carnarvon. They lived at Pixton Park, a slightly dilapidated fifty-four-room mansion set on a hill in the wild Exmoor countryside above Dulverton in Somerset. Her name was Laura

Herbert. She died when I was young but I tweely conceive that she and I had, in our brief knowledge of one another, a particular bond based upon our shared fondness for cows. At the end of her life Granny lived with us in 'The Wing' at Combe Florey, and every Saturday morning she and I went together to the cattle auction in Taunton. She held her trousers up with binder-twine, and I copied this. We were both at our happiest amid the mooing, bleating, pastoral whiffs and rustic tones of the Taunton cattle market. I once found a rubber milking teat lying in a field and put my penis into it in a bid to be funny. Alas, a red ant that lived inside it, resenting the intrusion, bit me. In tears I showed my rash to Granny. She looked at my swollen organ for a moment in silence. '*Not* very nice!' she said at last, rolling her r in heavy *gravitas*. They were the most comforting words I think I had ever heard. I miss her very much. But I am jumping ahead . . .

Evelyn and Laura's courtship had started in 1935. He knew when he converted to the Catholic faith that he would probably never be allowed to marry again as long as She-Evelyn remained alive. In the meantime he had proposed in vain to one nice lady and nearly impregnated another. When he heard that the latter might have his child he wrote in his diary, 'I don't care either way really, so long as it is a boy,' and a few days later, when she had got the all-clear, 'She says she is not going to have a baby, so all that is bogus.'

When Evelyn realised that the Catholics had left a loophole that provided, under certain strict conditions, for a previous marriage to be nullified,[1] he presented the Church with the plea that he and Evelyn Gardner had entered into their marriage on the understanding that if anything went awry they would divorce. The Curia, or Papal Court, accepted their argument and granted them an annulment on 4 July 1936.[2] For Evelyn it was the end of a sorry

[1] When I was married in 1990, the Roman Catholic priest, Father Caraman, asked me to testify that I loathed my future wife and had no intention of having children by her, so that should I ever wish for an annulment he could bear witness to my claim. I refused.
[2] Alec, She-Evelyn and others gave evidence at the tribunal. It has been asserted by several of Evelyn's anti-Catholic biographers that he induced witnesses to lie on his behalf. This, I am happy to say, is untrue and was disproved by the Latin court records of Decisio XLVIII of the *Sacrae Romanae Rotae Decisiones*, 1936.

process that had dragged on for several years. Laura was prepared to wait, but at times the wait seemed interminable. Five months before the annulment was granted he had written Laura a frank and eccentric proposal of marriage. He was thirty-two at the time, a famous novelist and a man of the world; she was a modest, shy nineteen-year old virgin:

> Tell you what you might do while you are alone at Pixton. You might think about me a bit & whether, if those wop priests ever come to a decent decision, you could bear the idea of marrying me. Of course you haven't got to decide, but think about it. I can't advise you in my favour because I think it would be beastly for you, but think how nice it would be for me. I am restless & moody and misanthropic & lazy & have no money except what I earn and if I got ill you would starve. In fact it's a lousy proposition. On the other hand I think I could reform & become quite strict about not getting drunk and I am pretty sure I should be faithful. Also there is always a fair chance that there will be another bigger economic crash in which case if you had married a nobleman with a great house you might find yourself starving, while I am very clever and could probably earn a living of some sort somewhere. Also though you would be taking on an elderly buffer, I am one without fixed habits. You wouldn't find yourself confined to any particular place or group. Also I have practically no living relatives except one brother whom I scarcely know. You would not find yourself involved in a large family & all their rows & you would not be patronised & interfered with by odious sisters-in-law & aunts as often happens. All these are very small advantages compared with the awfulness of my character. I have always tried to be nice to you and you may have got it into your head that I am nice really, but that is all rot. It is only to you & for you. I am jealous & impatient – but there is no point in going into a whole list of my vices. You are a critical girl and I've no doubt that you know them all and a great many I don't

know myself. But the point I wanted to make is that if you marry most people, you are marrying a great number of objects & other people as well, well if you marry me there is nothing else involved, and that is an advantage as well as a disadvantage. My only tie of any kind is my work. That means that for several months each year we shall have to separate or you would have to share some very lonely place with me. But apart from that we could do what we liked and go where we liked – and if you married a soldier or stockbroker or member of parliament or master of hounds you would be more tied. When I tell my friends that I am in love with a girl of 19 they look shocked and say 'wretched child' but I don't look on you as very young even in your beauty and I don't think there is any sense in the line that you cannot possibly commit yourself to a decision that affects your whole life for years yet. But anyway there is no point in your deciding or even answering. I may never get free of your cousin Evelyn. Above all things, darling, don't fret at all. But just turn the matter over in your dear head.

The courtship had been going for nearly two years, yet Laura had never been introduced to Arthur or K. She was extraordinarily incurious, and I doubt she had asked Evelyn if he had any parents let alone what they were like; in any case, Evelyn was in no hurry to draw them in. By the spring of 1936 the pair had agreed to be married in a pact between themselves. It was not, at that stage, an official engagement.

Laura's father had died when she was a child and her mother, Mary Herbert, now in sole charge, had virulent objections to the union, which were entirely snobbish. Many grand men had sought Laura's hand. Evelyn Waugh, though clever, famous and socially as well – if not better – connected than the Herberts, was not one of them. Mary Herbert thought her prospective son-in-law was a 'common little man', an *arriviste* who had already left a bad smell in the family with his failed marriage to her niece Evelyn Gardner. But Laura, in an uncharacteristic mood of rebellion, was flatly determined to marry him and nothing would sway her to the contrary. In the end Mary Herbert, like Lady Burghclere a few years earlier, had no choice but to concede.

On 23 September, K in Highgate telephoned Alec to discover that Joan had received a letter from Evelyn announcing his engagement. Arthur moaned into his diary: '*But he has not written to us!*' A week later K received a letter from Evelyn announcing that the wedding would most likely take place in February. Still Arthur had not been personally apprised and, as head of the family, was starting to feel hurt. In a short letter of congratulation he hinted, in the martyrish tone Evelyn loathed, that he was upset to be the last person informed of the good news. By way of excuse, Evelyn claimed that he had only just received the nod from the Catholic Church – in fact it had come four months earlier – and his future mother-in-law's withholding of her approval had delayed everything. Perhaps he did not want to involve Arthur in another snobbish, humiliating wrangle with yet another redoubtable Herbert matriarch.

My dear Father,

I hope that you did not think it unfilial to delay telling you of my engagement until it was settled. I know that you easily become anxious, and for the last two or three years there have been many causes for anxiety about the decision of the Curia. The case was only finally sealed and signed about two days ago [*sic*]. For various reasons Mary Herbert does not want the engagement announced until the end of December. However, everyone is now so far in agreement that it can be known within the family & I wrote to Joan and my mother – meaning of course that a letter should reach you too. Thank you very much for your kind wishes. I have sent your letter on to Laura. I know she will join me in gratitude.

She is very young, very thin, rather poor, dead silent, long nosed, laudably devoid of literary, artistic or social ambition, lazy, affectionate, timid, ignorant. I will bring her to see you at the first opportunity. Probably to dinner one evening next week, when I hope to be in London. She is the youngest daughter of Aubrey Herbert of whom you probably know more than I do. I gather he was a popular and prominent figure in his day. Her mother is a sporting Irishwoman with an interest in foreign politics. I can't hope that you will find much in common with her.

I shall never find a more suitable home than the one at Nunney (do you know it? The old Manor House was a farm, dilapidated but full of magic architectural features) but it is still doubtful – rather improbable – that I'll get it from the present owner, a homicidal squireen named Major Shore.

Yours affectionately Evelyn

The first meeting between Laura and the Waughs took place over dinner in Highgate on 6 October and went with a bang. In his diary Arthur wrote, 'Great preparations for Evelyn and Laura. The evening was delightful. She behaved charmingly; he was at his best and the dinner was good.' And on the next evening: 'K and I had a pleasant talk over dinner about our happy evening with Evelyn and Laura. I was very glad to see K so happy. By last post a little note came to K from Laura, thanking us for being "so sweet" which sent us to bed happier still.'

Two months later the engagement was official. K had offered the happy couple as a wedding present a little mahogany bureau of great sentimental value to herself, but Arthur was still dithering over what to give. In the end he settled for five pieces of silver and a small cheque. Evelyn wrote to Laura:

My papa says will we come and choose a bit of silver from what he has left of his grandfather's wrapped up in a flannel under his bed. Also he will give us £25 to buy 'something definite and lasting – to remind you of me'. I think that's decent considering his reduced circumstances and the fact that he forked out handsomely for my mock

marriage some years back. So what would you like? . . .
Will you choose? Now I will write my Nash's article. All
love E.

Two days after Arthur had sent the money to Evelyn he learned
that Laura's grandmother had given them £4000 and that Evelyn
had a £1000 cheque for a 'film scenario' in his pocket.

The wedding ceremony, which took place at a gloomy Catholic
church in Warwick Street, London went off without a hitch. The
congregation consisted of many grandees from Laura's side of the
family and a handful of Waughs. The service was followed by a
crowded reception that was all over by one o'clock. Arthur went
home for brown bread and cheese having enjoyed a 'capital
morning'. He was particularly pleased when Alec rang to say that
he had enjoyed the wedding too.

But Arthur's happiness was not destined to continue long
beyond that day, for he soon came to realise that he did not
especially like his new daughter-in-law. He found her distant,
impenetrable, enigmatic and disappointing. She, in turn, was
unimpressed by his flamboyant performances. An interviewer
who came to Highgate to write about Arthur for a series called
Publishers in Person recorded in that 'cosy abode of books,
manuscripts, pleasant chintzes a modern incarnation of Mr
Pickwick. He had twinkling eyes, rosy cheeks, silky white hair
and a pleasantly rotund figure', but none of it worked on Laura.
Soon her mind would be focused on cows and only cows. As
Evelyn's letter to Arthur had warned, she was not impressed by
other people, no matter who they were. As a literary man Arthur
was appalled by the vapidity of her letters. To Joan, he wrote:
'Certainly my two daughters-in-law write very differently, and
have very different temperaments. I shall never be able to make
anything of Laura. We live in other worlds and talk another
language. But I miss nothing. I find everything I want in Joan,
the daughter of my heart.'

Evelyn and Laura did not succeed in buying the manor at Nunney,
as Evelyn had predicted. Instead they settled for a beautiful Tudor

house with an elegant eighteenth-century façade, surrounded by parkland and mature trees, 120 miles west of London. Piers Court lay just outside the village of Stinchcombe, near Dursley in the Cotswolds. The Waughs called it 'Stinkers'. At last Evelyn was free of his father's house and his first years of marriage were consequently years of great happiness: a period of joy in a life that was otherwise clouded by depression and turmoil. He enjoyed decorating the house, designing shelves for his library, follies for the garden, filling the place with fine books, beautiful furniture and pictures. He had a remarkable eye for *objets d'art* and keenly collected Victorian paintings at a time when they were unprized and inexpensive. He bought Rossetti's *Spirit of the Rainbow* (a full-length charcoal nude), now in the Andrew Lloyd Webber collection. He bought a notable Arthur Hughes, *The Woodman*, and a striking narrative painting by George Smith, *Out Into the Cold World*, which depicts a beautiful bankrupted lady and her child being turfed out of their home following the death of her husband. In the fields surrounding the house Laura kept four dairy cows that to her were a source of inordinate pleasure.

The outlying cottages at Piers Court were filled with servants; others walked every day from the village. Many were from the Attwood family. There was Norman Attwood, the cowman and his sister Mrs Harper, who along with Gladys Attwood and Mrs Attwood, their mother, was supposed to do the cleaning but spent most of the morning squabbling with her family over cooked breakfast in the kitchen. The first cook was a refugee from Austria, Frau Müller, who made veal schnitzels until war broke out when she hid under a bed at Pixton in daily expectation of a summons from the Fatherland. Mr Ellwood was an efficient, Jeeves-style butler, imported from St John's Wood in London.

Arthur came to Piers Court only twice. The first of his visits (a year after Evelyn and Laura had moved in) took place towards the end of July 1938. By the time of his second visit, in August 1939, Evelyn and Laura had had their first child, a playful kitten of a girl called Teresa. Both visits were a success. Evelyn was at his warmest, friendliest and best disposed. He, Arthur, Laura and K spent the weekend dandling Teresa, playing chess, driving round country lanes, eating good food, sipping expensive wines and poring over *The Times* crossword puzzle. Arthur marvelled at Evelyn's good fortune, was delighted with the house and awed by Evelyn's wonderful collection of books. It must have been odd for him that both his sons, coming from a modest middle-class Hampstead background, were now set up in formidable English country houses surrounded by parkland and filled with servants. I suppose he was a little jealous.

Despite the success of his two visits Arthur was still no closer to understanding Laura. 'I must confess I cannot fathom Laura a bit,' he wrote to Joan. 'I don't know whether she has a very strong character, and is able to keep all her feelings to herself; or whether she is a case of arrested development soothed by the Papal dope. The only things I have ever discussed with her are cross-word puzzles and the question of whether Ellwood is actually married to Mrs Ellwood! Which does not get us very far along the beaten path of confidence!' His thank-you letter to Laura after his second visit took the form of a rhapsody in verse:

> How, Laura, can I hope in verse
> (For none has ever written worse)
> To hymn the joys of countless sort
> That greet the guests at Piers Court?
> I might essay it, if I could
> With Auden vie and Isherwood;
> I might, had I Rossetti's bloom,
> Revive the rainbow in your room;
> Or pass that snowy portal with
> The widow of the painter Smith,
> But, being a deaf Victorian bore,
> Such heights are not for Arthur Waugh.
>
> So let me rather sit and muse
> On memories I shall never lose:
> Of Evelyn's kindness, Laura's grace,
> And all the witchery of the place,
> Of Cotswold stone, and English lawns,

Of swooping knights and captive pawns,
Of lightning turns round tortuous lanes,
Of Tudor casements, Stuart vanes.
Unravelled clues myself have missed
(You champion crux-verbalist!),
Our host's illimitable wit,
(Heaven knows how much I envy it!)
And over all, urbane and free,
Your matchless hospitality.

O for another beaker blest
With that ripe nectar of the West!
O for the meals Frau Müller cooks;
O for a month with Evelyn's books;
O for the gentle evening hush;
The thoroughness of Ellwood's brush;
And sweet Teresa's plaintive moan,
'Mama is gone! Papa is gone!'
ME she will never miss – not she!
But I miss HER tremendously.

Dear Laura, for these golden days
Accept our gratitude and praise:
And if the Führer, blatant, blear,
Should spare us for another year,
And Peace return, on earth to reign,
I pray we may come back again.

Arthur Waugh
August xxiii: 1939

As we all know, the Führer did not 'spare us for another year'. Within nine days of the poem's conception he and his goose-stepping cohorts had rolled their tanks into Poland. Two days after that London and Paris had declared war on Germany. Within a month Evelyn and Laura, round wombed with a second child, had left Piers Court for Pixton where, on the top floor, twenty evacuee children from the

Midlands had been billeted. Their precious belongings were boxed up in the cellar. On 26 September a gaggle (if that is the right collective term) of Catholic nuns arrived at Piers Court to run it as a convent school for the duration of hostilities. For Evelyn and Laura the brief idyll was ended and the world was once again at war.

As a trained soldier in the Regular Army Reserve Alec was given immediate instructions by the War Office to report in uniform to barracks in Dorchester. Evelyn, by contrast, found it harder to get into the army. He was a brave man, excited by danger, always craving new experience, desperate to fight, and to avoid the tedium of a desk job in army intelligence, but as a thirty-six-year-old novelist, untrained in soldiering except for a few terms in the Lancing College OTC, he was not the obvious first choice for regimental colonels. Despite his good contacts, both Naval Intelligence and the Welsh Guards turned him down. I do not doubt that in the back of his mind lay memories of the little aura of importance that Alec enjoyed during the First World War and when he told his father of his efforts to enlist as an active soldier, he was disappointed that Arthur proved 'markedly unsympathetic to my project of joining the war'.

From that moment Evelyn resolved to tell his father nothing but the barest minimum about his movements. It was a plan calculated to agitate Arthur, but he believed there was no point in 'going through the motions'. He sensed that Arthur's interest in his war was dutiful and unsympathetic: all he really cared about was Alec. When Arthur asked Evelyn to let him know what he was doing he responded: 'But why? It is merely your idle curiosity!' There was no peace between them. Every time they met Evelyn upset his father. Sometimes, when he felt he had gone too far, he sent round a crate of Pommard in half bottles by way of apology, but the relationship did not improve. Arthur's heart remained with Alec, to whom he wrote in September 1939:

> Your cheerful letter, which arrived at mid-day, has done me more good than a half bottle of Pommard. I am so thankful that you are happy. What does income tax matter

compared with that? And if you get a comparatively safe job my spirits will not crack. My war is *your* war, 'because man's heart is small'.

Two months later, after the intervention of two MPs, Winston Churchill and Brendan Bracken, Evelyn was offered a commission in the Marines. A week earlier his son Auberon, my father, had been born at Pixton.

While Alec was stationed in Dorchester he met and fell in love with a six foot two giantess whose large bosoms bounced about on a level with his eyes when they danced together. Her father was Admiral Sir Arthur Duff, himself a titchy man but a formidable presence in Dorset society, and his daughter Joan was attracted to the diminutive male especially if he showed no awkwardness when they danced. Alec danced unselfconsciously with his face buried in her chest. He loved her black wavy hair, her blue eyes, her strong hairy arms and her deep *basso* voice. Oh yes, her voice! 'Talking to her on the telephone was a date,' he used to say. Dorset-Joan was given free run of Alec's bachelor flat in London for a modest pound a week. Between army duties in Dorchester and visits to his new, heffa-lump mistress there was no time for Alec to see the children or his wife, the other Joan, at Edrington.

When, at length, he was posted to Arras, Arthur and K went to the station to see him off. It was the same platform from which they had waved goodbye on that chill morning in 1917. Again the scene was emotional. K thought Alec looked splendidly youthful in his uniform, but Arthur only gazed upon his son's bald pate and sighed, 'The years pile on now.'

The train stopped for a few minutes at Basingstoke where Joan and the children had been asked to wait on the platform and wave a brief farewell. In the few short minutes that the train was stopped, Alec passed Joan his suitcase of civilian clothes and a bag of cricket paraphernalia, before saying goodbye to them all. 'I wonder when I shall be needing my cricket stuff next,' he wondered to himself as the train pulled out of the station.

* * *

The Dunkirk episode was not a triumph for British forces. On 23 May 1940 Alec was evacuated out of Boulogne. Though physically unscathed, he was shaken to have witnessed as much bloodshed during a single aerial bombardment of the harbour as he had seen during his spell in the mud of Ypres. A number of men were killed in front of his eyes, one of whom he had dined with that evening.

On his return to London he learned that his wife had made up her mind to close Edrington and return with her children to Australia for the duration of the war. Her departure was a bitter blow for Arthur who believed that, once she and the children were embarked for the Antipodes, he would never see them or the house again. He wrote to her in a desperate state:

My dearest Joan,

When I first heard that you and the children were going to Australia, I felt it was the last straw. In very truth I turned my face to the wall and wept. But on reflection I see that that was pure selfishness; and that it is the right thing for you to save the children the shock of a possible air-raid. I only hope the sea-voyage may be propitious; but I shall know no peace of mind until you are safe in Australia.

My dear, you can't think how I shall miss you. It is not that we meet so often; but the thought you are all so near and so happy has been a continual comfort. *'La reine est là bas dans l'île.'* I shall keep on hoping that we may meet again. If not, I want you to remember that in your sympathy and affection I have found continual peace, and that some of the very happiest days of my life have been spent at Edrington, with all you dear ones around me.

God bless you, dear, dear Joan – you and the children, and bring us all together again – 'Oh heart in the great dawn!'

Ever your loving and grateful
Poppa

In the first week of July Joan was packed and ready. Arthur and K rushed down to Edrington to say their last goodbyes. He was looking and feeling old. Afterwards he wrote to his friend Kenneth McMaster, transferring most of the emotion to his wife: 'K felt their departure very, very much. She mainly lives for those grand-children and the thought that we are not likely ever to see them again is a thought that we have to set aside. I write to Alec's wife every week, and she sends us splendid letters; but that is not the same thing as seeing.' The children were still very young: Andrew was seven, Veronica six, and Peter two. They remained in Australia until the war was over. Alec pondered on how different they would look the next time he saw them – if, that is, he survived the war. 'I was saying goodbye to their childhood,' he later wrote – but without emotion.

In Australia Joan received a long letter from Arthur every week and it is through these that the relationship between Arthur in his last years and his two sons is best recorded. Needless to say all references to Alec are glowing. A small spattering of examples should suffice:

1.9.40: We have had Alec here, waiting for his summons to Matlock, and he has been simply splendid. His kind-ness, consideration and unfailing cheerfulness have been an inspiration.

8.11.40: Alec has sent me a dozen *sauternes* which is *most* kind of him.

28.12.40: Alec has been most good to us, and wrote to me just before Xmas the best letter any father ever had from any son, to say he had found much comfort in having our hearth to come to in these days of comparative homelessness.

22.1.41: Evelyn and Alec dined in a smart restaurant in Leicester Square, which I expect *you* know, but I don't. I do hope Evelyn was decent to Alec, who is so uniformly

kind to everyone. Now that he comes to us practically
every weekend, we have always something to look forward
to; and though he is often too tired to talk much, it is a
great comfort to see him sitting here and to know that he
is safe and well.

But from these same letters it is painfully obvious that Arthur's
relationship with Evelyn was consistently bad. Evelyn was happier
now. He was interested in his work as both a writer and a soldier.
He was joyfully married to Laura. His circle of friends was extensive. Visits to his parents were a duty of obligation and he went to
them without enthusiasm or pleasure. They, he felt, did not care
for him. He, they felt, was bored by and ashamed of them. Unable
to hide his irritation and despondency, Evelyn, on his rare visits to
Highgate, succeeded only in making matters worse.

In 1938 Chapman and Hall, anxious that their most precious
asset should not desert them for a rival publisher, invited Evelyn
to join the board. Alec claimed that his father and brother worked
peacefully together at board meetings, but Arthur's diary does not
always support this: 'Chapman and Hall committee meeting. Evelyn
laid railing accusations against Gatfield for the way his book had
been produced and the "intolerable impertinence of his reply" . . .
an awful 40 minutes. Evelyn like a smouldering volcano.'

When, in 1941, two new men on the board tried to sack Evelyn,
who was receiving £150 a year but was unable to attend meetings,
Arthur was both loyal and uncharacteristically defiant:

I have told them that I shall vote for Evelyn, even if mine is
the only vote cast in his favour. One must stand by one's own
family, and I do think it rather lousy to try to oust a colleague
who is fighting for his country. Short-sighted policy, too, from
their own point of view, for Evelyn's tongue is bitter, and he
will not say much that is good of Chapman and Hall in the
days that are to come.

Away from the board room, things between Arthur and Evelyn
were less rosy. Evelyn was determined to keep his movements

secret from his father but when Arthur met an ex-Highgate school-boy from Evelyn's battalion and asked after his son, the young soldier (Thomas, by name) told him where the battalion was stationed and what it was doing. Evelyn was furious. 'He was all for getting the youth arrested, or disembowelled, or something lingering with boiling oil in it,' Arthur wrote to Alec. For years Evelyn had felt that his father did not care for him, but now it was Arthur's turn to feel the full force of Evelyn's rejection. In January 1941 Evelyn was granted a fortnight's leave. His one visit to Arthur was fleeting and cursory. In his diary Arthur had noted that Evelyn was 'very arrogant and dictatorial'. The full details were relayed the next morning in a letter from 'your loving Poppa' to 'My darling Joan':

Evelyn burst upon us. He rang up one day when we were both out. On our return Margery[3] reported 'Mr Evelyn wished you to know that he is at Claridge's.' K got busy with the telephone and he and Laura arranged to come to lunch next day. They came. She was looking rather fragile, but really very pretty. He has shaved off his moustache, which is an improvement, and put on a good deal of weight, which is not. I think he is trying to make himself look like Winston Churchill,[4] and with a little grease paint and a toupet, he might play the part. He was really very cold, arrogant and contemptuous. Considering this was the only time he was going to spare us out of a 15-day leave, I think he might have been a little more patient. I know that I make him itch all over. Everything I say puts his teeth on edge. Still it is an old story: 'Don't shoot the pianist, he is doing his best.'

[3] Margery Fox replaced Mrs Yaxley who had been the Waughs' daily help for twenty years. Arthur wrote to Joan in November 1940: 'You could not have a greater contrast than Margery Fox, a plump little dumpling of 25 . . . She has a "boyfriend" which always keeps a girl in a good temper. I have always found that if they get plenty of time to fornicate on Sundays the girls keep fairly cheerful during the week.'

[4] Evelyn, who was a friend of Sir Winston Churchill's son, Randolph, loathed Sir Winston because 'he was a rotten father'.

A month later Arthur was still stewing about that visit. He wrote to Kenneth McMaster:

> Evelyn, a Captain of the Marines, was in the Dakar fiasco and is now in a secret commando, of which we are allowed to know nothing. He never writes to us but a month ago he had 15 days leave, out of which he allowed us precisely two hours, when he and his wife came to lunch. From the time they drove away we have not heard a word from either of them. The fact is he is thoroughly ashamed of his parents and does his best to banish them from his conscience.

Father and son reached an impasse during the war years. They could not avoid aggravating one another. Alec believed it was because Evelyn and Arthur were so alike that they were unable to get on. In a generous portrait of his brother, written in 1967, he suggested:

> In later life Evelyn may have given the impression of being heartless; he was often snubbing, he could be cruel. But basically he was gentle, warm and tender. He was very like his father, and his father's own emotionalism put him on his guard. He must have often thought: 'I could become like this; I musn't let myself become like this.'

To prove his immunity to Arthur's worst fault – sentimentality – Evelyn struck attitudes of immoderate detachment, exaggerated often to the point of absurdity. The more emotional Arthur became, the more Evelyn vaunted his *sangfroid*. Or was it the other way round? In either case, they fed one from the other, locked in hopeless, tireless battle. In September 1940 Evelyn informed his father that Laura was pregnant with a third child, due in December. Later he wrote home: 'Laura's baby was born on Sunday and lived for only twenty-four hours. She was baptised, Mary, before she died and will be buried in Brushford Churchyard tomorrow. It was an easy birth, and Laura is in excellent health.' The letter went on: 'I have got three days' leave and return to my commando on Friday.

Life is more easygoing there than in the marines; many old friends and acquaintances are with me, and I find the life highly enjoyable.'

Arthur, who had craved a daughter all his life, was deeply shocked by Evelyn's apparent indifference to losing one of his own. He was also offended that the news had not reached him until the day after the funeral. In anguish he wrote again to Joan: 'There seems to be something quite pathetic in this little star of life, which just flickered and went out. She wasn't wanted and she did not stay. Evelyn announced her coming "to the regret of all and the consternation of some". Well, she didn't trouble them for long, and she is spared a great deal.'

The war had been interesting and unusual for Evelyn. He was sent hither and thither, from Cornwall to Scotland, from Gibraltar to Egypt. He assisted in the evacuation of Crete and the raid on Badia. Arthur and K relied on Laura to send them regular news but, as Arthur bitterly conceded, 'Letter-writing, at any rate to in-laws, is not Laura's strong suit.' It was true that she hated writing even to her husband and procrastinated in the hope that events would overtake her and no letter would be necessary – a dilatory attitude that exasperated her father-in-law: 'Whether Evelyn is still in Cornwall or transferred to the Mediterranean we have no idea and it is a worry not to know. I think K is going to write to Laura and find out; but I doubt if Laura answers for days and days. She is the most lethargic girl I ever knew.'

On the rare occasions that Laura did get round to writing, Arthur was far from satisfied. In September she wrote to him only to point out that 'Evelyn could not say where he was going, and said he did not know how long he would be away – maybe a month, maybe a year. The rest of his letter only dealt with what I was to do in case of invasion.' This was not strictly true. Evelyn's long letter to Laura contained news that Arthur would have liked to hear but Laura was too vague and lazy to pass it on. Steaming with tension, Arthur wrote to Joan: 'Evelyn, we presume, is in the Mediterranean, but we *know* nothing, and Laura's letters are like soppy bread dipped in tepid water.'

His anxiety was intensified by K, who seemed to be sinking into a deep depression. She missed her sons and her grandchildren but, above all, was terrified by the bombing in London. Laura had offered her parents-in-law refuge at a cottage on the Pixton estate but this was proudly declined. When Highgate was first bombed on 30 August 1940, K woke Arthur at 1.15 a.m. They took refuge for the rest of the night in a neighbour's basement. Tuppence, the poodle, showed no emotion and K hugged him tightly all through the night. Ten days later Arthur informed Joan:

> K is a very sad and ill-looking woman. It tears at my heart to have anyone say – 'Mrs Waugh is looking very ill. Can't you make her rest more?' But there is nothing any of us can do. I had a little walk with her the other day and she said 'My world has crashed about me. There is nothing more in life until this is all over. You must remember I am 70. If I hadn't looked it till now, it was because I was happy. Now happiness has gone and look what I am – an old woman. I am doing my best. You must be patient' . . . And indeed I am, and I do try not to annoy her. But my way of comforting is not her way of being comforted. And that is the conclusion of the whole matter.

North End and Highgate took another battering at the end of October. By this stage K was weary, pale and hollow-eyed. Arthur, certain that she needed stimulant, tried to press burgundy and port on her, but she would not touch them. Again he wrote to Joan:

> I am particularly troubled about K. She goes steadily on her way but everyone says how ill she looks; and the other evening when a bomb burst near us during dinner, she left the table and I found her sitting on the stairs, saying – 'Don't speak to me. I can't speak. It is shattering.' In five minutes she had picked herself up again; but a night later, when an explosion went off, she jumped up in a way that shows her nerves are all like harp-strings . . . No word of Evelyn. In the background of my mind is always a growing anxiety of what might befall him, now that the scene of

attack seems likely to shift to the Mediterranean. I expect K thinks of it also and all the time; but I don't mention it as I try to keep her mind off it – not that I succeed.

Arthur needed to hear from Evelyn if only to calm his wife's nerves. Life at Highgate was no fun when K was in such a state: 'We changed our dinner hour in the hope of finishing dinner before the bombs fell, as they upset K and she can't go on eating when the raid is near us. But that is no good, for last night, just as we were starting, the whole house shook and K retired into the bookroom and I had to dine alone. Later on she returned and had some rice and stewed pears – nothing more – and I don't think that is enough to dine upon.'

When at last news arrived from Evelyn in November 1940, just after the destruction of Arthur and K's neighbourhood by German bombing, the tone of his letter made Arthur miserable again. By this stage he was hypersensitive to Evelyn's slightest demur. He wrote to Joan and asked her what she thought of the tone of Evelyn's letter: 'I know that I am not apt to take Evelyn the right way, and perhaps his air of cold detachment is not so heartless as it seems to be.' Well, what do you think?

My dear Father,

My leave expires tomorrow and I am afraid that my return journey takes me up the West Coast and not through London. I do not however despair of seeing you and Mother fairly soon as I am trying for a transfer to a more melodramatic force than the Marines and if this comes off I will probably be in London for a day or so.

Chapman and Hall seems under very unliterary direction and I leave my fate to fortune. I do not think that there will be much use for small firms even those fortunate enough to have directors like Gatfield.

Laura is extremely well. I have a cold.

I hope the bombs hold off until my civilian wardrobe is evacuated – and longer still.

We went to Piers Court on Sunday and found the house

over-flowing with refugees, in good order, but the garden rapidly relapsing into jungle of the kind from which we rescued it.

Thomas was a great failure with our battalion and dismissed. I do not know his future. I found him a very affected and stupid fellow.

Sad about the destruction of North End but we have the consolation of many odious buildings that have disappeared. You cannot really make many mistakes with high explosive in London nowadays. Sorry about Holland House. The heir, Harry Stavordale, is in the force I seek to join.

Love from Evelyn

By September 1941 Alec had pushed his luck so far with chunky Joan Duff that she had upped and left him for another man. His mistake had been to move into his own London flat with her where his presence was immediately resented and she became short-tempered and poisonous. They remained friends although Alec's heart was broken. Evelyn noticed and wrote to Laura: 'My brother is deeply and genuinely in love with that giantess who came to lunch at the Perroquet.'

On 27 September the four Waughs, Arthur, K, Alec and Evelyn, lunched together for the last time. That evening Alec was leaving for Syria to act as a publicity agent to General Spears. Two days earlier he had broken the news of his departure to Arthur: 'Alec arrived in a car with much kit and went upstairs to pack,' wrote Arthur, in his diary. 'He gave me 6 bottles of sherry. He was very silent and thoughtful and I felt very sad.' He might be gone for two years or more and Arthur, 'the old sentimentalist' as he oft-times referred to himself, sensed that this might be their last meeting: he was seventy-five years old, tired, fat and ailing. By chance Evelyn was in town that day and rang to invite himself for lunch. 'As it turned out this was a very good move,' Arthur recorded, 'as he was amiable and cheerful and helped to stave off the anxiety of Alec's departure.'

For once Arthur decided not to wear his heart on his sleeve. 'Nothing is really so bad as we think it will be,' he had written in *One Man's Road*, 'the parting, the new venture, the unknown road, the shadowy corner – something, some power within ourselves or without, tempers the wind to the shorn lamb.' And so on this, the momentous occasion of his beloved elder son's departure to the war, Arthur restrained his emotions with a dignity that surprised everyone. 'This was an occasion that could have been sentimentalised,' Alec wrote later, 'but we treated the luncheon as though it were any luncheon. We did not make an occasion of it.' The final sighting came all too soon. 'He and Evelyn left us at 4pm,' Arthur wrote. 'It was a ghastly wrench to say goodbye to Alec, especially as he was so kind and gentle. But his taxi vanished through the drive and we were left sorrowing.'

The next day Evelyn wrote to Laura: 'Alec Waugh went off last night to embark for Syria. It is sad for my parents and for me as it means I now have them on my conscience.' He had just finished his latest novel, a light and amusing 'pot-boiler', as he termed it, about people jostling for purpose in the first years of the war. Arthur did not especially enjoy *Put Out More Flags*. 'Read Evelyn's book,' he scribbled in his diary, 'but can't get on terms with it. Hope it is *my* fault.' He wrote to Evelyn that he had not liked the beginning, that it picked up towards the end and that it was full of misprints. His letter also mentioned his worries about contacting Alec and revealed the sad news that Tuppence, the fearless poodle, had died. Evelyn replied:

Dear Father,

I am sorry to hear of the death of your poodle. You speak of it as having happened some time ago. This is the first news I have had. Please accept my warmest sympathy. I hope you will soon find another who will take his place in your heart.

Glad you liked most of *Put Out More Flags*. It is a minor work dashed off to occupy a tedious voyage, but it has good bits . . .

I am commanding a company again, living in squalor. We returned yesterday from a happy week at sea and re-embark next week.

A letter of yours was enclosed in your letter to me probably in error. It dealt with Beverley Nichols. Do you want this back? His inaccurate gossip about me caused pleasure on the lower deck but nowhere else.

You cannot expect to hear from Alec for some time after he arrives. I expect he is warm and content and in good company. We seem to have forestalled the German offensive in Cyrenia. I can't think what possessed the papers to forecast a triumphal advance to Tunis. We are lucky to hold the enemy at all. Syria should be safe until early Spring so don't fret about Alec.

Love Evelyn.

Arthur might have recognised a vignette of himself in *Put Out More Flags*. Although he had moved from Underhill a decade earlier, he continued to rhapsodise about the 'old' house and to extol the virtues of its 'little inglenook' and 'stout timbers'. He wrote to Alec that he had received a letter from Barbara Jacobs's sister who was sheltering from the Germans with her father at Paignton. 'She said that the return of war had brought back the past, and that she hoped we realised how much Underhill had brought into her life that she could never find at home. I wish the little place no better epitaph.' In *Put Out More Flags* Evelyn regurgitates Arthur's sentimentality about Underhill through Mrs Harkness, a minor character, whose house is inspected with a view to its receiving three evacuees:

Mrs Harkness pointed out all the features of the house with maternal pride . . .

'You may think me fanciful,' she said, remote and whimsical, 'but in the last few weeks I feel sometimes I can see the old house smiling to itself and hear the old timbers whispering, "They thought we were no use. They thought we were old stick-in-the-muds. But they can't get on without us, all these busy go-ahead people. They come back to us when they're in trouble.'"

'Agnes was always a poet,' said Mr Harkness. 'I have had to be the practical housewife.'

Evelyn's next book, interrupted by the war, contained a character based partly on Arthur and partly on his friend the solicitor E. S. P. Haynes, who had acted for him and Alec in their divorce cases. The first chapter of *Work Suspended*, originally entitled 'My Father's Death', later 'My Father's House' and finally 'A Death' marked a new depth of purpose in Evelyn's writing. In December 1941 he informed his father, 'My major work, unfinished in 1939, appears shortly as a fragment in Penguin . . . It is about a father with whom you will be unable to trace any similarities.' But Arthur did trace similarities and so, too, did Alec.

The father in question, Mr Plant, is a painter whose works are 'suffused with the spirit of Dickens'. He is an arcane type who lives on his own in a house not unlike Underhill in St John's Wood, dresses in the old-fashioned garb of the 1890s and considers himself the last survivor of his class. Arthur, recognising his own reflection, may have taken comfort in Evelyn's warm, serious approach, for Mr Plant is no straight gibe in the manner of Prendergast or Mrs Harkness. His son, the novelist John Plant, writing in the first person, visits his father's house after the funeral and gazes on a painting left unfinished at the time of his father's death: 'The four or five square feet of painting were a monument of my father's art. There had been a time when I had scant respect for it,' but in brooding on his father, putting his life's achievement into words, John Plant's esteem for him rises: it 'took form and my sense of loss became tangible and permanent'.

The first part of *Work Suspended* deals specifically with the physical, psychological and spiritual breaking of bonds between father and son. After his death Mr Plant's house is demolished. The total eradication of the father and his house enables the son to develop as an artist. There is a discernible parallel here between John Plant and Evelyn, who in the last nine years had severed ties with Arthur by marrying Laura, changing faith and moving away from his father's house as well as his sphere of influence. In *Work Suspended* Mr Plant is run over by a shady character called Arthur Atwater – 'Atwater the dreamer, Atwater the scout, Atwater the underdog' – and, as the plot advances, the reader is made dimly aware of Atwater's literary pertinence as the symbolic alter ego of John Plant, the son. When Plant Junior put a ten-shilling note into an envelope 'and sent it to the man who killed my father', the reader wonders if he is not complicit in his father's death. Since the book was left unfinished we shall never know what Evelyn had in mind. In any case the death of his real father soon intervened.

In London without Alec and Joan, Arthur kept himself busy. He continued to read manuscripts for the 'old firm', to chair the board, to walk on the Heath, to watch Highgate School cricket matches in the summer and to teach Victorian poetry to schoolchildren once a week through the winter. His diary tells of a full and busy life right to the end. Each day he wore a different tie given him by Alec, which, he believed, brought him good luck. If only Alec were there to straighten them! He wrote to 'my very dear Billy' at the end of 1942: 'Albert Knight came to tea with me last week and mentioned that his daughter has a way of pulling his tie straight which annoys him rather. I said that I too had a son who put mine in order, and oh, how I wished he were here to do it this moment.'

But time was running short and Arthur knew in his heart that Alec would never straighten another tie for him again. In the months remaining to him he adverted more frequently than ever to his own demise. It had long been a theme of his conversation – his father, the Brute, and his grandfather, the rector of Corsley, had been the same – but now, in the long, winding sentences about his past, his childhood, Midsomer Norton, Sherborne, the end was never far from his mind. Forty years earlier Arthur had bought the freehold of a burial plot in Hampstead churchyard and he walked there often to admire the spot and to ponder his interment there. Terrified that someone might usurp it, he staked his claim with his visiting card attached to a stick. Thirty years previously he had written detailed instructions for his family concerning his funeral arrangements and regularly refreshed their memories. His tomb-stone was to bear the legend from St John: 'And another book was opened which is the book of life.'

In his last two years, since Joan's departure for Australia, Arthur had found consolation in another quasi-daughter figure, the wan, pale, childlike, pre-Raphaelite-looking Elizabeth Myers. She was a struggling novelist in her late twenties when they first met. On 21 June 1942 she wrote to a friend: 'I was taken this afternoon to have tea with Mr and Mrs Arthur Waugh. Mr Waugh is a *glorious* old man. He is just like a character from Dickens, fat, smiling and wise, with a face like a lovely big red apple. I got on famously with him and we are to go again right speedily.'

Arthur was intrigued and excited by the young lady. In August he wrote to her: 'At present I know next to nothing about your life and want to know more, do come and have a long talk.' Soon they were the best of friends. He put pressure on 'the old firm' to publish her novel, *A Well Full of Leaves*, and invited her to attend Chapman and Hall board meetings. She proved a loyal and sympathetic confidante.

On her regular visits to Highgate Arthur told Elizabeth all about his childhood, about Alec, about Sherborne – the school, the town and the golden abbey in the west. He confided his loves, his hopes, his dashed ambitions and his childhood dreams. She, in turn, dedicated her book 'To ARTHUR WAUGH with Homage and Love.' She also dedicated a pagan stone to him, attaching to it the mystical petition: 'Not for a happy Death for him, for Death is always happy: but that he shall have a HAPPY DYING.' Three months later, transported in wonderment by his lively descriptions of Sherborne, and desiring nothing more than to see the enchanted place for herself, Elizabeth set off, with a letter of introduction from Arthur, to visit Littleton Powys, widower, writer and school-master who had been a pupil at Sherborne in Arthur's day. The old man showed her round the school and pointed out the plaques commemorating Alec's sporting triumphs – what a lovely day! Within a short space of time, Elizabeth and Littleton were married. But Elizabeth was herself terminally ill, destined to expire at the tender age of thirty-four.

In friendship to Arthur, Elizabeth assembled a book of his sayings and had it published in a twopenny paperback edition, by the city firm Tod & Co, as *Galaxy – a table-book of prose reflections for every day in the year*. Arthur, though flattered by her tribute, was anxious to avoid 'the implication that I have had this thing done to refresh my jaded reputation' and begged the publishers to put his name in as small a lettering as possible on the front cover. When Evelyn first heard of the book he was incredulous that anyone should wish to publish his father's lame ruminations. Arriving for luncheon with a black eye stitched up after a drunken brawl at his club, he was unaware that Arthur and K had read a report in the previous day's gossip column. When they asked about his eye he would only reply, 'Why the morbid curiosity? I am not going to satisfy it.' Arthur described the luncheon in a letter to Alec:

> At 12.30 on Thursday Evelyn and Laura arrived. He was in civilian clothes and had a bad looking eye. Very stiff and sarcastic. I mentioned the little book of 'reflections' from my books, which Betty Myers has made. He was, or pretended to be, consternated. 'Good God,' he said, 'what can she possibly find to collect? I hope she hasn't made you pay her a great deal for doing it?' I explained that she had already placed the book on a royalty and wiped the matter off the slate.

By a strange turn Evelyn found himself billeted at Sherborne, the town of his father's fondest reveries. In the autobiography of his late years Alec claimed that Evelyn's posting there had provided a belated bond between father and younger son, but there is no other evidence to support this. At the time Alec was thousands of miles away in Baghdad and was in no position to comment. He received only one letter from Arthur in which Evelyn's posting to Sherborne was mentioned, with an allusion to Evelyn's snobbery: 'He [Evelyn] said he was very much charmed with the country round Sherborne and thought of selling Piers Court after the war and settling at Melbury. I do not know the place but on looking up the Gazetteer I see that Lord Ilchester lives there, which may account for it.'

Evelyn's only surviving letter to his father from Sherborne contains a few gentle teases:

> I find Sherborne a wholly splendid town. The Digby Hotel is a disgrace but there is a pleasant black market place called Plume of Feathers where we lunch daily.
>
> Have you thought of retiring to the alms houses here? I have been over them and enquired into the conditions of life which I find highly luxurious – coal fires winter and summer, two pints of ale a day, the daily service of a barber and regular hours in church. I think it will solve the servant problem for you. The costume is very becoming but the women have foolishly discarded their crimson cloaks.
>
> Mrs Wingfield-Digby is a sad bitch.
>
> Someone called Wyatt-Smith claims acquaintance with you.[5]
>
> The boys of Sherborne seem a pusillanimous lot who all want to become government chemists. Only a dozen or so read classics. At the Jesuit day school in Glasgow for lower middle classes 300 boys do classics.

Best love Evelyn

Six months later, on 3 April 1943, Arthur had a setback that debilitated his writing hand and rendered him, at times, repetitive and incoherent. Evelyn recorded in his diary:

> I visited my mother on her birthday and found her alert and more cheerful now that her cook has come back and relieved her of continuous duty by my father's side. He is infirm and very deaf; his face seems fallen away at the side as though he had had a stroke. I am told that is not the case. I conversed by writing my replies on a sheet of paper and this seemed to cause him amusement.

[5] There were three Wyatt-Smiths at Sherborne with Alec – he must have been one of them.

Arthur was certainly in a bad way: a two-page letter took him over an hour to complete. His surviving correspondence from this time is in part illegible with long squiggles, deep knots of black ink with sudden jerky scratches clustered around the few words that are discernible. When Alec wrote from Baghdad to say that he had no wish to return to England except to see his parents, Arthur's reply contained all the robust old sentiments but the writing betrayed his body's weakness: 'Always the same old Billy! God bless you. The years go by and changes come but to me at least "You are alone the Arabian bird."[6] Ever your loving old Father.'

Arthur hoped to live at least until his golden wedding anniversary on 5 October, but in this harmless ambition he was sorrily thwarted. On 5 June he attended his last board meeting at Chapman and Hall, more than forty years after he had been appointed managing director: 'It really looks as though the old firm ought to live out its need for me,' he wrote to Alec. 'It will be very pleasant if we manage to keep light at eventide.' A fortnight later, on the twenty-fifth, he was drowsy and lethargic. The doctor came and said there was nothing wrong, but the next morning, according to K, 'all his functions ceased to exist'. By this she meant that he was peeing uncontrollably, all over the place. A nurse was called and he rallied after an injection to eat a normal lunch and to stay up for dinner. Then he wrote in his diary. For months his handwriting had been erratic, spindly and illegible, but on that day – his last – it was clean, round and large like a child's:

Fine day, morning after very good sleep. Dr Gretten called at 4 o'clock, he thought there was no immediate cause for anxiety. He made two changes in my medicine. Went to sleep: had to be woken up for dinner and before I had properly begun to eat feeling very dormant but otherwise amiable.

That night K slept on a camp bed beside him in his room. He was restless at first but later fell into a deep sleep from which he never awoke.

*　*　*

[6] He meant to quote Shakespeare's Cymbeline: 'If she be furnished with a mind so rare, she is alone the Arabian bird, and I have lost the wager.'

Evelyn and Laura, who were in London, came round at once. Evelyn arranged the funeral and they stayed with K in Highgate until it was all over. The church was full. They sang 'The King of Love My Shepherd Is' and 'Just As I Am.'

> Just as I am, though tossed about,
> With many a conflict many a doubt,
> Fightings within, and fears without,
> O Lamb of God I come.

In her diary K recorded a 'beautiful service' and sent Alec in Baghdad a follow-up letter to the telegram he had received announcing the death:

> It was dreadful having you so far away, darling Alec, you who had been everything to Father all his life. You should have been there to take your proper place at the funeral. Aunt Connie has written to you all about it. It really was a beautiful funeral, music, flowers and friends of long association all around him – just as he would have wished and the sun shone down on the scene.
>
> It is marvellous to have had Evelyn in London – he has seen to everything in a kindly and efficient manner. Another month he may have gone abroad and I don't know what I should have done without him . . . I have no definite plans except to keep this home ready for when you return.
>
> Good-bye darling Alec. I am so sad for you as well as for myself. I am so bad at letter writing, but I do love you.
>
> Your devoted Mother.

The obituaries were fulsome and generous. 'Mr Waugh was one of those who made history in the book trade not merely by re-establishing the fortunes of his own firm but by securing a much more enlightened policy of co-operation among those engaged in book production.' The Times published a warm tribute, a day before the funeral, that ended: 'In his talk he was always referring to his childhood and youth in the West Country. His affectionate pride in his two sons, Alec and Evelyn, entirely bridged any gulf that might have been presumed to exist between the literary standards of two writers so different from himself.'

Elizabeth Myers, who was fast gaining recognition with *A Well Full of Leaves*, wrote a letter of consolation to Alec:

> All my success I owe to your dear father. But I owe him much more than success for he gave to me all the wisdom and love I never had from my own father and these things will never be forgotten by me . . . We used to talk about you endlessly. He loved you as few sons are loved by their fathers and the mention of your name was enough to exhilarate him.

Elizabeth's transcendental vision, which had so endeared her to Arthur, is fondly recorded in a letter she sent to her friend, the dramatist and novelist Eleanor Farjeon, at the time of his death:

> Dear, dearest Eleanor,
>
> I can't trust myself to speak of our dear yet without breaking down. I phoned Mrs Bridges on Saturday night and it was hopeless, but she was very good to me and told me what I wanted to know above all – that the end had been peaceful. O, how I wish I could tell you, how powerfully I feel *that he is happy*. And what's more, I feel that he is much nearer to me than in life here. It isn't that I am sad; for death is so triumphant and lovely; it's just that I'm selfish.
>
> But Arthur is dead, he hasn't gone. He lives in you and me and all who ever came in contact with his midsummer sweetness. And he lives in his own ever loving presence. And he lives in the love of Littleton for him and for me and in mine for them. *What* I owe to Arthur Waugh!

Evelyn took Arthur's death in a loftier stride. In a diary entry, written shortly after the funeral he simply noted:

On July 24 my father died and Brigade HQ left London for 'Operation Husky'. It was an unfortunate coincidence as I was distracted from one by the other. I was angry with Bob for leaving me behind so easily. My father died with disconcerting suddenness. I spent most of the next few days at Highgate. The funeral was on the 27th at Hampstead. I spent some weary hours going through my father's papers and destroying letters. He kept up a large correspondence with very dull people. My mother's mind seems clouded by the business. Laura and I had Bron brought up to interest her.[7]

To all letters of condolence Evelyn replied with the same air of light detachment. Here is a typical example, sent to an old family friend:

Dear Tom

How very nice of you to write.
    You were always a most welcome guest.
    My father had been ill for some time but no one expected him to die so suddenly. It is a disagreeable world for the old and I think he was glad to leave it. His only regret would be leaving my mother.
    I am in a backwater of the war at the moment but hope for adventure soon.

Yours Evelyn

A week after the funeral, Evelyn, as he mentioned in his diary, rifled through his father's desk, filing or destroying papers as he saw fit. He was astonished at the size of his father's correspondence about Alec. Three days later, he posted a letter to his brother in Baghdad. Note the use of 'our' and 'my' in relation to their parents:

---

[7] Both his dates are wrong: Arthur died on 26 June 1943 and was buried on the twenty-ninth. Bob was Evelyn's commanding officer, Robert Laycock; Bron was his son, my father.

Dear Alex,

I wrote on your birthday too late to send you any good wishes.

You will already have heard the details of my father's death. It is lucky that I have been in England for this month. I go abroad at the beginning of August. If you could get home it would be a good thing as our mother is desornée [*sic*] and lonely.

My father's papers have been arranged in his bureau as follows. Top drawer: letters from or concerning you. 2nd drawer: papers of literary or family association. I have thought it best to destroy too little rather than too much. 3rd drawer: photographs which my mother wished to go through at her leisure. 4th drawer: literary work by our father.

My father left everything to our mother except his books which are divided between us. I am having a book plate engraved to mark his books so that eventually they can remain intact as a personal collection in our respective libraries.

My father's estate will probably be about £5000. This is clearly not enough to support our mother if invested in the ordinary way. Joan might care to make a covenanted allowance. The best thing would be for you to live with her; the next best that a friend should be found to share the flat. I hope that you will be able to get back to see to things after I have left.

Yours affectionately,
Evelyn

No sooner had Alec read Evelyn's letter than he received another and was startled to recognise the handwriting on the envelope. It was from his father, written just two days before his death and delivered to Baghdad a full week and a half after his funeral. Arthur's writing is so bad that many passages of this letter are indecipherable:

My most dear Billy,

I have been villainously guilty in my relations *vis à vis toi*, having had 3 really splendid letters from you and being prevented from replying by this exasperating failure of my hand. I was plugging away when your mother said 'My dear, you cannot possibly send that it is illegible.' So I tore my letter to pieces and had not the endurance to begin again. But here is another attempt which I hope may be more successful.

I am pretty well in myself, except for bad sleeping which is bound to knock me up. I feel very like the dyspepsia I got in 1931. At any rate I feel very much as I did then, before we went to Villefranche, but I have never felt anything like as bad as I was then.

My one pleasure has been watching the school cricket which has had many good days and successful wins . . . I never remember a boy not much higher than the stumps getting 102 not out twice as young Laws did while Maclure was getting 74 and 30 . . . and then . . . wickets . . .

Evelyn has been over to see us several Sundays. He has had Laura with him. He has been most agreeable and has brought me some wine . . . has been a great benefit . . . the best I ever drank. I have two full sized bottles and 4 half bottles. May the day come when we drink it together in the kingdom of our fate.

Evelyn is not at . . . is a sort of . . . hot dry. He has . . . is shouting that it does not suit . . .

Well, I have looked through what I have written, but I must confess that it has made me sad. So often I have said to myself – Well, when I am growing old and ugly, at least I shall have the old gift of communication and if I can still speak in the old language, I shall be able to bring the old look back . . . and . . . to the heart . . . the heart of Jacob! But alas it will not. I can see the old secret vanished and when a letter comes, my dear ones can no longer . . . The old clouds lose their colour in the sky. Never mind, God bless you, son of my soul, there will never be shadows in the . . .

With every tender remembrance . . . May every base be broad in honour . . .

Your loving and grateful
Father

X

Irritability

On the morning of 18 November 1939 Evelyn wrote in his diary:

At 9 I was telephoned to say Laura's baby had started. I drove over to Pixton. When I arrived soon after luncheon Laura had had morphia and was cheerful and in practically no pain. She grew worse and later in the evening the local doctor summoned help from Tiverton to induce the baby. A son was born shortly before midnight.

Laura and Evelyn were delighted when their second child turned out to be a boy. According to one of his earliest biographers, 'Evelyn's desire for a son and heir could not have been stronger if he had been a reigning prince.' I don't know how the writer knew this but let us, for the sake of argument, accept it. Although they were pleased to have a son, both Evelyn and Laura disliked babies. When telegrams of congratulation came in, Evelyn responded: 'Many thanks for your telegram. The midwife speaks highly of the baby.' In a letter to his friend Mary Lygon two days later Evelyn appears to have examined 'it' a little more closely: 'Laura has had a son. Will you be it's god-mother? It is to be called Auberon Alexander. It is quite big and handsome and Laura is very pleased with it. We would so love it if you would accept. Please do.'

I do not know how, why or when Evelyn was induced to call his child Auberon as it was the name of Laura's only brother whom he detested. In a passage excised by my father during Great-uncle Auberon's lifetime from the published version of the diaries, Evelyn had written:

> Laura's brother Auberon came for the night at his own invitation. He wished to discuss his career in journalism. We made him tell us something of his clownish courtship of Elizabeth Cavendish. Slow of speech, dirty of body, clumsy of movement, conceited, oafish – a horrible young man.

As their father was dead it fell to Auberon to give his sister away at her wedding. He was only fourteen and in the car on the way to church hot salty tears splurted on to his morning suit as he pleaded with his sister to abandon her plans to marry Evelyn: 'Oh, Laudie, Laudie,' he begged, 'you cannot marry that awful shit. It is still not too late to change your mind.' When Evelyn heard of this he was unforgiving.

Auberon's dislike of Evelyn was the aristocrat's natural dislike of the *arriviste* or, as my father preferred, the 'traditional jealousy between privilege and actual achievement'. Auberon was no fool. He spoke six languages fluently, had a natural and unusual wit and was adored by figures as random and far apart as Sir Isaiah Berlin and Karol, his Polish butler, but to Evelyn, who deplored his manner of speech, the habitual twisting of his wrists by his face as he spoke, and the suffocating odour of his scent that wafted oppressively around his person, Auberon was no more than a spoiled idler. It is true that he never achieved much in his life and frittered most of it in overeating, overspending, selling-off Herbert heirlooms and thus ensuring that no one could ever succeed him at Pixton.

Auberon was the third Auberon Herbert of a distinguished line. The name Auberon (properly pronounced Orbr'n) was invented, according to Evelyn, by Laura's great-grandfather, Henry, 3rd Earl of Carnarvon. The earl's younger son, Laura's great-uncle, was Auberon Herbert, the famous anarchist philosopher, whose own son (and namesake) achieved a modicum of renown as a one-legged airman who disappeared over enemy lines in November 1916 calling himself Lord Lucas. The *Oxford Dictionary of Names* thinks Auberon means 'noble bear', adding to this implausible definition 'as in Auberon Herbert and Auberon Waugh'. To the best of my knowledge there have only ever been eight Auberons and all descend from Henry Carnarvon. The name must never be confused with Oberon, a jealous fairy out of Shakespeare who pronounces it differently.

Arthur did not like the name; nor did he, or anyone else, make arrangements to see the baby until he was older. In August 1940 he had written to Kenneth McMaster complaining, 'Evelyn's wife went to her mother at Pixton Park, Dulverton. She had a son on November 27th last [*sic*]. She is expecting another in December. The Roman Catholic priests insist upon it.'

For the first six years of his life Auberon, or Bron, as he soon became, lived at Pixton. The war was raging and Evelyn, who was fighting for King and country and, in any case, had an edgy relationship with his in-laws, was seldom there, disdaining the place even when on leave. But the house was far from empty: it was filled with servants, old retainers, close and distant cousins, aunts, great-aunts, one step-great-great-grandmother and, on the top floor, twenty or thirty evacuee children from bomb-target cities in the Midlands. My father carried few memories of Evelyn at this time, and only muddled, disjointed impressions of his mother. He could just distinguish her from her two sisters, who also lived in the house. Laura was a mother in name only. As he later wrote: 'I was not aware that motherhood involved any particular emotional proximity.'

Neither Laura nor Evelyn was thrilled to have children. Laura had dreaded the prospect of girls. When her elder sister had a baby she wrote to congratulate her: 'I am so glad that you have got the baby over – it must be a relief that it's over – I am sorry it's a girl.' Perhaps Arthur was right that Catholicism drove them to have children. Evelyn, who eventually had seven children, once told my father that if he had not been a Catholic he would only have had three, but I wonder if even three would have been too many. He was lucky to

have had a war to go to. When he returned to civilian life at Piers
Court, his children immediately grated on his nerves; Bron was six
years old. In 1946 he wrote to his friend Lady Diana Cooper:

> I have my two eldest children here [Piers Court], a boy and
> girl, two girls languish at Pixton; a fifth leaps in the womb.
> I abhor their company because I can only regard children
> as defective adults. I hate their physical ineptitude, find
> their jokes flat and monotonous. Both are considered great
> wits by their contemporaries. The elder girl has a taste for
> theology which promises well for a career as Abbess; the
> boy is mindless and obsessed with social success. I will put
> him into the army later; meanwhile he goes to boarding
> school at the end of the month with the keenest expecta-
> tion of delight.

Lady Diana wrote to Conrad Russell: 'I think Evelyn's shrimp will
be much happier at boarding school than under Laura's wing. She
dislikes her children as much as their father does.' I do not know
how much of this is true or whether Evelyn and Laura's apparent
dislike of their children at this time amounted to anything more
than an assumed show of boredom, mock-humour and bravura.
Evelyn told Diana Cooper that 'for choice he would take his six
children to church at Easter, see them shriven and annealed and,
at the church door, slaughter the lot in their innocence and
absolution'.

'But what about *you*, Evelyn?' Diana asked him.

'O, I would repent at leisure and be forgiven.'

I think he was joking; if not he had a poor grasp of the rules
and arrangements of the Catholic game.

While Evelyn was rushing around at his war work, he instructed
Laura in her letters not to bore him with details of the children
and, in 1941 when he was contemplating his Christmas leave, he
wrote to her:

> If I do get leave it will probably be suddenly and the first
> you will hear will be a telegram summoning you to Claridges

where we must spend a day or two before thinking about the country . . . I shall not visit my children during this leave. They should be able to retain the impression formed of me for a further three months. I can't afford to waste on them any time which could be spent on my own pleasures. I have sent them some kippers as compensation.

Christmas the following year was just the same: 'I am very glad not to be with my children for Christmas. There is an hotel at Shaftesbury with a very splendid sideboard. I think we might take a weekend there soon when you are fuckable.'

Teresa, much loved by Arthur and K, was a sore irritation to both her parents in her early years. 'My father writes to say he looks forward to Teresa coming. Poor sucker.' But Arthur was delighted by his granddaughter and wrote a letter of fulsome praise that Evelyn, incredulous, forwarded to Laura: 'Here is a report on Teresa from my father which will interest and surprise you.' In 1942, when Laura was pregnant with a fourth child, he wrote to her suggesting names: 'JAMES if it is a boy; if a girl it is kinder to drown her than to bring her up like her poor sister. I note that you have recalled that wretched child just in time to scar it with chicken pox.' Laura wanted another son. Evelyn appeared not to mind: 'I am fretting about your anti-daughter feeling. You must not mind when this new baby is a daughter. Daughters are a great comfort to their parents compared that is with sons.'

At Pixton, Bron, his sisters and all their cousins enjoyed the sort of freedom that children seldom experience under the watchful eyes of their parents. The house was large enough for them to escape the gaze of grown-ups for hours on end and the grounds, with mature trees, rolling parkland, dilapidated stables and welcoming tenants' cottages, were as a paradise to a free spirit like Bron who, from the start, resented any intrusions on his liberty. The adults of the house rarely questioned what their children were up to. Discipline, such as there was, was usually delegated and usually physical. Mary Herbert, Pixton's matriarch, instructed her perfumed son Auberon to carry out the business of corporal punishment. As heir to the estate and Lord High Executioner of Pixton Park, this pear-shaped young man chose the grand hall as the setting for this important function. Small crowds of cousins assembled on the stairs, while evacuees were permitted to watch – and to gob, if they liked – from the second-floor gallery. At the bottom, beneath the portraits of his illustrious Herbert ancestors,[1] Auberon ceremoniously flagellated Bron, his little nephew, with an old golfing shoe that had belonged to Hilaire Belloc.

Laura, a heavy smoker with a fondness for sherry, was too lazy to carry out corporal punishment but she did not object to it in principle. From Pixton she wrote frequently to Evelyn to complain about Bron. Sometimes he replied with indulgence: 'I am sorry my poor son is so morbid and sensitive. He has a bad heredity in that matter.' At other times he advised physical retribution: 'I am sorry my son is so vicious. Why do you think yourself unable to whip him? He is really quite small. If you hold him firmly in one hand and lash out often enough and hard enough some blows are bound to fall in the right place.' Once, and only once, she chased Bron for a mile and quarter lashing his bare legs with stinging nettles whenever she caught up with him. But this was unusual behaviour: for the most part she kept herself at a distance from her children, neither hugging, chatting nor whipping. As my father later wrote, with a hint of bitterness, 'My mother did not feature in any particular way throughout those six years of my life at Pixton. Much of her time was spent serving in an Air Force canteen and in other vital war work.'

Evelyn might have thought or hoped that his long absences from Pixton would engender in his children some fond images of heroism, bravery, dashing good looks and doughty deeds that would make him especially interesting to them on his infrequent returns. He sent Bron a postcard photograph of himself, with a

---

[1] At the time of his birth rumours abounded that Auberon was the illegitimate son of his tutor and godfather, Hilaire Belloc, in which case he had no Herbert blood. A few surviving facts support the thesis. Belloc loved Mary Herbert and wrote poems to her. Auberon's physiognomy resembled Belloc's more than Aubrey Herbert's. Aubrey Herbert was not pleased by Auberon's birth. Unless baby Auberon was eleven months *in utero* he cannot have been conceived by Aubrey, who was in Albania. Belloc was a regular guest at Pixton in his absence.

gun in his holster, looking handsome in full military uniform in Yugoslavia.

> This is your Papa. Pin it up. I do not know when I shall come home but hope it will be soon. I shall expect you to read, write, ride and paint perfectly before I next see you.

> Your affectionate Papa EW.

But Pixton was no Underhill. The stream of anxiety and heady sentiment concerning Alec in the First World War found no parallel for Evelyn in the Second. Bron scarcely knew who his father was and did not much care one way or the other. His sister Teresa's first memory of Evelyn was of a red-faced, uniformed man appearing from a window at Pixton, shouting across the garden: 'For God's sake, someone take those children to the other lawn.' I think he wore the uniform on these off-duty occasions to excite his children, but it had little effect. Bron's first memories were no less depressing than Teresa's. He and all the other children were having tea in the dining room at Pixton when Evelyn, again in uniform, walked in. My father can take up the story from here:

> I had a particular passion for yellow jam tarts, but tarts of any colour were a delicacy, making their appearance on the tea table perhaps once a fort-night. The distraction caused by my father's arrival was too good an opportunity to miss. Within seconds I had cleared all the plates of yellow jam tarts and was shifting about ten of them into the pockets of my corduroy shorts, when there was a bellow from the door. My father, who attached greater importance to his paternity than I did, wished to know why his only son had not gone to greet him. The tarts, in broken and squashed condition, were extricated from my pockets and I was sent to bed in disgrace.

Alec Waugh's children, far away in sunny Australia, were brought up by Joan in the belief that their father was a gallant, handsome hero, such as they had read about in children's books and comic strips. When Peter, aged five, was asked what his father did in the war he replied proudly: 'He is admiral of the Jewish navy.' It was considerate of Joan to boost Alec to her children in this way, especially since his latest book, *His Second War* (1944), an account of his army service dedicated to the other Joan – giant Joan Duff ('O for the viols of her voice'), revealed no evident heroism on Alec's behalf. When the war was over and the little Waughs had returned from Australia, Joan assembled her children at Waterloo station to greet their father. They had not seen him for six years. Only the two eldest, Andrew and Veronica, had any but the dimmest memory of him. Peter, the youngest, had none at all. As the train emptied, with hundreds of soldiers pouring off it and diving into the arms of their loved ones, the three children trembled in anticipation.

'There he is!' cried Joan. Peter stepped forward immediately to shake the hand of the first lantern-jawed muscle-man to catch his eye and was pulled back sharply.

'Not that one, Silly, this one,' she said.

He looked in dismay at the small, bald, simian figure shuffling towards them along the platform with a heavy sack under his arm. It was not until Alec had tipped the taxi driver generously that Peter thought he understood the true nature of his father's heroism.

As soon as Alec was back, he was itching to be off again. After two days with his family at Edrington he took a train from Silchester to London. Evelyn met up with him briefly at one of his clubs and wrote to a friend:

> Alec arrived recently with many distressing nervous habits. He made a century against a minor public school. I asked him why he did not make use of one of Joan's cars. He said that if he were to do that he would not be able to commit adultery with a clear conscience. I asked him how often he had done so in the last five years. Five times. It hardly seems worth tramping the London streets for.

Within two months of his return to England, Alec was off again. 'New York,' he wrote, in the last of his memoirs, 'was the axis round which my world revolved after the war.' He arrived there in September 1945 and 'the next four months were as good as any I had known'. On his return in January 1946, he spent no more than two days with his family before setting off for a hotel in Devon to write a book on his own.

During the war, Evelyn had made a few stabbing efforts to get to know his son. He invited Laura to bring Bron to see him at a training camp in Hawick: 'Bring Bron and why not send Teresa to Highgate?' In August 1945 he took him to stay with the Churchills where little Winston, the Prime Minister's grandson of the same age, was marched out to entertain him. For the whole of their stay Bron delighted his father with his good manners, enthusiasm and humour. He fell into a bonfire but showed fortitude in the face of pain and, as Evelyn wrote to Laura, 'won golden opinions on all sides, even mine'. Indeed, he was so pleased with Bron that he decided to take him on to see K and a few of the sights of London. In three letters to Laura, Evelyn expressed how much he was looking forward to the trip and for two days went to considerable lengths to entertain Bron. From Evelyn's diary:

> On Wednesday I took him to the zoo which was crowded with the lower classes and practically devoid of animals except rabbits and guinea-pigs. On Friday I devoted the day to him, hiring a car to fetch him from Highgate and to return him there. I wore myself out for his amusement taking him up the Dome of St Paul's, buying him three-cornered postage stamps and austerity toys, showing him London from the top of the hotel, taking him to tea with his god-mother who gave him a sovereign and a box of variegated matches. Finally I took him back to Highgate.

All seemed to have gone well, until K asked her grandson how his day had passed. Evelyn was deflated by Bron's response and, feeling absolved from paying him any further attention, packed him back to Pixton in the care of his sister-in-law. That evening he wrote to Laura:

I have regretfully come to the conclusion that the boy Auberon is not yet a suitable companion for me . . . I took him back to Highgate in a state of extreme exhaustion. My mother said 'Have you had a lovely day?' He replied 'A bit dull.' So that is the last time for some years I inconvenience myself for my children. You might rub that in to him.

Three months before his infelicitous London excursion with Bron, Evelyn had published the novel for which he would become most famous. Several of his admirers were disappointed. In place of the dry hilarities of his earlier books, there was a new, alien mood of moist sentiment. At the time Evelyn was in no doubt that *Brideshead Revisited* was his finest work, 'my magnum opus', as he called it, but after a decade of reading and rereading it his confidence in the novel's opulent tone had started to wane. In his preface to the 1960 revised edition he explained how it had been written in the six months between December 1944 and June 1945 while he was convalescing from a minor parachute accident: 'It was a bleak period of present privation and threatening disaster – the period of soya beans and Basic English – and in consequence the book is enthused with a kind of gluttony, for food and wine, for the splendours of the recent past, and for rhetorical and ornamental language which now, with a full stomach, I find distasteful.'

Brideshead was begun only a few months after Arthur's death, but ideas for it had been brewing in Evelyn's mind for some time. The story is narrated as a flood of pre-war memories by an army captain whose battalion during the war is billeted to Brideshead Castle. Since his days at Oxford, the captain's life had been intimately connected with various members of the Flyte family, who had inhabited the castle until it was commandeered by the army. Many angles of influence came to bear on Evelyn during the conception of that scenario but I wonder if his billeting a year earlier at the Digby Hotel – amid the architectural splendours of Sherborne, its sandstone abbey, school, old associations of father and brother, now transformed to an army barrack – did not act as some sort of a spur to *Brideshead*. I wonder also if Evelyn's nostalgia for

Oxford before the war and for the imaginary Brideshead in the days when it was a home were not influenced to some degree by his perusal of his father's nostalgic autobiography shortly after the old man's death. In *One Man's Road*, Arthur had written:

> Oxford, who has welcomed so many armies home, now victorious, now again vanquished, but all alike her sons, Oxford seems to have suffered more than most from the brief but biting ordeal of war. I remember sitting in Tom Quad at Christ Church midway in the first year of hostilities, and wondering whether the place could ever be the same again as it was when we were young. Everything for which Oxford stood was at a standstill; the Colleges were barracks, the meadows drill yards; the long tradition of manners which 'makyth man' was broken.
>
> Today in the Broad and the High you can hear very little except the horns of the charioteer. The motor car indeed might be taken for the symbol of our era of restlessness and change; and nowhere does it seem so incongruous as under the shadow of Magdalen Tower. For the motor-car has turned every man's road into a railway. Never again will the journey be made in the steady, jog-trot fashion of my youth.

Brideshead Revisited abounds with similar sentiment: the same fruity nostalgia, the same juxtaposition of old architecture and modern vandalism, the same conflict of tradition and change, the same vein of rich, tea-cake prose. Evelyn, of course, was a finer writer than his father:

> Oxford — submerged now and obliterated, as irrecoverable as Lyonness, so quickly have the waters come flooding in — Oxford, in those days, was still a city of aquatint. In her spacious and quiet streets men walked and spoke as they had done in Newman's day; her autumnal mists, her grey springtime, and the rare glory of her summer days — such as that day — when the chestnut was in flower and the bells rang out high over her gables and cupolas, exhaled the soft vapours of a thousand years of learning. It was this cloistral hush which gave

our laughter its resonance, and carried it still, joyously over the intervening clamour.

Alec claimed that the new emotionalism of his brother's writing was directly caused by Arthur's death. Evelyn, he believed, had guarded himself against sentimentality all his life until, free of his father's example, he had found himself at last able to indulge his natural inclination.

A great deal of *Brideshead* is autobiographical. The hero, Charles Ryder, has much in common with the author, especially concerning the relationship between father and son. Ryder, a painter who, like Evelyn, serves as a captain in the war, has two children, one of whom is born while he is away on active service. When he returns on leave he shows no interest in his daughter and cannot even remember his children's names. Ryder's father, Ned, is a close, semi-affectionate portrait of Arthur.

During his university years Charles Ryder is in constant conflict with his father but, like so many of the fathers in Evelyn's novels, Ryder *père* is an eccentric who hides behind a screen of his own dottiness to deflect his son's arguments. Like Evelyn, Ryder finds his father depressing while others adore him, and like Evelyn Gardner, who described Arthur as a 'complete Pinkle-Wonk' in his velvet dinner jacket, Julia, Ryder's girlfriend, thinks that his father 'sounds like a perfect poppet'. Arthur Waugh's gasping asthma attacks are recalled in old Mr Ryder's 'snuffles'. Like Arthur, he refers constantly to his youth and how things were 'in my day'.

My father was in his late fifties, but it was his idiosyncrasy to seem much older than his years; to see him one might have put him at seventy, to hear him speak at nearly eighty. He came to me now, with the shuffling, mandarin-tread which he affected and a shy smile of welcome. When he dined at home and he seldom dined elsewhere – he wore a frogged velvet smoking suit of the kind which had been fashionable many years before and was to be so again but, at that time, was a deliberate archaism.

Like all fictional Evelyn Waugh fathers to this date Mr Ryder is distant, unhelpful, one might say uncaring, even a little malicious towards his son. But for all that he is an attractive character. His wry wit may be uncongenial to Charles but the reader delights in his parlour games and looks forward to his every appearance:

'It's a *very* long vacation,' he said wistfully. 'In my day we used to go on what were called reading parties, always in mountainous areas. Why? Why,' he repeated petulantly, 'should Alpine scenery be thought conducive to study?'

'I thought of putting in some time at an art school – in the life class.'

'My dear boy, you'll find them all shut. The students go to Barbison or such places and paint in the open air. There was an institution in my day called a "sketching club" – mixed sexes,' (snuffle), 'bicycles,' (snuffle), 'pepper-and-salt knickerbockers, Holland umbrellas and, it was popularly thought, free love,' (snuffle), '*such* a lot of nonsense. I expect they still go on. You might try that.'

The nuns removed themselves and all their paraphernalia from Piers Court on 12 September 1945. Evelyn moved back in immediately and the children returned from Pixton when the house was considered ready to receive them after Christmas. Boxing Day was spoiled for Evelyn by their arrival:

Teresa and Bron have arrived: he ingratiating, she covered with little medals and badges, neurotically voluble with the vocabulary of the lower middle class – 'serviette', 'spare room'. Only on points of theology does she become rational. By keeping the children in bed for long periods we managed to have a tolerable day . . . The children leave for Pixton on the 10th. Meanwhile I have my meals in the library.

When Evelyn was not avoiding his children, feeling irritated by them, dying of boredom in their presence, he made great efforts to entertain them. He taught them games, drew pictures for them, told fantastic stories of his childhood, rollicked with exaggerated laughter at their jokes and took them out for walks and on expeditions to local sites of interest. At Christmas he took them to the pantomimes at Bristol and Bath and bought 'trashy and costly' toys for their stockings. The strain of it all demoralised him. He could not sustain his interest in them for long – but he tried hard nevertheless. 'I went home for two nights to find my boy more personable and manly. I drew pictures, played games, climbed the roof and was exhausted.'

Evelyn was a bad sleeper, dependent for many years on a dangerous cocktail of alcohol and chloral. He did not have a natural gift with children and could not see them in any other light than as 'defective adults; feckless, destructive, frivolous, sensual, humourless' and, as such, they wearied him. Most of the evidence dragged out to prove his viciousness as a father is drawn from his own private diaries and letters; but, needless to say, they do not tell the whole story.

We are all bored by our children on occasion and the world might be an easier place if we were only frank enough to admit it, but modern parents tend instead to furrow their brows, force smiles on to anxious lips and talk down in sentimental goo-goo voices that sometimes stick even after their children have grown up. This, I believe, is the way to damage children. This is what Arthur Waugh did.

Christmas was always a bad time for Evelyn. I think he suffered from a problem that, since his day, has been identified as Seasonal Affective Disorder, or SAD, a lowering winter lethargy, now identified with a gene that once had something to do with our distant ancestors hibernating. I suffer from it too. In his least good book, an African travelogue from 1960, Evelyn explained his Christmas blues:

> Childermas is the Sabbat of *cafard*. I have just looked up this popular word in the dictionary and have learned, as no doubt the reader already knows, that its roots come from 'hypocrisy' and 'cant'. It is therefore peculiarly apt for the emotions with which the father of a family performs the jollities of

Christmastide. It is at Christmas, as a rule, that I begin to make plans for my escape, for, oddly enough, the regularly recurrent fit of claustrophobia always takes me by surprise. Writing now in high summer, it seems hardly conceivable that I shall ever want to leave my agreeable house and family. But I shall, next Christmas, and no doubt I shall once more find myself with no plans made.

The next Christmas was just the same. His diary entry for 23 December 1946 shows that it was, as usual, steering him into a heavy gloom:

The presence of my children affects me with deep weariness and depression. I do not see them until luncheon as I have my breakfast alone in the library, and they are in fact well trained to avoid my part of the house, but I am aware of the them from the moment I wake. Luncheon is very painful. Teresa has a mincing habit of speech and a pert humourless style of wit; Bron is clumsy and dishevelled, sly, without intellectual, aesthetic or spiritual interest; Margaret is pretty and below the age of reason. In the nursery whooping cough rages I believe. At tea I meet the three elder children again and they usurp the drawing room until it is time to dress for dinner. I used to take some pleasure in inventing legends for them about Basil Bennett; Dr Bedlam and the Sebag-Montefiores. But now they think it ingenious to squeal 'It isn't true.' I taught them the game of draughts for which they show no aptitude. The frost has broken and everything is now dripping and slushy and gusty.

I cannot read this passage without feeling a little sorry for Evelyn. It is all very well cooing, oohing and bridling on the children's behalf, but Evelyn was the sufferer here, not his children. There are times when my own brood affects me in similar ways, when I, too, seek refuge in the library from the tyranny of their noise and deadly paraffle of their physical presence. It doesn't hurt them. They are not damaged. Of course it would be ideal if I never had such hostile feelings towards them in the first place, but I do and I am stuck with it. Honesty is the only virtue left to a parent in this condition and Evelyn was unusually honest.

When my father published his autobiography in 1991 the press exploded with indignation over an anecdote concerning a bunch of bananas. The story, simply told, is that bananas were not available in England during the war. When the fighting stopped and the first shipments resumed the government decreed that every kiddie in the land should be issued with a banana coupon exchangeable for a free sample at his local greengrocer. Teresa, Bron and Margaret (or Meg, Evelyn's third surviving child) had apparently been apprised of the deliciousness of this tropical fruit and were greatly looking forward to tasting it. I shall let my father continue in the words that caused the outcry in 1991:

> When the great day arrived and my mother returned with the bananas, all three were put on my father's plate and before the anguished eyes of his children, he poured on cream, which was almost unprocurable, and sugar, which was heavily rationed, and ate all three. A child's sense of justice may be defective in many respects, and egocentric at the best of times, but it is no less intense for either. By any standards he had done wrong. It would be absurd to say that I never forgave him, but he was permanently marked down in my estimation. From that moment, I never treated anything he had to say on faith or morals very seriously.

Neither of my aunts, who were present at this débâcle, remembers the episode. I am not suggesting that my father invented it, only that he, like Evelyn, was unable to control his greed. A boy who, by his own admission, fills his pockets with jam tarts rather than greet his father back from the war is not in a strong position to moralise about other people's banana hogging. Nor do I feel heartbroken when a six-year-old is denied a new taste experience, as they usually fuss and spit it out. Of course it was greedy of Evelyn to scoff them all but it was also greedy of Bron to let it fester. No one comes out of this tale smelling of roses – but it was not the shocking example of parental cruelty that the press at the time tried to portray.

Laura's happiness at Piers Court was drawn mainly from her cows. She owned six or seven of them, some named after her daughters, all jealously guarded by herself and the cowman, Mr Sanders. Sanders had been imported from Pixton and Laura was a little in love with him. Evelyn affected to be unable to remember his name. Every year Laura's cattle made a loss, but never enough to dampen her enthusiasm for them. The happiest moments of her day were spent in discussing her herd with Sanders, pointing out the strengths and weaknesses of individual beasts, comparing moos with milk yields, moving them slowly from one field to another and wondering what to do with them next. Sanders had a room in the attic at Piers Court where, after two years, he died and his amplified and extended death rattle woke everyone in the house.

If Bron ever suspected that his mother was more interested in Sanders and her cows than she was in her children, he may have been right. I do not suppose that he resented this at the time, but later on, when he had become a father, these things rankled. In his autobiography he wrote: 'My mother had only a few cows and they cost a fortune to keep, but she loved them extravagantly, as other women love their dogs or, so I have been told, their children.'

From an early age Bron suffered from an 'alternating squint', which meant that one of his eyes was so badly aligned with the other that he suffered occasional spells of blindness. It was first diagnosed by a doctor in Exeter and Evelyn, on the advice of an exiled Pole living at Pixton, took him to a Harley Street specialist in January 1944, but the problem persisted. A year later Evelyn wrote to Laura from Dubrovnik:

> I am sorry Auberon's eyes are worse. It seems to me that the money we spent at the command of the Polish miner has gone down the drain. If he cannot see it seems to me hopeless leaving him in a class with children who can. Can

you not get him special tuition? He will grow up like an American if you are not careful. His cousin Andrew Waugh is to go to sea – a very good idea. I would send Auberon but eyes are particularly important to sailors. Can you make him a musician? I can imagine life so little without sight that I can advise nothing.

By the time Bron was seven urgent action needed to be taken and he was sent for an operation at a hospital in Bristol. Evelyn, perhaps remembering the trauma of his appendicitis at about the same age, was particularly kind, rushing back and forth from the hospital bringing, on one occasion, a box of white mice to amuse Bron in his convalescence. The ward sister was furious.

Bron came round from the anaesthetic to find he had been blind-folded and his arms strapped to the side of the cot to prevent him removing his bandages. 'I think it may have been the lowest moment in my life,' he later recalled. 'Although equable by nature, I have never felt such rage as I felt then.' When, at last, his arms were untied, he was flogged by the nurse for scratching at his bandages. Many years later, when he was famous, she wrote to him begging his forgiveness.

A letter from Laura to her sister, Gabriel, sent at the time of Bron's operation, affords a glimpse of the whole tragic episode from a mother's perspective:

Darling Gabriel,

. . . I suppose you have heard about my madness at last Friday's sale – I went mad and paid £108 for I think the most beautiful Guernsey cow I have ever seen. Sanders and I fell in love with her from the moment we saw her and we waited until the end of the sale for her and then the bidding went haywire and we found we had paid this colossal price for her. We were still not upset because we thought her such a wonderful cow but when we got her home we found she was only giving one gallon a day – though she was sold as giving four gallons and feeding her calf. It is all most peculiar. She has a magnificent udder, not at all pendulous but silky and rectangular and firm. Just like all the pictures of perfect udders you see in farming papers. Anyhow Sanders and I are feeling very sad, foolish and perplexed as we really cannot see what to do with the beastly animal. Yesterday she improved faintly and gave 18lbs – anyhow don't make a story about it – I feel far too deeply.

My life at the moment is hellish – I motor every week into Bristol for Bron to do eye exercises which take half an hour – all the rest of the week I seem to spend in shopping . . .

All my love to you, Laura.

In 1948 a new nanny arrived at Piers Court. Vera Gilroy was the eldest of nine children from an impoverished mining family of the Merton Colliery in County Durham. When she came down by train to Gloucestershire she knew little of the ways of an English country house. She was just fifteen and very innocent, expecting Laura to greet her at the station in long silk robes and a diamond tiara. Instead she was met by a scruffy woman – with tousled hair, in rough muddy trousers held up with binder-twine – who drove her back to Piers Court in a rickety old pick-up truck. Her heart sank when she realised this was the lady of the house and it sank further when she met Bron. 'Do my hair!' he ordered her imperiously – but soon she got the hang of him and they became firm friends. The children adored her. She was not much older than they and later, when she was married and calling herself Vera Grother, Bron and Meg would descend on her cottage in the village to smoke cigarettes away from the disapproving glare of their parents.

Laura was not cold but her head was in the clouds and she was never demonstrative. In her heart I think she was a sad person. Like Evelyn, she did not possess a natural gift of communication with the young, but her affection for her children increased as they grew older. Evelyn, on the other hand, cared too much. His irritation, especially with the elder two, was engendered by their failure to reach the high standards he set for them. He minded how they spoke, the words they used, the clothes they wore, the books they read – he passionately wanted them to shine. When he found Teresa reading a women's magazine given her by one of the staff, he snatched it away and tossed it ostentatiously into the fire. When Vera gave Teresa a children's novel by Nancy Breary for Christmas he confiscated it. Vera was terrified, but the next day Evelyn came into the nursery with the novel in his hand, 'Vera is a genius! This book is awfully well written,' he proclaimed and returned it to Teresa.

Clothes were a problem. Laura was not interested in buying new ones so all of her children were fitted out in scruffy, falling-to-bits hand-me-downs from cousins or servants. When the girls were sent to boarding-school they had no knickers. Laura asked Vera to sew up the fronts of some of Bron's old underpants to give them a more feminine look, but Vera, appalled on the girls' behalf, snuck out to Dursley and bought them some proper kit with her own money. In the holidays at Piers Court Bron mostly wore his school uniform as there was nothing else on offer. He was given an air-gun and a chemistry set for making bombs – in those days you could order the ingredients for nitroglycerine from an inexpensive shop in London. He walked around the house with a binder-twine belt, like his mother's, tied over his school blazer with several dead sparrows dangling from it. These, added to the mixed and spilled contents of his chemistry set, combined into a pungent whiff that radiated outwards from him – far more deadly than his Uncle Auberon's *Aqua di Selva*.

Evelyn deplored his children's scruffiness but was too lazy to do anything about it himself and unable to galvanise his wife into action. When he noticed a bowl of rotting fruit on the kitchen table he said to Laura: 'If that bowl is not removed by tomorrow luncheon I shall throw the contents at you.' The next day the fruit was still there. Laura stood erect, fuming but rigidly accepting her punishment, as Evelyn, in front of two of his children, launched one after another of the rotten fruit at her, until the whole of her upper torso was splattered and drenched in over-ripe flesh, pips and skins.

Of all his children, Evelyn was particularly hard on Bron. He recognised that the boy had spirit, but worried that he was doomed to waste from an early age. He expected too much of him too early, without having the patience or gentle nurture to help him along. 'I find my children particularly charmless,' he wrote in 1947. 'I am attempting to give Bron some extra lessons. He is lazy but not very stupid.'

Although Evelyn was a younger son, the ownership of Piers Court inspired him with an old-fashioned passion for primogeniture. There was a triangular pediment on the front elevation, which he had decorated with a plaster escutcheon of the Waugh coat of arms, and in 1941, when he was stationed in Cairo with the Royal Marines, he made a will leaving the house to Bron. Piers Court should have belonged to Laura since it was due to the £4000 wedding present from her grandmother that they were able to afford it, but Evelyn had paid for it in advance with his own money and was, therefore, able to dispose of it as he saw fit. His 1941 will stipulated: 'I devise all my freehold estate unto my trustees upon trust for my son Auberon Alexander Waugh as and when he shall attain the age of twenty-one.' Laura was unhappy with the will and wrote to tell him so. Evelyn replied: 'The will you criticise was made under legal advice and is perfect. Piers Court is not entailed and on Bron's dying intestate after me goes to his next of kin, yourself. If Auberon dies before me and I do not make a new will, the bequest to him is void and Piers Court goes to you.' But this did not answer Laura's gravest objection: that if Bron inherited Piers and died leaving it whimsically to a third party, she would be homeless. Eventually the will was superseded by a fairer division, but for the time being Bron was officially 'son and heir'. It is odd that Evelyn, who had so strongly objected to his father's banner welcoming home 'the heir to Underhill' should have devised a will based on the inequalities of primogeniture. My father often used to call me 'my son and heir', though he impressed on me from the start that this was a term of endearment not a title conferring advantage over my siblings in the posthumous division of spoils or any sort of meal ticket.

As 'son and heir', Bron was taken by his father on holiday to the South of France, for weekends with friends and on trips to London. His wine glass was filled higher than those of his siblings, and at

Piers Court he was the only child to be allowed a room at the front of the house, next to his parents. The rest were billeted in the servants' and nursery quarters at the back. But Bron's special status was not in all ways to his advantage. More was expected of him than of his brothers and sisters, and Evelyn was particularly unforgiving of his weaknesses. Vera tried her best to stand between the dragon and his wrath; so, too, did Laura, often pretending it was she who had broken a plate or lost a book to shield her children from their father's rages. If Bron entered the room with his hair improperly brushed, Evelyn shouted, *'Out!'* He would ask him without warning impossible questions about Pythagoras, the history of the Romans, Catholic doctrine, or the works of Shakespeare, and when his boy failed to supply the correct answers dragged him into the library for summary instruction. Bron always left the room in tears. On the way to Sunday mass Evelyn would ask him:

'Pray, what do you propose to celebrate this Sunday, Bron?'

'Today, Papa, is the third Sunday before Lent.'

'Good boy, and what do you call the third Sunday before Lent?'

'What do you call what?'

'I am not asking what *I* call anything. I am asking *you* what *you* call the third Sunday before Lent.'

'Septuagesima, Papa, I call it Septuagesima.'

If he failed to answer correctly, a stark, sour coldness would descend from his father's body and seep like a nasty vapour towards him. To spare Bron these humiliations Vera instructed him before mass every Sunday: 'When Mr Waugh asks you what Sunday it is you must tell him it is St Andrew's Day . . .'

Bron held Vera in special affection, as she seemed to fill the gap between his father's hostility and his mother's detachment.[2] After the war, when Evelyn's star had risen in the United States following the success of *Brideshead Revisited*, both he and Laura were often away from home. Vera took on the role of replacement mother.

---

[2] Evelyn was also very fond of Vera. He took her to the cinema to see *The Third Man* with Graham Greene; took her father on a boat trip up the Severn River and gave her a signed photograph of the family inscribed: 'For Vera with love from many old friends including Evelyn Waugh.'

She wrote with news of the children to Laura, who responded with stories of her travels, and asked after her cows rather than her children. Bron's close bond with Vera continued even after he went away to school. A letter he sent to her when he was thirteen in his first year at Downside survives. She was engaged to be married to Terry Grother:

> Darling Vera,
>
> Just a line to wish you a very happy birthday and to tell you how my heart and soul have been pining for your divine company . . .
>   Papa wrote me a letter of 3 pages – 20 words of which I could read and that's all . . . Could you, for I'm sure Mummy forgot to tell you – send off the scout uniform of mine . . .
>
> PS: Don't show this letter to Terry or he will use it in the divorce proceedings after you are married, as a love letter.

Alec's elder son Andrew had been taught no Latin in Australia so he couldn't pass his entrance examinations to Eton and Winchester. Instead he was sent to Alec and Joan's measly third choice school – Sherborne. Alec did not take anything like as keen an involvement in Andrew's Sherborne career as Arthur had taken in his. A few visits, a few letters, but he was not especially interested. Joan derided Sherborne to her sons as a dim, lower-class establishment. She had received a proposal of marriage from a viscount shortly after accepting Alec and tended, in consequence, to look down upon the Waughs. Alec, on the other hand, believed he had done Joan a favour in marrying her.

He was disappointed also by the physical and mental shape of his children after their long sojourn in Australia. None of them knew any Latin. Peter, who was seven, could not even spell Waugh. At least Andrew should be good at cricket. In the summer holidays Alec enrolled his elder son for coaching at Lords, but was 'shocked' to discover that Australia had taught him nothing of the game. 'He had no idea of the technique of the left shoulder; he swung across the ball.'

Alec did not follow his sons' school sports with any great interest, or read to his children as Arthur had, or attempt at any stage to inspire them with a love of literature and poetry. When he saw Andrew wearing the familiar school uniform for the first time he felt 'a quirk of responsibility for him'. But the quirk did not amount to much and nor did it grow into anything more substantial. As a father, Alec was notable by his absence. When a concerned friend once asked him, 'But how will your children ever get to know you if you are always away from home?' he answered, 'They can read my books.' But he made no effort to ensure that they had copies of them. (Most, except *The Loom of Youth*, were out of print within fifteen months of publication.) The separate parts of his life were still contained, as they always had been, within 'watertight compartments'. In his autobiography Alec was frank about his sloppy fathering:

> My conventional civic duty was clearly to devote my ener-
> gies to my family, to reforging links with them, to planning
> for their future, to making amends for the six years' separa-
> tion. That was my civic duty. Yes, I know, I know. I had been
> six years away from my family, but I had also been six years
> away from my desk. I put the claims of my writing first. Time
> was running out. I had to make the most of the time still left.

Sad. Most fathers do not see their paternal responsibility as a 'civic duty' but Alec was an unusual man. He insisted on a stark choice between work and family, but never suggested that the same choice might apply between work and his mistresses, work and cricket, work and golf, work and his various gentlemen's clubs. All other things could be fitted in; it was only his family who couldn't. Nor was he being truthful in asserting that he had deserted his desk for six years. In that time he had produced two novels, a military memoir and several short stories. Evelyn was highly critical of *His Second War* and accused Alec of writing with 'an air of affectation' – 'All your slang is unfamiliar and uncongenial to me . . . If you must write in the first person give the chap a name. Sentences beginning "Himself" where "Alec" or "I" are needed, depressed me.'

Alec wrote to his mother: 'I have just received from Evelyn a typical letter about *His Second War*. He seemed to think the book quite good. His tone was of course very patronising. I think he thinks he is being funny.' Alec was well aware, and had been for fifteen years, that while his brother's literary star twinkled high in the night sky his own flickered dimly low in the twilight haze but, to his eternal credit, he never expressed a squeak of jealousy.

After Arthur's death Alec continued to search for his father and sensed that Arthur was trying to get through to him 'from the other side':

My father used to burn a powder called Himrod's Asthma Cure. It had a very peculiar and pungent smell. One morning soon after my return from the Middle East, I walked into what had been his bedroom and my nostrils were assailed by the familiar smell. I mentioned it to my mother. 'It is extraordinary,' I said, 'how the smell of Himrod lingers. It was very strong this morning.' 'But that's impossible,' she said. 'He never burnt Himrod after we moved into this flat. Besides I've had the room repainted.'

My father's hatred of discipline in all its guises magnified itself at All Hallows prep school, a draughty converted Victorian mansion, not far from Midsomer Norton, in east Somerset. Evelyn had painted a rosy picture of the English boarding-school system, and the poor ginger-haired, freckle-faced fellow had swallowed it, hook, line and sinker. Bron set off on his first day with the broad smile and swinging gait of someone expecting a treat. He arrived at the imposing gates of All Hallows 'a midget in new school outfit', holding his father's hand, on 28 January 1946. He was the smallest and the youngest boy in the school. In his diary Evelyn wrote of the headmaster and his wife: 'Dix had little presence. Mrs Dix seemed trustworthy.' As far as Bron was concerned Francis Dix – the white-haired, white-moustachioed, flagellant, voyeur, paedophile headmaster – had far too great a presence in his life over the next six years. For though Dix might have cowered and winced in the glaring presence of Evelyn Waugh he was a ferocious monster with his boys.

Bron was proud that his father struck terror into the heart of Dix, even though later in life he recognised that his father's awesome personality was the cause of much of his apparent unhappiness:

> My father was a small man, scarcely five foot in his socks, and only a writer after all, but I have seen generals and chancellors of the exchequer, six foot six and exuding self-importance from every pore, quail in front of him. When he laughed, everyone laughed, when he was downcast, everyone tiptoed around trying to make as little noise as possible. It was not wealth or power which created this effect, merely the force of his personality. I do not see how he can have been pleased by the effect he produced on other people. In fact he spent his life seeking out men and women who were not frightened of him. Even then, he usually ended up getting drunk with them, as a way out of the abominable problem of human relations.

During term-time Evelyn put in occasional appearances at All Hallows. He agreed one year to present the school prizes but embarrassed Bron by wearing a flashy bowler hat and following with exaggerated, theatrical attention Dix's every movement as he performed a set of conjuring tricks. Evelyn must have remembered how embarrassed he had been at Arthur's 'incorrigibly theatrical' Dickens readings in his childhood yet he, too, was an 'incorrigibly theatrical' father to his children. Curiously, as the years rolled by, he became more and more like his father. Bron, on the other hand, moved in the opposite direction, and became less and less like Evelyn as he grew older.

In the 1930s Evelyn was a figurehead of the younger generation. He stood for all that was fast, brash, witty and loud, but after the war he transformed himself into an old-fashioned clown not unlike his father. He wore outmoded and outlandish suits and hats, insisted on changing for dinner, surrounded himself with Victorian furniture and bric-à-brac and, like his father, appeared to the world as an arcane eccentric from a Victorian novel. He affected to despise modern gadgetry, especially the telephone and wireless, yet he loved the sit-on lawn mower at Piers Court (until he crashed it into a thicket) and was overjoyed in 1961 with his purchase of a washing-up machine, expressing his great satisfaction with it in a letter to his daughter Teresa:

> Since you emigrated you have become part owner of two Holman Hunts but an acquisition which excites more pleasure and interest is an engine for washing plates. Since our last servants left, washing-up became a great bore so I invested in a white expensive object which instantly blew up filling the pantry with steam and shards. Yesterday a mechanic came out and restored it since when it has become an object of worship like a tractor in an early Bolshevist film.

Evelyn wrote of Arthur, in *A Little Learning*, that 'his melancholies were brief and quickly relieved'. In this respect he was unlike his father. He suffered from deep, intractable depressions all his life. Boredom was his greatest enemy and it haunted him throughout his days. Fear of it and cravings for shock or excitement are classic symptoms of a depressive disorder. Evelyn, as I say, was a brave man but the stark horrors of boredom terrified him.

21 March 1943
A night disturbed by a sort of nightmare that is becoming more frequent with me and I am inclined to believe is peculiar to myself. Dreams of unendurable boredom – of reading page after page of dullness, of being told endless, pointless jokes, of sitting through cinema films devoid of interest.

Even his foreign travels failed to stimulate him. In *Remote People*, an African travel book written in 1931, he described himself as 'desperately and degradingly bored', as 'a martyr to boredom'. During four days in Abyssinia he experienced boredom 'as black and timeless as Damnation; a handful of ashes thrown into the eyes, a blanket over the face, a mass of soft clay, knee deep':

> No one can have any conception of what boredom really means until he has been to the tropics. The boredom of civilized life is trivial and terminable, a puny thing to be strangled between finger and thumb. The blackest things in European social life – rich women talking about their poverty, poor women talking about their wealth, weekend parties of Cambridge aesthetes or lectures from the London School of Economics, rival Byzantinists at variance, actresses off the stage, psychologists explaining one's own books to one, Americans explaining how much they have drunk lately, house flies at early morning in the South of France, amateur novelists talking about royalties and reviews, amateur journalists, quarrelling lovers, mystical atheists, raconteurs, dogs, people who try to look inscrutable, the very terrors, indeed, which drive one to refuge in the still remote regions of the earth, are mere pansies and pimpernels to the rank flowers which flame grossly in those dark and steaming sanctuaries.

Boredom and irritation characterised Evelyn's attitude to his children during the holidays at Piers Court. 'My two eldest children are here and a great bore,' he wrote, to his friend Nancy Mitford. 'The boy lives for pleasure and is thought a great wit by his contemporaries. I have tried him drunk and I have tried him sober . . .' When he tried Teresa drunk she had a terrible hangover the next day and so did he, and her dry, grating voice annoyed him all the more. Evelyn encouraged his children to drink from an early age, insisting it was beneficial for them to do so: full glasses of wine for the eldest, half-glasses for the next and so on down to a liberal thimbleful mixed with water for little Septimus.

'Children all home. Teresa's voice odious, Bron lazy, Margaret stupid but charming, Harriet mad.' He did his best to entertain them but he was never strong enough to keep up the effort for long – he put too much in and felt he got too little out – so that by the end of each school holiday no one was happier than he to see them return to school. 'At last the holidays have come to an end,' he wrote in 1948. 'In my most miserable school days I did not welcome the end of term more gladly.' As the holidays dragged on, he found his disgust with his family grew past bearing and took refuge in the library, banning children from the front of the house, or stole away to London for refreshment. In his absences from Piers Court the children played happily, noisily and freely around the house; but even then no one dared enter the library. In 1954 Evelyn wrote to Nancy Mitford:

> My news are the great news that all my children have at last disappeared to their various places of education. My unhealthy affection for my second daughter has waned. I now dislike them all equally. Of children as of procreation – the pleasure is momentary, the posture ridiculous, the expense damnable.

Evelyn's disillusionment with his second daughter, Meg, was short-lived. Like Arthur, his grandfather and his great-grandfather before him, Evelyn elected one of his children as the favourite. From the age of nine Meg was the chosen one, carried around, hither and thither, like a lucky mascot or sausage dog puppy. She accompanied him on trips to Italy, Greece and South America, and for weekends in the country, to London and out to the cinema. His relationship with her was exclusive and, as she grew older, bordered on the incestuous. It is a miracle that none of his other five surviving children seems to have minded a jot. When Nancy Mitford wrote to Evelyn, 'I hear your daughter Teresa is beautiful and fascinating, how lucky for you', he replied, 'My daughter Teresa is squat, pasty-faced, slatternly with a most disagreeable voice – but it is true that she talks quite brightly. She has cost me the best part of £1500 in the last year and afforded no corresponding pleasure. Margaret remains the star of my existence.'

On the last day of the holidays Evelyn allowed the children to choose a dinner menu – when Teresa asked for Brussels sprouts, he was furious. The table was laid with the finest silver and after dinner everyone was encouraged to make speeches. Evelyn rose to his feet, in white tie and tails, with long lines of shining medals pinned to his bosom, and expressed, in the simplest and most eloquent terms, his unbounded relief at the impending departure of his flock. But the children detested their boarding-schools and their father's speeches wounded them grievously. As Bron later wrote:

> The most terrifying aspect of Evelyn Waugh as a parent was that he reserved the right not just to deny affection to his children but to advertise an acute and unqualified dislike for them. This was always conditional on their own behaviour up to a point, and seldom entirely unjustified, but it was disconcerting, nonetheless, to be met by cool statements of total repudiation.

The occasional flashes of warmth, humour, generosity and kindness for which Evelyn was beloved by a large circle of close friends were not then so obvious to Bron. He was terrified of his father and took pains to avoid his company, as Evelyn took similar pains to avoid Bron's. He told me he was grateful for Evelyn's obsessive devotion to Meg as it deflected his father's gaze from himself. Out of Evelyn's sight Bron was permitted to do almost anything he wanted. The grounds at Piers Court, though not on the scale of Pixton, were extensive. He had a room at the back of the house for chemical experiments, smoking, secret drinking, shooting out of the window and listening to loud music on his gramophone. Holidays at Piers Court, especially when his father was away, were invariably happy.

XI

Fantasia

Evelyn, thanks to his good, solid Protestant upbringing, detested Bron's inability to tell the truth. Most children lie to get themselves out of trouble or to secure themselves a third helping of pudding or some other juvenile advantage, and Bron did all these things, but also he lied for the fun of it, for no possible gain other than sheer joy of invention and the pleasance of deceit. I understand and admire this attitude in young children. When my wife was pregnant with our first child, my mother-in-law asked me what sex I hoped the baby would be. 'I don't particularly mind,' I replied, 'so long as it's a liar.' She was shocked, but a child is no good unless it is charged with fantasy and confident enough to foist it upon others.

From his earliest days Bron's lies took fabulous form. He told his grandmother at Pixton that he had seen evacuee children eating rat-poison. He hadn't – but they had spat on him from the second-floor gallery during his Uncle Auberon's ritual floggings and he desired vengeance. In the identification parade that followed he picked out two or three of the meanest-looking, who were promptly whisked off to hospital in Exeter to have their stomachs pumped. The lie was never detected and he got away unpunished but many others were exposed. When he was three and a half his cousins inscribed a slate 'Bronnie is a liar' and appended it, out of reach, to the trunk of a tree. Try as he might, with sticks and with stones, he was unable to dislodge it. In January 1944 Evelyn wrote to Laura:

Your son has had his hair cut in Highgate and looks very neat. My mother thinks him in indifferent health and more ignorant than on his former visit. He appears to be happy with her and expresses his preference for Highgate with greater strength than mere civility requires. His untruthfulness is confirmed; he persists in asserting that he and my Aunt Constance climbed the high iron fence surrounding the cricket field.

During his time at prep school Bron told his father a lie for which he was never fully forgiven. He claimed that a boy called Lavery had taken a ten-shilling note from him with the intention of throwing it away because it lacked a metallic line through the middle. According to Bron, Lavery did this to *prove* that ten-shilling notes without metallic strips were valueless. Evelyn asked Bron if he had actually seen Lavery throw the note away. No, he hadn't. At this Evelyn wrote a stern letter to Lavery's father accusing his boy of theft and instructing Bron to write a similar rebuke to Lavery, demanding his ten shillings back. Both Lavery and his father denied the charge, so Evelyn, determined to resolve the matter with a letter to the headmaster, asked Bron: 'Are you absolutely sure, before I write this letter, that you are telling the truth?' At which point Bron crumbled and told his father that it was all a pack of lies.

In his book my father suggests that the whole story was a fantasy that ran out of control, that he had no intention of accusing Lavery of stealing the money, only of engaging his father in an interesting conversation about metallic strips and proving his point about their value. He was highly acquisitive at this time and obsessed by money. He might have accused Lavery of the crime in the hope of getting Evelyn to redeem the loss – if so, it was a cunning schoolboy ruse that backfired. I wonder, even, if it is true that Bron, as he claimed in *Will This Do?*, confessed the lie to his father, or whether Evelyn found out by other means. His diary entry is ambiguous: 'I fasted and gave up wine during Holy Week and attended a number of religious services. I made the disconcerting discovery that Bron's tale of Lavery's theft was pure invention.'

Whatever the truth, one thing is certain; that Evelyn trusted Bron little thereafter. He was no fool. He could see that his son was a crafty, devious and slightly delinquent boy of a type who would have fared well in Fagin's army of Victorian pickpockets. Bron made cunning swaps with his brothers and sisters for any of their possessions that he coveted. When a great-aunt died and her property was distributed equally among the children, he bartered with his siblings until he had collared the lot and they had nothing. Throughout his life he honed his skills as a master barterer and was brilliant at it. He could have cleaned out every stall in Marrakesh for a couple of dirhams, if he had put his mind to it. I remember a beaming smile as he left a shop with an ornament having paid thirty-five per cent of its asking price. 'How did you get it so cheaply?' I asked him.

'I told the fellow I didn't need it, didn't like it and didn't want it,' he replied.

He took me once to the flat of a painter of pornographic capriccios in Florence. The artist – who was English – greeted us at the door. 'I am in a great hurry,' Papa said, 'as I have left my family starving in a restaurant without any money.' The artist, who was ingratiating, showed us round his studio with pride. Fourteen or fifteen diligently executed oils of people exciting one another in the nude were arranged along one wall. Papa looked pleased with them all and his enthusiasm was spotted at once by the artist.

'So, how much are they?'

'The small ones are a thousand pounds each and the large ones three thousand five hundred.'

Without a flicker of hesitation Papa said, 'I'll take that one, that one, the small one over there and . . . perhaps, yes, I shall have the one with the lady in the mask as well.'

'All four?' cried the artist, barely able to conceal his glee.

'All four,' said Papa. 'For three hundred and fifty pounds.'

The painter was visibly shocked. 'All right,' he demurred, in a whisper, between his teeth.

Papa produced the cash from his wallet and we left, smirking, with the paintings under our arms.

* * *

In the spring of 1949 Alec decided to apply for American citizenship; it meant that he would no longer be able to spend any more than ninety-two days a year in England. In reality he stayed at home for considerably less than this allowance permitted and the time spent with his children had long since been whittled down to only a few weeks at Edrington each year. When not in America he visited the Caribbean, the Seychelles, or spent his months writing novels at the Hôtel Escurial in Nice or the Hôtel Velasquez in Tangier. His children looked upon his visits to Edrington as they might the arrival of a favoured god-parent or a grandfather. He was friendly and polite with them, he did not argue with their mother and seldom disciplined them. Once he picked Peter up and hurled him out of a window, but that was an aberration and he felt guilty about it for the rest of his life. He was neither lavish with gifts nor prodigal with praise but he left them in no doubt that, had he bothered to spend more time at home, he would have been a fine father.

In America Alec lived out of suitcases in hotels. He had no home of his own there, but the nomadic life suited him well. All that he needed to complete his bid for freedom was a divorce from Joan. The idea was first mooted on his return from Baghdad after the war. News of his intentions reached his ageing mother in the spring of 1946. She wrote to her son, begging him to reconsider:

Darling Alec,

Please don't think me interfering — and truly your well-being and happiness is [sic] all I care about — but is this disturbing step your only way of finding it? Up till yesterday I thought it was entirely Joan's desire and that she wished to marry someone else, but yesterday she was in tears at breakfast time — I don't know what letter had disturbed her — and later she spoke of this divorce and said it was entirely your wish; that she wouldn't go through with it but for you; that she was used to living a lonely life and could make her own life. I know you cannot happily lead a domestic life with her all the time, your tastes are so dissimilar and she would not expect you to. Now have you

considered this grave step from every point of view? Family
life is a very precious and interesting thing. Have you
considered what it means living outside the pale of all its
goings on, its gatherings and celebrations, birthdays and
Christmases? To be an outsider of all this? You have a very
charming family and you cast away much. Each year as
they grow up brings them into closer companionship with
you: and are you doing them a wrong not sharing their
homelife and bringing matrimony into contempt?

Darling Alec, forgive me for writing to you like this;
and I will stick to you and defend you whatever aunts and
friends may say. And of course it will be a great blow for
the Norton aunts, for I do not know what the feeling of
the church is for the 'guilty' party. Then, in time of sickness I cannot bear to think you would have no home to
go to. As long as you have me I love to think you would
come to me – but sometimes I think I grow old.

I know this is a rotten letter so tear it up and forget
about it, but believe that I love you dearly and only wish
for your happiness and that you should do what is right;
and always I love you, and am always your loving

Mother

As soon as Alec's American citizenship had been granted, he arranged
a secret divorce in Reno. Desperate that his mother should not
discover his plan he employed the best under-cover techniques he
had learned during his time in Baghdad to ensure that the press
would not get hold of the story. In his petition he claimed that Joan
was guilty of 'mental cruelty' for refusing to allow him to keep a
dog at Edrington.[1] After two months' residence in Carson City,
pretending to friends and family that he was writing a book, Alec
succeeded in procuring the necessary papers. Evelyn was not told
and did not discover that his brother was *die-vorced* (as he pronounced
it) until 1962.

[1] There were, in fact, two dogs at Edrington, both loved by Joan.

K never did discover the truth. Nor were Alec's children informed. Peter only found out when he was eighteen during an altercation with Joan: 'You should know – you're married to him after all,' he said.

'Well, no, I'm not, actually. You see, your father and I were divorced many years ago.'

K, who was not, as can be seen from her letters, an especially literary person, lived on at Highgate in her dotage superintended by her housekeeper, Mrs Yaxley. When Evelyn sent her copies of his books she was more interested in their covers than their contents but, with the friction between her husband and son now ended by Arthur's death, she began to enjoy her status as mother to such an important writer. In 1950 when Evelyn sent her a copy of his novel *Helena*, she wrote to him: 'It is terribly sweet of you giving me one of your beautiful copies of *Helena*: I am most grateful and appreciative. It is a joy to handle such a perfect piece of book making: the luxurious paper – wide margins – clear type all delightful in which to read the work of my genius of a son.'

In later years Evelyn found visits to her flat irksome. He was bored by her company, then filled with self-loathing at his inability to attend to her more charitably. 'Damn, damn, damn! Why does everyone except me, find it so easy to be nice?'

K wrote to him on his fiftieth birthday in October 1953:

Many happy returns for your birthday. Fifty years, half a century, what a lot of years that seems! And what a lot you have accomplished in that time! I do thank you for all you have brought to my life – all the happy memories and all those sweet early years. I know I have failed you often, but I have loved you always, and my mind glows with thoughts of you, and pride in your distinguished achievements.

Arthur had left her everything he had except his books, but it was not enough to live on. Evelyn set up a generous trust for her remaining years, to which Alec (much to his brother's irritation) was unable to contribute. Alec persuaded K to make Evelyn her sole heir, instructing her solicitors to draft a will that would leave him nothing. At first K was horrified at his suggestion: 'Your father would turn in his grave at the "heir of Underhill" being disinherited,' she said. But Alec was adamant. 'I am abroad for nine months of the year,' he told her, 'and am not able to accept the responsibilities proper to the head of the family. Evelyn is in a position to accept and should be rewarded.'

Bron and the other grandchildren visited K regularly in London and she came occasionally to see them at Piers Court, but in her last years she was too feeble to endure much movement. Evelyn invited her, reluctantly, to live with him at 'Stinkers' but she declined, struggling on for another year at Highgate until, in early December 1954, aged eighty-four, she died in her chair with a cup of cold tea in her hand. On 7 December Evelyn wrote to Bron at Downside:

My dear Bron,

Granny Waugh died yesterday, very peacefully. Mrs Yaxley came into the drawing room and found her dead in her chair after tea. It is how she hoped to die. For the last two years, as you know, she has been very weak. Please pray for her. I wish you had known her when she was young and active. That is how I like to remember her.

The funeral is at Highgate on Thursday afternoon. I do not think it is feasible for you to go to it. Teresa will be coming from Ascot — not the other children. If however you very much wish to come, I shall not forbid it. We shall be at Hampstead Lane at 12.30. The service is at 2 and you would have to make your own way back immediately afterwards. You must decide for yourself if you wish to come and make your own arrangements.

Ever your affectionate papa
E. Waugh

In his autobiography Papa announced that he had been forbidden to attend his grandmother's funeral as he was in disgrace. As the letter shows, this was not quite correct.

'One's enthusiasms are a solitary affair,' my father would say to me. 'You cannot expect to share them with others.' This particularly applied when I was playing the piano, listening to the gramophone or scraping on my viola in the bathroom. I wonder if it was something that Evelyn had said to him. Perhaps not: it never occurred to Evelyn that his enthusiasm for the Roman Catholic faith should not be shared or, rather, inculcated into his children. As the years went by Evelyn's Catholicism deepened. From *Brideshead Revisited* onwards all his novels contained a Catholic theme. He went regularly on retreat to monasteries to pray, hired only Catholic nannies for his children and reduced his non-catholic circle of friends to a handful. He might have expected his beliefs to prove as valuable to his children in later life as they were to himself, but history should have taught him that the zeal of the convert is seldom passed down on the hereditary principle.

By 1950 he and Laura had six surviving children: Teresa, Bron, Meg (sometimes Pig or Hog to her father), Harriet (or Hatty), James and Septimus. They were all sent to Catholic schools, encouraged and tested by their father in their devotions and given (more than any other type of present) religious books and religious artifacts. When Meg wrote to Evelyn from her boarding-school at Easter to tell him that all the other girls' parents had sent Easter eggs, could she have one too, he wrote back: 'I won't send you an Easter egg. You must nibble bits of the other girls'. Perhaps as a reward for your great unselfishness I will send you a little book of devotion instead.'

When Bron was fourteen he made a will. Evelyn was appointed executor, Vera Gilroy (Nanny) and Norman Attwood (Farm Hand) were witnesses to his signature. Listed among his possessions at that time were:

A blue china statue of Jesus, a rosary from Jerusalem fashioned in dried olives, a jewelled cross from Portofino, a mother-of-pearl cross from Jerusalem, a Pope-blessed rosary from Rome, the Midsomer Norton family Bible, a Roman Missal and a *Missale Romanum* (separately itemised), a bronze medal of St Gudule Church, a bronze medal of St Peter's Basilica in Rome and a mother-of-pearl Jerusalem picture of the nativity.

Having divided his belongings more or less equally among his siblings Bron left to his father: 'As the executor of my will Mr Evelyn Waugh (novelist) should legally be granted nothing, but may take, a discreet time after my death having elapsed, £100, or whatever remains of it after my burial and any possession of mine unbequeathed to another.'

From All Hallows Bron was sent, aged twelve, with a scholarship to the Benedictine monastery school of Downside in Somerset where his great-grandfather, the Brute, had been the school doctor. On hearing of his scholarship Evelyn sent a telegram: 'ADMIRABLE BOY . . . PAPA.'

For a while at Downside, Bron behaved well, but a thick streak of anarchy was never far from the surface. Gossip lit up Evelyn's day, and Bron was aware that the best way to his father's heart was to entertain him with letters of scandal or high adventure from school. Bron's writing style shows surprising confidence for a fourteen-year-old:

Dear Papa,

Many happy returns of the day – I am sorry that I have no present for you, but I send my love instead.

Yesterday was Field Day with its usual purgatory. There was a howling gale and, as a brilliant new idea, we were loaded with 50lbs weight of equipment precariously strapped on with rotted webbing. We were given ten blank rounds each, but as we did not see any enemy all day, we were ordered to shoot them off at a bit of heather which was said to look like a disguised enemy scout. Major Page, our illustrious commander, was wildly excited, blasting off red, green and yellow lights at the rate of seven a minute. We have an enormously keen Company Commander who crawled 600 yards on his stomach to whisper to someone that he should rub mud on his face . . .

All my love and many happy returns
Bron

When there was nothing to report Bron enjoyed hinting darkly:

No news here. We dug up a cow's tooth. There is rather a mad monk who wants to see you when you come down – he is called Dom Meinrad and spends his time making bombs in a little shack a good way away from the abbey. There are wild rumours about him, all scandalous and unmentionable.

All my love
Bron

Evelyn's letters to Bron were usually warm and chatty, with only the odd sentence of reproach:

Dear Bron,

Pray accept my congratulations of your attainment of 15 years. May your sixteenth year start prudently. Give up this nonsense of beer drinking and smoking with local poachers. Eat heavily. Wash down crumpets and cakes with refreshing cups of tea. Keep good company.

I was sorry not to be able to meet you on Saturday. I gather that you are not keen to go to the mountains this year. Perhaps next year you will be able to make up a party of friends.

Juliet Smith, who I think was with you on Lord Camrose's yacht, came to luncheon here on Sunday. She spoke only of the intestines of the smaller mammals.

You will be sorry to hear that I am in pain from rheumatism of the right knee.

Perhaps you would like to open a correspondence with this black boy (or perhaps girl?)?

I have at last finished the book I was writing.

Here is a pound — not for tobacco or beer.

Your affec. papa
E. Waugh

At Downside religious discipline was exacting. On Sundays each boy was required to spend two and half hours praying in the chapel. Devotions started at seven thirty in the morning with low mass, and continued through the day with compline, high mass, a long sermon called sodality, vespers and benediction in the evening. The boredom was excruciating. When Bron tried to set up an alternative religious entertainment in the form of satanic black mass meetings in the chemistry lab, he was discovered and caned. The monks enjoyed whipping boys as a release from the constraints of their celibacy and my father, throughout his life, always claimed that to be beaten was a small sacrifice for a boy and a great treat for a monk. Both he and I earned the record in our schools for the most beatings in a single term but I have not inherited his gift for forgiveness.

At Downside boys were expected to bend over with bare bottoms. Francis Dix at All Hallows used to order them out of his classroom to his study where they were instructed to await his arrival with their trousers down, prostrate over his desk. As he often forgot to return to his study after class, boys were left stranded in that position for hours, not daring to move. At my school we wore trousers for our beatings and, after careful experimentation, I discovered that the whippee could put on up to sixteen pairs of rugby shorts under his trousers before they bulged enough to be detected by the whipper. Only one master regularly disobeyed the rule about trousers and beat my bare bottom with the palm of his hand. It did not hurt as much as a cane – and far less than a gym shoe – but it was more humiliating than either. After his spankings he used to hug me tightly, his forehead pressed against mine and the rest of me enveloped by his large tummy and fat, red, flaky face.

'You know why I did that, don't you, Alex?'

'Um, 'cos I was bad, sir?'

'But specifically. Why did I do it, Alex?'

'Er, because I threw a billiard ball at Henderson, sir?'

'No. I did it because I love you. Now, come here. Come closer. You understand. It is because I love you and wherever you are in the world at any time, if you are in any sort of trouble, you must call me. Yes? Promise?'

'Promise, sir.'

'All right. You may go.'

In my experience, corporal punishment was of no benefit. When people are treated like animals they descend to the bestial mean.

Within a few terms of his arrival at Downside Bron's attitude to rules, discipline and authority had deteriorated. He took his gun to school and hid it in rented rooms in the village that he was using as headquarters for his newly founded Downside Numismatic Society. His interest in coins was not affected, but it was partial: the society's chief concerns were smoking, drinking, shooting and gambling with cards. Bron invoked the law of trespass on all prefects who threatened to disturb their meetings. When he discovered an air-pistol on the headmaster's desk that had been confiscated from another pupil, he removed it and shot a boy called Gregory in the leg; when asked for an explanation, he stated that he had intended only to stir up the gravel beside Gregory's feet.

Evelyn had warned the monks at Downside that his son had a 'defective sense of honour' and asked them to report regularly on his progress. In the holidays he tried to monitor Bron's behaviour more closely. In reply to a weekend invitation from Randolph Churchill in 1953, Evelyn wrote:

Laura, who, alas, will be busy with farm and children all summer, sends her love and regretfully declines your kind invitation. The boy Auberon Alexander is available for little Winston's entertainment. His chief interest is shooting sitting birds with an airgun and making awful smells with chemicals. He is devoid of culture but cheerful and greedy for highly peppered foods. If not closely watched he smokes and drinks. Shall I bring him for the first weekend of August?

After Bron's first year at Downside the monks were far from pleased with his progress. They enjoyed writing to Evelyn and receiving his witty replies. Bron, they said, was spiritually idle, his attitude to religion was cynical, he appeared to enjoy breaking school rules, he did things 'just to annoy' the teachers and went about the school with a superior air. Evelyn wrote to Bron from Jamaica where he was staying with his friends the Brownlows:

Dear Bron,

I was sorry not to see you before your return to Downside. Had I done so I would have offered you sage advice. I got the impression that last term you were going a bit far in your defiance of school rules. I should hate you to be low spirited and submissive, but don't become an anarchist. Don't above all things put on side. It is an excellent thing to see through the side of others – particularly of youths who think they are young Gods because they are good at games. But they at least are good at something. There is no superiority in shirking things and doing things badly. Be superior by cultivating your intellect and your taste. Enough of this, but pay attention to it . . .

I wish your mother were here with me. She would not like the bats which fly about the verandahs in the evening in hundreds. I left her cold and sad. I hope she is now at Pixton recuperating.

Lord Brownlow's son has just failed to get a commission in the Grenadiers – a sad warning to boys who give themselves airs. Take heed.

Tiny humming birds are hovering round the flowering trees. It is really most agreeable here.

Your affec. papa
E. Waugh

Despite Evelyn's counsel, Bron's behaviour worsened in the months that followed. Evelyn threatened to pack him off to the colonies — a one-way ticket to Australia — if he did not pull himself together, but two months later he received a flood of letters from the headmaster complaining that Bron was more unmanageable than ever.

Passmore, as the headmaster was called, had an evil countenance. He filed his teeth and was unable to eat without half-masticated lumps of food slipping between the gaps and staining his habit. He was phenomenally fat. He loathed Bron, and having beaten him to within an inch of his life for smoking, drinking, insolence and general insubordination, he was presented with a petition signed by the boys for his removal as headmaster. It was all Bron's idea. 'We the undersigned members of Downside School, would respectfully beg of the Rt Rev. Father Abbot to consider their plea for a new headmaster.' Bron signed first and fetched forty other signatories, some of whom lost their bottle and scribbled out their names when Passmore vowed to whip every boy on the list. When he addressed the school next morning at assembly Bron made mocking gestures, huffed, puffed and rolled his eyes to the heavens. In noisy asides (sometimes louder than the speech itself), he appealed to fellow pupils at every passing platitude. For this he was beaten again, and again, and again, but Bron accepted his floggings with insouciance and a proud curl of the lip. As one of his persecutors later wrote to remind him: 'You ruled your little empire of friends with ruthless efficiency and gave every impression of complacent triumph over the ineffectiveness of authority.'

Between Passmore and Evelyn it was agreed that Bron had fallen into bad company and that the best thing for him would be to change house in the winter term of 1955 and so he was moved from Roberts, under the housemastership of Dom Hilary Steuert, to Caverel, presided over by an unctuous, hairy Welshman called Dom Aelred Watkin.

Father Aelred was infatuated with Evelyn and consequently delighted to have Bron in his house so that he could bombard the famous novelist with a hundredweight of letters every day. Before informing Bron of his fate, Evelyn wrote to Father Aelred on a done deal:

Dear Fr Aelred,

Ever since the Headmaster told me that you had kindly consented to take Bron into your house, I have been on the point of writing to thank you. It is an act of charity.

He is not at all a vicious boy or ill-mannered, but I think he is listless, lazy, conceited and not completely truthful. He has no respect or liking for his present house-master. I think that this is the stage in his life when he must be in contact with someone he does respect and like. I am sure you are the man.

Fr Aelred, excited by such flattery, wrote back immediately: 'All I really wanted to say was that of course I shall be only too glad to help you – and Bron – in any way I can . . . I much hope he will always feel himself able to speak freely to me, for then things always go so much more better [sic] . . .'

Evelyn, unfazed by such a blatant exhibition of illiteracy from his son's tutor, sent a curt postcard to Bron: 'Your headmaster has kindly consented to transfer you from Fr Hilary's care to Fr Aelred's. You will find him a man deserving of your full respect and I hope you will make a new start in his house and redeem your past mistakes.'

Bron was appalled that his own father should have connived with the hated monks to remove him from his house and all of his closest friends without any prior consultation with him. In reply he wrote coldly to Evelyn on his new Downside Numismatic Society letterhead:

Dear Papa,

Thank you for your postcard which arrived this morning.

Since you are obviously resolved to effect the transfer I cannot dissuade you. It is unprecedented in the history of the school to change house outside Junior House, let alone approaching the fourth year here. You made the decision ignorant of the constitution or opinion of the school and could not have realised how drastic such a course is. Your esteem for Father Aelred and my indifference towards Father Hilary are hardly sufficient grounds to justify the step; nor will my circle of friends change with my house, or if it does, it will be for the worse; Caverel House under Father Aelred's ministrations is by far the most vicious of all.

However since the decision is made I can do nothing; even if Passmore decided to change his mind, he would hold such a transfer over me as a threat.

Frankly, I would rather the ticket to Australia.
Bron

It was a hopeless case, a battle that Bron could never expect to win. Evelyn's reply was the last word in the matter:

My dear Bron,

Don't write in that silly tone. No one has any motive with regard to you except your own welfare. No decision is absolute yet. If you have a better suggestion to make I shall be pleased to hear it.

I warned you at the beginning of last term that you are heading for trouble. You paid no attention. I need not repeat what I said to you at the end of the holidays. I could not tell you then what I had in mind for your future, as I had left the Headmaster to make his own arrangements in his own time with the house-masters. I fully realise that it is a most unusual kindness of the headmaster's to allow you to change houses. My first idea was to send you to another school. It is possible that Stonyhurst might take you, but I should have to ask them to do so as a favour, and I cannot do this unless you are confident that you intend to behave yourself. If you go there as Psmith and Mike went to Sedleigh, determined to sulk, it would be hopeless.

You have made a mess of things. At your age that is not a disaster, but you must help yourself. Your future, temporal and spiritual, is your own making. I can only provide opportunities for your achievements.

Your affectionate papa
E.W.

Fr Aelred used Bron's turmoil as an excuse to worm himself deep into the fabric at Piers Court. He came to stay, several times, ostensibly to talk about his charge, but mainly to excite his host into helping him with his mother's memoirs of his grandmother[2]. Evelyn did not think they were good enough to publish but continued to revere Fr Aelred and all Catholic clergymen with the same unquestioning gusto as Laura revered her cattle. Fr Aelred got away with much. He wrote often to update Evelyn on Bron's spiritual progress. 'I find it very hard to sum up Bron at the moment. I don't think he is irreligious, though I don't think religion means a great deal to him . . .' His points were often clumsily expressed, but Evelyn, usually a stickler for the finer points of language, seemed not to care. 'To a boy of Bron's cast of mind religion frequently seems something bourgeois; a mere sanction imposed upon the infringement of certain tiresome and unexciting virtues . . . I believe we shall have just to wait and watch and pray.'

Lying. He has lied to me this term (to my knowledge) but when I put it to him he admitted it. I believe in his case that it is fear that causes it – not fear of anything concrete but just fears. He is lacking in real confidence and so likes to appear brighter. I'll just have to work away at him. But it will have to be the work of grace – he has few natural

---

[2] In the guests' bedroom at Piers Court, Fr Aelred would loudly chastise himself for things he had said at dinner. His howls were heard right through the night. At breakfast he was always tired and bruised.

virtues — but supernatural ones, though harder to acquire, are the most worthwhile and the answer to every problem in him is a religious one, as you say, and the building is slow work and transformation almost imperceptible. But I think the beginnings are there.

Bron's end of term reports — all of them — abound with adjectives like 'glib', 'slovenly', 'superficial' and 'slack': 'It surprises me that so intelligent a boy should have such a callow fondness for un-tidiness and casual disregard for normal house discipline. Apart from these defects he is a cheerful and agreeable member of the House.' Before long Bron got the gist of what was going on and altered his attitude so that at least Fr Aelred's reports to his father would read more favourably: 'I feel very happy about Bron this term, he really seems to be taking religion more seriously.' As a further measure to quell Bron's exuberance and make him more religious, Evelyn had asked the razor-toothed headmaster to interview him once a week. Bron had no idea that his father was complicit in this arrange-ment and was working on other fronts to win paternal approval. In the spring of 1955 he wrote a series of short stories on broadly religious themes and sent them, unsolicited, to magazines for publi-cation. One, 'The Twelve Caesars', went to *Everybody's*, *John Bull* and the *Evening Standard*. To *Esquire* and *Colliers Magazine* in New York he sent 'The Cheerful Chivalry,' while *Lilliput* and *Clubman* got 'The Mills of God'. Only *Lilliput* showed any interest and then only because they had noticed that the author was the son of Evelyn Waugh. The editor wrote to Bron to say that he would like to run 'The Mills of God' but was unenthusiastic when Bron replied that he wished the story to appear anonymously:

> To be frank, we think *The Mills of God* is very good but it is not the sort of short story we normally consider publishing. I fully understand your reluctance about using your father's name in any way but I think it would justify the use of a piece which is out of character with us, if we were to mention who had written it. This could be done discreetly and in a way approved by yourself. I don't suggest for a

moment that it should appear as though the story is being published because your father is Evelyn Waugh. Nevertheless I think it adds considerably to the interest of the reader to find the son following in a famous father's footsteps.

We won't discuss payment until you have reconsidered this position. Meanwhile I will retain the story.

Inevitably Bron's desire for cash prevailed over his scruples about the use of the family name. Within days an agreement was struck: 'Thank you for your kind acceptance. I will guarantee that we will be discreet. I suggest we pay you 25 guineas. Perhaps you will let me know if this is acceptable.'

Of course it was. Bron had never had so much money in his pocket before. He wrote to announce the good news:

Darling Mummy and Papa,

The most wonderful thing has happened – I have sold that pathetic short story of mine for a perfectly monstrous sum, with which I hope to do great things. It is true that the magazine which bought it is not the most cultured or edifying in circulation, but Papa has written for it, and it pays 10 guineas for the wettest story imaginable – every time I read it it seems worse. The money has not arrived yet, but the offer has, which I promptly accepted. It's really too good to be true and after the exams I intend to turn out enough short stories to swamp the offices of every magazine in the country. They asked for a photograph of myself and I sent them a wonderful one in Victorian costume. I don't know if they will put it in but if they do it will be too gorgeous.

No news – it has been a very quiet term so far and will probably continue so, as I have to see the Headmaster every week so that he can get to know me. I have the horrible feeling always that I am being psychoanalysed by him, which is all too depressing.

I do wish I had written the story under a pseudonym – it is so futile.

All my love Bron

P.S. I have joined the League of Empire Loyalists which is wonderful fun. I have to circulate pamphlets throughout the school and other schools. I have sent them to 30 people at Ampleforth, 3 at Eton, 1 at Stowe and hundreds of others. It is an Imperialist movement which is always marching around London with banners and loud-speakers in vans. I received 3 letters today from fellow Imperialists, which always give me a thrill.

AW

Observant readers will have noticed that the ten guineas mentioned to his father was less than half the sum that *Lilliput* had actually agreed. On the manuscript letter Bron has violently scrubbed out '25' and replaced it with '10'. I imagine he did this for fear that his father would consider him rich enough to survive without paternal tips and allowances. Apart from this small lie, Bron's letter seems to have hit the spot. Nothing could please Evelyn more than the idea of his eldest son joining the 'family business':

My dear Bron,

I congratulate you with all my heart on your success with your story. You have not named the discerning magazine – *Everybody's* perhaps? Anyway it is an agreeable thing to see one's work recognised. I look forward greatly to seeing the issue. They won't pay you until the end of the month in which it appears. That is the usual practice.

Your hairless uncle Alec has also had a success at last. His latest book has been taken by the American 'Book of the Month', serialised, filmed – in fact the jack-pot. It is very nice for him after so many years of disappointment and obscurity. He has not drawn a sober breath since he heard the news.

Your uncle Auberon's hopes are less rosy,[3] but your mother, grandmother, aunts and pig-walloper[4] have had and are still having a highly enjoyable time in Sunderland. Your mother still believes she has been in Sutherland.

I am glad the headmaster is paying attention to you. His aim I think is to find whether it is better to continue your education or to send you with a changed name and £5 to Australia.

I trust your Empire League is not under the auspices of Sir Oswald Mosley? If it is you will end up in prison like my old friend Diana Mitford.

Think of all lonely schoolboys on Ascension Day in memory of your father in 1916.

Your affec. papa

The League of Empire Loyalists was a mildly ridiculous, pseudo-sinister right-wing organisation that stood for 'the resurgence at home and abroad of the British spirit and the conscientious development of the British Colonial Empire under British direction and local British leadership'. Bron joined, not because he felt strongly about colonialism, but because it excited his passions for secrecy to be attached to an organisation outside the school funded by a shadowy figure known to members only as 'RKJ'. Evelyn regarded Bron's involvement as harmless folly and in July 1955 acceded to his son's request to travel to London to take the secretary of the League to the annual Downside Ball where they hoped to recruit new members to the cause. Bron left home on 25 July with a bottle of his father's gin and caught a bus to Gloucester. At Gloucester station he grandly offered the gin to railway staff on the platform, then boarded the train for London. He didn't make it to the dance. Evelyn's diary records a partial version of events:

[3] Bron's uncle, Auberon had hoped to be elected as the National Liberal MP for Sunderland but failed.
[4] Alick Dru, married to Bron's aunt Gabriel, used to beat his pigs savagely in order to tenderise the meat.

Bron left early by bus for London to stay with a school friend and go to the Downside dance. At 2 o'clock Laura and I took the children to the cinema in Dursley. We were greeted by the manager saying that the Stroud police wished to speak to us. They said that a youth had been arrested incapably drunk carrying Bron's suitcase. From their description it was plain that the prisoner was Bron. We drove to Stroud and found him white and dirty eating a bun. He had a third of a bottle of gin, of the brand I drink, in his possession. We took him home and sent him to his room. Later he said that he missed his bus to Gloucester, spent all his money in the White Hart buying a bottle of gin, drank most of it at Gloucester Station, conceived the idea of travelling to London without a ticket and with 2d in his pocket. When arrested he gave a false name and address and was identified by correspondence in the suit-case. Inquiries at the White Hart in Gloucester elicited the reply that no bottle of gin had been sold that day. We told Teresa and Margaret, leaving the rest of the household, I hope, in ignorance. An evening of ineffable gloom.

In Bron's first novel, *The Foxglove Saga*, written five years later, a boy called Kenneth is discovered by his father drunk on his stolen whisky and, as in the Gloucester incident on which it was based, is sent to bed to await his father's wrath on the morrow.

Kenneth thought how pathetically unsure of himself his father looked standing alone in the drawing-room trying to appear Victorian and strict. It was not as if his father had any sanction he could apply. It was not like school where they could beat you into a jelly, and Kenneth reckoned he was slightly stronger than his father . . .

As he lay in bed he prepared speeches to make to his father in the morning; jewels of sarcasm and wit came into his mind, and every possible point his father could make was antici-pated, and a devastating reply contrived. Eventually a witti-cism so bold and yet so exactly on target came into his head that he switched on his bedside light and wrote it down in

Biro on the back of his hand. Then he switched off the light and composed himself to sleep . . . When he woke up he had a nasty taste in his mouth and his stomach felt slightly queasy. As he washed he found that he had written indelibly on the back of his hand the words *Buggers don't bite*. He couldn't think what it meant although he remembered that it had seemed frightfully important at the time.

Evelyn turned up at the juvenile court in Stroud wearing an ostentatious checked cap. Bron pleaded guilty and was fined ten shillings. When Evelyn was invited to take the stand he doffed his cap to the magistrate and said simply, 'I beg you to regard the incident as a disastrous experiment rather than as a mark of viciousness and depravity.'

For the rest of that long summer holiday as Bron awaited his return to the unknown and unwanted world of Fr Aelred's Caverel House, he was in disgrace with his father. Before long Evelyn became so depressed and irritated by his presence that he packed him off to stay on his aunt's farm at Nutcombe, in Somerset. Evelyn's exasperation may be traced through his diary:

10/8/55: Back from London. To my annoyance Bron is still here. I was promised his absence. The children greeted my return with illuminated addresses and Septimus in fancy dress presenting the key of the front door.

15/8/55: Early Mass. Bron left for Nutcombe. In spite of my earnest prayers I was delighted to see him go. The household became happy once more and we began to plan an outing to Birmingham Art Gallery and Stratford Theatre. Displeasure takes the form of boredom with me nowadays.

21/8/55: Communion, praying again for charity towards Bron. By telephone the glad news that he is prolonging his stay at Nutcombe.

14/9/55: Bron was returned to Downside. We dropped

him there after a visit to my Raban uncles and aunts. Clusters of unprepossessing boys were lurking round the drive and gates. Laura gave him £4, his allowance for a quarter in advance, most imprudently. He immediately joined the corner boys, perhaps to drink and smoke. A cheerful dinner in his absence.

Evelyn's prayers for charity towards Bron were more readily answered when his son was out of the house and he could channel such charity as he possessed in the direction to which it was best suited: letter-writing. His letters to Bron, of which some eighty survive, cumulatively testify to the warmth, kindness, solicitude and urbane, gossipy good humour that characterised his paternity at its best. Any son would have been proud to be the recipient of such a correspondence. In his first letter to Bron in the new term, he described Alec's daughter's wedding and his plans to sell Piers Court, which, now threatened by road-widening schemes and spreading conurbation, was no longer desirable.

Dear Bron,

I hope you are comfortably established under Father Aelred and are making some desirable new friends. Please inform me what studies the headmaster has prescribed for you.

You did not miss any great pleasure or amusement at your cousin's wedding. It was highly respectable and dull. She looked very personable.[5] I knew no one of the hundreds of guests. Nor did your uncle Alec. A Protestant Bishop performed the ceremony, the Hyde Park Hotel provided their regular wedding fare. It was all very middle class.

Septimus, as you would expect, was widely admired. I must admit the little darling looked well and conducted himself without reproach. Even your half-great-uncle George was inconspicuous. A thoroughly tedious afternoon in fact.

---

[5] The wedding of Alec Waugh's daughter, Veronica, to Christopher Keeling.

Next day your mother and I went to Brighton returning in time to show an insane baronet over the house, but he was not quite insane enough to purchase it. Portlip has been bought so it seems probable that we shall all be here at Christmas.

Ever your affec. papa
E. Waugh

All references to Septimus are glowing and it might be tempting to deduce from them that he was Evelyn's favourite son, but I do not think it true. Of his three sons Evelyn was predominantly interested in Bron who craved his father's attention and made sure he got plenty of it. He was more ambitious for Bron than for any of his other children. Septimus, as the youngest in the family (ten years younger than Bron and only sixteen when his father died), was treated with the extravagant indulgence usually shown by rich old American women for their Chihuahuas. Evelyn never showed the slightest interest in James, his second son. The two youngest children were grouped together in Evelyn's mind as 'the boys', but with Septimus always preferred. 'Your brother James is home dull as ditchwater; your brother Septimus bright as a button.'

James was intelligent in mind and able with his hands but, like his mother, he was fundamentally lazy, unambitious, unrealistic and undemonstrative. Evelyn bullied him. 'And now,' he would say to assembled guests after dinner, 'and now my son James will tell us an amusing story.' Poor James would leave the table in tears. At best Evelyn found James 'quaint' and expected him, without conviction or interest, to follow the traditional path of an English gentleman's younger son by entering the army or the Church. He had no expectation for him as a writer, believing him devoid of literary taste. 'James is reading P. G. Wodehouse with great seriousness. "Don't you find it funny, James?" "I think this book is meant to be serious, Papa." The book was *Carry on Jeeves*.' Later, in despair at James's lack of literary curiosity, he bribed him to read one of his own books. James chose *The Loved One*, Evelyn's shortest novel, and sat for a while sighing over the first page in the drawing room. When Laura announced she needed help topping and tailing beans in the kitchen James, not usually keen on that sort of thing, leaped to his feet and forgot all about the book.

On Evelyn's fifty-second birthday, 28 October 1955, James presented him with a metal crucifix; Meg gave him a rosary she had made at school. Bron, who had telephoned Meg to ask the date of their father's birthday, forgot to write or send a present. Perhaps he had meant to offer birthday salutations in a letter of the twenty-second but, with all the excitement of being given the part of John Worthing in his house production of *The Importance of Being Earnest*, he must have forgotten. Throughout his life Evelyn took birthdays seriously. He enjoyed giving and receiving presents and regarded his eldest son's forgetfulness as a slight.

Dear Bron,

Thank you for your letter.

I am glad to hear you have so good a part in so good a play. Are strangers admitted to the performance? I should like to see it.

The chief event here has been my 52nd birthday which was celebrated with all suitable pomp. Rich gifts were brought by the representatives of all civilised nations and many barbarous tribes. The silver band played continuously from dawn to dusk. Pontifical high mass was celebrated in Dursley church. In the evening an ox was roasted in Miss Hooper's hut and eaten by Lady Tubbs.[6]

Your mother's cowman, whose name escapes me — Christopher? — broke his legs with a motor bicycle and your mother has to milk twice a day for the next three months. It is a grievous imposition which makes it impossible for her to leave home. She found a substitute for one week-end. We visited your sisters at Ascot who ate more than was decent.

[6] Lady Tubbs: a figure of fun in the neighbourhood. Married to Colonel Alan Durand in 1944, but styled herself according to her first marriage to Sir William Tubbs, first and last baronet, who died in 1941.

Your brother Septimus continues to give unusual pleasure.

I am appalled to hear of the Abbot's sacrilege in allowing televisions into the Abbey. I hope the place is struck by lightning.

Ever your affec. papa
E. Waugh

On Bron's birthday, a month after Evelyn's, he received a tie (which he did not like) and a letter from his mother. He replied to Evelyn:

Please excuse the extreme squalor of this letter – it is being written in a prep and must somehow look like an history essay. Thank you very much for the magnificent birthday present – I have not had the opportunity to wear it yet, and have contented myself with peering in the mirror; after my vile act in forgetting your birthday you could have been quite justified in ignoring mine entirely.

Bron had been present at Piers Court a year earlier when men from the BBC had come to interview his father. They had tried to humiliate Evelyn with impertinent questions about his moral values: 'In what respect do you as a human being believe that you have primarily failed?'; 'Have you ever wanted to kill somebody?'; 'You are a fairly facile writer?' When asked, 'Do you find it easy to get on with the man in the street?' Evelyn replied, 'I've never met such a person.' And when pressed as to whether he would be prepared to execute a man, he answered: 'Do you mean actually do the hanging?'

'Yes.'

'I should think it very odd for them to choose a novelist for such a task.'

After the interview Bron noticed the malign effect of the interview upon his father, and commented, 'They did not like you much, did they, Papa?' In his autobiographical 'conversation piece', *The Ordeal of Gilbert Pinfold*, Evelyn turned the remark round: 'When they were out of sight down the turn of the drive, one of the children who had been listening to the conversation in the van said: "You didn't like those people much, did you, Papa?"'

At this time Evelyn was ill, suffering from a surfeit of chloral bromide mixed with too much alcohol, fibrositis in his legs, a filthy cold, persecution mania and depression. To improve his health he decided to take a cruise to Ceylon but once on board ship suffered a breakdown with hallucinations and debilitating barminess. Laura wrote to Bron at Downside:

> Darling Bron,
>
> Papa told me to tell you he had not written because he was not well. I hope he will come back soon. Otherwise I think I will fly out to him on Sunday week as it is beastly being ill the other side of the world. In the meantime please pray that he may swiftly recover and return home. I do not mean that he is dangerously ill but just very unwell.
>
> My cow called Margaret has had a heifer calf but it is not nice and I shall not keep it . . .
>
> All my love to you, Mother

Evelyn's hatred of the BBC predated the Piers Court interview but was especially virulent in the year that followed. He had detected an underlying malice in the interviewers' questioning and in *Pinfold* had criticised the menacing, 'insidiously plebeian voice' and the 'hint of the underdog's snarl' in the leader. The thought of these terrible 'electricians', as he called them, trampling with their cameras and microphones upon the sacred apse of Gilbert Scott's spectacular abbey at Downside horrified him. Bron wrote to reassure his father:

> The televised High Mass was not quite as awful as it might have been. There was a host of ugly little men chewing gum that crawled up and down the aisle with lots of rope

etc. Two cameras flash red and green lights on you as they swing enormous 3 foot noses in every direction.

The Abbey is now swamped with letters from 'Mother of six, Birmingham' who are, apparently, flocking to the church as a result of the performance.

But two days later something much more interesting happened at Downside than the televised mass. I do not think that Bron *deliberately* burned a large part of the school to the ground, though he might have done it accidentally while playing around with matches and cigarettes. The blaze was reported in the national press, which was where Evelyn first heard of it. In a letter to his daughter Meg at Ascot he hinted that there had been something fishy about it: 'Have you read about the Downside fire? By curious good fortune all the buildings which were scheduled for demolition have been consumed. They were well insured. No other buildings were affected. If the property belonged to anyone other than monks one might suspect arson.'

In his autobiography my father claimed that Evelyn always suspected him of having caused it. When Evelyn asked him outright Bron brazenly refused to enlighten him either way; he used this inflammatory technique often in his life. I remember the press once got hold of some cock-and-bull idea that Papa was the 'fifth man' in the Burgess-Maclean-Philby-Blunt spy ring. The telephone rang all day and to each journalist Papa politely replied, 'I can neither confirm nor deny that I am the fifth man.' Curiously his name appears on a list of British spies on the Internet even though in his several attempts to secure full-time employment in the Secret Service he was unsuccessful. Whether or not he struck the match that caused it, the fire at Downside filled him with exquisite sensations of anarchic happiness that remained with him for the rest of his life. His letter to his father reflects this joy:

The great fire was immense fun; the circular you got from the headmaster keeps just within the bounds of truth, although it does not give a glimmering of what actually happened. Besides the gym, which, as he says, is completely destroyed, three dormitories (not two) are left without a stone upon a stone, and one is badly damaged. The linen room, containing the whole school's sheets etc has been completely destroyed. One class room has been pulled down because it was unsafe. 'The boy's behaviour was, in all cases, exemplary.'

The school divided, more or less, into three distinct sections: those who were confined into their dormitories, not being able to escape at an early stage, then those who gallantly tried to put the fire out, and then the reactionary group who tried to let it burn. More hoses were squirted at the boys than at the fire. The headmaster was equally delighted with both groups – he was torn between the conflicting emotion of the thought of the insurance (a claim for £40,000), the love of a bonfire, and his duty to the insurers. The other monks did not attempt to conceal their delight. Father Hubert van Zeller danced in front of the fire singing the *Te Deum* off key. Another monk rushed into Father Wulston Phillipson's room (some thirty yards from the fire) and started throwing the wireless out of the window, breaking pictures, jumping on gramophone records etc.

I managed to get out of the dormitory while a riot was taking place at the other end, down in the hall. I joined a group of other boys who had escaped and were busy throwing their corps uniforms into the blaze. I managed to grab a hose from a semi-stupefied fireman and was the first (of many) to squirt the headmaster. The Tusk was wildly excited, squirting himself with synthetic foam, until he looked like a Christmas cake Santa Claus. The flames were now raging some thirty feet above the top of the gym. Among the junior boys there was a general tendency to be heroic, but since there was no one to be rescued and they had no one to practise their Boy Scout training on, they had to content themselves with running everywhere very usefully, and running the gauntlet of our hoses, which knocked them down like nine-pins.

I joined the Headmaster who was standing with the Abbot instructing the firemen as to which parts of the building they should let burn, and which parts they should squirt so long as they stopped if the fire showed any signs of abating. At 3.00 a.m. the fire reached its climax. While it roared and hissed some fifty feet above the roof, while iron girders became white-hot and crashed in twisted shapes on to the floor, while over 2000 gallons of water were being pumped every minute at enormous pressure from some forty hoses, while all this was happening, boys were still running up and down to the Barlow top dormitory with tooth-mugs full of water.

With that horrible bureaucratic outlook which always prevails in schools, work has been resumed as usual. Boys are sleeping on mattresses in the class-rooms, Old House, even Old Chapel, but still things go on. Gym is being held out of doors.

The whole of the prefabricated area of school – about 2 acres – is now a pile of rubble with twisted bed frames here and there. The fire was definitely a good thing.

All stories in the papers about 40 boys being rescued by monks are quite untrue – they were made up by myself and Mark Sykes for the reporters' benefit. I was televised by the BBC and ITA hunting, distraught, for lost belongings. Actually we were looting the remains of the signals room. I found one charred toothbrush.

Must end up. Hope but not expect to hear from you about possible plans for next Sunday.

All my love
Bron

If Bron had been responsible for the Downside conflagration – and on reflection I think that he probably was – he executed the task imperfectly. As his letter to Evelyn grudgingly admits, lessons were immediately reallocated to places that were undamaged and the desperate boredom and routine of learning and discipline continued. Within a month Evelyn had caught Bron lying again. On his return for the Christmas holidays, Evelyn gave him a lecture and five pounds; Bron explained to him that he was unhappy at school and wished to leave. Evelyn refused to allow it, telling him that he must work for a scholarship in English or history to Oxford or, failing that, must join the army. No sooner was Bron back at school than Evelyn sent him the forms:

> I met the present adjutant of the Blues the other evening and he said you should join the regiment. You can decide when the time comes (if your school record renders you acceptable to either) between Blues and Coldstream. Nothing is lost by applying now.
>
> Will you therefore sign and post.

But Bron was having none of it.

Just as Evelyn had appealed to Arthur to remove him from Lancing in 1920 and been refused, so history repeated itself with Bron. Back at Piers Court Evelyn was feeling the pinch: most of the servants had been dismissed and he wanted to sell up. The following correspondence of four consecutive letters tells its own story.

10th February, 1956

Dear Papa,

> The term has run about three weeks now, and it has become increasingly apparent to me, at any rate, that I am unlikely to coin an award in either English or History. This letter is not written in a fit of depression or fury, but is the result of several months' consideration. My stay at Downside is costing you a great deal of money, and, should I go to university, I will cost you a great deal more. I am doing very little good at Downside for the school or for myself, and I really think it is a mistake to go on paying for an education which is neither a pleasure nor a profit.
>
> Not long ago you mentioned you had some influence in the hotel-trade. If I entered this there would be no need for a University education. I already possess two advance level passes, and, if I stay on, the most I can hope to gain

this year is another two; if I stay on another year it is possible that I may coin an award that would be either worthless or nearly worthless to you financially, and would have cost you well over £500.

It would be convenient if I could get my two years basic-training in the hotel trade before National Service. In this way I would not completely waste the next two years, which seems to be inevitable otherwise.

If you write to Father Passmore I think he will raise no objection to my removal at the end of the term: our increasingly bad relationship renders this by no means improbable in any case.

Please believe me when I say that this letter is not the result of a fit of depression.

Love Bron

Dear Bron,

I have written to enquire at what age apprentices are taken into the hotel trade. I think you are still too young but I don't know. Meanwhile think and *pray* about your future. This is an occasion that will affect your entire life.

I have much sympathy with your restlessness with school life. I felt as you do at your age, asked my father to remove me, was resentful at the time when he refused. Now I am grateful to him.

If there was anything you ardently wished to do — go to sea, learn a skilled trade etc — because you felt a real vocation for it, I would not stand in your way. I believe you think hotel-keeping simply a means of leaving school. That is a very poor motive for taking a job and hotel-keeping is not a craft which fits you for anything else. If you fail in that you will be further from starting anything else. 'Previous experience: two years as kitchen boy, waiter, lift-man, book keeper' is not a high recommendation for any other appointment. If you leave school now you will not get a commission in a good regiment. Perhaps you will not get a commission at all.

Most of the interest and amusement in life come from one's friends. All my friends are those I made at Oxford and in the army. You are condemning yourself either to a lonely manhood or one among second-rate associates. All because you lack the will power and self-control to make a success of the next eighteen months by co-operating with those who have only your own best interests at heart, throwing yourself into the life of the school and doing your work and obeying the rules. At your age, wherever you go, you will find yourself under discipline much less humane and benevolent than that of the monks.

You have a sense of humour and a good gift of self-expression. On the other hand you are singularly imprudent and you have a defective sense of honour. These bad qualities can lead to disaster.

My financial interests have no bearing on my wish for your welfare. I am sorry you should suggest that they might.

Your affectionate papa
E. Waugh

19th February, 1956

Dear Papa,

After the Headmaster's letter I find I am in the novel position of trying to persuade someone how badly I am doing in work. I am not going to quote marks at you, but it is a fact that in a class of singularly backward boys I am not among the first three. I am fortunate enough to get along well with my tutors, which accounts largely, but not entirely, for the good half-term reports the Headmaster received.

However, be that as it may, everything you said in your letter was absolutely true. It would be useless to pretend

I had a vocation for the hotel-trade, or any other at the moment. I regarded it simply as a way to get out of school. If leaving school at 16 does entail all the disadvantages you mention – a friendless life, and an army career in the ranks – it would be silly to leave now. On the other hand I can see no way in which the next two years will not be wasted here.

You mention throwing myself into school life. I have tried all the methods – I speak at debating societies, found others, and attend all the high-brow philosophical discussions, and even attempt to edit papers. What more could be desired? Games are quite out of the question, and anything else is hardly respectable.

You mention obeying school rules. I am convinced that school life would be insupportable without breaking them. The only alternative to a life of pleasure is games, which I am unable to enjoy in the smallest way.

However hard I work it is almost impossible to excel at an entirely new subject among people who have been studying it for three years.

My relationship with the Headmaster makes any advancement in the school extremely unlikely, and even Father Aelred, with whom I am consistently on the best of terms, can not help me in this.

Love Bron

Dear Bron,

I am delighted to hear that, unaccustomed as you are to public speaking, you have won the debating prize and are going to Sherborne with the team. You will not, I think, hear your cousin Peter speak there.

The only honest answer to your letter is this: growing up is a disagreeable process for most men. You have to grow up somewhere. Downside seems to me the best place, but I am always open to other suggestions. If you leave prematurely everyone will always think you were sacked. To be sacked from school is not absolutely fatal but it is a grave disadvantage for the early years of whatever career you decide on. I am pretty sure it will prevent you getting a commission in any Household regiment and would make entry into Oxford more difficult.

I could probably get you into Stonyhurst, but as it is school itself, rather than Downside, that you dislike, I don't see the advantages unless it enabled you to shake off undesirable friends. But one can make undesirable friends anywhere if one has the taste for them.

I don't suppose you want to go to Dartmouth?

I see no reason why, once you have passed into Oxford, you shall not spend the last two terms before going up at a foreign school learning a language.

In the hope of understanding you better I have been reading the diaries I kept at your age. I am appalled at what an odious prig I was. Debating, boxing, ragging the OTC, intriguing for advancement, atheism and over-eating seem to have been my consolations at Lancing. One great advantage you have on me is the contact with a place of prayer. Don't neglect that advantage. Your spiritual and moral welfare is the main thing of absolute importance.

Your affec. papa
EW

Bron stayed at Downside for one further term, at the end of which, shortly before Christmas 1956, he was awarded an open exhibition in English at Christ Church College, Oxford. There seemed no point in his staying on. Evelyn and Passmore both agreed that his continued presence at the school would be painful and counterproductive to all concerned. Father Aelred wrote to congratulate him: 'You may not believe me, but I'm sorry you are going and I shall really miss you . . . although you have burned your fingers one way and another, you have learned much and God has taught you much.'

Two years of military service was, at that time, a compulsory duty for all fit, young men of Britain. All they had to do was cough with their testicles in the cupped, enquiring hands of a medical orderly, and they were in. The test was hard to fail, but at least the choice of whether to attend university before or after the army lay open and Bron decided that his interests would be best served by getting his National Service over and done with, and the university agreed to hold his place until October 1959. For some reason that I have not been able to divine, he did not inform his father of his decision until April the following year. In the meantime, it was agreed that Bron should travel abroad and con a foreign tongue until September. Had he chosen to go up to Oxford before the army he would have found compulsory National Service abolished by the time he left; but he could not have predicted this in 1956. When Evelyn heard of his son's decision not to delay military service he wrote, 'I am very glad you have decided to try for the army in September. I am sure you won't regret it in later life.' As things turned out, his decision to put the army first proved a grave mistake that, I believe, contributed to my father's untimely death.

XII

Under Fire

Evelyn and Laura moved from Piers Court to Combe Florey at the end of 1956. For six months, while the house was being renovated, Septimus (who was six) stayed with Vera Grother at her cottage near Piers Court. Neither of his parents visited him during this time. Evelyn had grown bored with 'Stinkers'. He enjoyed making, decorating and improving houses, but once these things were done he lost interest. He remembered with pride his brief apprenticeship in carpentry at Southampton Row when he had made an attractive mirror with the Waugh family crest fixed to the top, which hangs at Combe Florey, and a table that seems to have been lost. At Combe Florey he followed the carpenters and skilled artisans from room to room, discussing dovetails and tools, arranging for a panel to be inserted here, a boxed bath there. His mother wished he had never become a writer, and blamed his tortured personality on his literary career: 'If it hadn't been for She-Evelyn, he might have designed lovely furniture,' she once remarked plaintively to Alec.

'But, Mother dear, think of the books he has written.'

'I know, Alec dear, I know, but furniture is so useful. Besides, he would have been happier designing furniture.'

Combe Florey House was much larger than Piers Court. It came with a resplendent archway gatehouse dating from the twelfth century (refitted at the end of the sixteenth), two cottages in the village and just about enough land for Laura to continue in her loss-making dairy ventures. Evelyn paid £7500 for it — three-quarters of his annual income at that time. The manor house, formidable and square with an enclosed courtyard in the middle, is perched on a hill overlooking the medieval church on one side, with sweeping views of the Quantock Hills on the other. It was built in the reign of Charles II and constructed of an extraordinary reddish-pink sandstone common to only a small number of villages in the area. In the eighteenth century the front door and windows were aggrandised with magnificent Gibbsian surrounds and Evelyn rebuilt the stone perron to put it in symmetry with the front elevation. All the rooms are large, high-ceilinged and rectangular. The house's finest internal feature, a spectacular pine and softwood staircase with three twisted balusters to the tread, was fitted at the time of a grand remodelling in the 1730s. Bron and his siblings adored Combe Florey, but Evelyn, who at first saw in it 'possibilities of beautifaction', was never happy there.

'If only I were a pansy without family cares I would make it a jewel,' he said. Was it pansyish to have all the doors and skirting-boards painted in black gloss and the hall decorated in red flock, or brocade, wallpaper once popular among Indian restaurateurs but now out of fashion everywhere? At first Evelyn had grand plans to redesign the gardens and change the windows, but within a few years he had run out of money and lost interest in the world around him. The bookshelves, beautifully designed to fit the library at Piers Court, looked small and out of place at Combe Florey, but his expanding collection of Victorian paintings and furniture suited the house. The atmosphere was eccentric and lugubrious. A couple of mad Italians cooked, chauffeured and served at table, loudly accusing each other of adultery as they did so. Two ladies from the village helped to clean, but otherwise there was no one in the house. In the garden Coggins ruled, quickly securing himself a foothold in Laura's heart with recondite judgements on the state of her cows and the needs of her plants. When the Italians left he spread himself out for most of the day on a grubby *chaise-longue* in the kitchen to discuss udders while Laura podded the peas and stirred the stew. After Evelyn's death she gave him a large chunk of woodland within spitting distance of the house. He, or his descendants — I forget which – built a large, flat, plain bungalow upon it, surrounded by a six-foot-high orange security fence. Evelyn referred to him always as 'my rival Coggins', and shortly before his death conceded wearily to my father that 'Coggins has taken complete command of all your mother's affairs.'

At Combe Florey Evelyn wrote only one novel, his last, the final instalment of his trilogy about the Second World War, deemed by many of his critics to be the crowning glory and masterpiece of his literary career. It was called *Unconditional Surrender*. As with all of Evelyn Waugh's books, the trilogy (later recensed as a single volume under the title *Sword of Honour*) was essentially autobiographical. His novels, should you be asked, are best read in the order that he wrote them. Characters reappear, appropriately aged, from one book to the next; themes are kneaded, clarified, developed, enriched, juggled, sometimes discarded, sometimes resolved, along the winding, tipsy and often chaotic road that runs from *Decline and Fall* (1928) to *Unconditional Surrender* (1961). I can think of few novelists whose complete oeuvre comprises such a tightly woven canon as Evelyn Waugh's.

The father-and-son relationship provides one of the central themes of his fiction, running, almost obsessively, through every book. But not until his last novel does the reader get to witness a father–son relationship that is even partially successful. In *Unconditional Surrender*, for the first time, a father is seen to take his paternal responsibilities seriously and the advice he gives to his son is both meaningful and beneficial. To Evelyn, full realisation of his own father's worth only became apparent after Arthur's death. The same is true of the Crouchbacks in *Sword of Honour*. Gervase Crouchback may not be scrupulously modelled on Arthur Waugh, but there are, as with most of Evelyn's fictional fathers, strong similarities. When he dies (like Arthur) suddenly and peacefully in 1943, his son Guy, serving as a soldier (like Evelyn), is fortunate (like Evelyn) to be stationed in England. At his father's funeral Guy 'followed the familiar rite with his thoughts full of his father . . . His father had been a "just" man; not particularly judicious, not at all judicial, but "just" in the full sense of the psalmist . . . To Guy his father was the best man, the only entirely good man, he had ever known.'

A year after the publication of *Unconditional Surrender* Evelyn further settled his account with Arthur in a long article for the *Sunday Telegraph* entitled simply 'My Father'. Some of it I have already quoted. It is warm, generous, loyal and forgiving. Alec read it with trepidation and was amazed by the charity with which Evelyn portrayed the man with whom he had shared so many stressful antagonisms. Even Arthur's literary recitations in the book-room at Underhill, which Evelyn had so detested at the time, were handsomely praised:

> The happiest conjunction of my father's literary and theatrical tastes was in his reading aloud. This, for many years, was a feature of our family circle. It was never educational in intent. It was a shared delight, but it was also the basis of a generous education and of the recognition that education was something to be enjoyed, not the subject for schools. Some of what he read aloud was pure entertainment – the dramas of his youth which he would re-enact with vivacity. He also read us most of Shakespeare and Dickens, much of Thackeray and Trollope and of the staples of Victorian prose, but it was in reading poetry, with the fewest dramatic effects and the most reliance on rhythm and consonance, that he was most memorable to me. Indeed I have never heard him excelled except by Sir John Gielgud.

I do not wish to accuse Evelyn of rewriting or covering-up history with these lines. I am sure he remembered as he wrote them the extent to which Arthur's book-room readings had caused him to bridle, but as a father himself he could now look back on Arthur's efforts in a kinder light. As he recorded in his diaries at the same time as this article was written: 'Those who most reprobate and ridicule their fathers – e.g. Samuel Butler and Osbert Sitwell – were not fathers themselves.'[1] Evelyn, who was always intensely self-critical, came to believe in his last years that Arthur had been a far

---

[1] All printed versions of Evelyn Waugh's diaries have a mistake here: 'Those who most reprobate and ridicule their fellows . . .' The original clearly says 'fathers'.

better father to him than he was to his own children. In his diaries
he confessed to having nightmares in which he was reading aloud
endless tedious books to his family. He read occasionally to his girls,
not so much to the boys, but the strain of it wearied him. Now,
nearly twenty years after Arthur's death, he placed a new value on
the childhood his father had given him and, perhaps, felt guilty at
the cavalier manner with which he had treated Arthur in his last
years. The point is best reflected in the final paragraphs of his article:

> My father and I were never intimate in the sense of my coming
> to him with confidences or seeking advice. Our relationship
> was rather that of host and guest. He stayed with me in the
> country. I regularly dined with him in Highgate. The war took
> me away but I was doing a spell of duty in London at the time
> of his death.
>
> I am now the father of three sons. I have very little knowl-
> edge, or curiosity, about what they think of me. They are always
> polite. I have tried to fulfil the same duties to them and
> provide the same amusements as my father did to me. I lack
> his gift of reading poetry and his liveliness.
>
> I think I am less good company to them than he was to
> me, but I think I am kinder than my grandfather [the Brute].
> Perhaps host and guest is really the happiest relation for father
> and son.

A year after this article was published Evelyn set to work on the
first volume of his autobiography, *A Little Learning*, in which he
devoted more than an entire chapter to Arthur while to his mother,
whom he loved a great deal more, he ascribed a single paragraph.
The last lines of the chapter on Arthur are as redolent and fond a
tribute as any father could hope from a son:

> My father never, in adult life, aspired higher, nor did he ever
> repine at his lack of excellence. His primary, overriding,
> instinctive aim was to make a home.
>
> There were times when I was inclined to regard his achieve-
> ment as somewhat humdrum. Now I know that the gratitude

I owe him for the warm stability he created, which I only dimly apprehended, can best be measured by those less fortunate than myself.

On the other hand, I do accuse Alec of attempting to rewrite history. His motives, as I have said, were driven in part by guilt at having been his father's favourite. In his first autobiography, published in 1962 and dedicated 'To the memory of my father, ARTHUR WAUGH, with a love that the years have deepened', Evelyn is hardly mentioned. He wrote in that book:

> The reader may be surprised at finding so little here about Evelyn Waugh. If I were not myself and if I were to pick up the autobiography of Alec Waugh, the first name that I should look up in the index would be Evelyn Waugh. I am sorry to disappoint that curiosity . . . but I lack the key to Evelyn. I cannot enter imaginatively into the mind of a person for whom religion is the dominant force in his life, for whom religion is a crusade, as it is with Evelyn . . . So I shall confine myself reluctantly to this brief fraternal tribute of gratitude for the great pleasure that his books have given me and for the high honour they have conferred upon the name of Waugh.

I do not think that religious differences provide an honest excuse for the omission. The truth is that Alec was afraid to write about his brother while he was alive. After Evelyn's death in 1966, he wrote freely about him in *My Brother Evelyn and other Profiles* (1967); *A Year to Remember* (1975); and *The Best Wine Last* (1978), and even introduced him as a semi-fictional character in his last novel *The Fatal Gift* (1973). In all of these he attempted to portray his brother's relationship with Arthur as rosier than it really was. 'Evelyn and I,' he claimed in *A Year to Remember*, 'never failed to express appropriate gratitude for the devoted love that our parents gave us . . . we enjoyed our parents' company and they knew we did.' He approached the editor of Evelyn's diaries to persuade him to cut rude references to Arthur from the printed version. When he was going through correspondence, he threw away or crossed out whole sections that refuted the cosy-family-unity version of events that he preferred. When Arthur's letters to Kenneth McMaster briefly came into his possession Alec scribbled violently over the sentence 'The fact is he [Evelyn] is thoroughly ashamed of his parents and does his best to banish them from his conscience', though it can still be read by holding the paper upside-down and shining the light through it from behind.

In his documentary accounts Alec was unwilling to admit the truth of Evelyn and Arthur's bad relationship but he was more candid in his fiction. The best example can be found in his 1934 epic novel, *The Balliols*, a 500-page family saga that begins with a man building himself a house in North End Road, Hampstead in 1907. He is Edward Balliol, director of the old City firm of Peel and Hardy. He has two sons, Hugh, the elder whom he prefers, and Francis, who is clearly based on Evelyn. Hugh serves in the First World War and afterwards joins his father on the board of the company, while Francis, a schoolboy during the war, is ignored by both his parents. Edward's 'capacity for curiosity had never been fully exercised on Francis', we are told. 'He had begun by thinking him a nuisance. Later he told himself that the child was his wife's concern. And now when she was too busy with her war work, he had grown into too confirmed a habit of ignoring Francis to take a very real interest in his concerns.' Francis is well aware that his father considers him a second-class son. '"No one is really bothering about me:" thought Francis: "no one ever has; no one ever will." And that old feeling of being alone, neglected, unaided, "out of things," that had made him reserved and secretive as a child, volubly rebellious during his first terms at school, made him now ruthlessly resolved to decide his future for himself.'

The phenomenal success of Alec's 1955 novel *Island in the Sun* made him a rich man. In fact, he earned more from this one book in the two months *before* its publication than he had made from all his other novels put together. New fame and fortune distracted him from gloomy ideas of suicide. Only a year earlier he had been swallowing mouthfuls of barbiturates in the hope of ending it all. Nobody seemed to be interested in his work any more, least of all in the short stories that for fifteen years had kept him in reasonable income. He could, of course, always have returned to England. Joan had never taken Alec's Reno divorce seriously – nor did she believe in the legality of it. As far as she was concerned Alec was welcome to return to Edrington at any time; but as he later recalled:

> I could not picture myself abandoning my immigrant status in the USA and returning to Edrington with 'my tail between my legs'. I could not subject myself to that humiliation nor, if I did, should I have been a very satisfactory person about the house, either as a husband or a father. I should no longer be able to take a pride in myself; and when a man cannot do that he is better somewhere else.

The sudden and unexpected success of *Island in the Sun* could not have been more timely. Alec's English agent complained that it was too long and needed cutting. For the first time in his life Alec ignored his advice and sent the book directly to his publishers in America. The next thing he knew was that his novel had been bought by *Ladies' Home Journal* for a princely sum. Three days later it had been taken up as the Literary Guild selection for January; and the next day a telegram arrived to say that the Reader's Digest Condensed Book Club also wanted to serialise it. Then Hollywood jumped in. Within four weeks Alec had made quarter of a million dollars and more was on the way. The film version of *Island in the Sun*, directed by Robert Rossen, starring James Mason, Joan Fontaine, Harry Belafonte, Dorothy Dandridge and the young Joan Collins, was the most talked-about film of the year. Alec's steamy yarn centred on two adulterous interracial romances and a murder on a West Indian island. The film's title song soon became a chart hit around the world:

> This is my island in the sun
> Where my people have toiled since time begun
> I may sail on many a sea
> Her shores will always be home to me

My father used to play the record on his old Pye gramophone, singing and dancing round our Wiltshire sitting-room. 'The influence

of the Waughs is spreading!' he used to say, as he took the record off.
And indeed it was, for the world-famous reggae label, Island
Records, was named after Alec's book and from this we might
conclude that were it not for the 'influence of the Waughs' no one
would ever have heard of Bob Marley. (Alec's other strange claim
to fame was that he invented the cocktail party by serving a rum
swizzle to astonished friends who thought they had come for tea
at his flat in Earls Terrace in the spring of 1924. Within eighteen
months early-evening drinks parties had become an established form
of social entertainment right across the civilised world.)

Alec was disappointed that neither his father nor his mother had
lived long enough to witness the grand success of *Island in the Sun*.
K, no doubt, would have found it all too sexual. The film gave
Dorothy Dandridge the chance to appear as the first black woman
to have an on-screen romance with a white man. It was this, and
the black-white relationship between Harry Belafonte and Joan
Fontaine, that caused the stir. *Island in the Sun* is actually quite a
boring and cautious film and seeing it today I struggle to understand how it could have been such a sensational cult controversy
in the fifties. *Tempora mutantur . . .*

Though Alec's triumph succeeded in lining his pockets it did
not, alas, bring him any closer to his family. In fact, the opposite:
it held him longer in America. His eldest son, Andrew, grew into
a handsome man with an eye, like his father, for the ladies. When
they met they discussed sexual intercourse, sometimes in front of
the rest of the family. Andrew once described to his father the
sensations of a 'spine-shattering fuck'. Alec thought about it for a
minute before answering competitively, 'Yes, I seem to remember
one like that too.' Joan employed, at that time, a demented Polish
husband-and-wife team who lived in the attic and served at dinner.
One day the husband accused Andrew of using the glue from his
model aeroplane kit to anaesthetise his wife and rape her while she
was comatose, and from that moment went around the house
calling him 'Die Focker' under his breath. When Alec heard the
story he was perplexed and slightly jealous. 'Why doesn't he call
me Die Focker? Surely he means me?'

* * *

Evelyn at the time of his first marriage in 1929.

Barbara Jacobs: the snapshot that Alec took with him to the trenches.

Alec the young officer, at the time he wrote *The Loom of Youth*, 1917.

Joan with Alec at the start of their marriage, he in his golfing kit.

Alec with Andrew and Veronica moments after the Prime Minister's declaration of war in September 1939.

Andrew, Alec's elder son, as a handsome teenager posing with a pipe.

Peter, Alec's equally handsome younger son, emulating a cowboy.

Father and son: Alec and Andrew at a garden party in 1950.

Evelyn and Laura at their wedding in London, 17 April 1937.

Bron in his school uniform during the holidays at Piers Court, 1947.

Evelyn eyeballing his youngest son, Septimus, at Piers Court, 1955.

Family and staff at Piers Court, 1947. Evelyn in the centre sits between his wife and mother. Elwood, his butler, stands behind him, while Teresa and Bron create a symmetry at his knees. On the far left, Gladys Attwood, a cleaning lady, holds Hatty's hand. James sits on his mother's lap and Meg stands between her grandmother and old Mrs. Attwood on the right. The young girl, top right, is Vera (beloved Nanny), and next to her is Norman Attwood (one of a string of beloved cowmen).

A painful moment in the Morning Room at Combe Florey, 1965. Left to right from the back: James, Papa (holding me and my sister Sophie), Granny, Grandpapa, Aunt Teresa (with her son, Justin), Aunt Meg (with her daughter, Claudia). Kneeling in front: Hatty and Septimus. Sitting on the floor bawling: Meg's eldest daughter, Emily.

Bron, a teenager,
posing at Piers Court,
1955.

Bron, a man of the world, posing at Combe Florey, 1990.

First steps to a literary career? Me aged eleven months in the library at Chilton Foliat.

At Chilton Foliat, 1969. Mama and Papa behind, Sophie holding Nat, Daisy looking serious, Biafran Dozie Chukwuka trying to puff his cheeks, and me looking priggish.

Father-and-son competition at Butlins, 1965. The winners were No. 41. Papa was reviewing the famous holiday camp for the *Daily Mirror*.

Bron at Piers Court aged twelve, 1952.

His grandson Bron aged six, 2004.

Suave? Attractive? Interesting? My family trying to maintain Victorian dignity, 2004. Me and Eliza and (from left to right in front) Mary, Bron and Sally.

For most of 1957 Bron's relationship with his father was epistolic. He took his 'year out' in Italy, and from September was stationed at army barracks in Windsor. Only for the first month and a half of that year was he at Combe Florey, getting on his father's nerves. Evelyn wrote to Meg at the end of January: 'Bron seems unable to move himself abroad. He sits all day smoking cheroots, reading P. G. Wodehouse, and occasionally goes out at dusk with a gun and brings back a pheasant.'

A fortnight later Bron was in Florence. Evelyn had asked his university friend Harold Acton, living with his mother in her opulent villa just outside the city, to keep an avuncular eye on Bron and to give him money as and when he needed it, which Evelyn would repay to Acton's account at the Heywood Hill bookshop in London. Acton was delighted by Bron and wrote to his old friend: 'He strikes me as a charming chip off the not so old block, in certain ways uncannily like you.'

In Florence Bron supplemented his income by holding out a hat to passers-by as his friend from Downside, Rob Stuart, drew kitsch, weeping Madonnas on the pavements in chalk. He also gave misleading English lessons to a surgeon and his wife:

> I simply sit down, give the old man Wilde's *Intentions* to read aloud and fill myself with their wine and food. Yesterday, after an exhausting day, I fell asleep which was embarrassing. My corrections of his pronunciation had become more and more erratic. 'Gilbert lowed' he used to read, 'Gilbert laughed' I said; 'Gilbert laughed' he repeated – 'lowed' said I automatically. He seemed very impressed with the eccentricity of the English language when I left.

Rob and Bron earned enough in their various ways to buy themselves each a motor scooter and to dine on most evenings at the best restaurants in Florence. Days went by in happy indolence, peppered by insignificant adventures that Bron amplified, exaggerated and embellished to make them more amusing in his letters home. Evelyn's genial unruffled responses to his stream of calamitous endurance were commendable. Among the various adventures he reported to his father were:

1. He was sitting peacefully in a train when a rifle bullet shot straight through the window passing out the other side. A minute later the window shattered into a thousand fragments.

2. He had crashed into a policeman on his Vespa.

3. His friend's motor scooter had exploded 'scattering red hot metal everywhere'.

4. He had fallen among 'terrible painted hags' – 'cackling prostitutes' – in a northern district of Rome.

5. At the Mille Miglia motor-race he had seen a car spin like a top out of control and crash into a tree 'within ten yards of me'. The Dutch driver was killed. 'When the ambulance arrived the people in it had great difficulty getting near the poor man, and the only person for whom an instant passage was made was a newspaper photographer who snapped the driver's death agonies quite dispassionately.'

6. 'We left Assisi vowing not to stop again until we arrived at Rome. At night the only traffic on the roads is enormous, double-loaded lorries driven by the criminal population whom it is too dangerous to lock up. Over great mountain passes, time and time again they tried to murder us, and at every all-night inn where we stopped they were boasting of the people they had murdered that day. It was a charming mediaeval pilgrimage and even if there were not gallows at every cross roads, there were the hulks of crashed motorcars as an edifying admonition.'

Most of Bron's letters contain wild exaggerations and downright lies. In one from Bologna (the only surviving letter to Evelyn addressed 'Darling Papa') he claimed to suffer a 'lunatic experience' similar to Evelyn's recent bromide-poisoning hallucinations from which he had forged his autobiographical novel, *The Ordeal of Gilbert Pinfold*:

As I was writing this letter over a cup of coffee in the Piazza del Duomo, I had one of those lunatic experiences which can only happen when one is alone. A gruff, nightmare voice said in the language of Texas: 'Odd stuff all this, very odd.'

I: 'Yes.'

It: 'People odd too, don't you think?'

I: 'Yes.'

It: 'Do you suppose they think we're odd?'

I: 'Very.'

It: 'Venerably?'

I: 'Venerably.'

It: 'You did say venerably?'

I (beyond caring): 'Yes.'

It (as I thought): 'I was kidding.'

I (alarmed): 'Where? That is odd.'

It (after a pause): 'I don't know that I like you.'

I never heard it again, nor did I see the person responsible. It seems to come straight out of Muriel Spark's book about madness. Very worrying.

With love from your affectionate son, Bron

When *The Ordeal of Gilbert Pinfold* was published a month after this letter was written Evelyn gave Bron a smart presentation copy and inscribed it: 'For Auberon Alexander in the hope that Pinfold's trouble is not hereditary.'

In another letter to his father from Italy Bron described his experiences with a German criminal and pathological liar:

We had a very exciting week recently harbouring a confidence trickster. We met him in a bar in the cheaper part of Florence and he told us that he was a German student called Karl von Schmidt (which made us suspect him immediately – de Smith indeed!) However he wanted lodgings and so we gave him the address of our own lodgings which were far cheaper than his present ones. We left the bar at about 12, and at 3.30 a.m he burst into our room saying that he had lost the key of his car and he demanded a bed. So we sat up with him playing poker dice, at which he was lamentably bad and lost 3000 lire – next day he wanted to borrow money so I gave him a couple of hundred hoping to get rid of him. Not a bit of it; he reappeared for lunch to say that he would pay the landlady for a month in advance. This went on for a week, when he told us that he had paid her, which he hadn't, as we well knew. He had told her we were his friends and she now asked us to pay for him. So I picked his pocket while Rob showed him some paintings and extracted the necessary money. Next day we decided to expose him. The German Consulate had never heard of him, nor did he have a motor car. We decided we should be armed in case he turned nasty so I solemnly filled two socks with sand from the banks of the Arno and we waited for him to reappear, but he never did. Great anti-climax to an exciting week. He had an extraordinary streak in him that he always proffered a lie at any stage, and we had great fun spotting the contradictions, which were frequent.

I suspect this story to be almost entirely fabricated. It has that ring about it. In an untitled novel, never published, Bron described two seventeen-year-old English boys who spend their year off together in Italy. The book contains a scene in which one of them attempts to write a dutiful letter home to his father.

Dear Papa, he wrote in his crabbed painstaking hand, *Jonathan and I arrived safely in Perrugia*. What else could he tell him? . . . *Also there is a very amusing German student here called von Schmidt.* What could he tell his father which would make Schmidt sound interesting? He decided to invent but his imagination was not as forthcoming as Jonathan's. *He has a very lively trick of drinking beer while standing on his head*, he wrote, and then wondered if it struck the right note of gay, sophisticated, cosmopolitan life he had intended. He crossed it out and wrote instead: *He does the most amusing parodies of German opera, especially Wagner.*

Evelyn was richly entertained by Bron's correspondence and sent friendly letters in return, but at heart he was not a happy man.

His depressions were growing deeper and more frequent, and he was falling out of love with the Catholic Church:

Dear Bron,

Thank you for your letter. I hope you spent longer in Rome than you intended and did not waste too much time in forums and imperial ruins but instead explored some of the superb renaissance areas of the city.

I spent the last four days of Holy Week at Downside. Did you know a boy named Mortimer? If not it is too late. They buried him on Easter day. Poor Fr Passmore was much occupied with this sad event. Otherwise I am sure he would have joined with the other monks in sending his love. There were none of my particular friends at the monastery this year and I found the time, impoverished by the new liturgy, hanging rather heavy . . .

The monks advise that you ride your Vespa armed with a pistol. I don't.

Your affec. papa

While Bron was in Italy Evelyn's parental attentions were consumed by his favourite child Meg who was falling off the rails at Ascot. She had broken out of her bedroom at dead of night for a picnic feast on the golf links, had swallowed a phial of mercury, which she had stolen from the chemistry cupboard, and had, according to her Mother Superior, 'reached the stage where tolerance is no longer practicable. Her conduct and attitude are wholly to be deplored. It is so sad that she can only use her strong personality just now in a negative and destructive way.' The nuns asked Evelyn to come and talk to her.

Meg wrote to her father in distress:

Darling Papa,

You and Mummy are the kindest parents anybody could

ever have. You are the most wonderful father. I long to leave this place because it is really the separation from you and Mummy I mind more than anything. But I realise that if I do leave I am proving myself a coward and a failure. I cannot bear the idea of you having to be ashamed of me and I think you would if I proved myself incapable of a boarding school.

O Papa I cannot come to a decision. I loathe this place and feel it is too late to start again. But I have many friends and a few whom I am genuinely fond of. I would make no friends at Taunton but I do not mind that. To live at home with you and Mummy is all I could wish for.

Papa, please tell me truthfully soon if you would mind, if you would be ashamed. I know it is cowardly . . . but is there any point in making myself miserable when I needn't be?

Papa, you know me as well as I know myself, please decide for me. I trust you, I do not trust myself.

Evelyn's immediate decision was to remove both Meg and her sister, Hatty, from Ascot and send them to a Catholic school near Combe Florey in Taunton.

I have hired a punt. Your first duty will be to clear the island in the lake of all vegetation. You will have many arduous duties to atone for your naughtiness at Ascot. I am not ashamed of you. I think it is best for you to leave. No one is going to persecute you. But remember you are *not* returning in triumph and mustn't expect red carpets and silver bands . . .

I hope this doesn't seem a cross letter. I am not cross with you sweet Meg.

Papa

When Bron joined the army in September 1957 he was eighteen years old. His initial posting was to the Royal Horseguards HQ at

Combermere Barracks, near Windsor, then to the Guards depot at Caterham and finally to the Officers Training School at Mons Barracks near Aldershot. As Evelyn had predicted, the contrast between Florence and the army was a rude one and Bron hated every minute, especially at Caterham. His parents sent him cakes, books, magazines and letters. 'Thank you very much indeed . . . I cannot tell you how comforting it is to think that there are benevolent agencies working somewhere outside this wilderness of malice and violence and stupidity.' After a weekend visit to Combe Florey, where Bron escaped the 'depravity and ugliness' of the army, Evelyn wrote to Lady Diana Cooper: 'My son Auberon has grown very tall and handsome but is losing his wool.'

Bron's passing-out ceremony was in March 1958. He wrote to his parents: 'If all goes well I pass out on Thursday 20th – I don't suppose you would like to attend the parade, but I have been told to ask you.' He might not have 'supposed' that his parents would like to attend but he was nevertheless disappointed when they didn't. However, by the time he came to write his autobiography in 1990 he had decided that it was 'probably a good thing':

My parents did not attend the passing-out parade at Mons, alone, I think, of all the parents involved. In a way this was probably a good thing, as my father would probably have worn his grey bowler or Brigade boater, and my mother, although the kindest and sweetest of women, had no great sense of style. She had one fur coat, of astrakhan, but it was at least twenty years old and had lost much of its fur. It had once had rather a smart belt, but this had long been replaced by binder-twine.

So unembarrassed by any eccentrically dressed parents I was taken out by a brother officer and his mother to the Hog's Back Hotel, outside Guildford, where we ate *canard à l'orange* and returned feeling slightly sick.

After 'passing-out' Bron was sent on active service to the Mediterranean island of Cyprus, but not before a short sojourn at Combe Florey. 'Bron has got his commission in the Blues,' wrote

Evelyn proudly to Lady Diana Cooper, 'many sons of old Blues failed. He must have guts, he succeeds. Scholarship at the house and now this. But he's a queer morose boy, sloping round the woods with a gun alone or playing light opera on his gramophone. Teresa has had a dazzling term academically. But Meg for me anytime.' Evelyn's attitude to his six children is succinctly summarised in another letter from this period 'Bron is going bald, Meg is fat as suet. Teresa dirty. Hatty dotty. The little boys just little boys.'

In 1958 Cyprus was a Crown Colony, where British troops were engaged in holding the peace between rival factions of Greeks and Turks while the governor, Sir Hugh Foot, worked out a plan for sovereign independence. The Greek majority wanted the island to be part of Greece, although they fought among themselves as to how, where and why. The Turkish minority wanted *taksim*, or partition, whereby the island would be split and they would govern their own half.

By the end of 1958 twenty thousand British troops were stationed there: riot, shooting and bombing between all factions were on the increase. There was no war, as such, only regular small acts of terrorism. In April, seventy-five explosions, accounting for twenty-six murders, were recorded on the island; in May, there were twenty-seven bombs and fifteen murders. Life for the British troops was exciting. There was no front-line action, but they occupied their time swaggering around with machine-guns, looking wary and important, guarding, searching, arresting, checking, shooting at trees or tin-cans, blowing up rocks and wooden sheds for the sheer fun of hearing a bang.

Bron, as a second lieutenant in the Royal Horse Guards, had command of a handful of men and found the experience of being saluted, being abroad in the sunshine and being an officer in a smart regiment an exhilarating contrast to the undignified drudgery of military training at Aldershot.

> So much happens here that I really cannot think where to begin [he wrote to his father]. Life is immensely exciting and unbelievably comfortable. Nearly every day we are out on some raid, roadblock, search or patrol.

They say they are going to start ambushes again tomorrow, but everybody rather doubts it. At the moment they are not shooting much; although one cornet claims he heard bullets whistling past him, nobody believes him. Bombs however are exploding at the rate of three every 24 hours, and we sometimes go rushing to the scene; quite often the Cypriots blow themselves up as they are not very expert in handling them.

Evelyn, who liked nothing more than the excitement of military action and was at that time engaged in writing a sanctimonious biography of a priestly friend, was, I suspect, a little jealous of Bron's Cyprus adventure. When his son's commission papers arrived at Combe Florey Evelyn turned them over and over, rummaging through drawers to compare them with his own:

A document came to you from the War Office which I opened hoping to save you trouble. It is your commission. I take it that you would sooner it was kept here. The Queen's copper-plate hand has deteriorated since her father's day, as have her titles of honour. George VI described himself on my commission as 'by the Grace of God of Great Britain and Ireland and the British Dominions beyond the seas, King, Defender of the Faith, Emperor of India etc'. Your Queen describes herself as 'Head of the Commonwealth'. However, though inferior in station she has the same view of you as her father had of me. You are her 'Trusty and well beloved'. She reposes 'special Trust and Confidence in your Loyalty, Courage and Good Conduct'. You score over me in one particular. I was charged to 'exercise and well discipline in arms both the inferior officers and men serving under me'. You are to 'exercise and well discipline in their duties' (not so good) 'such officers, men *and women* as may be placed under your orders from time to time'. I was never given charge of women. Congratulations. Treat them severely.

As the author of such off-beam epistles as this one, it was courageous of Evelyn to criticise Bron's letters home for being too
concerned with his military exploits. Was there nothing more
amusing he could report from Cyprus? What wild flowers had he
seen on the island? What did he eat for breakfast? Had he met
Evelyn's friend Lord So-and-so's son or the Marquess of Whatnot's
boy? Bron replied in ironic tone:

> I am sorry that I was not sufficiently explicit in my last
> letter. I have met the Dunnes. I have not met the Fox-
> Strangways. There are several species of plant in flower,
> but I am unable to identify them. I arise at 6.15, being
> called by my servant. I have breakfast at 6.35. The first
> parade is at 7.10. The crews then retire to their vehicles
> until 12 o'clock and then that is the end of my working
> day, unless we are being sent out on a patrol, roadblock
> or ambush. These occur about three times a week. We do
> not catch anyone. The last is the most boring as we sit all
> night in an olive grove from 7pm to 4.30am and see no
> one and drink something disgusting called self-heating soup.
>   Randolph Churchill arrived here, was fêted by Colonel
> Julian and asked for your telephone number, which I had
> forgotten, but he said that he would get hold of it.
>   Drink in the mess is enormously cheap, outside unbe-
> lievably expensive. We are only allowed into four approved
> bars/restaurant/nightclubs at any of which a glass of
> whisky costs 19/6; in the mess it costs 4d.
>   The day is spent sleeping, playing bridge roulette
> pontoon murder backgammon dumb crambo.
>   We have to carry guns everywhere. I cannot hit a human
> sized target at 10 yards with 20 shots once with my assured
> pistol, which I am constantly in fear of losing.
>
> Love Bron

And that was Bron's last letter to his parents from Cyprus.
  Evelyn wrote to his friends: 'Cornet Waugh is enjoying himself

top-hole in Cyprus,' and, on 9 June 1958, he wrote, with his fingers crossed, in a letter to Lady Diana Cooper: 'My boy is a cornet of horse. I hope he has some fighting.' How could he have known as he wrote those words that on that very evening his eighteen-year-old boy would be lying on the thin, hot road between Guenyeli and Orta Keuy slumped in a pool of his own blood, gasping for his life?

I never saw my father's bare arse or his exposed genitals and am glad of that, as a passing glimpse of either might have traumatised me for life – I am indebted to his modesty. Others – friends from school – who regularly witnessed their parents' trooping the corridors or even the kitchen stark naked felt perfectly at ease with the situation. I have heard it said that the regular spectacle of a naked parent is good for the growing child – it turns him into a man, or something like that. Perhaps I was too neurotic as a youth, but the fear of chancing on a friend's father's backside on an alien landing made me a reluctant guest in all their houses. I may have lost a few friends because of it.

The rights and wrongs of parental nudity are complicated. They always have been. Don't expect any help from the Bible. God punished Ham for peeping at his father as he lay naked in a drunken stupor; elsewhere the patriarchs clasp their fathers' pricks while making solemn promises to them. So, Christians, what line are we expected to take? In the nineteenth century Lord Esher shared his bathtub with his son through the entire period of his education. Both Esher and little Reginald ended up lunatic but their example does not seem to have stalled the naturist movement. Evelyn wrote to his eldest daughter, Teresa, in June 1961:

> Yesterday's *Sunday Times* had an article on paternity by Mr Mathew M.P. He said it was essential to the happy relations of fathers and children that they should congregate at bath-time. The children should stand around their father's bath. The spectacle of his nakedness and wetness while they are clothed and dry established confidence and equality. I am sorry I failed you in this.

I wonder if harboured recollections of naked fathers are more likely to puncture or augment the sexual confidence of young males. I wonder, also, in my own father's case, if his erotic sensibilities were not slightly impaired by the seminal shock of seeing (aged three) his nonogenarian step-great-great-grandmother naked in her bath. Her name was Grace Wemyss: she was his mother's mother's mother's stepmother. 'How beautiful you are looking today, Granny Grace,' he is said to have said. Evelyn, oblivious to the psychological damage this grotesque spectacle might have inflicted upon his little boy, wrote proudly in his diary: 'Auberon surprised her in her bath and is thus one of the very few men who can claim to have seen his great-great-grandmother in the raw.'

For fear of damaging my own children in this way I have ordained that they are never to look upon, to witness, even to ponder for an instant my *zones privés*. When I caught my son standing on a bucket to ogle me through a downstairs lavatory window I lectured him on the sin of Ham – no apology. In fury I composed a short verse for the moment and ordered him to recite it by heart within the hour or lose his claim to supper:

> I do not wish, nor ever have,
> To see thee, Daddy, on the lav,
> And though, I s'pose, thou art oft bare,
> 'Tis thy concern and thine affair.
> For he is but a craven fool
> Who muses 'pon his father's tool,
> Or creeps and peeps and tries to spy
> What lies within poor Papa's fly.
> So when thou next perchance be nude
> Fear not lest prying eyes intrude,
> For I who hold thee, Daddy, dear,
> Know well thy law and won't go near.

J. R. Ackerley, writing about his brother in his memoir *My Father and Myself*, described Peter's 'thin white buttocks and abnormally long dark cock, longer than my own or any other I had seen'. This, I think, is going a step too far and I would never venture to such a treatment of my own father even if I had that sort of information to hand. No – the subject only arises here because the rest of Papa's body, that part which I was permitted to see on the occasions of his swimming on our long summer holidays in the South of France, made a profound impression upon me.

For those who were unaware, the only clue to what lay beneath his shirt was the evidence of his left hand. A translucent scar ran past his thumb to a plump reddish mound, which was all that remained of his left index finger. It horrified my schoolfriends, and he relished the sight of young people recoiling from his deformity. He used to regale them with stories of how his finger had been bitten off by a Royal Bengal Tiger, caught in the string of a kite during a hurricane or had dropped off, quite inexplicably, that very morning.

If his left finger stump was disconcerting to behold, his back and chest were far worse. The front left side of his chest was gravely disfigured, as though the whole area from his left nipple to his armpit had violently imploded. On his back he had a scar two inches thick that ran from his shoulder to a deep, dark crevice behind his left elbow. This, to the squeamish, was a frightful sight.

Exactly what happened on 9 June 1958 is still shrouded in mystery. My application to the historical-disclosures department of the Army Records Office was returned only after six months of pestering with a heavily censored account of the official inquiry into the accident and a dossier of 'top-secret' information (sent to me in error) relating to my cousin Peter Waugh's hush-hush operations in the 9th Lancers.

One version of the accident was narrated by my father in an article, entitled 'The Ghastly Truth', that he published in the *New Statesman* fifteen years after the event:

> It was a very pleasant day with a school of Turkish policemen passing to and fro, being taught how to ride motor-bikes. We had been told to fraternise with them and they with us, so we waved enthusiastically every time they passed, waiting for one of them to fall off and cheering every time it nearly happened.

I had noticed an impediment in the elevation of the Browning machine-gun in the turret of my armoured car, and, having nothing else to do, resolved to investigate it. Seizing hold of the end with quiet efficiency, I was wiggling it up and down when I noticed it had started firing. Six bullets later I was alarmed to observe that it was firing through my chest, and got out of the way pretty sharpish. It may encourage those who have a fear of being shot to learn that it is almost completely painless, at any rate at close range with high velocity bullets. You feel a slight tapping and burning sensation and (if shot through the chest) a little winded, but practically no pain for about three quarters of an hour afterwards when, with luck, someone will have arrived with morphine, if you are still alive.

My first reaction to shooting myself in this way was not one of sorrow or despair so much as mild exhilaration. I lay down behind the armoured car and explained what had happened in words of a few syllables, to incredulous murmurs of 'coo' and 'cor', while an enterprising corporal climbed into the turret and tried to stop the machine gun. He managed it about 250 rounds later when the belt was nearly exhausted and a huge hole had been dug in the Kyrenia road. That is my memory of the incident, although there is no particular reason why people should prefer it to other versions.

Alternative accounts of the accident circulated then and continue to circulate to this day. Some said that he was shot in the back by his own men. My aunt Hatty believed that his corporal accidentally fired on him as he emerged from a building that was being searched for traces of the friends of the EOKA terrorist, Colonel Grivas; some say that one or both of his testicles were shot off. The *Daily Express*, in a front-page news story headlined 'Evelyn Waugh's Son Badly Wounded', claimed that the accident took place in the middle of a village, darkly hinting that a third party might have been involved. 'He was hit by a burst from a Browning automatic when it was accidentally fired.' The *Daily Mail*, also on its front page, went a step further:

MRS WAUGH FLIES TO BEDSIDE OF WOUNDED SON
Mrs Evelyn Waugh, wife of the novelist, will fly to Cyprus
today to visit her 18-year-old son, accidentally shot by one of
his men while patrolling curfewed Nicosia. His mother said:
'My flight has been arranged by the Red Cross and I hope to
leave London Airport early tomorrow. My husband will remain
at home.'

The Times announced that 'Second Lieutenant Oubyn Waugh' was
'accidentally shot during anti-riot operations in the Nicosia area'.
According to the report of the Army's internal investigation, Bron
'declined to make any comment or give any explanation' at the
time. Afterwards he signed a statement claiming that no one was
in the Ferret car or in any of the other cars. Of the soldiers who
were with him, none appears to have seen what happened. He was
entirely on his own, out of sight of his men, privately, incompe-
tently, mending his gun.

Evelyn's decision not to fly out to his son's bedside is hard to
understand. The doctors all assumed that Bron would die. To Lady
Diana Cooper he wrote, four days after the accident:

> Laura is in Cyprus with Bron. His life is very precarious.
> He seems to have had more than one bullet in lung and
> spleen. Details are wanting, but it sounds as though he will
> never completely recover. I shall go out to travel home with
> Laura if he dies.
>
> One good result of the newspaper reports is that monks
> and nuns and priests all over the country are praying for
> him. Prayer is the only thing.

Evelyn was furious with Bron: he took the view that he had shot
himself in a flagrant act of exhibitionism and was consequently a
disgrace to the Waugh name. The reason that 'details were wanting'
was that Evelyn had an eccentric distaste for the telephone and
refused ever to answer it. News of Bron's condition had to be telephoned to Laura's sister, Bridget, on a farm twenty miles away; she
drove to Combe Florey to relay it to her brother-in-law. When

Laura's letters from Cyprus started to arrive, Evelyn put a stop to Bridget's visits. At home, working on his priestly biography, he refused to allow any conversation about Bron's trouble. The original excuse for not flying out was that his friends Henry and Pansy Lamb were coming for the weekend and could not be put off. Later he modified this: prayer was the only solution to Bron's predicament and his own presence at his son's bedside would be of no use to his recovery. If I were a psychoanalyst I would plunge at this point into an interpretation of Evelyn's behaviour based on his experiences in the First World War when his father fussed and flapped at Underhill with anxiety over Alec. I would ascribe Evelyn's cold, detached reaction to Bron's pitiful condition as a subconscious reversal, a reaction against the memory of that trauma of 1918, an attempt, perhaps, to break away from his upbringing etc. etc. However, I am not a psychoanalyst, so I shan't 'go there' as they say. I leave it instead for others to decide – what do you think?

On the roadside Bron was given the last sacraments as he and his troops waited anxiously for medical assistance. On the way to the Royal Military Hospital in Nicosia the regimental doctor stood over his bed reciting the De Profundis while Bron spluttered responses through mouthfuls of blood. On arrival he was operated on immediately. With feeble implements and astonishing skill, the army surgeon diligently removed his spleen and two ribs; a third rib was wired together. Bron's left hand was also seriously damaged. Attempts were made to revivify his left index finger, which had been dislocated and fractured by one of the bullets, but if they failed, he was warned, it would have to come off.

Sifting the evidence from a ball-and-claw footed armchair in Combe Florey Evelyn smelt something fishy about the circumstances of his son's accident. Laura's first letter implied that it might have been Bron's fault for failing to unload the gun and that he would probably have faced a court-martial had he not been so badly injured. In her second letter she announced that everyone had fortunately agreed that it was no one's fault except the gun's: 'Apparently no one was to blame – it was the machine gun in the turret of an armoured car and no one was in the armoured car at the time and no accident like that has ever happened before. They think it must have been the heat but even so they cannot really understand it.'

A hurried investigation team hastily decided that Browning sub-machine guns can quite easily fire off 250 rounds all by themselves and the case was closed. Writing to his friend Ann Fleming nine days after the accident, Evelyn observed:

> It has been an anxious week but today the news from Cyprus makes it seem probable that Bron may survive. He stopped six bullets and has had a lung, his spleen, two ribs and part of a hand removed. Few people can have lived after such a fusillade. All done by the unaided and independent action of a new-fangled machine-gun. I have known many good soldiers hit by their own side (including a post-humous VC) and several rather moderate soldiers who shot themselves, but this is the first time I have known the weapon take control.
>
> It is the end of his army life, I am afraid, but the surgeons seem to think he may be fit for all but the most strenuous activities one day.
>
> Will you please give this information to anyone in London who enquires?

Unable to move from his bed, Bron impressed everyone with his bravery. The heat in Cyprus was stifling – often as high as 108°F during the day. Matters were not improved by painkillers which made him hallucinate, an abscess in his chest which had to be drained every other day of poisonous fluids, and a running high temperature of 102°F. For a week he was unable to speak more than a few stuttered words as his mouth was filled with tubes and the effort exhausted him. Laura saw him for fifteen minutes twice a day. As he strengthened, the length of her visits increased. For weeks on end he received no word from his father or from the rest of his family in England. Every day Laura begged her husband to write, but he did not respond:

11th June: I think it would be a good plan if you all started writing to him.

17th June: Do write to him and get everyone else to too. He longs for letters.

18th June: Do please write to him and get all the Herberts to write. He does long for letters.

19th June: He has received no letters. Please get everyone to write to him, he longs for it and all he thinks about is Combe Florey and the family.

20th June: Do get everybody to write. He longs for news and things to take his mind off his present life and he can't read books yet.

On 21 June Laura received a telegram from Evelyn wishing her a very happy birthday – but still nothing for Bron. The first and possibly the only letter he received from his father in Cyprus arrived on 22 June. Sadly it has been lost. By this stage Laura's implacable calm was fraying:

Do please *write* and get lots of other people to write it doesn't matter what, loving letters, newsy letters, anything. But Bron is often in pain and often pretty dopey but what he likes are things to either take his mind off his pain or else to meditate dreamily about. So far he has only received two letters, one from you and one from Margaret, and as the days go by it is such a disappointment to him. He particularly requests that there should be no let up in the prayers for him – he feels he needs them badly, especially now. I am so glad I came out to him, I think it does make a big difference. I read to him a lot now.

All the while Bron was painfully aware that his mother wanted to get back to England. He pleaded with her to stay, and the doctors backed him up, impressing on her the importance of her bedside vigils:

> He hates me being away and says if only he has someone to talk to it makes the pain and the heat more bearable. Also I do quite a lot of swabbing his face and giving him cold drinks and bullying nurses to move him when his bed sores get too uncomfortable.
>
> He announced today that if he died he implored us to have him flown back to England and buried there. He could not bear to be buried in Cyprus.

Laura was uncomfortable in the heat and felt herself to be a terrible imposition on her host, the governor. She did not think she had the right dresses to wear, bought a couple of new ones, felt frumpy in them, and wrote to Evelyn for instructions on etiquette and procedure at a governor's abode. 'As soon as it is safe for me to leave,' she wrote, 'I shall return.' She was missing Evelyn, missing her marigolds and, above all, she was missing her cows:

> Could you please deal with a couple of farm problems – will you tell Giovanni to give 1 spoonful of cow-cake daily to Magdelen and Desdemona this week and 2 spoonfuls daily to them from next Monday – Also is Lucy still giving 40lbs a day milk she had better be artificially inseminated next time she comes bulling with the Aberdeen Angus bull. If she is not giving as much as 30lbs I do not want her served at all.

Bron fought on courageously in the expectation of imminent death. His sister Meg had written to say she had given up ice-cream in some superstitious bid for his recovery; but he did not trust her and worried that if she had even a small taste of it he might die. He was also anxious that the family might soon lose interest in praying for him and precipitate his demise. For week after feverish week he lay in agony, clinging to life by the slenderest of threads. A small improvement on one day was invariably followed by a major setback requiring surgical adjustments on the next. The searing heat rendered doctors and nurses as dizzy and delirious as their patients. Laura reported, 'Today was the hottest thing I have ever known. We just sat and panted opposite each other. It was too hot to talk or think . . . Oh how I long for the coolness of England!'

For two days after the arrival of those letters from Evelyn and Meg, Bron tried his best to write a reply. The note he finished after two days' intensive labour was never sent, but it has survived. It was written in a jagged pencil script that is in places illegible:

Dear Papa, Meg, and everyone at Combe Florey,

Thank you all for your letters. They are an enormous comfort. But Mummy has lulled you into a false idea of my condition. While in *no* danger now of dying I am in daily . . . agony. Doctors stick needles into me to drain fluids, my back where the bullets came out . . . and sore . . . with pain . . . so KEEP praying please. The heat is appalling.

It was rather worrying earlier on to think my life depended on Meg not eating ice-cream. What would have happened if the temptation had proved too great?

All my love,

Many many thanks for the letters and please KEEP PRAYING

LOVE BRON

Laura's hoped-for return on the twenty-first was delayed by further setbacks and complications on the twentieth. Bron was not taken off the danger list until the twenty-ninth and it was only then that she felt it safe to return to her husband and her cows. After her departure for England Bron languished in Cyprus for a further week and a half before he was transported on a stretcher by military plane to a hospital at Millbank in London, but his problems were far from over. It was a further nine months and twelve operations before he was fit enough to be discharged from hospital.

On his arrival in England Evelyn was not present to greet him.

Instead he had decided to honour the foundation of the city of Munich with readings – which the Germans would not understand – from his books. He did, however, send a letter:

My Dear Bron,

Welcome home. I am delighted that you have escaped from the torrid and treacherous island of Cyprus. I wish I could come and greet you but I have a long-standing and very tedious engagement in Germany. It started as a treat for your mother, who now can't come with me. I am being paid to stand up in a theatre in Munich and read aloud for an hour to an audience of Huns who think that such a performance will somehow help celebrate the 800th anniversary of the foundation of their city. I am sure neither the Huns nor I will enjoy it.

Teresa who, insanely, means to spend August in Turkey will visit you, then your mother, finally I. I cannot tell you when dear little Septimus will arrive. Your grandmother has dashed off to persecute Lord de Vesci but no doubt she will soon be at your bedside.[2] She is well known to raise all invalids' temperatures five point degrees.

I hope you get a decent room to yourself overlooking the river. If the walls seem bare tell your neighbour Sir John Rothenstein[3] to bring round a few of the fine paintings he keeps hidden in the cellars of the Tate.

For spiritual comfort summon Mgr. John Barton, 43 Palace Street, Victoria 7635, a learned, very tall, slightly bawdy prelate who has been praying for you.

The pea-hen has laid two more eggs and is sitting. The pea-cock is so bored we can't keep him out of the house.

Yours ever affec. E.W.

---

[2] Bron's grandmother, Mary Herbert, was the only child of the 4th Lord de Vesci. The Lord de Vesci mentioned here was her first cousin, Yvo, who died a month later on 28 August 1958.

[3] Director of the Tate Gallery from 1938.

On the day that this letter was written Evelyn learned that his friend Lord Stavordale's son, Stephen Fox-Strangways, had been killed in action in Cyprus. The boy had been in Bron's regiment and had visited him in hospital the day before he was hit by a terrorist sniper in Nicosia. My father claimed he was shot coming out of the hospital, but I am not sure that was true. He was twenty years old. Evelyn was devastated by his death: all his stifled emotions about Bron suddenly vented and expressed themselves in a welter of grief at the Fox-Strangways' assassination. From Munich he wrote to Nancy Mitford:

> Thanks awfully for your letter about Bron. It was an anxious three weeks and painful for Laura who had to spend them under armed guard in the great heat, which she hates. It is Harry Stavordale who has been struck down. You saw? His only surviving son murdered. Tragedy doesn't seem appropriate to him and Nell. There is no conceivable human mitigation for their suffering.

To another friend Evelyn wrote from Munich: 'I have been hit very flat by Harry's tragedy . . . In a way I feel it is more poignant for Bron's recovery.' But Bron was still far from well. Evelyn saw him for the first time on his return from Munich, probably on 15 or 16 July, more than five weeks after the accident. When he arrived Bron was asleep and by his bed, written in his son's jagged invalid hand, a note:

> Memorandum: Waugh to Dr——
> Duties expected by Mr Auberon Waugh of his orthopaedic advisers:
> 1. Constant attendance and advice in orthopaedic matters
> 2. Curative treatment
> 3. Sobriety in dress and behaviour
> 4. A proper regard for the relationship between patient and physician. Given this day.

Evelyn immediately made arrangements for Bron to be transferred to a more comfortable hospital. When he finally talked to his son he was life-enhancing – witty, warm, sympathetic, clever, profound. If Bron had borne him any grudge for not writing or not rushing to his bedside in Cyprus, all was now forgiven. As soon as he was transferred to the better, cleaner, more ably administered Rock-Carling Ward of the Westminster Hospital he wrote to his father. Still, on 28 July, he thought he might die. The abscess in his back had developed into chronic empyema, or accumulation of pus, in the chest cavity. Too embarrassed to express his love to Evelyn's face he put it in a letter, sealed it up, wrote on the back 'For my father E. Waugh in the event of my predeceasing him, Auberon Waugh', and sent it to his bank in Oxford with instructions to pass it to his father after his death. The bank held on to it until Evelyn died in 1966, when they returned it to my father. Embarrassed, he buried it at the bottom of an old tin chest and thought no more about it. Written on the envelope in a bank clerk's hand are the words: 'He does not wish his father to know of the existence of this letter.'

Dear Papa,

Just a line to tell you what for some reason I was never able to show you in my lifetime, that I admire, revere and love you more than any other man in the world.

My possessions belong to you in any case, and will obviously be retained, divided or jumble-sold at your discretion, but I should very much like my collection of gramophone records to be given to the Grothers (that is Vera and her husband).

Love Bron

On 2 August Evelyn went to London for his second visit to Bron – his first in the new hospital. He wrote to warn of his arrival and Bron replied:

Dear Papa,

I should love to see you on Saturday and Sunday, more than

anything in the world, but the pleasure will alas be confined to gazing on your features as I am speechless at the moment with a sore throat. But you can read to me or we can pass each other little notes, or big ones for that matter. I can't remember exactly when Mama said she was coming but if this reaches home in time could she load herself with patent medicines instead of peaches, as the hospital despises them but can't cure me with its own mixtures.

Letters and gifts arrive daily from the whippery. The great whipping man himself was here yesterday, jovial but surprisingly sober; I didn't taunt him with the second-hand wax earplugs his wife had sent me a few mornings before.[4] With him, and smelling like Cleopatra in her barge on her way to meet Antony for the first time, was Uncle Auberon.

Don't come during an authorised visiting hour, but walk in any other time. You won't be treated with the reverence you found at Mill Bank, and which is your due anywhere, because nobody here has ever read a book in their lives, which is rather a relief for me as it saves me many impertinent enquiries. But play the poor parent from Somerset and they will be as plasticine in your hands.

Auberon brought some chicken paste and promised to bring oysters, champagne and *foie gras*. Whipper brought some greengages and promised nothing, but encouraged Auberon in his fantasies. W. also lent a very pretty picture book of Baroque by a German.

Nowadays I neither sleep nor eat nor talk. I feel the only way to remain human is to write long bad letters to everyone.

Love from your affectionate son, Bron

Still too unwell to undergo the major operation that doctors had in mind, Bron was transferred yet again to another hospital. No sooner had he arrived than he received a letter from his father

---

[4] The 'whipper', as mentioned, was philosopher and farmer Alick Dru, married to Laura's eldest sister, Gabriel Herbert.

there stating that he was not rich enough to continue the monthly allowance he had been giving him and that since Bron was in hospital he probably did not need it anyway. Bron ripped up the letter in a fury. 'I wept bitter tears of rage when I read it,' he remembered later.

Dear Papa,

Thank you for your letter. Far from being upset by your action, I am enormously grateful that you should have been so generous as to continue my allowance up to this moment. I hope that you soon overcome your financial difficulties. Mushroom growing is said to be remunerative or you could open a lodging house.

Before long Evelyn's temporary feelings of warm solicitude had turned to irritation that Bron was being spoiled by streams of guests at his hospital bedside. In August he wrote to Bron's godmother, Mary Lygon:

Auberon Alexander is having his character undermined by well disposed people who pamper him sitting round his bed and satisfying his every whim. He will be in hospital for many weeks and all the good done by the army at Caterham and Mons is being undone and he will be a sponger all his life. Jolly lucky if he can find people to sponge on, say I. I can't. My daughter Margaret is the joy of my heart, perhaps what you were to your father, only she does not bring me cocktails in my bath. My daughter Teresa is in Constantinople. I will not tell you of my other children, they live with rabbits and are mentally retarded.
      Auberon Alexander is in Sister Agnes's Home in Beaumont Street. Perhaps you will go and beat him and rob him and undo the bad work of others.

In the middle of October Sir Clement Price-Thomas, the distinguished surgeon who had ostentatiously failed to cure George VI of his lung cancer and eventually died of it himself, decided it was time to cut off Bron's left index finger. Of all his injuries, the depredations to his left hand were among those that upset him the most and the amputation of his finger, though a minor operation, was a distressing emotional experience. Evelyn wrote to comfort him:

Dear Auberon Alexander,

The man who calls on you purporting to be my brother Alec is plainly an impostor. Your true uncle does not know your whereabouts and supposes you to be here convalescent – as witness this card which came with a volume of his describing the more obvious and picturesque features of the West Indies. Did your visitor offer any identification other than baldness – not an uncommon phenomenon? Had he a voice like your half great uncle George? Did he wear a little silk scarf around his neck? Was he tipsy? These are the tests.

Your sister Harriet tells me you are to be operated on this week – the ponderous and intricate machinery of Sir Clement's mind having at last come to movement. I hope you enjoy the anaesthetic and that your awakening is not too disagreeable. Your mother told the Jesuits that you were to be operated on last week and they all prayed hard. I daresay God can postpone the effects. He must anyway be awfully bored at the moment with all the prayers for Pius XII who is already sitting pretty. Much better to pray for Chips Channon whose case is more precarious.[5]

Your Aunt Gabriel is obsessed by the need to lend you a relic of the true cross. Contrary to all experience she thinks it safer to send it by hand of Herbert than by post.

Your sister Margaret had a sharp attack of alcoholic poisoning, as the consequence of having been put in charge of the wine last weekend.

I resolutely deny myself butter potatoes bread etc and am shrinking in girth in a most encouraging way. My life otherwise is without interest.

[5] Pope Pius XII and Sir Henry Channon had both recently expired.

Mr Coggins broods about your condition perpetually.

Your affec. EW

On 17 November Bron spent his nineteenth birthday in bed at the Westminster Hospital where he had returned for further operations. Evelyn sent birthday greetings from Combe Florey:

My dear Bron,

Many happier returns of the day. It has been a year of triumph and disaster, has it not? I am sure you feel very much more than a year older. To have looked into the throat of death at 19 is an experience not to be sneered at.

I am dispatching your sisters to you, one today, a second on Monday. I have no other present than the blameless quills. Some time I hope very soon you will need a civilian wardrobe which will cost over £100. That must be your birthday and Christmas present. It is important to start out with a sufficiency of proper clothes.

Your mother tells me you are now a civilian and pensioner and that your pension may be delayed. If you are short of money I will, of course, advance it.

Your Aunt Bridget tells me you think of chucking English Literature as a school. If your college will let you, I strongly advise it. It is a fatal school for anyone who may, as I hope you will, become a writer. History, even read as sketchily as I read it, is a good school. Modern Greats now called something like 'P.P.E' provides general knowledge. I think you might find Law too inhuman. But you are master of your fate and captain of your soul now you are out of your teens.

A suggestion – why not read a lot of French? Light literature if you like. But a long spell in bed seems a good chance to enlarge your vocabulary and idiom.

I will call next Sunday.

Your affectionate papa
EW

That Christmas Evelyn, desperate to escape from his family at Combe Florey, decided to take Meg for three days' fun in London. Together they went to see *Peter Pan* and the first London production of Eugene O'Neill's *Long Day's Journey into Night*, which Evelyn described as 'an intolerable Irish-American play about a family being drunk and rude to one another in half-darkness'. On Christmas Day he took Bron out of hospital to lunch at the Ritz where they were moved to pity at the spectacle of rich old pensioners sitting unloved and on their own, with paper crowns on their heads, joylessly stuffing Christmas fare. Isn't it odd how these little things stick in the mind? My father never forgot it and used often to mention these people, holding them up to his children as a 'parable of human selfishness'.

Harriet (or Hatty), Evelyn's fifth child, suffered from dyslexia but no one in those days, neither her parents nor her teachers, was able to diagnose it. Evelyn concluded that she was backward and in letters to friends wrote her off as 'my dud daughter'. At Combe Florey she and her brother James had become obsessed with the breeding, stroking and avid petting of rabbits. Evelyn, who had cherished his own rabbits as a boy at Underhill, was at first enthusiastic but after a while began to see in Hatty and James's undiluted enthusiasm only further indication of their mental derangement. Hatty's favourite, Gabriel, and another called Raphael fell to the myxomatosis virus in December 1958, but James had cunningly taken a pair to school which, despite masculine names – Michael and Harvey – succeeded in breeding together a whole new generation. Back at Combe Florey in the Christmas holidays Evelyn complained that the rabbits were not entering enough into the spirit of the season and gave them each a goblet of vodka to perk them up. They expired of alcohol poisoning on New Year's Eve.

XIII

Leaving Home

So Bron finally escaped the privations of the Westminster Hospital in March 1959. A *chaise-longue* was brought by cattle truck from Laura's sister's house to Combe Florey for the purposes of his recuperation and for four months he languished upon it, daydreaming, smoking, reading P. G. Wodehouse, occasionally poking his nose out of doors and, much to his father's irritation, dropping matchsticks and ash all over the floor. Evelyn was abroad for a lot of this time but not long enough to diminish his irritation at the continued presence of his convalescent son. Oxford awaited, but that was not until October. In the meantime it was agreed that as soon as Bron was on his feet he should go abroad.

Despite his enormous fame, both at home and in America, Evelyn was again beginning to feel poor. The tax burden in those days was punitive, and he could no longer afford more than a skeleton staff. He was depressed, sozzled, inactive, bored and looking forward to death. His children continued to irritate him – all, that is, except Meg. To her he wrote on Bron's return from hospital: 'Darling Hog . . . Please marry someone very rich very soon, let him die, then you can set up house for me on a luxurious scale. I would not mind your having one daughter if she were like you. No sons please.'

In November 1958 the War Office medical board pronounced Bron unfit for 'any form of military service under existing standards' and his commission was relinquished on 15 January. Shortly before his departure for France the famous photographer Mark Gerson came to Combe Florey to take pictures of the family. Evelyn insisted that Bron dress up in his Royal Horse Guards uniform for a picture but Bron, no longer a soldier, was reluctant to do so. A battle of wills ensued, which Evelyn won. I remember photographers coming to Combe Florey to take pictures of my father and his similarly insisting that I take part. I loathed doing so, but Papa could be quite demanding: 'Look, you bugger, we have to keep the show on the road.'

Evelyn thought Gerson's picture of Bron in his uniform dashing and sent copies of it to grand Catholic friends whose daughters, he hoped, might take a fancy to him. One of these was Lady Acton whose fourth daughter, Jill, seemed just the ticket: 'How does Jill like the photograph of Cornet Waugh?' Evelyn wrote. 'He has just gone off today to the South of France. How I despise those who go there in summer.'

Bron set out for France with eighty pounds in his pocket, planning to spend six glorious poolside weeks with some exceedingly rich Herbert cousins at their southern French villa at Valescure before moving on to his uncle Auberon's hilltop castle at Portofino in Italy. To his astonishment the Valescure millionaires decided to charge him for food, wine and restaurant meals. Within a few days he was forced to the sorry conclusion that he could no longer afford their hospitality. Uncle Auberon was not ready to receive him at Portofino so he set off instead for a lodging house in Bologna, which he remembered as being exceedingly cheap two years earlier. On arrival, with nothing to do and no money to spend, he decided to write a novel. Years later he thanked his stingy cousins for their parsimony without which he might never have launched his successful career.

Bron's letters home from Bologna contain an even balance of extravagant sightseeing news and urgent requests for money. The tone is jocular, never timid. He told Evelyn that the novel he was working on was based on his experiences in hospital and Evelyn was at first delighted to hear that his son was making a serious attempt to join the family business. He had always hoped that Bron would become a writer and had urged him to have a book out by the time he was eighteen. The hospital *mise-en-scène* seemed a good one:

My Dear Bron,

Augustus Hare says of Bologna (in 1876) that it has 'an agreeable society of well-informed resident nobility'. I trust that you have the entrée into these circles and are not alienating them by scattering matches on the floors of their palaces. Hare also says that all the beauties of the city may be seen in three days and he was not a hustler.

So I imagine that you are occupied with writing. The theme of 'operations' is extremely popular with middle-aged literary subscribers, here and in the USA. I think a light treatment of your hospital experiences would find a publisher and a public . . .

What Bron had not told his father was that his 'hospital' novel opened in a school – a Benedictine monastery school rather like Downside. When the news reached Evelyn he wrote immediately to Bron:

I enclose a catechism. Your grandmother (on Harriet's authority I think) has told the monks at Downside that you are composing a diatribe against them. I am confident you are incapable of ingratitude to these patient and magnanimous men. Pray bear in mind that until you are 21 you cannot legally publish a book without my consent as you are incapable as a minor of signing a contract. I do not anticipate having to withhold my imprimatur. Your best course, I think, will be to have it typed and sent to Peters[1] asking him to find a publisher without disclosing your name. It will be more gratifying to have it accepted on its own merits than on my, or my brother's, notoriety. As soon as it is accepted you can claim it and publish under your name.

[1] A. D. Peters, Evelyn's literary agent. Alec had been one of his first clients.

The best restaurant in Genoa is named Pichen.

Your affec. papa

Perhaps Evelyn's letter sounded more severe than he had intended. Bron wrote back to tell him that he was, anyway, losing heart. Evelyn returned with a postcard urging him to continue, finish the work and send it to his agent. The Downside problem was 'not grave', he assured him.

More important to both Bron and Evelyn was the question of money. Evelyn worried about the cost of sending Bron to university, while Bron, who had taken to eating nasturtium leaves from public gardens, was desperate to survive the next three weeks until he joined his rich uncle at Portofino.

Dear Bron,

There used to be very comfortable charabancs with very polite drivers which stopped at cafés and restaurants and places of interest between Ravenna and Bologna but that was in the good days of Il Duce.

I am told that £450 is not enough for an undergraduate. The President of Trinity told me £600 enabled a man to live as he and I did on £300. I went down deep in debt. I hope you won't. I will make up your total income to £650 for the next three years. If your pension goes down, my allowance will go up. I don't know whether the House will let you have your full £50 exhibition. If they do I will give you £284. I will also, of course, settle your current tailors' bills. After October, unless for special emergencies, the £650 must suffice for all requisites and pleasures. You will not be charged for board here during the vacations but will have to pay for travel. It would be well worth your while to apply for the best rooms in college. I will advance you the Caution Money and Deposit (not out of your allowance). These sums should be repaid when the college repays them, for the education of your younger siblings.

. . . Your account at Barclay's, Oxford, is guaranteed by me. If you run short of money do not borrow from Auberon. Make him cash a cheque for you. It will be honoured. The Inspector of Taxes has sent you £2.8/–.

This letter seems to be all about money. An absorbing topic in old age.

When I visited Bologna there was a dead saint, dressed as a nun, sitting in an armchair. One could shake hands with her. Can one still? She is called Catherine and died in the 15th century.

Your affec. papa, EW

Bron made an effort to find St Catherine although probably not as large an effort as he maintained in his letter:

Dear Papa,

Thank you for your letter and for your nice settlements . . . I have searched high and low in Bologna for St Catherine; I went to the Central Tourist Office and produced my passport and demanded to be allowed to shake her hand but they seemed puzzled and a little shocked. I have approached begging friars and one-eyed guides, but they all claim ignorance of her. The best they could do was show us the body of a Cardinal Rocca which was not nearly so good. I think that she must have rather retired from social life since the good old days.

'Money,' Bron wrote, 'is also a fairly absorbing topic in extreme youth.' Please, he begged, could his father send thirty pounds on to Portofino and to Bologna: 'Two five pound notes in separate envelopes – my criminal acquaintances tell me that you should wrap the notes in carbon-paper to elude a device employed by the Excise man to detect the Lavery line in bank-notes.' In his autobiography Bron suggested that Evelyn had deliberately ignored his request for money but this was not true. His father did immediately as asked but, for some reason, the money failed to arrive. After a short wait Bron wrote again, complaining that he was at Death's door and would expire if the money was delayed a day longer. He may have pretended not to have received it. He was still very duplicitous in those days. In any case, by the time he received Evelyn's postcard he was already safely ensconced at Alta Chiara, his uncle's castello in Portofino:

> Dear Bron,
>
> I am distressed to learn of your starvation and the loss of the notes I sent. Each in a separate envelope, wrapped in carbon-paper. One included a card from myself so I shall no doubt be subject to criminal proceedings unless, as I hope, your servant in Bologna stole them.

Between school and university I spent eight months in Paris telling my father that all I needed for the whole period was two hundred pounds: I could earn the rest when I got there. 'No chance,' he said. 'You'll be begging me for money within a month.' Did I detect a sneer? I think so. In Paris I succeeded in living from hand to mouth by teaching English and the violin to children of rich parents, but nobody warned me of the half-term break when every Parisian child of the middle class evacuates the city for the pleasures of *la campagne*. For three days I stared at my last ten francs wondering whether to exchange them for a Camembert or a packet of cigarettes. In the end I decided the fags would be a greater comfort. For seven days I ate nothing at all, filling my belly with water in the hope of relieving the hunger, but was determined not to ring my father or to give him an ounce of I-told-you-so satisfaction.[2] On the eighth day I gave a violin lesson to a six-year-old. '*Oui, très bon*,' I said hazily, as the boy scraped his way through 'Twinkle, Twinkle' with a green bogey stuck to his left index fingernail. As soon as the money was in my hands I staggered to a burger

[2] I have since been informed that hunger, like any other pain, is easily relieved by aspirin.

bar called O'Kitch, ordered a large *O'Kitch et frites s'il vous plaît*
and vomited the first two mouthfuls over the floor of the restaurant – a Pyrrhic victory against my father. I don't think he ever
noticed that I had not asked him for money and I was too well-
mannered to point it out.

Money continued to be an absorbing topic for father and son while
Bron was studying at Oxford University. He tried but failed to live
within his means. Evelyn was not ungenerous and bailed him out
several times, sent him bottles of sherry and lent him several grand
pictures to adorn his rooms, but Bron set his heart on better rooms
for which he would need even grander pictures:

> Thank you for your post-card. Do please come and see
> my rooms at any time, but I am afraid you will see nothing
> new. The room is simply a white cube, and the only saving
> features are your own Solomons and the drawing of the
> Vatican. If I manage to get the room upstairs I shall need
> many more pictures – things like King George III – in
> order to preserve its dignity – what happened to Queen
> Charlotte? If she's still around she would do . . . Have you
> bottled any more sherry? If so can I come and pick it up
> on Friday? I shall telephone on Thursday to confirm it. I
> would very much like to bring a few people to show off
> the pictures to, and Papa, and the cows, and the works.
> They would be very nice, need nothing to eat (perhaps a
> little drink) . . . They would need no reparations, would
> break nothing, drop no matches. Is the thought more than
> you can bear? It would be the greatest pleasure to me and
> them.

At Combe Florey Evelyn was welcoming to all Bron's friends, though
he enjoyed teasing them as Charles Ryder's father in *Brideshead
Revisited* had teased Charles Ryder's guests. One of Bron's university friends was asked: 'Pray, what would you care to drink?' 'A
glass of sherry, please Mr Waugh.' 'Turtle soup? I fear we have no
turtle soup.'

Everyone appeared to be afraid of Evelyn — except Laura, who stamped on his feet when he was being recalcitrant, Meg, who brazenly admonished him for drinking too much, and Bron, who barracked and joshed him as though he were one of his own raffish student contemporaries. As Bron later put it:

> At about this time I began to be quite fond of my father, never having liked him much in childhood or early youth. As I prepared to leave home and set up my own establishments elsewhere he became more tolerant of my various failings, and in the last five years of his life we enjoyed a distinct cordiality.

At Oxford Bron made many friends. In the first few weeks he was ecstatically happy, writing to his father, 'Oxford is the most tremendous fun but it cannot possibly last. Either we shall all get a lot nastier or we shall all be sent down very soon I fear. There are more nice people than I realised existed in the country or the world.' As he predicted, his joy could not last for ever. The novel he had written in Bologna was he decided NBG — No Bloody Good. He put it away in a drawer and started another, a feeble rant about adolescent sexual frustrations that was never published. He spent too much money, as all students do, fell in love with the wrong girl and did no work.

Within a month of his joining the university he was involved in a car smash that nearly killed him. Once again Evelyn was reluctant to attend his hospital bedside. Writing to his eldest daughter Teresa, he informed her:

> I am sorry to tell you that your brother, Bron, is again in hospital. On Thursday night a car full of undergraduates on their way to a party in Hampshire ran headfirst into a lorry. Bron was not driving, I am glad to say, but he is the worst injured. He has cracked his skull and will be laid up a long time . . . he is conscious, in great pain, drowsy and forgetful. His life is not in danger but it will be a setback to his university career. Your mother is going to see him

on Tuesday. We have had no report of the accident but I presume the undergraduates were at fault. The driver, young Lennox-Boyd, is reported to be dangerous on the roads. If you do not hear to the contrary you may assume that Bron is making a satisfactory recovery. We shall know more after your mother has been to Winchester. I presume he will have another Christmas in hospital.

On a second visit Laura took Evelyn to Winchester with her, but he did not go into the hospital, preferring to visit his donnish friend John Sparrow, instead.

During his convalescence Bron decided to take another look at *The Foxglove Saga*, the novel he had written in Bologna and, much to his surprise, found it brilliant. He particularly chortled at the inventiveness of his dénouement, a savage and surreal episode in which a hairy-legged baby (Tarquin) scratches out the eyes of his adopted mother (a pious, cold-hearted do-gooder called Lady Foxglove) as she attempts to kiss him on the lips. Without telling his father or showing him the manuscript, Bron spent the Christmas holidays at Combe Florey furtively perfecting it in his bedroom. When it was ready, he had the manuscript typed and, in mid-January 1960, sent directly to Jack MacDougall, managing director of Chapman and Hall. Perhaps he should have sent it elsewhere, or even, as his father had suggested, anonymously to the agent A. D. Peters, but he needed money badly and Chapman and Hall, who had a sixty-year association with the Waugh family, seemed an expedient choice. Mr MacDougall telegraphed him by return:

ACCEPT FOXGLOVE WITH PLEASURE HORROR AND DEEP ADMIRATION STOP MANY CONGRATULATIONS = JACK

In his follow-up letter he wrote, 'I suppose you were born with a first-rate prose style, for I cannot think how you could have acquired it so soon: there are no signs of the beginner in the writing of this book . . . Have you shown it to your parents or to anyone else?'

Of course Bron had not shown it to anyone. Evelyn was overjoyed

at the news that his son's book was going to be published but Bron
would not let him read it until the proofs were ready at the end
of February. Evelyn wrote to his son at Oxford on 7 March:

Dear Bron,

Your sister Margaret and I returned on Thursday night
from an instructive visit to Rome and Athens. We are in
good health and found your mother in the same condition. I
fell upon *Foxglove Saga* and read it with great delight. I
congratulate you. It is original, lively and well written; far
better than I or your uncle Alec wrote at your age. I
particularly enjoyed the army episodes. I am confident that
you will get encouraging reviews. I don't think you can
hope for great financial success but it will be proof of
ability and promise which will ensure respectful attention
when you come to apply for employment. I urge you,
however, not to abandon the idea of taking your degree.
To go down without one is not a deep disgrace but it is
a minor disadvantage. When you come to seek a job the
lack of a degree will be a slight bias against you in most
occupations. You are at your ease in Oxford. It is a place
with numberless opportunities for enjoyment. Your difficulties, you say, are financial. These, I think, must be the
result of gluttony. The world is full of much more expensive
restaurants than can be found in Oxford. You will not
solve your problem by changing your address. Do not
count on any great gain except in prestige from your book.
Prestige is more enjoyable at Oxford than in Paris, London,
New York or Bologna. Make the most of it.

The copy of *Foxglove* I have read is, I know, uncorrected.
I enclose a list of some *errata*. Note especially: the more
fantastic the incidents of the book, the more important to
preserve plausibility in detail. There is no point in setting
your school in N. Ireland where it could not exist and from
which a sick monk would not be transported to a London
hospital. If Lady F. was Lady Julia Something she would

still be Lady Julia when married to a knight; not Lady F. You suggest that young Foxglove has a long career in the army and then sharply curtail it. I think it is a great mistake to call your characters (in the narrative, not in the dialogue) sometimes by their surnames and sometimes by their Christian names. I *think* (and this is purely a matter of taste) that it is a mistake for the author to lapse into slang when the book is not written in the first person. But, perhaps, you have changed all this in your revision. It is a mistake to use the name 'Smith-Bingham', a small identifiable family. You have great ingenuity in inventing names. I *think* you introduce the position of O'Connor *père* as editor too late. The hospital scenes at the beginning are admirable. I especially enjoyed the incident in which Foxglove gets the credit for laying a false scent for O'Connor. The book is full of excellent jokes. Too much stealing perhaps? Theft should be an outrage not a normal form of conduct if it is to be funny. 'Hen' 'Ken' admirable joke. As many others.

. . . Try living as I do on one square meal a day. It was enough for Petronicus and too much for Byron.

The Guinness Family has opened a hotel in Venice. Suck up to Lennox-Boyd and point out, if you are sent down, that his reckless driving is responsible for your failure and perhaps he will find you employment there. It is called Cipriani's.[3]

Don't get bored with your book before publication. Keep revising until the last moment . . .

Yours affec. E.W.

In the month before publication Bron attended a string of balls and parties in and around Oxford. A surviving letter to Evelyn describes a long list of them in heady, inebriate detail and ends:

Last night I was at a very pleasant dance given in Sussex

---

[3] Lennox-Boyd's mother was a Guinness girl.

at which there was a room entirely given over to middle-aged love and all the little debutantes stared wide-eyed through the windows at the gross figures sprawled over sofas. My examinations start tomorrow and so I am spending a quiet evening with my books. I should be disagreeably surprised if I do not distinguish myself.

He knew he had not done nearly enough work to pass, let alone distinguish himself. In truth he was confident of failure. No miracle could save him but he needed money from his father for a holiday in Rhodes. By the time the results were published Bron would be safely abroad. In his autobiography *Will This Do?* he claimed to have artfully wheedled the money from his father; Evelyn, in a letter to a friend, put it the other way round: 'Bron said I looked corpulent. He has come down and I am trying to bribe him to go abroad. He shows a painful affection for home life.' Bron was still in Rhodes when an open postcard from Oxford University arrived at Combe Florey with 'FAILED' stamped in red ink on one side.

On his return he was presented with a stark choice by the university: resit or get out. Sensing the first flowers of literary success with *Foxglove* he decided on the latter but declared, to his dying day, that his ejection from Oxford was the biggest single humiliation of his life. Evelyn did not seem to mind too much: he said it was 'foolish' of Bron to be sent down but blamed the university's draconian rules of matriculation for his leaving. That week he wrote to inform Bron's old Downside master Aelred Watkin:

Bron's failure in schools was a great surprise to him but he is not cast down because at the moment he is flush of money, having received ample advances on his book and having not yet understood that he will have to pay tax on them. I have set him to read Cyril Connolly's *Enemies of Promise* as a warning of the hazards of literature as a profession and I think he would like to find employment.

He made a lot of friends at Oxford but he was never captivated by the university as I was. Perhaps it is less captivating these days. He might just as well have been living in barracks at Windsor for all the part he took in real Oxford life.

There are indications that his novel is going to have a success. Not perhaps the best thing for the formation of his character but very convenient for my pocket.

Yours affec.
E.W.

In the run-up to the publication of *Foxglove* Bron had sent proof copies to many of his father's literary friends. Most were genuinely impressed. Graham Greene wrote to him, 'You are going to suffer a lot of irritation when reviewers compare you to Evelyn, but *The Foxglove Saga* has only one parent and stands magnificently alone.' John Betjeman described Bron as a 'born novelist' and Malcolm Muggeridge thought *Foxglove* 'the most brilliant work by a young author' that he had read in years. But some of Evelyn's more prudish Catholic friends were disgusted. One of them, Douglas Woodruff, wrote both to Bron and to Evelyn urging them to withdraw 'this revolting, callous and filthy book'. Evelyn wrote back:

Dear Douglas,

Bron is away at the moment. I am sure that he will receive your criticism with proper respect but I do not think he or the publishers will think it feasible to stop the book appearing in its present form.

I read it with relief that it was neither blasphemous nor salacious and, to my taste, 'the coldness' of the cruelty made it inoffensive and fantastic. I hope you are wrong in supposing it will do him or anyone else any harm.

Shortly before *The Foxglove Saga* was published, Bron took a job as copy editor at a magazine called *Queen*. When the novel came out it was an instant success. Most of the critics praised the work for its freshness and originality. John Davenport, in the *Observer*, hailed Bron as 'the new voice of the decade', while the most offensive review came from Quentin Crewe, a wheel charioteer, who resented the attention the book was getting at a time when no one was showing the slightest interest in his own recent treatise on the Japanese. 'Only the son of one of the literary establishment would have got this book published with so much publicity,' he wailed, in the *Sunday Express*. 'I can say without doubt that it is one of the most heartless disagreeable books I have ever read. Contempt reeks from every page . . . For what? For nothing but the hope of a joke. A joke which never comes. No sadistic, perverted, vulgar trick is missed. No object achieved.' Strangely, at the time he wrote that review, Crewe was Bron's boss at *Queen*. Evelyn disliked the magazine. 'Bron,' he wrote, 'has become involved in a very common paper called *Queen*. Not, as you'd think, about buggery. A sort of whining *Tatler*.'

He urged his son to resign as soon as the review appeared. 'Do not be deflected from destroying Crewe,' Evelyn wrote to him. 'Take the line "and this is the man who dares set himself up as a critic".' Bron, obedient to his laws, pursued Crewe with merciless onslaughts for the next forty years but he needn't have bothered. Crewe's sneering made no impact: by November the book had sold fourteen thousand copies in hardback and was reprinting. Bron's small advance of £150 from Chapman and Hall had been supplemented by £1500 in serialisation rights from the *Daily Express* and $2000 from the American publishers Simon and Schuster. By the end of July he had found a new job as a sub-editor on the *Daily Telegraph*, the same paper to which his grandfather, Arthur Waugh, had for thirty years, contributed a weekly book review.

Evelyn was convinced – correctly as it turned out – that his son's success would not be repeated. He was worried also that Bron would squander his money before paying tax on it and that his sudden fame would go straight to his head and ruin him. When a friend wrote to him in praise of the book Evelyn responded on a postcard: 'I am most exhilarated that you enjoyed *The Foxglove Saga*. My first instinct was to send your letter to the author. Then reason intervened. I don't want him to get a swelled head or still less a swelled idea of his expectations. I enjoyed it too.' Martin Stannard, in his often ponderous two-volume biography of Evelyn, claimed that Evelyn (who at this time felt his own creative powers were fading) was jealous of his son's success, but I can find no evidence to support this. He was delighted by the 'undeserved' success of *The Foxglove Saga*; he thought it was a very funny book; he helped to publicise it in the *Daily Mail*, to antagonise those critics who had insulted it and was demonstrably proud to be the father of its author. 'I rejoice in your success,' he wrote to Bron. 'Regard it as a lucky win at gambling – not likely to be repeated. Think of your Uncle Alec who had a great success at your age and waited 40 years for another. But enjoy it to the full while you have it.' In September he read the book for a second time with 'enhanced enjoyment'.

Evelyn recognised that the best passages in *Foxglove* were based on Bron's personal experience. Rashly, or perhaps typically for a first novelist, Bron had used all the experience he had – school, the army, hospital – in writing it and had left himself very little (other than a single inebriate year at Oxford) to draw upon for his next novel. To gain more experience for another novel Evelyn urged him to find an interesting job. Bron's natural enthusiasm for mendacity and subterfuge suggested the intelligence services – an area in which Evelyn had many useful contacts, not least his old drinking companion from Oxford, Roger Hollis, at that time the M of James Bond – head of MI5. The Waughs have, for three generations, maintained cordial links with the Secret Services, though we're not supposed to talk about them. Hollis arranged for Bron to meet Admiral Sir Charles Woodhouse at Carlton Gardens on 13 July. The interview, which was of an exploratory nature, went well enough and Frank Pakenham, later Lord Longford and Bron's godfather, worked behind the scenes to advance his cause. A second series of interviews was proposed for September, by which stage Bron had arrogantly assumed that he was in. Evelyn wrote to him beforehand:

> You have an interview in London on 19th for your Foreign Office job. It is in fact the first of two days' interviews . . . you will need to see your barber and rearrange your wardrobe. Frank Pakenham has been to great trouble on

your behalf. He learns that at your first interview you made a generally favourable impression but the examiners feared that you might find the restraints of the service irksome. Hatty went to a party and was greeted at once with 'we hear your brother is in the secret service'. It is important that you should refrain from boasting.

Over the next three years Bron tried three times to join the intelligence services but was turned away on each occasion. It is surprising after so many rebuffs that he should have continued to help them on an *ad hoc* basis. One of his MI6 friends later told him that his efforts to join between 1960 and 1963 had been thwarted by Martin Dunne, an army associate who had been lampooned as a callous prig in *The Foxglove Saga*. Dunne's letter of reference had stated that, to his certain knowledge, Bron was unfit to join the service. The letter was dragged out of his file and held against him on each reapplication. Spurned by the intelligence services, Bron turned his talents reluctantly back to journalism.

After his book was published Bron felt rich and set himself up as a dandy bachelor-about-town in a small but luxuriously panelled Edwardian apartment on Clarges Street in Mayfair. Determined to transform it into a 'veritable palace', he bought expensive pictures from the galleries in Bond Street, antiques, carpets and bibelots, writing excitedly to inform his father of all his latest purchases. He commissioned suits from Evelyn's tailors in Savile Row, dined at expensive restaurants, and at the weekends went shooting with grandees in the country.

But the more money Bron earned, the more convinced Evelyn became that he was headed for bankruptcy. 'After your 21st birthday,' he wrote to him, 'I shall not bore you with advice. Meanwhile I urge you to examine your surtax position. It is a deadly encumbrance to be in debt to the government. They always win. When you say that you will enjoy 70% of your present earnings, my heart quails for you. 30% seems a more probable figure. Have you consulted an accountant?'

But Evelyn need not have worried: my father might have been

a little eccentric in his financial affairs but he was also prudent. He was terrified of debt and, to my knowledge, never had an overdraft. The accumulated funds in his current account made him sublimely happy – so much so that he used to send me into Taunton to get a statement from the cashpoint machine so that he could gloat over it with a beatific smile and a glass of gin. He liked to carry large sums of cash around with him wherever he went. His wallet always had two or three hundred pounds in it.

Throughout his life he was wary of financial advice, never buying stocks or shares, shunning Lloyds Insurance schemes, gilts, bonds and all forms of high-street usury. His only investments were in precious metal. Like a pirate of the sixteenth century he surrounded himself with great piles of gold and silver – krugerrands, Maria-Theresa silver thalers and, at one time, a large box of solid silver ingots.

When I was about ten years old I removed a bag of treasure from his library and buried it somewhere in the garden. It contained, if I remember correctly, around twenty silver coins of great antiquity. A week later I decided it would be fun to dig them up again but couldn't for the life of me remember where they were buried. I confessed tearfully, but Papa didn't seem to mind. Years later I took a metal detector to the area where I thought the treasure had been hidden and still could not find it. Perhaps one day someone will retrieve that hoard only to have it confiscated under the avaricious terms of Treasure Trove.

Bron's enthusiasm for precious metal started with the Downside Numismatic Club and continued throughout his life. With his money from *Foxglove* he bought his first collection of solid silver bars. Evelyn thought it a sign of dementia. When he realised that Bron was never going to marry Lady Acton's daughter, Jill, he wrote to his friend to console her:

> I think Jill is well out of Bron. He is rather mad I think. His collar drawer is full of what look like slabs of chocolate in silver paper and are really bar silver. He has taken grand rooms in Clarges Street, goes shooting with the nobility and entertains extravagantly. Every time I see him

he is wearing a new set of clothes. My beloved Margaret
I see all too little . . . Also, I forgot to say, Bron's teeth
are black.

Any lingering hopes that Bron might still be in line for a marriage
to Jill Acton were finally dashed at the end of February 1961 when
he surprised his family with a peremptory announcement of his
engagement to Teresa Onslow. On hearing the news Evelyn wrote
to Lady Acton, Jill's mother:

> Dearest Daphne,
>
> Hard tidings.
> My son, impatient at the curb put on his passion by
> Jill, has become engaged to a Protestant girl. I am very
> sorry it is not your dear daughter. Match-making must be
> postponed now unless you can make your eldest son marry
> my idiot daughter, Harriet. My non-idiot daughters both
> have their absurd affections engaged elsewhere. Perhaps the
> Maltese journalist would take idiot Hatty?

Lady Acton's second son, the Maltese journalist, became professor
of dogmatic theology at the Westminster Diocesan Seminary and
never married. Hatty, on the other hand, married the American
art critic Richard Dorment. Her eldest sister, Teresa, married an
American academic (John D'Arms) and moved permanently to the
United States in 1961. Meg, much to her father's chagrin, was
married in 1962. Evelyn wrote, 'Your sister Margaret has fallen
deeply in love with a penniless stockbroker's clerk named
FitzHerbert. He seems a pleasant young man. They will be married
(I hope) without celebrations, but it is hard to discourage the ambitions of brides.' He did not want his 'eye-apple' to marry at all but
realised that he could not easily forbid it. 'She wants children,' he
wrote sadly, 'and that is a thing I can't decently provide for her.'
Giles FitzHerbert, he believed, had 'a rather common way with
him', an 'oriental face' and, he suspected, might be 'some sort of
crook'. He was twenty-seven, had taken a job in stockbroking on

his engagement, but seemed to have done nothing much before that. Later he joined the diplomatic service and ended his career as British ambassador to Venezuela.

Evelyn poured out his anguish at losing Meg in his last work of published fiction called *Basil Seal Rides Again*, a long short story about a fat, fifty-eight-year-old father conniving to thwart the marriage plans of his beloved daughter. His closest friends teased him about the semi-incestuous nature of his relationship with Meg. None could have failed to notice how Basil Seal's obsession with his daughter Babs had been drawn from real life:

> His daughter wore very tight, very short trousers, slippers and a thin jersey . . . Two arms embraced his neck and drew him down, an agile figure inclined over the protuberance of his starched shirt, a cheek was pressed to his and teeth tenderly nibbled the lobe of his ear . . . He disengaged himself and slapped her loudly on the behind.

'I feel that with Meg I have exhausted my capacity for finding objects of love,' he wrote, to Diana Cooper. 'How does one exist without them? I haven't got the euphoria that makes old men chase tarts. My ghastly brother calls them "pipe lines" through which he is refuelled with youth. Not for me. Did I tell you my brother has written an autobiography in which he says: "Venus has been kind to me"?'

Evelyn told his friends not to congratulate him on his acquisition of a son-in-law but on 'my great beauty of character in surrendering my daughter to Fitz Giles'. Meg, for her part, tried to reassure him that her marriage to FitzHerbert would not alter their perfect relationship:

> I haven't really thanked you properly for being so kind about my engagement – you are the best father anyone can ever have had in the history of the world – really no flattery or sucking up – I think that. And there need be no divorce between us – I will come home just as often for weekends – Giles won't mind.

Meanwhile James, who was studying at the grim Catholic monastery school of Stonyhurst, was told by his father to become a Catholic priest. He refused and was instructed to join the army instead. When he wrote to Evelyn begging to be allowed to go to Oxford, he was branded by his father as a 'coward' and a 'disgrace' – 'My son James is a thorn. Won't go into the church or the army, smokes cigarettes and can't take his hands out of his pockets. My youngest son is a jewel but I suspect he will grow up homosexual.' In a similar round-up of his sons to another correspondent Evelyn wrote: 'My youngest son is a saint, my second son a dutiful bore, my eldest son was a fiend at puberty but lately much improved in character.'

If Evelyn had a snobbish bone in his body, which maybe he had, he should have been pleased that his future daughter-in-law, Teresa Onslow, though not of the Catholic faith, was blue-blooded. She was the daughter of the 6th Earl of Onslow and directly descended from more British monarchs than George VI, who was King of England at the time of her birth, but due to the speed of their engagement Evelyn hardly knew her. In a letter to his publisher he bewailed: 'It is distressing that my son should think of marriage at an age when he should give himself to the education of *a femme du monde de quarante ans*, but, as you remark, in the age of miscegenation it is agreeable that he should have chosen a consort of his own class.'

Teresa Onslow had visited Combe Florey only once before Bron announced his intention to marry her. On that occasion Evelyn had taken an instant liking to her. She was humorous, sharp and unafraid of him. At dinner on her first night Bron had casually turned to his father: 'Papa, do you like Penelope Betjeman?'

'If you are asking me if I have fucked her, the answer is "yes".'

Teresa was unfazed by her future father-in-law's eccentricity and Evelyn admired her all the more for it.

The first Evelyn and Laura heard of Bron's marriage plans arrived by letter on 21 February:

Dear Mummy and Papa,

I wondered if I might return this week-end to Combe

Florey, although I am afraid it will be a fleeting visit, to arrive on the Saturday and leave on the Sunday.

I would like to discuss with you a plan about which I am afraid you may have misgivings, to say the least. I propose, despite my extreme youth, and my uncertain and at times irresponsible temperament on which it has been your painful duty from time to time to remark,[4] to take a wife and marry her.

I am terribly sorry to be doing something which might incur your displeasure. I only ask that you accept the matter and, if you can, give us your blessing. I am well aware of all the objections to the step, and I respect them. From being an elegant and well-to-do bachelor whose irresponsibility can only harm himself I shall be a poor married man, in the prime of his life, committed to a life of hard work and staid behaviour with a wife and family to support. I can only hope and pray that all will be well.

Teresa Onslow, whom I love, has said she will become my wife and submit to instruction from the Church.[5] Her mother has agreed. Although she has not much money, she has some. My own income as you know, amounts to £1600 p.a. of which £450 is tax free. Although very poor we shall not be grotesquely poor, and this figure does not include any sums I may earn from time to time writing books or other things.

I know that you will counsel delay, but my mind is certain, and living so close in London and seeing her so often, a long engagement would become a farce. In any case the life of a rich bachelor, although seemingly enjoyable and sensible, is really awfully pointless and selfish and mean. Although extremely young I do not think that celibate existence has many more surprises, lessons or pleasures for me. I am extremely lucky to have such a charming and

---

[4] Evelyn had written to Meg a few months earlier: '[Bron] is a moody, nervous boy with, so far as I have seen, no sense of responsibility.' Bron may have been hinting to his father that he had seen this letter.

[5] But she refused to become a Catholic.

lovely girl fond of me, and feel confident it would not happen again. My hair and teeth are falling fast, and if I do not marry soon I shall have to be content with Miss Catcheside.[6]

. . . I shall live in Islington in an old but spacious house. Please take it seriously.

Lady Onslow's address is at 47 Chester Row, SW1. I should like to announce the wedding after I have seen you next week-end, or it might out, and the final disgrace of all is to see it in Wm Hickey before it has appeared in *The Times*.

Please do not be distressed by it all.

With love from Bron

Laura replied by return:

Darling Bron,

Well you could knock me down with a feather. By all means come this weekend, as early as you can Saturday. Car or train?

I will attempt to cook you some good meals —

All my love
Mother

The sharpest embarrassment of any marriage arrangement is often centred on the pre-nuptial meetings of in-laws. Bron told his father that he need not bother to see Lord Onslow but Evelyn wrote to him anyway to explain that his daughter was making an imprudent choice in marrying his penniless, irresponsible and slightly mad son. Lord Onslow replied:

---

[6] Unappealing neighbour from Stinchcombe.

Dear Evelyn,

Many thanks for your very kind letter. If I may say so, I found your son a most charming young man and I feel that in this changing world one should not obstruct the young in a matter such as this.

Money certainly 'oils the wheels' but it is not everything. That they should be happy long after we are dead is all that matters. I do not think I need bother you to come to London – but next time you are up we might meet together especially as I have not seen you for a long time.

Yours Arthur

Evelyn bridled when anyone but his closest friends called him by his Christian name and he thought it odd of Lord Onslow (whom he hardly knew) to call him 'Evelyn' in lieu of 'Mr Waugh'. His eldest daughter's wedding to John D'Arms took place on 3 June 1961; Bron and Teresa's less than a month later on 1 July. Evelyn stipulated, 'Neither Teresa nor the young American shall call me Evelyn.' His first meeting with Bron's future mother-in-law, Lady Onslow, was not a success. Bron had written in advance to warn his father:

Dear Papa,

I hope you enjoy your luncheon with Lady Onslow. It is very kind of you to put yourself to all this trouble. You will find her a nervous woman, but not unintelligent. I should say that it is a great sorrow to her that her daughter is marrying a Catholic, although she is determined not to influence her in any way in the matter. Please make it quite plain to Lady O that you have absolutely no capital at all. I have told her, and she realises it, but is advised by some lunatic lawyers or relations that you must, and suspects, I think, that you have been keeping me in ignorance of it. Lord Onslow is exceedingly genial about the whole affair.

Evelyn and Lady Onslow met for lunch at the Ritz Hotel. Both were early. He found her 'nervously and unreasoningly anti-Catholic'; afterwards she turned up several times at Combe Florey. 'I returned rather travel worn to find Pamela Onslow installed here – *not* refreshing.' At the time of her daughter's wedding she was in a jittery state, behaving badly about money, rude about and to Bron. Evelyn objected to her receiving telephone calls at midnight. Bron wrote nervously to his father: 'I hope the Pamela visit was not too disastrous – she is scarcely sane, I am afraid. If she tries to come and live with us I shall poison her (secret).'

Two weddings within a month were more than Evelyn could bear. 'My life at the moment is hideously overshadowed and agitated by weddings. I have a daughter marrying a studious and penniless Yank in a fortnight and, hard on that, a son marrying a pretty, well endowed English girl. But the turmoil and expense are damnable.' His daughter Teresa was married in Taunton, near to Combe Florey, so he could hardly avoid it. Bron's wedding was to take place in London with a reception afterwards at the House of Lords – this Evelyn hoped to miss. Ideally he would have liked both weddings over and done with as a single event:

> My daughter Teresa has returned from Massachusetts very lean and spotty. I had envisaged a card:
>
>
>
> The Earl & Countess of Onslow
>
> &
>
> Mr & Mrs Waugh
> Request the pleasure of your company
> At the marriages of their daughters
> Teresa
> To Mr A. Waugh and Mr J. D'Arms respectively
>
>

But, alas, it seems T. Onslow will not become Catholic so she and Bron would not be admitted to the sanctuary but would have to stand outside the rails. This would cause offence to Lady Onslow. Both weddings fill me with gloom.

Immediately after the D'Arms wedding Evelyn retired, bilious, to the library and composed there a short recessional:

> The tumult and the shouting dies;
> The D'Armses and the Waughs depart;
> Still stands the mound of dough and ice –
> Vain product of the baker's art.
> The wedding-cake is with us yet,
> Lest we forget; lest we forget.

Bron wrote to reassure Evelyn that the cake contained a mountain of healthy, sustaining ingredients and he should tuck into it with relish. He was aware that his father was wondering how he could get out of coming to his own wedding: Evelyn's record for turning up at his son's events was poor. I have already recorded that he and Laura were the only parents not to attend 'passing out' at Mons. They also ducked Bron's twentieth birthday party, fearing press photographers, and Evelyn flatly refused to attend his twenty-first. This was a lavish affair at the Hyde Park Hotel paid for by Chapman and Hall out of their profits on *The Foxglove Saga*. The party was crowded with important people – the Prime Minister, the Duke and Duchess of Devonshire, Sir Isaiah Berlin and many of Evelyn's closest and oldest friends – but Evelyn and Laura stayed at home. He had written to Bron a fortnight before: 'Your publicity has been such that no cocktail party could enhance it.' Bron (in handwriting that suggests he might have been drunk) wrote back to both parents: 'I am awfully sorry you can neither come to the party. People will say. And lots of really quite nice people are coming. Still. I have so much news but no time. I keep buying Christmas presents for Papa, but none for anybody else.'

Evelyn got it into his head that the Onslows had invited four hundred farm labourers to the wedding, none of whom had been in their employ for more than a year. At first he announced that he would be staying at home, but Laura protested. His next plan of escape was to attend a rival society wedding that was due to take place on the same day. Viscount Encombe was marrying the absurdly named Countess Claudine Maria Olga Columba Fidelis von Mountjoye-Vaufrey et de la Roche of Vienna. Uncle Auberon chose this event over his nephew's. Laura forbade Evelyn from attending the Encombe gig and Bron wrote a week before the ceremony to make sure: 'I look forward to seeing you on Saturday. I hope you will have the fortitude to remain throughout the reception – at any rate until the handshaking and photographing are over.' But Evelyn saw another opportunity of escape when Meg announced that she had a tummyache. Two days before the wedding Evelyn sent a postcard to Bron at Clarges Street: 'Your cousin Antonia has sent what she thinks is a paper-knife but I think it is a skewer. It is of white metal, possibly silver, certainly not modern. Your sister Margaret has the grippe. I may have to stay and nurse her while your mother attends your nuptials.'

Laura acted with uncharacteristic resolution in hauling Evelyn by car up to London, but on the morning of the wedding he refused to get out of bed. She had to drag him out and forcibly dress him. July 1, 1961, was the hottest day for years, and Evelyn was sweltering, crusty and uncomfortable. When he saw the wedding photographs in the next day's newspapers he was horrified by his own obesity and started immediately on a purgatorial diet. But nothing could save him now. He had started on a long, declining slide; a deep, painful and unbudgeable depression that would hound him to an early grave.

Alec made nibbling attempts with his younger son, Peter, to reproduce something of the old father-son bond that he had enjoyed with Arthur, but his efforts were dilatory. He simply wasn't around often enough. If Peter was Alec's favourite child he failed to notice it until he read his father's last memoir, published in 1978: 'My father was no longer there,' Alec wrote in *The Best Wine Last*, 'and Peter was; Peter who would later fill the role of *copain* in my life, was to take in a sense my father's place of confidant and companion.' But how was Peter expected to fill this role of *copain*? Alec saw his children only for a few weeks of the year. For most of the time he was flitting like a brightly coloured butterfly in striped cricket blazer and broad brimmed cha-cha hat between New York, the Mediterranean, the West Indies, the Seychelles and the South China Seas.

More interesting to Alec than his family were his writing, his hankering for fresh experience on which to base novels and the rejuvenescence he experienced during copulation. In 1954 he fell in love with a divorced forty-year-old American mother of two. Virginia Sorenson enjoyed a brief period of fame in America as the author of children's books and novels about her traumatic Mormon upbringing but now, I believe, her reputation has extinguished. By 1963 she was agitating for marriage with Alec. The idea of settling down with Virginia appalled him; besides, he had his 'pipelines' – girlfriends – in other places, one in France, one in Tangier, another in England. He liked it that way. But Virginia was persistent: if he wouldn't marry her she would leave him. Alec wrote despondently to Evelyn in mid-August:

> Almost certainly during the next month I shall be going through a form of legal marriage with Virginia Sorenson – an American writer – with whom I have been cohabiting intermittently for the last nine years. It is my hope that this covenant will not have any effect on my present way of life; I don't plan to put down roots anywhere. I am for the first time in my life doing something which I know is wrong. Please say a prayer for my imperilled soul.

But before he could marry Virginia Alec had a redoubtable hurdle to jump in the shape of his former wife and the mother of his children. Joan told him that if he married Ms Sorenson she would throw his cricket kit, his books and all the rest of his possessions out of Edrington and he would never be welcome there again. In the interests of peace, and to maintain the slender thread of his relationship with his three children, Alec postponed his plans.

In the spring of 1969, he was in Washington when a telephone call came through from England to say that he was urgently needed at Joan's bedside. She was dying. She told him she was leaving the house to her elder son. Alec asked Peter to sell his library of several thousand books on a 20 per cent commission. What pictures and furniture he owned he gave to Andrew. His papers, he decided, would be sold to the University of Texas. Two years earlier he had presented Sherborne School with the manuscript of *The Loom of Youth* and a bound volume containing all the correspondence concerning the novel's great controversy – letters from Arthur Waugh, Arnold Bennett, H. G. Wells, and many others.

Immediately after Joan's funeral, Alec set out possessionless with a new spring in his step for Alexandria where, by arrangement, Virginia was waiting to greet him and to insist, once again, that they be married. This time he bowed to the inevitable, accepting patiently her little Mormon hand.

> This was the end of many things for me [he wrote], of my marriage, of my home, of my life in England. In a way too of my fatherhood. I remembered how when my mother had died I had lost touch with a whole group of family friends of whom she had written to me. The same thing would happen now with Andrew, Peter and Veronica. They would be on their own. They had come into their inheritance. I had no place any longer in the direction of their lives.

Neither before nor during his marriage to Virginia did Alec let up in his quest for sexual experience. I suspect he was driven by a morbid fear of failing potency. One of my uncles remembers him in Tangier slapping his maid's bottom each time she passed him. 'This way I keep my powers *à point*,' he said. In his sixties he took medical advice on sexual stamina and boasted to his brother that he had found the perfect cure for impotence. 'My brother Alec,' Evelyn wrote to Ann Fleming, 'has fallen victim to the continental regime of aphrodisiac injections and is leading a life that is not seemly at his age.' The treatment may have had a warping effect on his mind for, as time went on, the sexual content of his novels increased. His first big book after *Island in the Sun*, entitled *Fuel for the Flame*, was loaded to breaking point. He sent a copy to Evelyn, who wrote back to congratulate him: 'It was extremely kind of you to send me your new novel. I have so far read only fifty pages but there have been five fucks already. I look forward to many more.'

Evelyn did not live to read Alec's later novels. In one called *The Fatal Gift* (1973) an aunt canes her twelve-year-old nephew during the school holidays. The boy enjoys this so much that the very thought of his next visit inspires an erection. His aunt is especially talented at thwacking a particular area of his bottom that is erogenous – a zone that his housemaster always misses. After each beating she holds a damp flannel over his cock to achieve detumescence. 'I shan't be using this flannel again,' she said to him, after his third stay. 'Next holiday you will be too old for it. I'll show you what to do instead.' I have often wondered if this form of seduction is not based on a real life experience that Alec had had with one, or more, of his maiden aunts at Midsomer Norton. Connie? Elsie? Trissie? We shall never know.

There is a popular game in which children entangle themselves, giggling, on a plastic mat. An adult version may be attempted by re-enacting a lesbian love scene from Alec's 1970 novel *Spy in the Family*, although I think it may be impossible.

> At one moment they had swung into reverse, their knees drawn close under their chins. Lying on their right sides, Myra's left foot pressed against Anna's shoulder-blade; Anna, her left leg drawn under Myra's, pressed her foot under Myra's arm; her left hand, from beneath her leg, was clasped around the small of Myra's back. Myra's own left hand was curved between Anna's thighs. Their breasts were held apart by a confusion of knees and elbows, but each was completely, intimately exposed to the other's darting tongue.

On the back of the book's dustjacket – it is subtitled 'an erotic comedy' – a large photograph of the simian roué in his mid-seventies grins benevolently. His waist has spread, he wears a striped shirt and an MCC blazer and, round his neck, a silk foulard scarf. What had become of Alec? Where had the bright-eyed eager Sherborne youth gone? The boy who had immersed himself in Swinburne, Turgenev and Byron, and once hoped, with his father, that he would become a great English poet? From 1955 all he desired was to have one more literary success on the scale of *Island in the Sun* – just one. His attempts to achieve this goal were craven and it was not to be. In his last years his literary judgement waned but he was far from giving up, obstinately producing two thousand handwritten words a day until, in September 1981, he suffered a series of strokes and shortly afterwards died at the grand old age of eighty-three. His last years, spent cooped up with Virginia at 717 Bungalow Terrace, Tampa, Florida, were not his happiest. But, for all the roaming spirit of his lifetime, he expressed a wish to be cremated and for his ashes to be interred in the same grave as his father and mother in the Hampstead churchyard near to Underhill.

> When they bring back that thing that once was me
> And lay it in some quiet grave to rest,
> Say that a weary river, long distrest
> With aimless wanderings winds at length to sea.

How prophetic 'The Exile', a poem he had written as a sixteen-year-old at Sherborne, turned out to be. Alec was a less than aver-agely attendant father yet his children and a phenomenally wide circle of friends were shocked and saddened by his death. 'I have not seen nearly as much of my children as I would have liked,' he wrote at the end of his life. 'I have been a casual father. But their company has immeasurably enriched my life. I hope I have not been a nuisance to them.'

Shortly after his death, his wife Virginia wrote to Bron: 'Alec loved you so very much and often said he felt closer to you in certain ways than to any of his own children.'

As a writer Alec had a special sympathy with Bron that was absent from his relationship with his own sons – but he had never encouraged them to write and consequently neither did. Andrew went into the Navy and later into Lloyds Insurance; Peter pioneered an innovative photographic technique called photoaquatint, then retired to a hermetic life of clocks and pedigrees in an ancient mill house near Reading. Veronica is a furniture restorer.

My father was no great champion of Uncle Alec's novels, but he admired his fluent prose and was inordinately fond of the man. Alec's last letter to him from Tampa is dated a few months before his death: 'I am doubtful if I shall ever return to England. I am rather feeble on my pins and only have one real meal a day. But I do not repine. We are well content here and we rely on seeing you one day very soon, your devoted Uncle Alec.' They never met again.

In his obituary essay for the *Spectator* my father wrote a moving tribute:

> In old age Alec resembled nothing so much as a tortoise – toothless, slow-moving, unaggressive, benign, with a little piping voice so soft as to be almost indistinguishable. Like a tortoise, his natural equipment was designed more for survival than for battle and conquest. But he was a Waugh and I find myself inexpressibly bereaved.

There is no point in pretending (nor did Alec try to pretend) that he was anything but a minor writer, yet he took a certain pride in his craft and at their best his books are eminently readable. He was genuinely proud of his younger brother's success: 'Evelyn's fame has inflated my stock upon the literary bourse,' he used to say. In 1955 he supported Evelyn in a libel action against the *Daily Express* newspaper, travelling from Tangier to London to testify that his brother's books were far better than his, far more popular and sold in greater numbers. The loyalty, affection and pride with which he regarded his complicated younger brother were all remarkable and it is in these spheres that I detect in my Great Uncle Alec flashes – no, glimmers perhaps – of greatness.

The years between Bron's marriage and Evelyn's death were of happy association for father and son. 'In his later years my father had lost all terror,' Bron wrote in his autobiography, 'becoming bland and benevolent, and genuinely pleased to see his eldest son, daughter-in-law and grandchildren . . . Where before he had been gloomy, bad tempered and on occasions aggressive, he became benign and affectionate.' He attributed Evelyn's change of attitude to a dental operation in which he had all of his teeth removed without anaesthetic. Arthur Waugh had his extracted in the same way, and Evelyn had been impressed by his father's fortitude. I think it was for this reason that he declined the dentist's painkillers.

Bron and Evelyn's lately happy relationship might have been terminated prematurely in 1962 if Evelyn had discovered that his son had talked about him to a journalist on the *Sunday Telegraph*. The story, simply told, was that Evelyn had turned down an invitation to lunch with the Prime Minister because he felt that it was being offered as a sop in lieu of a knighthood. At the time Bron was working at the *Telegraph* and shuddered to see an angry letter from his father sitting on a colleague's desk. 'Dear Papa,' he wrote, 'I have just read your letter to the *Sunday Telegraph*. They are delighted with it. It was not I who sold you to them, although I had a theory as to who did.'

By a stroke of good fortune Evelyn happened to have told the story to Pamela Berry, an old friend of his and the wife of Lord Hartwell, the *Telegraph*'s proprietor, and thus it was she, not Bron, whom Evelyn was convinced had betrayed him.

Dear Bron,

Of course I never suspected you of betraying me to the *Sunday Telegraph*. The culprit was Pam who is now known alternatively as 'Little Miss Judas Sneakhostess' and 'Lady Randolph Grubstreet'. Alas pressure from the Prime Minister obliged me to withdraw my letter – or rather compassion for his secretary P. de Zulueta, a decent young man, who got into very hot water with the P.M. for instigating me to write.

There used in my youth to be much indignation and contempt for 'sneak guests' – impecunious young men who sold gossip to the papers. 'Sneak hostesses' of ample means and no motive but malice are a new development.

I have contented myself with warning Lord Hartwell against his butler who as the only other person in the room besides Pam must be in illicit communication with one of his editors.

The breach between myself and Pam is final. I do not think this will affect your position in any way. You got the job without my assistance.

It is, of course, possible that Evelyn suspected it was Bron all along, but he had other reasons to be annoyed with Pamela. She was trying to bully him into letting her have a picture of his that she coveted – a Fleet Street scene by Atkinson Grimshaw. Eventually he gave it to her but, in the meantime, he enjoyed telling his friends that he would never speak to her again.

Throughout the slow, dispiriting decline of his last years Evelyn continued to take a moderate interest in Bron's career. He abhorred the *Sun*, the *Mirror*, the *News of the World* and the *Sketch*, to which Bron had contributed in his early days, but was filled with pride and admiration when, in February 1963, he started a discursive column in the *Catholic Herald*. Within weeks the letters page was jammed with correspondence from those wanting Auberon Waugh sacked versus those wishing to compliment the editor on hiring such a bright new columnist.

Evelyn wrote often to compliment Bron on his pieces and followed every controversy with keen interest, occasionally chipping in himself under the *nom de plume* Mrs Teresa Pinfold. 'Some lunatic this week suggests you were brought up in affluence. Little does he know . . . I hope you are keeping a scrap book of the cream of your columns and of the controversy . . . It is rumoured that the *Catholic Herald* is up for sale. You should be represented as its chief asset – as indeed you are.' But Bron was attracting not just angry letters to the paper but libel actions as well. One came from the author and academic C. P. Snow, who objected to the accusation that he had ambitions to 'take over the reins of government', and another from the philosopher Bertrand Russell for a slur on his moral integrity. 'If ever a philosopher has deserved his cup of hemlock, Lord Russell has,' the article stated. Russell, through his solicitors, pursued the *Herald* for a retraction and damages, claiming that Bron's article had insinuated that he was 'guilty of the conscious and sustained corruption of youth to serve the international ends of communism'. Evelyn wrote to comfort Bron: 'Don't worry about Bertrand Russell. There is no chance of a jury supporting him on any subject. Anyway the law courts are so congested that he will be dead before the case is called.' The Russell case never came to court but the *Herald* sacked Bron all the same. Evelyn promptly cancelled his subscription. After that he continued to read Bron's journalism in other papers and comment upon it. In one he found a sentence he disliked, cut it out, stuck it on to a postcard and sent it to his son: 'Unhappily expressed. E.W.'

Bron's second novel *Path of Dalliance* drew heavily on his short experience of Oxford University. He refused to show it to his father until it was published. Evelyn was worried, writing to his daughter, Teresa, in America: 'Bron is being very secretive about his new novel which appears in ten days' time. He wrote it with unhealthy speed and I have fears that its reception may disappoint him. Critics are always eager to welcome new talent and then to discourage it.'

When *Path of Dalliance* was published in November 1963 reviews were mixed. John Betjeman compared it to Dickens and Freya Stark to Shakespeare. Alec wrote to Bron: 'I think *Dalliance* has cleared your road; it proved that *Foxglove* was not an isolated firework display. A genuine career is on the march. Salutations.' But Evelyn felt the opposite. He regretted that Bron had rushed it. Parts were 'very funny' he thought, but others were 'a bore . . . He should have taken more trouble over his second book – always a difficult one.' *Path of Dalliance* confirmed Evelyn in his opinion that Bron would probably never manage to support himself as a novelist. Six days later he wrote to wish him well for his birthday. My mother was pregnant: I was *in utero*.

Dear Bron,

My best wishes for your birthday. I hope that the coming year will find you the father of a son as worthy of your devotion as you have been of mine. Also that you will be in honourable employment . . . Teresa tells me you propose to call a daughter Charlotte – very nice. For a son why not Alexander Foxglove Brideshead Pinfold Clandon Forty-Martyrs Dillon?[7]

---

[7] Alexander, a Waugh family name; Foxglove, Brideshead, Pinfold are all Waugh books; Clandon, the Onslow family seat; Dillon, Bron's mother-in-law's maiden name; Forty-Martyrs – why not?

The false teeth that Bron believed to have been the cause of his father's improved demeanour felt uncomfortable in the mouth and resulted in a loss of appetite that precipitated his mental collapse. Changes to the Catholic liturgy, a reluctance to write any further novels, too many contracts for non-fiction books he was not interested in writing, boredom, punitive taxation, gin, paraldehyde, the 'abominable problem of human relations' – there were many reasons for Evelyn's decline in the 1960s. However, Bron, unlike Meg, was not someone in whom Evelyn chose to confide, though occasional hints of depression sneak into his letters:

Dear Bron,

I was very sorry to have to ask you and Teresa to postpone your visit. The truth is that the house has been too much frequented of late; we have no servants; I have work to do and there is much to be done in securing the house against burglary during our absence. We hope very much you will both come in the Spring.

Bron replied, 'I am sorry to hear the house has been too much frequented of late, and would not wish to do anything that might aggravate such a state of affairs.' A similar outburst of self-pity from Evelyn prompted Bron to offer his parents the dedication to his third novel, *Who Are The Violets Now?* in 1965. Evelyn had written a stark list of bullet points:

Dear Bron,

Thank you for your letter.
    Was M. de Vogue your host at Epernay?
    I look forward to your novel.
    I caught a glimpse of you and Teresa on the platform at Newbury. I was returning from a funeral – the only social functions I now attend.
    I congratulate you on acquiring a Canaletto . . .
    Your mother-in-law was making a tour of the criminal

classes of Wessex and kindly included us.

Neither your mama nor I have been very well lately.
My love to Teresa, Sophia, etc.

EW

Bron replied:

I am sorry to hear that you are both unwell. Would the
dedication of my new novel to you both be of any
comfort? It is a small return indeed for all the education,
nourishment etc that I have received from you over the
years, but it would give me great pleasure if you were to
accept.

If the idea gives you no pleasure, perhaps you would be
kind enough to tell me soon, as the book goes to press on
Monday, and there will be no time to alter the page proofs.
As it stands, the dedication is simply: 'For My Parents'.

I think it is livelier than the last effort. If it fails, I shall
dedicate myself to some serious occupation like accoun-
tancy, or the prison service.

Ever your affec. son
Bron

Evelyn was touched by the dedication but in the depth of his
depression found himself to be more interested by the behaviour
of his peacocks than by anything else:

Your mother and I are greatly exhilarated at the prospect
of your dedication of your novel to us. Thank you very
much indeed. It makes us more eager to read the book.

I am happy to announce that pea-hen has hatched two
chicks of indeterminate sex but apparent health. We are
going to great trouble to nurse them through their adolescence with various chemicals. It is some consolation to me.

This time Bron allowed his father to see the proofs in advance of publication. Evelyn replied to him cordially:

Dear Bron,

The proofs of your new novel arrived yesterday and I spent a very happy day in reading it. I congratulate you on the best constructed and controlled work you have yet done and am very proud that it should be dedicated to me. I hope it achieves the success it deserves.

I think the quotation from which the title is derived ought to appear on the title page. It is obscure to those as ill-educated as myself.[8]

I find it curious that you should demonstrate intimacy with the underworld of urban lodging-houses and tea shops which surely you have never experienced; but the picture is convincing.

A few slips: Carlton House was demolished a century before your book. Do you not mean C. H. Terrace (pp 27, 33); *Altera persona* seems unfamiliar to me (117). Do you not mean *alter ego* as on p. 189? p. 140, l. 15 delete 'and'. p. 173, l. 13 delete 'ex-' p. 36 insert? after 'happens'.[9]

I greatly admire the continued and varied use of the pet animal motive.

My love to Teresa, Sophie and Alexander,

E.W

Evelyn's last two years were spent in a welter of ascetic boredom and self-loathing. 'I am low spirited, old and very easily fatigued,' he wrote to Meg in 1964, 'and I find all human company increasingly distasteful.' Even his usual winter escape to foreign sunshine now

---

[8] Shakespeare's Richard II, act V, scene 2. Duchess of York: 'Welcome my son: who are the violets now that strew the green lap of the new come spring?'

[9] None of these corrections was made to the first edition.

seemed futile to him: 'I am seedy and idle and woebegone. It is the time I normally go abroad but there is nowhere now I wish to go.'

Meg tried everything to alleviate his wretchedness, offering to spend her weeks at Combe Florey or for him to live with her in London. 'I can't bear thinking of you in despair,' she wrote. 'Darling Papa I love you so much – please don't be unhappy.' But he was not for saving. His depression was fixed.

At the same time he was suffering bouts of acute paranoia, convinced that a Catholic newspaper had sent spies to Combe Florey to check how often he was going to church. At Mass, believing the 'True Faith' to have been destroyed by the stupidity of the modern church he heckled and groaned from the back row as the priest trilled out the new liturgy. 'I am toothless, deaf, melancholic, shaky on my pins, unable to eat, full of dope, quite idle – a wreck.' All he wished was for death.

The end came suddenly in the downstairs lavatory at Combe Florey just before lunch on Easter Sunday 1966. He was only sixty-two when he fell to the floor under the octagonal red light that, a hundred years earlier, had hung in the hall at Midsomer Norton illuminating the Brute as he castigated his servants. A hundred miles away at our rectory home at Chilton Foliat, my sister and I were eating sausage mashed in the French way with *petits pois* and gizzards, cooked, spiced and served by our crawly monoglot nanny, Lolita. Our parents had abandoned us to share a leg of lamb with a bookmaker called Wyatt and his new Hungarian wife at their house near Devizes.

Evelyn (who had been jovial all morning) had left the drawing room looking pale but amiable. Half an hour later he failed to appear for lunch. After an episode of gonging in the hall, Septimus (sixteen) tried the door of the downstairs lavatory. It was locked from the inside. He took a ladder out to the place we call the Crystal Palace and erected it where he could climb up and look in through the high lavatory window. From the top of the ladder he saw his father slumped, motionless – dead, in fact – on the lavatory floor. He called in panic to his older brother James, who clambered in through the window, stepped nimbly on to the cistern and over his father's body to unlock the door from the inside.

Once it was opened, Evelyn was dragged out into the passageway.

He had a severe cut on his forehead where he had presumably knocked himself falling against the door handle. Septimus and James went upstairs to get blankets while an eccentric Irish baking lady, called Maureen Regan, attempted to revive the corpse using the old mouth-to-mouth resuscitation formula. Her breath was unavailing but her valiant efforts earned her the title 'Nurse Regan', and, in the pride of it, she continued to bake delicious soda bread for a cadet branch of the family until, many decades later, she, too, was gathered, senile and decrepit, to the judgement of her Maker.

The doctor pronounced his verdict on Evelyn several hours later. Everyone in the house deflected their grief to the problem of Bron. Where was he? What if he learned of his father's death from the radio? Quick – ring Chilton Foliat. The monoglot couldn't say where Bron had gone so Granny decided to ring the police. My parents returned from their paschal beano with the Wyatts to find a copper rehearsing grave expressions at the front door. If Papa's autobiographical account is to be believed, the news of his father's death came to him as a relief – not least because he feared for a moment that something untoward might have befallen his children. 'Just as school holidays had been happier and more carefree when my father was away, so his death lifted a great brooding awareness not only from the house but from the whole of existence.' Bron was grateful to his father for dying early, while Margaret found in her Catholic faith a philosophy for rejoicing and wrote to Evelyn's old friend Diana Cooper to cheer her:

> Don't be too upset about Papa. You know how he longed to die and dying as he did on Easter Sunday, when all the liturgy is about death and resurrection, after a Latin mass and holy communion, would be exactly what he wanted. I am sure he had prayed for death at Mass. I am very, very happy for him.

After the policeman had returned to his kennel in Hungerford, Papa set off for Combe Florey on his own. When he arrived it was past midnight, everyone except his brother-in-law had gone to bed and Evelyn's body had been removed from the house. A nauseating smell of paraldehyde filled the hall. 'I noticed a small pile of excrement on the carpet outside the downstairs lavatory,' he later recalled. 'Others must have noticed it too, but, being Waughs, they all pretended not to have done so until the daily help arrived, when it vanished, without anything being said.'

This small observation from his autobiography caused great dismay to many of Evelyn's friends when it was published in 1991. Why so tasteless? Don't all people defecate in death? Was it really necessary to bring this unseemly matter to the public's attention twenty-five years later? Why did you do it, Bron? I never asked him. All I can do is to offer a mixed bag of possibilities and excuses:

1. He could not resist a lavatory joke even one that intruded on the sombre reflections of his father's demise.

2. He wanted to shit on his father's memory.

3. The sight of his father's faeces – the last tangible sign of his living body – subconsciously replaced the catharsis that seeing the corpse might otherwise have afforded him.

4. He wished to portray himself and other members of his family as uniquely unimpressed by dung, death and other worldly horrors.

Perhaps the truth lies in a *mélange* of all four but I doubt it. I think the answer to the great shit question lies elsewhere:

Evelyn Waugh's death was a blow, keenly felt by many of his fellow novelists, among them Graham Greene who recalled his shock on hearing the news in a haunting radio commentary. 'It was Easter Sunday symbolising his religion,' the great novelist lugubriously intoned, 'and he died [*long pause*] on the lavatory [*long pause*] symbolising his humour.'[10]

---

[10] Graham Greene was convinced that Grandpapa had killed himself by pushing his head down the lavatory and filling his lungs with water, a rumour hotly denied by members of the family.

I suspect Papa would have agreed with Greene's theory about the symbolism of his father's lavatorial exit. Perhaps he would even have stretched the theme a little further. You see, Evelyn Waugh was always performing, always theatrical, always unpredictable. His role at home combined that of the stern Victorian paterfamilias with court jester. He was, of course, supremely witty – 'he scarcely opened his mouth but to say something extremely funny' – but he also revelled in the physical buffoonery of a knockabout circus clown. He would clutch his groin with both hands and waddle across the drawing room to explain to his children what 'syphilis' meant. He would roar like a lion from the cellars at Piers Court or tumble ostentatiously from his seat, groaning on the floor in exaggerated reaction to a slight or passing remark. He was a master of macabre slapstick, and that pile of shit, if not his funniest, was, at any rate, Evelyn Waugh's final joke: the great saltimbanc's farewell somersault. Papa must have seen it this way and included it in his book for the honourable purpose of giving credit where he felt credit was due. Very filial.

By some meteorological fluke it was snowing at Evelyn's spring funeral in Somerset and everyone was worried that the hearse might slip off the drive and upturn its load into the green, goose-shit lake below. The ceremony was attended by family and close friends. Evelyn was deeply mourned. Outsiders might have shuddered at the hard external impression of a bully, a bigot and a snob, but despite all his foibles he was adored by a wide circle of intimate friends. The world of literature also bemoaned his passing. To Graham Greene his death was likened to the loss of a commanding officer. John Betjeman wrote to Bron:

Dear Bron,

Your father was one of the only great people I ever knew – loyal, secretly very kind, generous, and oh my goodness how piercingly funny. You have his genius and he recognised it. This consoles me a bit. I know we are meant to think leaving this world is a triumph, so it is. All the same there's a sense of emptiness without Evelyn for those of us left on earth who knew and loved him and I hope you won't mind my pouring out my sense of loss on you; perhaps sharing it may help me. Even if it adds to your troubles don't let it add to your correspondence. R.I.P. I'll remember you all in my Anglican prayers, Yours

John B.

Evelyn was buried in the grounds at Combe Florey. A week after the funeral a Requiem Mass was held at Westminster Cathedral, which coincided with the State Opening of Parliament a quarter of a mile away. Dozens of MPs chose to pay their final respects to the great English novelist rather than to sit through the Queen's speech, and the cathedral was packed.

My father once said that if an afterlife existed the last person he would wish to meet there would be Evelyn Waugh – he always referred to him as 'Evelyn Waugh', seldom 'Papa' or 'my father'. Bron was only twenty-six years old when his father died. I think by the end of his own life he had become muddled between his 'affec. Papa' and the public figure – the world famous writer, Evelyn Waugh. After decades of pondering, of contemplating a memoir of his father, of diligently managing the Evelyn Waugh Estate – the public and private Evelyn Waugh seem to have merged in his mind into one obstinate, irreduceable, slightly disagreeable, groan-causing blur. Poor Papa.

XIV

My Father

I have read many books written by sons about their fathers and none is particularly happy. I think immediately of the great denunciations – Edmund Gosse's excoriation of his father Philip Henry in *Father and Son*, Samuel Butler's of Thomas Butler in *The Way of All Flesh*, and Moritz Thomsen's extraordinary autobiography, *My Two Wars*, which begins with the memorable first line, 'This is a book about my involvement with two outrageous catastrophes – the Second World War and my father' – but it doesn't seem to matter if the author loathed his father or adored him, the relationship is not one that ever seems to work.

Perhaps it is the same for all sons: a childhood of trust (sometimes hero worship) leads to an adolescence of disillusionment and rage. In the busy years that follow we try to ignore our fathers and concentrate on feathering our nests without them; and when, at last, in fair round belly and seasoned middle age, we think ourselves emotionally ready to review the relationship with equanimity, we usually discover, to our dismay, that we have arrived on the scene too late. By then our father's star is fading, obscured in mists of eccentricity and semi-senile detachment. Sooner or later it will fizzle out altogether, but a father's death resolves nothing. While the son remains conscious the relationship never ends. Neither does it flourish. Instead it trundles round and round on an axis of the mind, suspended, unclosed, incomplete. *Most* unsatisfactory.

I adored my father, more, I suppose, than he adored me, or at least I thought about him much more than he thought of me – but I do not repine, as the Wavian[1] saying goes, for that is the nature of any father–son relationship. A father may have many children to add to his many concerns but a son has only one father, the 'august creator of his being', who chooses where he lives, where he goes to school, what he might find funny and, to a certain extent, what he thinks. Fathers are more important than sons, and therein lies the problem.

My own father was not a conventional parent in the Hollywood or BBC sense. He never kicked a football around the garden, never played frisbee, never took me camping or white-water rafting. He did not construct models of Lego or castles of sand; he took no interest in my homework or my school marks or whether I made it into the school cricket team. He was, above all, a literary man, but he did nothing to inspire in me a love of books. He never read aloud, never suggested titles I might enjoy. He recommended nothing and never discussed literature or writers. He once offered me a pound to read William Golding's *Lord of the Flies*, not because he thought I would benefit by it but because he discovered the book had been plagiarised from W. L. George's *Children of the Morning* and needed someone to remind him of the plot so that he could make a case of it in the *Spectator*.

His article appeared in December 1983 when Golding was in Sweden picking up the Nobel Prize for Literature. It ended:

> My researches suggest that W. L George had two sons by his second marriage to Helen Agnes Madden, who died in Houston, Texas, in 1920, so it seems by no means impossible that he has descendants. I am not, of course, suggesting for a moment that Mr Golding might like to share his prize money with them, but it would be a kind thought to send them a tin

[1] The adjective 'Wavian' meaning 'of or pertaining to Evelyn Waugh or his family' was coined by the Jewish mimic and railway enthusiast John Sutro in the 1950s as a counterpart to the word Shavian, which describes things to do with Bernard Shaw. Some dictionaries offer the alternative Waughian but this is ugly and incorrect. I would have called this book *Waviana* if I had thought anybody would understand.

of pickled herrings or something of the sort on his return from Sweden.

Papa was what would nowadays be termed a workaholic. He was the most prolific journalist in England. At home he slogged at his desk from the crack of dawn until lunchtime, was back in the library after lunch until supper, and often retired there after supper as well. He never took a holiday and wouldn't stop even on Christmas Day. In France, at a farmhouse in the Aude to which we repaired every summer, he wrote his articles in an open barn, occasionally shaking a fist when his children crunched the gravel too noisily in front of him. He could not live without his work and, on the rare occasions that he rested, would feel distinctly queer. 'For a week I have done no work at all,' he wrote in his diary, 'and marvel at the stamina of the English, who somehow manage to do none all their lives. After a few days, I found myself in a state of nervous exhaustion and moral collapse.'

Most of my memories derive from mealtimes where he sat, at the head of the table, polite, quiet, never holding forth, usually attentive and always extremely funny. My mother led the conversations. He loved wine and managed to fill nine cellars at Combe Florey with top-class ports, burgundies and Rhônes, which he poured generously down the gullets of his family and guests. I was treated to the best vintages of France at every meal from the age of twelve. He insisted that it be uncorked at the proper time and in order to get it right for the evening would ask as he sat down to lunch, 'Pray, what are we having for supper?' which always made my mother very cross. Like his uncle Alec, he treated the drinking of wine as a ritual but, unlike his uncle Alec, always spilt large amounts of it on the table.

The best wine only begins to develop – open out, show a leg or whatever – once it is in the glass. Within the space of two hours a wine which has lain undisturbed for twenty or thirty years will run the gamut through tight, suspicious puberty, vivacious adolescence, joyful awakening, sensuous maturity, fat and crumbling middle age to sour, crabbed senility.

I learned from him everything I needed to know about wine and in my period of refusing to be a writer he tried to encourage me to become a wine merchant instead. Until the last two years of his life when his appetite failed him his greatest pleasure was food. He would eat almost anything except cabbage, which reminded him of Downside, and turnips, which reminded him of the barracks at Caterham. He was breathtakingly generous at expensive restaurants. Secure in the knowledge that he had never vomited since childhood, he went out of his way to experiment with exotic and, to many, unpalatable dishes. He tasted crocodile meat in Cuba, dog in the Philippines, raw horse in Japan, toad in Egypt and snake in northern Thailand. For a while he encouraged us to eat the squirrels at Combe Florey until we cooked one in red wine sauce that looked and tasted as we all imagined rat to look and taste. He never forgave the socialist governor of Szechuan, China, for preventing him eating a giant panda. My brother Nat has inherited Papa's enthusiasm for rare and exotic delicacies and cannot be trusted to sit by a swimming-pool without shoving every passing insect into his mouth. Ants, he says, are nice and lemony; fried wasps, no good.

Outside his annual trips to a health farm Papa never dieted (distrusting those who did) and blocked his ears to faddish advice concerning starch and protein, salt and blood pressure and the dangers of cholesterol:

Dieting has emerged as public health enemy number one; worse than eggs, milk, cheese, saturated fats, tobacco, alcohol, sex, meat, vegetables, potatoes, unsaturated fats, soft drinks, fast food, botulinus toxin and any known form of nerve gas yet developed. It destroys the brain cells and permanently impairs mental performance, distorts moral perceptions and tends toward unsafe driving, removing all libido while making the dieter more prone to HIV and its concomitant scourge, Aids. It adversely affects foetuses and is linked with an increase in cot deaths. It makes those who fall victim stupid, mad, ugly and boring.

Over the years he put on a lot of weight. In his prime, he was 'a fine figure of a man' – at least, that was how he would have described himself. This, by extrapolation, meant narrow shoulders, thin, elegant limbs, a fattish neck and, for most of his adult life, a firm, round, Buddha-like belly that was a delight to admirers of both sexes and of all persuasions. Most sons are wrong about the handsomeness of their fathers. My own little boy rates me above James Bond – deluded fool. English fathers are not particularly handsome (they look horrid in supermarkets) – yet I believe my own to have been an exception. True, his looks were unconventional by the James Bond standard: he was bald on top with thick curls of golden ginger hair at back and sides, which he tried to flatten in the mornings with a powerful-smelling unguent. One of his eyes failed to align when he looked sharply to the right. He wore round, wire-framed spectacles – and, for a while, a Beatles pair set with tinted yellow glass. But for all this he was, as I say, a good-looking man. He had light blue humorous eyes, a fine masculine nose, a pleasantly cleft chin, and a noble, wise, philosophic shape to his head. He was not particularly tall (let us say five foot eleven), but when the subject arose, he would produce a measuring tape from the library, run it under his shoe, round his Buddha-like protrusions, up his forehead and along his crown, stopping only when he was sure that at least six foot two of it had been unravelled. He insisted that he was taller than both of his sons, which he wasn't.

He was not a vain man but, like his own father, there was something of the dandy about him. He loved fine clothes – silk ties, handmade shirts and expensive leather shoes. His cupboards, both in London and at Combe Florey, groaned with suits and jackets, tailor-made, of every cut, colour and cloth. At weddings he wore his father's sealskin top hat with a frock coat, which would have looked out of date on Arthur Waugh, that he had had especially made. Except in the most severe heat, he always wore a tie. One summer he grew a handlebar moustache, which made him look like a motor-bike queen on the Earl's Court Road *circa* 1968: 'Every man must grow a moustache or a beard at least once in his life,' he said – one piece of his advice I have never taken. His family thought he looked loathsome with that on his face.

We seldom talked about his father as the subject invariably bored him. I remember one brief effort because it went something like this.

'Papa, was Grandpapa clever?'

'Very.'

'I mean, was he good at chess?'

'A grand master.'

'What about maths? Was he any good at maths?'

'Stupendously so.'

'Advanced maths?'

'Timmy, you're boring me.'

He never called me by my real name. For the first eight or ten years of my life I was addressed simply as 'Fat Fool'. Not that I minded. There was affection in his tone so I wore the 'insult' as a badge of honour. One day someone earnest must have told him to desist and 'Fat Fool' disappeared to be replaced with a string of names that weren't mine: Timmy, Roge, Nige, Jockey, Wilf – anything would do so long as it did not involve him in too much thought. I don't think he ever called me Alexander. Perhaps the closest he came to it was 'Arlex' in a satirical Scottish accent. When my father-in-law (also Alexander) came to stay, Papa threw up his hands in dismay. 'This is all too confusing,' he said. 'I shall have to call you Billy One and Billy Two.'

I must now interrupt this swinging portrait of my father to give a brief account of my own circumstances and the role I think I have played in this unfolding drama.

I was born in December 1963, conceived (according to some calculations but not others) near Treviso in Italy at the house of a one-eared Arabist called Dame Freya Stark. I have been told that the nearest village was called Arsehole, though this strikes me as unlikely.[2] I was my parents' second child and their first son, the

---

[2] Asolo is a possibility.

first male Waugh of the fourth generation from Arthur. Perhaps it was this that stirred feelings of patrilineal pride in the hearts of my grandfather and great-uncle Alec. 'Grandfathers prefer grandsons,' Evelyn said, when I was born. Papa told me that he was 'pathetically pleased and proud to have a grandson'. Alec wrote offering his detached congratulation: 'It is fine that the name of "Waugh" has been maintained.' Grandpapa funnelled his pleasure into the embellishment of a silver plate and tankard – family heirlooms that had been given him by Arthur on his twenty-first birthday. By looking into my mother's pedigree he had established that a shield could be drawn in my name and filled with sixteen patterns (or quarterings), each pertaining to one of the sixteen families of my great-great-grandparents. The resulting peacock-tail display (which I think is called an 'armorial achievement') was engraved all over the tankard and the plate in such a way that it ruined the look of both. Grandpapa gave them to me as christening presents and I treasured them until the day they were snatched by burglars during a raid on our house in London in 1992. I expect they have since been melted down for their silver content.

Evelyn's exuberance at the birth of his first grandson was tempered by anxieties about Bron's career. Papa was just twenty-four when I was born and without gainful employment, as they say. What was left of his last book advance was running out and he had been sacked by the *Catholic Herald,* yet continued to employ a daily help, a French maid and a maternity nurse. Evelyn sent some money to his daughter-in-law and wrote to a friend in the BBC begging him to find a job for his son: 'I ask a boon. Please find remunerative employment for my son Auberon Alexander in your broadcasting service . . . I think the boy could be useful in the BBC. He has two children to support.'

The money was well received, but it did not solve the long-term problem. Bron sent part of it to some bribable nuns in Cornwall asking them to pray for his success at a third interview with the intelligence services. Their prayers fell on deaf ears and MI6 once again turned him down. His hopes now rested on a possible job with the *Daily Sketch* and an interview with the BBC:

Dear Papa,

Thank you for your extremely generous present to Teresa.
It may yet make the difference between honourable penury
and public disgrace. I now feed six mouths completely, as
well as clothing and keeping them warm. Lolita eats three
loaves of bread a day and even our daily woman has fallen
to eating my food, which makes a seventh mouth. I shall
see that the servants starve first.

Evelyn wrote back: 'I hope you insinuate yourself into the BBC –
a safe and reasonably honourable concern. The *Sketch* would be
shameful. Provincial papers have a way of suddenly ceasing publication. Make Lolita keep to a diet of bread – much cheaper than
the fresh meat demanded by English servants.'

Crisis was averted when Bron found himself a job on the *Daily
Mirror*. It was not especially well paid but he wrote little for the
paper, spending most of his time in the office working on his
third novel. His career as a journalist only came to life after
his father's death. The spark that ignited it took the form of a
review of his father's obituaries for the *Spectator* in May 1966.
Papa was embarrassed by it later but at the time it was seen as
a *tour de force* of vituperative journalism, which led directly to
his appointment, aged only twenty-seven, as the *Spectator*'s
political correspondent.

Despite Evelyn Waugh's enormous and beneficial contribution
to English letters many of his obituaries were cavilling, sour and
inaccurate. *Time* reported:

In the last ten years of his life Evelyn Waugh was a flabby old
Blimp with brandy jowls and a menacing pewter complexion
. . . he lived in an eighteenth-century country house 140
miles from London where he played the country squire with
a conservatism that soon became simply amniotic [?] . . . And
then last week on Easter Sunday, home from a Mass sung (to
his crusty satisfaction) in Latin, he climbed the stairs to his
study and died of a heart attack.

Urged on by his mother, who was 'baying for blood', Papa's counter-attack was swift as well as sympathetic:

> If the purpose of this advanced style is to inform the public, they have been cheated. My father did not die of a heart attack, nor did he die in his study which is on the ground floor. The Mass he attended was not sung. He never at any stage played the country squire, having no interest in local affairs or rustic pastimes, and probably never spoke to more than half a dozen people in the neighbourhood. It is true that he lived in the country, as do many writers, and in a large house because he had a wife and six children to accommodate. Those who saw him in his last years will know that they were probably the most mellow and tranquil of his life – certainly much more so than the preceding ten. In the final years he worried about some work he had undertaken and was distressed by the extraordinary simple-mindedness of Catholic bishops, but to me he was never so benign or so gentle.

The kernel of Bron's defence against Evelyn's critics is best illustrated by a single paragraph that sums up the stolid attitude to his father that lasted him throughout his life and formed the basis of almost every conversation I ever had with him about Grandpapa:

> The main point about my father, which might be of interest to people who never knew him, is not that he was interested in pedigree – it was the tiniest part of his interests. It is not that he was a conservative – politics bored him. His interest was confined to resentment at seeing his earnings redistributed among people who were judged more worthy to spend them than he. It is not that he was tortured by class aspirations – he was not. It is not that he had a warm and compassionate heart – warm and compassionate hearts are two a penny. It is not even that he was a Catholic – there are 550 million of them and a fair number must be Catholics by conviction. It is simply that he was the funniest man of his generation. He

scarcely opened his mouth but to say something extremely funny. His house and life revolved around jokes. It was his wit – coupled, of course, with supreme accuracy of expression, kindness, loyalty, bravery and intelligence – which endeared him to everybody who knew him or read his books.

Papa's review went on to attack several other obituaries, including one in the *Observer* by the writer and broadcaster Malcolm Muggeridge. 'I am twenty-six,' Papa wrote, 'and have a reasonable chance of surviving him [Muggeridge] . . . my pencil will be out, my throbbing compassionate heart in my hand, when the unhappy event occurs.' This was followed by a merciless mock-obituary of Muggeridge in pastiche Muggeridge style. The unhappy event actually occurred twenty-four years later, when Muggeridge was eighty-seven, and my father wrote in the *Daily Telegraph*: 'Like many wise old birds he attracted the attention of ornithologists from all over the world. Now he has finally dropped from his perch, they will have to go away. There is nothing to be said about him which he has not said himself many times over.'

Soon after I was born my parents moved from London to an attractive rectory house in the village of Chilton Foliat, near Hungerford in Berkshire. I think Grandpapa came to visit us there only once though I do not remember the occasion. Five years after his death we moved into Combe Florey and Granny took all her things across the Crystal Palace into the North Wing. Ten years earlier she had been forced to sell her cows when the taxman forbade Evelyn to offset her farm losses against his literary income. Their departure was greatly mourned but she let the fields to the village butcher and watched his heifers grazing there instead.

I spent many absorbed hours with her in this occupation and on good days when they escaped through holes in the wire I was allowed to chase them through the woods, waving laurel branches and shouting, 'Get ye o'er ther, yer girt flummins.' I always spoke to cows in a Somerset accent. In the evenings I brought my toy plastic cows round to the Wing and spread them out across Granny's kitchen table. With these she taught me the tricks and techniques of the cattle trade: herding, milking, curing, sexing, how to put a ring in a bull's nose without enraging it. I soon became as obsessed as she. Perhaps I flatter myself in supposing that my indefatigable willingness to join with her in endless bovine conversation elevated me in her heart to the honoured position vacated by the deaths of Sanders and, more recently, of her gardener at Combe Florey, Walter Coggins. My father had murdered him – or so Granny always claimed – to avenge his cruel treatment of Grandpapa's peacocks. The first time she accused Papa of killing Coggins was during a quiet moment at Evelyn's funeral. The gardener had disappeared at the time of Evelyn's death. 'I know where you've hidden the body,' she hissed at him; but a week later Coggins reappeared at the kitchen door stinking of alcohol. He had been on a blinder.

On the night of 16 June 1973 Granny came to supper and left the table early, saying she was feeling unwell. I was sitting at the far end nearest the door to the Wing, and as she passed I looked at her white, anxious face and thought to myself: She is going to die tonight.

Next morning I came down to breakfast to find my father on the telephone in tears. It was the first and last time I saw him cry. She had died of pneumonia in the night.

I cannot easily explain how Granny, who was so strangely detached from the world and all the people in it, came to be loved so passionately by those who knew her – but that was how it was. Anthony Powell described her as 'extremely dim to put it mildly', but he hardly knew her and his reckoning was erroneous. She was clever in many ways – much cleverer in some than Powell. I am sure she could have completed *The Times* crossword in the time it took him to digest the first clue, but she was no show-off. Papa believed her to have been more remarkable than his father, and felt her death more deeply than his. Her humour was warm and her personality gentle. She was companionable. I particularly liked the smell that attached to all her jerseys – sherry, French cigarettes and dog baskets all blended into one, a lovely Granny fragrance.

Combe Florey House, as I first remember it, was a shambling fortress of creaky stairs and alien smells. Chief among its attractions

— at any rate to a seven-year-old boy — were a life-sized carved wooden lion in the hall; Victorian painted furniture by William Burges; a stuffed white owl whose wing I could remove by lifting the glass dome that covered it and yanking; a wooden bagatelle board; cattle grids; delicious Guernsey cream; a crystal chandelier that tinkled when you punched it; a ferocious gander called Captain, whose attacks we fended off with umbrellas; incomplete sets of cards, sherbet fountains, bottles of ink. In the years after Evelyn's death Granny put the house on the market but when prospective buyers came round she poured buckets of water through the floorboards and ordered her dog, Credit, to shit on the carpets and pee against the curtains. If anyone was brazen enough to put in an offer after that, she declined it.

The library, when we arrived, was empty. Every shelf, desk, sheaf of paper, even the pens and the wastepaper baskets, all Grandpapa's books, his bound manuscripts, diaries and precious collections of Victorian chromo-lithography, his first editions, second editions, inscribed editions, books by his father, books by his brother, carpets, paintings and carved animals — the whole lot was sold in 1968 to an opportunist in a Stetson called Harry Ransom on behalf of the University of Texas. Ransom's original concept was to set up, brick for brick, shelf for shelf, the Evelyn Waugh Library at Austin, but my father died in the belief that once the deal had been struck and everything transported to Texas, Ransom had never got round to unpacking the crates. This may be true. Papa's attempt to swap some of the Texan plunder, in particular the furniture and pictures, for four thousand items of Evelyn's incoming correspondence came to nothing.

At Combe Florey Granny made no attempt to reconvert the gutted room to better use. It just lay at the front of the house, vast and derelict. By dismantling the library she had effectively extinguished the spirit of Evelyn's personality from Combe Florey. It was as though the heart of the house had been plucked from it — is that what she really wanted to do? My father and his sister Meg believed that she sold the library *in contumeliam puerorum* — or, to put it in plain English, to annoy her children. If that had indeed been her aim, she certainly succeeded in it. Evelyn had left her plenty of money but, in the hands of a perverse solicitor who dripped it to her in tiny increments, she was constructively encouraged in delusions of poverty. The deal with Texas – $8500 for the whole lot – included items that were not even part of the library: a marble bust of Evelyn by Paravicini that was in the dining room, two seventeenth-century globes that stood in the hall. Grandpapa had spent far more than $8500 accumulating his books alone. I don't understand how Granny came to be so ill-advised. I don't know *what* she thought she was doing.

For a quiet lady who hated the public gaze she surprised all who knew her in the short interval between her husband's death and her own, by letting off two wreaking petards. The library sale was the first; the publication of Evelyn's diaries the second. She had not even read them before she sold the rights to the *Observer*; neither did she consult any of her children. My father later wrote: 'Like many of the upper class she had a hatred of publicity, but also a passion for selling things. Any crooked timber merchant who came to the door could persuade her to sell him an avenue of mature oaks for £15 a tree.'

When the diaries started to appear in lurid weekly instalments she regretted what she had done, hoping that the fuller version, in book form – which she did not live to see – might, one day, repair some of the damage. To those who had already formed the view that Evelyn was a callous snob, the diaries confirmed their prejudice. For some reason people thought he should have paraded his virtues in his diaries and have ever since held it against him for not doing so.

It is debatable that Evelyn intended them to be published. He left no instructions, and some of his children took the view that their publication was a betrayal of his memory. My father was not among them. 'The main thrill in keeping a diary,' he wrote, 'lies in the secret hope that it will be published one day and astound the world. I see it as a sort of private exhibitionism like that of a woman who locks herself in her bedroom alone and takes all her clothes off, imagining that 100,000 people are feasting their eyes on the spectacle.' He did not mind in the least about all the rude references to himself. If anything he agreed with his father's assessment. Reviewing the diaries for the *Spectator* in 1976, he conceded that 'growing children are seldom very elegant, amusing or smart and I think it was this vulgarity that my father resented most'.

Papa sympathised with Evelyn because I think he also found children a little vulgar, his own included. At times he resented our sloppy speech, our gross appetites for junk food, sweets, plastic toys and baggy clothes. Most of all, he hated the sight of us in gym shoes, but while his father would have ordered him from the room with cries of 'Out!' – Papa's method was to block his nose, pull an imaginary lavatory chain and a disgusted face, and leave it at that. In *Cakes and Ale* William Somerset Maugham, meditating on the tribulations of a writer's life, concludes: 'But a writer has one compensation. Whenever he has anything on his mind, any emotion or any perplexing thought, he has only to put it down in black and white, using it as the theme of a story or the decoration of an essay, to forget all about it. He is the only free man.' Having liberated myself from the obstinate problems of time, God, and now fathers and sons, I can wholeheartedly agree with Maugham's point and am sure my father would have felt the same. He, too, used his writing to free himself from the irritations of life and the problems of human existence:

> Young people wear sneakers, trainers and other forms of tennis shoe all day long. These are always rubber soled and often with a top of some synthetic material which makes the feet sweat and smell and grow fungus. When one thinks how strict the health fanatics are about every form of food, drink and cigar, pipe or cigarette, you would think they would show some concern about these pools of sickness and infection at the bottom of everyone's legs. It may take a year or two for the baneful effects of this footwear to be noticed – nearly four centuries elapsed between the introduction of tobacco by Sir Walter Raleigh and the setting up of ASH, the organisation of anti-smoking hysterics – but I would not be surprised if most of those smelly feet eventually had to come off.

By the time we moved to Combe Florey in 1971 the name Auberon Waugh was quite well known among intelligent, educated English folk. Five years later it was a household name throughout the land. His fantasy diary published in the fortnightly satirical magazine *Private Eye* attracted a cult following, and in 1976 a television series in which he excoriated the working class attracted equal amounts of adulation and opprobrium in Britain and beyond. The unpredictable Libyan head of state, Colonel Muammar Gaddafi astounded his people by claiming that Auberon Waugh was his favourite author, while the Queen of Holland told her courtiers that she subscribed to the magazine *Books and Bookmen* only to keep up with the wit Auberon Waugh.

In late September 1976 while she was absorbing herself in the latest edition Papa was watching television in the kitchen at Combe Florey. He rarely switched it on but when he did it was always for the pleasure of laughing at pompous, self-important people. That evening he was confronted by a tanned, meaty face with a heart-throb Australian accent. The programme seemed pretty dull to me – another earnest world-affairs round-up seen from a slightly whining, socialist perspective – but my father thought it extremely funny and could not contain his merriment. The presenter was called John Pilger. In his diary Papa noted:

> Something about the bottomless stupidity and deviousness of Pilger's face had me in stitches even before the extraordinary announcement at the end that the views expressed had been Mr Pilger's own. This idea that Pilger himself thought up all those *kindergarten* opinions put me in such paroxysms as might easily have been mistaken for the last stages of rabies. It was at that point that someone wisely telephoned for an ambulance.

I remember the incident well: wonderful to see him so happy; horrid to see him so ill. Papa never forgave Pilger: the hearty laughter he had provoked somehow disturbed the delicate equipoise of the old Cyprus wounds in Papa's back and chest. For six weeks he hovered between life and death at the Westminster Hospital. Those who had not seen the funny side of his anti-working-class broadcasts clapped their hands with glee. My mother rushed up to London, leaving her children at Combe Florey to fatten themselves on a rich diet

of melted Mars Bar and vanilla ice-cream, served daily by an indulgent aunt. From my bedroom I wrote to Papa with the news of
ten separate village sex scandals that I thought would amuse him.
My letter ended: 'I hope you are feeling better. I think you are
extremely nice and I know lots of people who have seen your television programmes on the television and they all said that you were
very good and interesting.'

This was not quite true. In fact, I remember people telling me
that my father was a shit because of his 'radical' views. Over the
years I got used to it. If they weren't brave enough to say so
outright they simply asked, with a slippery smirk, 'So, what's it like
being the son of Auberon Waugh, then?' People have walked away
from me at parties as soon as they learned who my father was, and
I was once head-butted by a violent oaf in Manchester wishing to
protest against one of Papa's recent pieces. Blood streamed from
my face as I crouched on the floor and the maniac tried to kick
my head off. Eventually he was pulled away, shrieking and cursing,
'Your fucking dad's a fucking tosser.' On a separate occasion I was
grabbed by the neck and shoved against a wall by the son of a
Labour MP who thought that by throttling me he might rid the
world of some minor aspect of the Auberon Waugh canker.

My father's articles made humourless and pompous people shake
with uncontrollable rage. In 1985 *Private Eye* pretended to sack
him. A flood of letters came in protesting that the magazine without
the 'comic genius' of 'this latter day Samuel Pepys' was not worth
reading. At the end of the column the editor wrote: 'As a result of
the above letters Mr Waugh has been re-engaged.' In the next issue
furious enemies wailed their resentment of the 'balding vulgar
little egotist', 'this slimy lower class rat, this stammering old hooray
henry, this perpetually wanking rotten gritter and ubiquitous AIDS
carrier'.

John Pilger, I have learned from one of his friends, was so terrified
of my father that he used to blanch at the sound of his name. Papa
never seemed to care how many people appeared to hate him. It
amused him to be insulted just as it embarrassed him to be praised.
He did nothing to court popularity: 'Anyone who applies the concept
of popular approval to any aspect of his life's philosophy or behaviour

is building his house upon a pile of shit,' he used to teach me.

When people met my father for the first time they invariably came to the same conclusion: 'Isn't it odd that this rude, abrasive and opinionated journalist should be such a mild-mannered, diffident and pleasant man? He must have a split personality.' I never saw it like this. Knowing the man first, I can only perceive his articles as having been written in the same benign, liberal and humane tone as that with which he presented his observations in private. I have never understood why people thought his writing cruel, malicious or offensive. It was mischievous certainly, often teasing, often outraged, always clever and always funny, and beneath everything he wrote, behind the hot words and bandied rebukes, there always throbbed, as far as I could tell, the steady beat of a warm heart.

People were terrified of meeting my father. They imagined him to be sharp, aggressive and impatient of other people's opinions, but he was none of these things. I only once ever saw him be rude to anybody – a whining American lady with blue-rinse hair in the Doge's Palace, Venice, who abused him for walking the wrong way down a thin passage between galleries. I was twelve, standing right behind him when the argument began. 'Go away you ugly old tart,' I heard him say to her – what a hero he was to me that day.

In October 1977 he received, out of the blue, a letter from Lionel Grigson – son of the famous poet Geoffrey Grigson – complaining that he had read in the *Guardian* Diary that Papa was among the signatories to a letter attacking the Catholic Institute of International Relations for its 'alleged pro-guerrilla stance' in Rhodesia. 'Your views are becoming more and more odious every day. You seem to be turning into a grotesque parody of your father,' Grigson wrote, ending his letter: 'I've noticed a similar pro-Rhodesia tendency in other things of yours. I would like to have thought that you were at least a pleasant person to know, but you have finally convinced me that this cannot be so. Yours coldly, Lionel Grigson.'

Papa was, as I say, a very polite person, but when kicked, he liked to kick back and, as a self-proclaimed 'master of the vituperative arts', invariably came out on top. His reply to Lionel Grigson's assault is a good example:

Dear Mr Grigson,

How queer that I have no recollection of signing any letter about Rhodesia and think it most unlikely that I did so, but as I have not seen the piece in the *Guardian* Diary to which you refer, I do not really know what you are talking about. I seem to remember signing a letter complaining about the impertinence of the Catholic Institute of International Relations in presuming to speak for the Catholic Church. I should also suppose that only a moral cretin would support terrorist activities in Rhodesia, however just their aims. But I have never written on the subject of Rhodesia, despite writing three articles a week on current affairs for the last ten years, for the good reason that, unlike you, I have never been able to decide the exact rights and wrongs of the situation there. So when you say you have noticed a pro-Rhodesia tendency in my writing, you are talking rubbish.

You are right when you suggest that whatever gratitude I may owe to your father for his devotion to English literature over the last 50 years does not extend to his son, of whom I have never heard until this moment. I would write in stronger terms except that I suspect you may be mad, when you write these pompous, twerpish letters to complete strangers and sign them 'Yours coldly'. So I will end with a cordial invitation to piss off, or as the Americans say, go fuck yourself.

Yours sincerely,
Auberon Waugh

Papa never took much interest in my education, resigning himself early to the disquieting truth that I had only two solid talents, both of them 'soft options': art and music. He was not a discerning critic of either. I think he liked oil paintings of animals and I know he adored Gilbert and Sullivan and traditional church hymns. He used to sing a lot – 'When I Am King of the Boeotians', 'Take a Pair of

Sparkling Eyes', 'Lily the Pink', 'She Was Poor But She Was Honest', '*Chi del gitano I giorni abbella*' – he sang them all with reckless disregard for the rules of rhythm and pitch, but always with gusto as he crossed the hall from the library to the kitchen. Since he died I cannot hear these songs without feeling tearful.

I am grateful that he did not ram religion down my throat in the way that he had had it rammed down his by Grandpapa. We were not sent to Catholic schools; nor were we given prayer books and religious bric-à-brac for Christmas. For a while he drove his children dutifully to Catholic Mass in Taunton. My mother, an Anglican of sorts, did not come with us and we sat in the back seat of the car chanting noisily 'Boo to Churchy! Boo to Churchy!' I like to think that it was this act of rebellion that eventually persuaded him to discontinue our Sunday trips to St George's, but in his autobiography Papa gave an alternative explanation:

> For many years after my father's death I continued to go to church faithfully every week. It was only when I came to accept that the services would be completely unrecognisable to him, that the new religion had nothing whatever to do with the church to which he had pledged his loyalty, that I felt I could distance myself . . . Whatever central truth survives lies outside the modern church, buried in the historical awareness of individual members. Or so it seems to me. But whenever I have doubts, it is my father's fury rather than divine retribution which I dread.

Much fuss and comment arose from a passage in the foreword to *God* in which I recounted how Papa had offered to pay me the sum of my advance for the book if I would cease to work on it and decline to have it published. Perhaps he feared divine retribution or his father's fury, but I doubt either to be the case. As I wrote at the time, 'He never asked what line the book was taking nor had he read a word of it and I never learned what lay behind his eccentric gesture.' He believed that 'man's relationship to God is an intensely private affair, the most intimate and personal of all his relation-ships'. It may be that he thought my snooping in the Almighty's pants drawer was vulgar, but I believe that the real reason he wanted me to abandon the book was that he thought I would cock it up. He never had much faith in his children's competence, always assuming that whatever new project they were embarked upon would end in catastrophe and disgrace. Had he lived to read *God* I am confident he would have been amused by it. Perhaps he would even have made space in his *Daily Telegraph* column to plug it.

The bravery of his nepotism was stunning. When he believed that his children had done something well (and only then), he suffered no qualms or moral misgivings over the propriety of extolling their work in public. His paeans to his children often took poetic form. They were always sincere, and if the underlying emotion might have been one of relief that, for once, they had not botched things up, spontaneous pride usually overwhelmed it. For all his apparent detachment, for all his strong opinions, he was at heart a modest man for whom life's value was intrinsically bound to the welfare of his children. 'The best monument one can leave nowadays,' he wrote, 'is a clutch of children who are not spoiled, over-supervised psychopaths. The time is surely past for building more lasting memorials than that, and we should concentrate on self-effacement.'

Despite this long-term philosophy I do not doubt that, from time to time, the presence of his children depressed him as grievously as it had depressed his father, but he was better-mannered than Evelyn and made an effort to conceal his negative feelings. He never lost his temper with us, he was never in a rage, not even a mock one, and was never – well, hardly ever – sharp with us. No doubt he was often bored by our conversation, irritated by the physical presence of his boys especially, and exasperated by what he called the 'plastification of Combe Florey', which meant the strewing of toys around the house. Like his father he had a sensitive ear for language and recoiled from schoolyard jargon and solecisms of grammar but, unlike his father, he endured them all with muffled groans and saintly patience.

At times he was visibly stunned by the fatuity of our remarks but, in kindness, was more inclined to blame our teachers than ourselves:

British teachers, instead of filling their pupils' heads with a lot of boring, out-dated rubbish about contraception, abortion, and how to masturbate, should teach each generation an entirely different language. Only those who wish to promote strife for their own sinister purposes can seriously pretend that there is anything to be gained by the generations talking to each other.

More irritating to him than children were the modern, go-ahead parents who talked in quasi-cute tones to curry favour with their offspring. 'Kiddie love' that confronted him in every paper was a sure sign of the guilt parents felt for disliking their children intensely. 'The English show their hatred of children by dressing them in hideous clothes called anoraks and romper suits, stuffing them with sweets, refusing to talk to them and sending them out of doors whenever possible in the pathetic hope that someone will murder them.' He was allergic to the whole concept of 'kids'.

London children, or 'kids' as they are rudely called, have taken to crawling down sewers, where they could be overcome by lethal gases and pick up infections, according to the Thames Water Authority. Experts think the new craze is brought about by a children's television programme showing some mutant turtles who live in the sewers, apparently without harm to themselves. This explanation strikes me as unlikely. Children who watch television all day seldom have time to do exciting things like explore sewers. A possible explanation is that they are trying to escape from television, but I doubt that, too. The terrible thought occurs to me that if there were indeed a significant migration of London kids into the sewers, it could be the result of a dawning existential suspicion that this is their destiny, this is where they really belong.

His boys were met with more disapproval, I think, than his girls – particularly at and after puberty. I greeted him and bade him goodnight with a kiss until I was twelve when suddenly, one night, he held his nose, stuck out his tummy and shook my hand instead.

*   *   *

Politically my father was neither left nor right wing, but was bored by politics and regarded all politicians with scorn. 'That is my political creed so far as I have one,' he said. After his attacks on the sloth and avarice of the industrial working class in the 1970s he was branded by many as a right-winger – even a fascist by some. Others saw his detestation of capital punishment, of harsh prison sentences, of war and of British isolationism as signs of inner left-wingery, but in truth he despised all positions, especially extreme ones: 'I see nothing to choose between the National Front and the Race Relations Board,' he wrote. 'Both are a collection of bores and busybodies and both are harmful to the extent they are taken seriously.' Socialism, he believed, impoverished not only the wealthy but also the poor that it was designed to enrich: 'The trouble with socialism is that in the process of keeping the workers poor, oppressed and docile it must depart so far from its own sustaining rhetoric of liberty, equality, fraternity, prosperity and workers' control as to create a psychotic society requiring mass imprisonment.' Capitalism, on the other hand, was only marginally better, for it carried with it the seeds of its own destruction and led inevitably to a degraded world of 'noise, smell, dirt and accompanying moral pollution'.

> A nation's prosperity is no longer measured by infant mortality, deaths in childbirth, incidence of rickets, deaths aggravated by malnutrition. These are so small as to be negligible. In a proletarian technological age prosperity is measured by numbers of motor boats, transistor radios, foreign holidays, hideous new accommodation for the working class and their recreational appetites. It is something to be regarded with abhorrence by the cultivated or reflective mind.

I think his politics are best described by the term 'liberal anarchist', driven as they were by a conviction that all politicians are demented by *Machttrieb* – a manic desire to impose their decisions on other people. 'Politics is for social and emotional misfits,' he wrote, 'handicapped folk, those with a grudge. The purpose of politics is to help them overcome these feelings of inferiority and compensate for their

personal inadequacies in the pursuit of power.' His faith in the political system was shattered early on. 'The problem with democracy,'
he wrote, 'is that it is not democracy at all but a zealotocracy or rule
by enthusiasts. This is a polite way of saying that as many bossy people
as possible get a chance to throw their weight around. It may be lovely
for bossy people who like deciding how the rest of us should live,
but it is hell for those at the receiving end.' As political correspondent for the *Spectator* he spent many years observing politicians from
the press gallery in the House of Commons, and it was from up there
that he formed his views on political motivation.

> The yells and animal noises which the nation listens to on the
> radio programme *Today in Parliament* have nothing to do with
> disagreements about the way the country should be run, or
> how much fuel should be given to old age pensioners at
> Christmas time. They are cries of pain and anger, mingled
> with hatred and envy, at the spectacle of another group exer-
> cising the 'power' which the first group covets; alternatively,
> they are cries of alarm as the group in 'power' sees its terri-
> tory threatened. Old age pensioners are mad if they think
> anyone actually cares about their wretched coal.

When a campaign was launched to make MPs put in longer hours
he was furious: 'The last thing we want from MPs is greater produc-
tivity. Since 1979 alone, they have passed enough footling and
oppressive new laws to last a hundred years. They should be offered
half the pay for half the hours, with an open invitation to go on
strike for the rest of their natural lives.'

I have dwelt at length with Papa's politics as I believe they go
some way to explaining not only his philosophy of fatherhood but
his philosophy of life. At its core was a hatred of bossing in all its
manifestations. That is why, as a child, I was seldom if ever disciplined
by him. He believed that good behaviour, particularly good manners,
were taught by example and could never be learned from orders
and instructions, or from any system of contrived or spontaneous
punishment. All his instincts were geared to identifying bossing

with a view to ridiculing and disobeying it. Once, walking into Westminster Abbey for a memorial service, his eyes alighted on a circular traffic-style notice – a picture of an ice-cream with a diagonal red line drawn through it. 'Fascists!' he said, as he walked past. If he had had time I am sure he would have doubled back to buy an ice-cream and lick it noisily during the service.

When scootering by a river in France, he saw a sign proclaiming *'Inderdiction formelle de jeter dans l'eau et sur ses dépendances des animaux morts (volailles comprises) et des ordures – Decret du 6–2–32 Art. 56'*[3] and immediately set off to find a dead animal.

It had never occurred to me before that it might be fun to throw dead animals into the water but this notice, advertising a formal interdiction, could only be interpreted as an open invitation to join in what was presumably a traditional French sport. It was beyond reasonable hope that I would find a dead chicken or duck, but I remembered seeing a dead hedgehog on the road some miles back. Unfortunately it proved inseparable from the tarmac of which it had already begun to form a part, and it was while I was trying to run over a green lizard, the size of a small crocodile, that I fell off my Mobylette and suffered the sort of injuries which would cause any self-respecting British worker to draw sick benefit for a year.

By following my father's anarchist lead and aping it studiously, I found myself frequently in hot water at school. Complaints about the injustices of schoolteachers were listened to sympathetically. In my second year I conceived the notion that a maths teacher was guilty of hiding samples of women's underwear in a locked cupboard in his classroom. Unable to force the doors I threw the whole cupboard down a flight of stairs in an effort to break it open and reveal his dirty secret. For this I was rusticated. Papa took the view that I had for once, shown bravery, skill and considerable enterprise, and wrote to the headmaster recommending that I be awarded school colours for my actions.

[3] 'It is forbidden under the Decree of 6 February 1932 (Article 56) to throw into the river or leave on its banks dead animals (including poultry) and rubbish.'

Vandals are practically never caught and one seldom has the opportunity of hearing the vandals' point of view. 'Senseless' is a word usually applied to these acts, but when one grasps the simple proposition that vandals obviously enjoy breaking things, then vandalism is no more senseless than playing tennis.

When a chemistry master put down his pipette to give an impromptu speech on the evils of *Private Eye* Papa sent him a card with a hand-drawn eye on it and the warning 'PRIVATE EYE IS WATCHING YOU'. I was encouraged to look out for signs of power mania in my teachers and, as soon as I spotted any, to denounce and despise them. This, on reflection, was counterproductive, and might have played some part in my poor academic record. Through Papa's eyes I came soon to the conclusion that all but a handful of the best teachers were enslaved to their *Machttrieb* and consequently treated the school, for the whole time I was there, as a battle turf on which to frustrate, insult and abuse them – not as a place of learning.

Teachers live in a small world and their job is an unpleasant one. Among the few consolations it offers is an aura of semi-divine omniscience which enables them to patronise and feel important. This is what is threatened every time a pupil raises his hand with the correct answer. How pleasant it must be for a teacher, as he ignores the raised hands in front and approaches some bemused oaf in the back who hasn't the faintest idea what he's talking about, to imagine he is making his contribution towards a fairer, more equal, society in the future.

When I failed to get into Oxford University (dimness?) Papa didn't seem to mind in the least. He probably thought that a music degree was a footling waste of time anyway. I applied to New College, where Arthur Waugh had scraped his third in Greats, and was rebuffed after a single, rather silly interview with a thin man who liked only eighteenth-century French organ music. I missed nothing by going to Manchester instead, but felt a deep sense of shame at being the first Waugh in four generations to fail his Oxford entrance. After university, like all penniless ex-students, I needed to find a job. Papa tried to steer me from music with enticements to set me up as a wine merchant operating out of the cellars at Combe Florey and living at the end of his drive in the gatehouse. It was a similar offer, oddly enough, to that which the Brute had put to his son, Arthur, three generations earlier. I am confident that my father and I could not have worked together happily, any more than Arthur and the 'son of his soul' could get along at Chapman and Hall between 1919 and 1926. Papa once suggested that we collaborate on a musical, but I am glad I did it with my brother Nat instead.

When Papa first took on the editorship of the *Literary Review* I supplied him with cartoon strips published, for some forgotten reason, under the *nom de plume* of Erin. I usually telephoned to discuss the content of each drawing before setting to work on it and when I proposed a hospital scene in which a wife gives birth to a two-headed baby he was delighted. Each head was to resemble one parent's face and the envisaged punchline was a picture of the father reaching across the maternity bed to knock one of the heads off with his fist. What Papa and I could not agree upon was whether it was funnier for the father to punch off the head that looked like his or the one that resembled his wife. I cannot remember which of us took which line, only that we squabbled over it like alley cats at full moon, that it was the worst and also the last cartoon I ever produced for him. It was at about this time that he kicked me out of his flat in London for leaving it in a mess.

My brother Nat confused him utterly. His relationship with Papa was different from mine. He did not respect him in the grovelling way that I did but teased, cajoled and gave him silly names. In return for being called Nige, Bernie or whatever, Nat gave Papa ridiculous names of his own invention, Celtic Woman, Reggie the Stiff, Anus Buster – anything that came into his head, often very obscene. 'You fail to convince me,' Papa once said to him at dinner. 'And *you* fail to convince *me*,' Nat retorted. Papa looked bemused, and Nat walked over to him and, to everyone's amazement, gently rubbed his hands on the crown of Papa's bald head. 'Quintus,' he said, with a mock sigh and a honeyed tone, 'we can't go on like this.' Nat refused to treat Papa as anything other than an intimate object of affectionate mockery – a campaign strategy that was only partially successful.

My brother is a very funny man. His humour is what you might call 'off the wall', 'zany' – 'lateral-thinking on boost', as one observer described it. When the late Willie Rushton met Nat for the first time he said he had never encountered such comic genius since the early days of Peter Cook. From the moment he left school Nat decided to roam the world in search of adventure and he found plenty of it. He has starved in the Indian desert, contracted malaria in the Congo; he has been thrown into prison in Colombia, car-jacked in Nicaragua, had his heel bitten by a baby crocodile and his posterior shredded by the sharp teeth of the Komodo dragon. Adventure follows adventure wherever he goes. Recently he found a lobster crawling across his garden in France, sixty miles from the sea. An ethnic guitar he brought back from South America as a present for his mother-in-law contained chagas larvae, which hatched into beetles, crawled out of the instrument, killed the dog and rendered his mother-in-law insane. I don't think there is a tropical disease left for him to catch. He has suffered them all with resilience, and continues to erupt periodically in blotches and sweats from ailments contracted in countries he visited many years ago.

For a while Nat lived (doing what?) in El Salvador. He was impossibly hard to contact and my parents were in a permanent state of anxiety. Months went by without any answer to their letters sent on Nat's recommendation to '*post-restante* Santa Ana', and the atmosphere at Combe Florey was pregnant with tension. Each time the telephone rang everyone raced towards it in the hope that it might bring news of Nat. On one occasion it was an unidentified Irish voice: 'This is the IRA,' he said. 'We've rigged yer feckin' house wit' Semtex and it's gonna blow in twenty minutes.' 'Oh, fuck off,' said my father, and hung up irritably. Another month passed and still no word. Then, as we were adjusting ourselves to the grimmest of all possibilities, a postcard arrived with an El Salvadorian stamp addressed to 'BIG BRON BROWNING at Combe Florey House':

Happy Birthday Jacob,

It doesn't seem so very long ago that we were celebrating your 35th down at Lowcombe Manor. The wine flowed a little too freely that evening. I will never forget how the light of Roger's fire played havoc with your profile. Yet despite these distractions you still found time to share some of your Tantric wisdom with yours truly, Gustav.

Papa received the card with mixed emotions of dismay and delight. He was flummoxed and, with no details as to what 'Gustav' was doing, how he was faring or when he was planning to return, continued to fret for his safety. After several further months of unknowing he tried to lure Nat back with the promise of a flat in London, which, he said, if Nat returned by a given date, he would fill to the ceiling with *foie gras*. The message got through to whatever Borstal-prison Nat was sloughing in and his reply, addressed on the envelope to Amos 'Aubs' Waugh, was received at Combe Florey three weeks later:

My Lord,

Your generosity, your letter and your *foie gras* concept have lifted me from a state of pancake-eating decrepitude into one of smiling evangelical good will. I now find myself winking at taxi-drivers, licking clean the scars of the infirm and at times blessing the very devil. That you, Sir, should have been the catalyst for such a turn-around fills me with filial pride and not a small amount of desire. For to my eternal shame I cannot always distinguish between these twin feelings of kinship and lust that slumber within me.

The news about the flat is particularly exciting, although I know better than to get over-quinnied in view of the calamities that life invariably throws at us. Have I done right, Father?

Yesterday I was chased round the cathedral district of Santa Ana by an enormous reptile the size of a fattened

Dobermann and was later told that the monster was an asexual herbivore — yet it clearly wanted something from me.

Lots of love Tonino

At games Papa was fiercely competitive. Though no athlete (I never saw him run) he put so much of his heart into matches of croquet, bridge, ping-pong and a foreign dice game called Perudo that his opponents often felt it would be cruel or rude not to let him win. He cheated without qualm. I once abandoned a bridge table because he was cheating too much — telling his partner exactly what cards were in his hand as she was bidding — and he went around for weeks telling everyone I was priggish. At croquet I know I could have beaten him many times, but he loved the game unrestrainedly and believed himself a champion at it. There seemed no point in spoiling the occasion and I deliberately missed hoops and posts to let him win. I can hear to this day his gloating squeals of delight each time I missed, unaware that I had done it on purpose, that I had missed the hoop for *his* sake. It is strange how sons feel guilty if they beat their fathers at games. Septimus told me that Evelyn, fed up with his sighing, had said to him, 'If I hear you sigh one more time I shall kick you.' When the next sigh fell on the silent air Evelyn duly leaped to his feet: 'Right, I am now going to kick you.' Septimus set off round the kitchen table with his father in sweaty pursuit. After a couple of circumnavigations he realised that something was wrong. 'This is ridiculous,' he thought. 'I could carry on running round this table all day. Papa is far too fat and slow to catch me ever.' Out of mixed feelings of guilt, compassion and shame, Septimus stopped running to allow his father to catch up and kick him.

At ping-pong Papa won plaudits for his ferocious darting backhand, but none of his other shots worked. Occasionally, when he lost to dinner guests, he would wake me in the night with pleas to come downstairs and restore the family honour. I put on games shorts over my pyjamas so that my penis would not loll out during the match. Once he woke me to defeat a homosexual friend who had claimed to be ping-pong champion of southern England: 'You won't be needing those,' he said, as he saw me, bleary-eyed, reaching for my shorts.

Papa never kicked me; nor did he ever raise a hand against me. Only once did I suffer a physical assault from him. My crime was breaking free of my au pair's hand and jumping in front of moving cars on my way to and from the village primary school at Chilton Foliat. It was an exciting game while it lasted and I, only six years old, was intoxicated by the effect that my small presence had on fast-moving traffic. I could stop cars, buses, ambulances – bring walloping great juggernauts to a screeching halt simply by leaping in front of them and waving. When news of my antics reached my father he resolved to stamp them out by any means. My sister and I used to clap and shout, 'Hooray,' when he returned home from London – which was exactly what we did on this occasion. He ignored Sophia and rushed straight at me, like an angry beast at the Plaza del Toros, and hurled me on to the floor. I was too startled to cry, but Sophia became almost suicidal with grief on my behalf. As I lay, slightly dazed, on the carpet, Papa delivered a brisk, rehearsed speech in a high staccato tone (to which I did not attend) before sweeping from the room like a princess in a huff. He was acting, of course – and badly at that – but it had its effect and I never played Jump-in-Front-of-the-Bus again.

My decision to join the 'family business' and earn a living as a writer was not taken lightly. Of course, I knew from the moment I left university that I would probably end up writing but put it off for as long as possible, hoping pathetically to earn enough money at other things to avoid my literary conscription. But it was not to be. For nearly ten years I frenzied away producing records, composing music, drawing cartoons, setting up a publishing company – for a while I acted as a concert agent and a classical impresario – but to whatever trade I turned my hand I invariably found myself losing money, or interest or both.

Papa was not enthusiastic about any of my careers in music and maybe a little ashamed of some. In the manuscript of his autobiography he wrote of my mother being pregnant in 1963 'with a second child later to emerge as our son Alexander, the musician'.

At some stage in the proofing he must have thought better of this and changed the sentence to: 'The child which turned into my elder son, Alexander, has been a source of growing pride and pleasure ever since.' I won important prizes for my records, but when one of them was nominated for a Grammy Award and Papa looked blank and bored when I told him, I resolved, in a petulant, adolescent way, never to inform him of any of my successes again. He was much more enthusiastic when Nat and I scooped the 12th Vivian Ellis Award for Best New Musical with a black comedy farce called *Bon Voyage!*. It took three years to get the thing staged and in that time, as he danced around the kitchen listening to a demotape of the music we had composed, there was a spark in his eye that seemed to say: 'Look here, you bloody fools, you're going to end up with egg on your faces.'

Papa was genuinely delighted when I returned from a trip to Sri Lanka to announce my engagement to Eliza. His notice of it in *Will This Do?* — if read by a crackling book-room fire with a glass of gin in the hand and a sentimental smile on the lip — might even pass for a nocturnal emission of Arthur Waugh: 'Nine months later my son Alexander announced his engagement to Eliza Chancellor, beautiful, clever, warm-natured elder daughter of our friends Susie and Alexander. For the moment, at any rate, the cup of happiness seemed to be full.' He adored Eliza and I think his love for her made him fonder of me than he would have been had I married anyone else. Our copy of his autobiography is inscribed: 'For Alexander and Eliza with fondest love from their proud parent, Bron.'

In April 1998, after the births of two beautiful, exciting and unusual daughters, Eliza and I had a son. He was Papa's sixth grandchild and his first grandson. We decided to call him Auberon but had forgotten to ask Papa in advance if he minded. As soon as the boy was born I telephoned Papa who was overjoyed and rang my sister.

'Good news! Eliza and Alexander have had a son.'

'Hooray. What is he to be called?'

'Oh, I am so glad you have asked me that,' he said, puffing with pride. 'They are going to call him Papa.'

Two years later the handsome boy with golden putto curls pulled a glass lamp down on his face amputating his right cheek. His parents were beside themselves with worry as he was rushed off by ambulance to hospital in Taunton. Two days later, bruised, bloodied and stitched, the boy was presented to his grandfather. Papa admired his wounds in silence before declaring: 'A definite improvement.'

In my reluctance to become a writer I ought to confess to an element of intergenerational competitiveness. Had I not been a Waugh perhaps I would have sprung to my duties sooner but, as it happened, other members of my family seemed to be dominating the court. In journalism I sensed that whatever talents I possessed were probably best suited to some sort of fantasy comment column on current affairs, but Papa was the king of that sphere and I could see no possibility of entering it while he continued to rule. As for novels, well, would you write a novel if your grandfather were Evelyn Waugh? The only feasible possibilities seemed to lie in the direction of non-fiction books and classical-music criticism. At least in these two I might be free to welter and groan, to experiment and make my own mistakes outside the long reach of my ancestors' peerless precedent.

So it was in 1991, when all else had either failed or bored me, that I entered a bizarre competition, which led to my appointment as opera critic on the *Mail on Sunday*. Within less than a year I followed the editor, Stewart Steven, to the more dignified and influential post of opera critic at the *Evening Standard*. 'Congratulations,' Papa said. 'You have the job that every middle-aged pooftah in London is dying for, and you have it for life.' These words diminished me as I had no wish to be stuck for ever in a room with such a low ceiling; neither did I get much pleasure from depriving 'every middle aged pooftah in London' of his heart's desire. So I resolved to give it up in five years.

Whenever furious letters poured into the paper objecting to my reviews, Mr Steven offered me a pay rise, and when he told my father, some time later, that never, in all his forty years of journalism, had he encountered such a monumental effort to dislodge a journalist from his spot, Papa was so proud that he gave me a magnum of 1966 Château Le Gay, Pomerol, to celebrate. But my resolution to stick with the *Standard* for five years turned out to be pointless for after only four Mr Steven retired as editor and was replaced by a pasty-titted war-and-blood-sports man called Max Hastings who, for at least a decade, had been my father's editor at the *Daily Telegraph*. Hastings, under pressure, hired a novice to run the arts pages. All the old hissings and snarls that, for four years, had succeeded only in raising my salary suddenly found fresh hope in the waxy ears of Hastings's impressionable minion. My contract was not renewed. Hastings wrote me a letter of dismissal, which reads like something between a craven plea for forgiveness and a schoolgirl Valentine card: 'On a personal level, I shall regret the change because like all your family you have always seemed the most charming and sympathetic of companions . . .'

Papa's fierce loyalty swelled to console me. 'Hastings is no good any more,' he declared, in a lugubrious tone. A few years later, as he lay in a bewildered state only weeks from death he asked: 'Remind me. Why do I hate Max Hastings?'

'Because he sacked me, Papa?'

'Oh, yes, of course. *What* a twerp!'

For all his loyalty at that time, I think, in his heart, he still regarded opera criticism as a pooftah's profession and thought me well out of it.[4] I can date the moment when he ceased to regard me as a maverick or loose cannon fairly precisely. It was in the last week of May 2000, less than a year before his death, when he read my book called *Time* at Shrublands health emporium in Suffolk. It had been published a full nine months earlier and had been selling well, both in England and America, due to feverish public demand for

---

[4] When Papa used the word 'pooftah' he did not necessarily intend the meaning 'homosexual'. I think he employed the word in the much same way as Evelyn had used 'pansy'. The best explanation to all this can be found in a letter Papa wrote to *The Times* editor Harold Evans in September 1976: 'My father used the term "pansy" to describe anyone connected with the Arts, or who, in conversation, demonstrated greater knowledge of the arts than seemed normal or proper to him – i.e. more than he himself possessed. It was also used as a description of expertise: children's damage to furniture would be judged by whether it could be mended by a carpenter, or would require a pansy to come from London to restore the damage.'

explanations of the phenomenon in the great champagne run-up to the new millennium. Since I had not heard a squeak from him concerning it, I assumed he had dipped in and found it wanting. In fact, I think he was delaying the fearful hour in the hope of finding press reviews that would reassure him it was all right. But none came so he had to start without them. The first I knew about it was when I opened the *Telegraph* on 31 May:

> . . . And so I turned to a study of *Time*, the unusual treatise by Alexander Waugh which has just been published in America amid scenes of what can only be described as hysteria. The book, which is a masterpiece, sold more than 10,000 hardback copies in this country despite receiving only two or three notices. The reason why the English literary establishment ignored the book is only in part because literary folk tend to be timid and jealous and only quite intelligent. The main reason is that *Time* is an extraordinary book, unlike any which has been written before or since. It cleverly produced huge amounts of information in a witty monologue which is also highly enjoyable.
>
> Since the death of the novel and the discrediting of poetry, this type of prose, using irony and wit to impart condensed information, may become the new literary art form. A pity if they say the Americans thought of it first.

I cannot describe how happy and grateful I was when I read these words. It didn't matter that people would inevitably say, 'He only wrote that because he was your dad.' I didn't care. Others may read it as they wish. As far as I was concerned it was a rare and personal message – after a lifetime of doubting and quavering confidence, a final thumbs-up to his elder son. At last I was doing something he understood, and it wasn't music.

I suppose, when I think of it, that all of us Waughs only became writers to impress our fathers.

Six months later the stage musical that my brother and I had been labouring over for goodness knows how long at last went into rehearsal in Notting Hill Gate. Papa was immensely enthusiastic but he knew his time was running out. 'If I should die in the middle of the run, you will carry on, won't you?' he asked. He was relieved to make it to the second performance and came once more before his final collapse.

I intimated at the start that when he said to me on his deathbed, 'Everything's going to be dandy,' I was irritated at the vanity of his words, but now, with the benefit of hindsight, I think I know what he meant. Perhaps it is too quaint to suggest that he held on just long enough to see *Bon Voyage!* but I happen to believe that to be the case. It was no matter of chance that his last published words should have been a short warm vote of confidence in his two sons. It was published under the title 'Hope for the Country' in his *Way of the World* column on 16 December 2000 just a month before he died. I believe he planned it that way.

> It would be absurd for English parents to suppose they have given birth to a modern Shakespeare, although I am afraid this may be quite a frequent delusion, and it helps to explain all the slim volumes of 'poetry' that continue to appear 14 years after the death of Betjeman.
>
> Not so many people will be tempted to indulge the hope that they have somehow produced a new version of Gilbert and Sullivan, but I must admit that I confronted the possibility when I went to see *Bon Voyage!* on Wednesday evening . . . In the spirit of the times, it may be found slightly rougher than anything that would have been encouraged at the old Savoy Theatre under D'Oyly Carte, but the same humour is there, the memorable, even breathtaking tunes and above all the same assurance that there is an intelligent, sceptical England surviving under all the rubbish we see on television. *Bon Voyage!* is a delight and a joy, and I am proud to have fathered the two geniuses responsible for it.

I know that A. N. Wilson and V. S. Naipaul are not alone among serious writers in believing Papa to have been greater in stature than his father. I am not inclined either to agree or to disagree with them but am proud of both and believe that the legacy of each complements the other. Papa was philosophically far more stable than his father, his writing less arch. I also think he was a nicer man. Like Evelyn, he believed this world to be a 'vale of tears' but his constitution was stronger than Evelyn's and he saw no reason to relapse because of it into blank depression, drunkenness or rage. Despite his unique cleverness, originality and humour he was, at heart, a man of simple convictions: 'I would be surprised,' he once wrote, 'if there is any greater happiness than that provided by a game of croquet played on an English lawn through a summer's afternoon, after a good luncheon and with a reasonable prospect of a good dinner ahead.'

I am grateful to him for many things, not least that he broke with the otiose propensity to favouritism that had characterised the Waugh line for at least five generations. He provided a more stable upbringing to his four children than he himself had ever received, and left more goodwill towards the name than he had inherited from his father. Papa was the most impressive man I have ever met. He was a loyal, generous father and a brilliant writer.

I am honoured to be his pale shadow.

To Auberon Augustus Ichabod Waugh
A letter of explanation

Dear Bron,

Have you read *Fathers and Sons*? Of course you haven't: you are only six. If you do and are wondering what to make of it all, I should explain:

You were named Auberon in honour of my father – I wish you had known him better. The name Augustus means 'magnificent' (which you are). You were not given it in order to be reminded of the bisexual, flame-eyed triumvir of Ancient Rome. Ichabod in Hebrew means 'the glory is departed'. Strange? Well, should you ever feel that you have let down the line, which I sincerely hope you won't, you can blame it on your parents for having given you such an unpropitious tag.

Bear the name of Waugh with pride. It is not a satchel of rocks, or a blotchy birthmark, or a tuxedo with medals for you to swank about in. Do not let it browbeat you into thinking you have to become a writer, that it is your destiny or your duty to do so. It isn't. There is no point in writing unless you have something to say and are determined to say it well.

Beware of seriousness: it is a form of stupidity.

Fear boredom.

Never use the word 'ersatz'.

Good luck. The road ahead is tough and tricky.

'May every base be broad in honour'. What does that mean?

Your ever loving and devoted father,
Alexander Waugh

To laugh often and love much; to win the respect of intelligent persons and the affections of children; to earn the approbation of honest critics and endure the betrayal of false friends; to appreciate beauty; to find the best in others; to give one's self; to leave the world a little bit better whether by a healthy child, a garden path or a redeemed social condition; to have played and laughed with enthusiasm and sung with exaltation; to know that even one life has breathed easier because you have lived . . . that is to succeed.

Ralph Waldo Emerson – (I think)

Milverton, August 2004

Acknowledgements

I can think of millions of reasons why most of the people who helped me with this book might rather I had not written it. Thank you Mama, Sophie, Daisy and Nat. Thank you Selina Hastings for giving me your stupendous Evelyn Waugh Archive – what generosity. It will be well looked after. Thank you Peter Waugh for your constant flow of information, for permission to quote from Alec Waugh and for your support and encouragement during the whole period of writing it. Thank you Andrew and Veronica for the trusting loan of letters and photographs, to Septimus, James and Hatty for agreeing to impertinent probings about your childhoods and to Aunt Teresa and the Evelyn Waugh Estate for permission to quote from Grandpapa's writings and for the loan of many of his unpublished letters. Thank you also to my father's cousins Robin Grant and Polly Mellotte; to his aunt Bridget and to his nanny, Vera Grother. Thank you Alan Bell for your colossal donations to my Wavian archive and to Vidia and Nadira Naipaul for getting the whole project off the ground in the first place.

Thank you to all those who put themselves out to clarify facts, lend me papers, grant me permissions, find me books or to help me in any other way along my path. Thank you especially: Gillon Aitken, Mark Amory, Robert Murray Davis, Richard Dorment, Tim Heald, Richard Ingrams, Charles and Mary Keen, Candida Lycett Green (for permission to quote John Betjeman), Thomas Meagher and Saen Noel (from the Alec Waugh Collection in the Special Collections at Boston University), Cristina Odone and Richard Oram (from the Evelyn Waugh Collection at the University of Austen, Texas), Michelle Paul (at the British Library), Dr Huw Ridgeway (Sherborne School), Jo Roberts-Miller (at Headline), Douglas Russell, Jennifer Scalt (Univeristy of Toronto Library) and John Howard Wilson. What a lot of kind people – thank you all.

Permissions:

Arthur Waugh books, letters, diaries quoted by permission of Teresa Waugh of the Arthur Waugh Estate; Alec Waugh books, letters, poems, diaries quoted by permission of Peter Waugh from the Alec Waugh

Estate; Evelyn Waugh books, letters, poems, diaries quoted by permission of Teresa D'Arms from the Evelyn Waugh Estate; and Auberon Waugh books, letters, diaries quoted by permission of Teresa Waugh of the Auberon Waugh Estate.

All photographs are from private collections except:

Insert A:

Page 2 – Dr Alexander Waugh (*Boston University*)

Page 3 – K and Arthur Waugh (*Boston University*)

Page 7 – Evelyn and Arthur Waugh (By permission of *The British Library*)

Insert B:

Page 4 – Auberon Waugh (*Jane Bown*), Evelyn and Septimus Waugh (*Hulton Archive*)

Page 6 – Auberon Waugh at Combe Florey (*Daily Mail*)

Page 7 – Alexander Waugh (*Camera Press*), Bron and Alexander Waugh (*Michael Ward, Sunday Times*)

Bibliography

The lists contain only those published items quoted from or referred to in the text

ARTHUR WAUGH

Fiction and poetry:
Gordon in Africa [Newdigate Prize Poem] (1888)
Legends of the Wheel: Poems (1898)
Galaxy: A Table-Book of Prose Reflections for Every Day of the Year, chosen and
    arranged by Elizabeth Myers (1944)

Non-fiction and autobiography:
Schoolroom and Home Theatricals (1890)
Alfred Lord Tennyson: A Study of his Life and Work (1892)
Robert Browning: A Biography (1900)
Reticence in Literature: And Other Papers (1915)
Tradition and Change: Studies in Contemporary Literature (1919)
A Hundred Years in Publishing: Being the Story of Chapman and Hall Ltd (1930)
One Man's Road: Being a Picture of Life in a Passing Generation (1931)

ALEC WAUGH

Fiction and poetry:
The Loom of Youth (1917)
Resentment: Poems (1918)
Pleasure (1921)
The Lonely Unicorn (1922)
Kept (1925)
Three Score and Ten (1929)
So Lovers Dream (1931)
Thirteen Such Years (1932)
The Balliols (1934)
Island in the Sun (1956)
Fuel for the Flame (1960)
A Spy in the Family (1970)
The Fatal Gift (1973)

Non-fiction and autobiography:
The Prisoners of Mainz (1919)
Public School Life: Boys, Parents, Masters (1922)
Myself When Young: Confessions (1923)
On Doing What One Likes: Essays (1926)
The Coloured Countries (1930)
His Second War (1944)
These Would I Choose: A Personal Anthology (1948)
The Early Years of Alec Waugh (1962) [autobiography 1898–1930]
My Brother Evelyn and Other Profiles (1967)
A Year to Remember: A Reminiscence of 1931 (1975) [autobiography]
The Best Wine Last (1978) [autobiography 1932–1969]

EVELYN WAUGH

Fiction and poetry:
Published in *Evelyn Waugh Apprentice* (ed Robert Murray Davis) (1985):
    The World to Come – A Poem
    Fragment of a Novel
    Conversion – A School Play
    The Balance (1926)
    Edward of Unique Achievement
    The Tutor's Tale (1927)
    Too Much Tolerance (1933)
Decline and Fall (1928)
Vile Bodies (1930)
The Man Who Liked Dickens – Short Story (1933)
A Handful of Dust (1934)
Mr. Loveday's Little Outing and Other Sad Stories (1936)
Work Suspended (1942)
Put Out More Flags (1942)
Brideshead Revisited (1945)
The Ordeal of Gilbert Pinfold – A Conversation Piece (1957)
Unconditional Surrender (1961)
Basil Seal Rides Again (1963)
Sword of Honour (1966) [a single volume recession of *Men at Arms*, *Officers and Gentlemen* and *Unconditional Surrender*)

Non-fiction and autobiography:
P.R.B: An Essay on the Pre-Raphaelite Brotherhood (1926)

Rossetti (1928)
Labels (1930)
Remote People (1931)
Edmund Campion (1935)
Ronald Knox (1958)
A Tourist in Africa (1960)
A Little Learning (1964) [autobiography, part I]
A Little Hope (unpublished) [autobiography draft for part II]

AUBERON WAUGH

Fiction and poetry:
The Foxglove Saga (1960)
Path of Dalliance (1963)
Who Are The Violets Now? (1965)

Non-fiction and autobiography:
Country Topics (1974) [collected essays from the *Evening Standard*]
Four Crowded Years (1976) [diaries]
In the Lion's Den (1978) [collected essays from the *New Statesman*]
A Turbulent Decade (1985) [diaries]
Another Voice (1986) [collected essays from the *Spectator*]
Waugh on Wine (1986)
Will This Do? (1991) [autobiography]
Way of the World (3 vols: 1994, 1997, 2001) [collected pieces from *Daily Telegraph*]

DIARIES AND LETTERS

Arthur Waugh's diaries (1930–1943) are held in the Special Collections Archive at the Mugar Memorial Library in Boston. Some of K's diaries are there also while others remain in a private collection. Evelyn Waugh's diaries are in the Harry Ransom Humanities Research Centre, University of Texas at Austin. An edited edition (*The Diaries of Evelyn Waugh*, ed. Michael Davie) was published in 1976. Dudley Carew's diaries are also in Texas. References to Auberon Waugh's diaries relate to those he published in *Private Eye* between 1970 and 1986.

Many of the letters quoted in this book were hitherto unpublished and in private hands. The most significant sources of published letters are:

The Letters of Evelyn Waugh, ed. Mark Amory (1980)
The Letters of Nancy Mitford and Evelyn Waugh, ed. Charlotte Mosley (1996)
The Letters of Ann Fleming, ed. Mark Amory (1985)
Mr Wu & Mrs Stitch: The Letters of Evelyn Waugh and Diana Cooper, ed.
   Artemis Cooper (1991)

The most significant letter collections from public libraries are as follows:

Alec Waugh Collection in Boston holds a large archive of Alec's incoming
correspondence including many letters to him from K and Arthur and
some from him to his parents, as well as Alec's notes on his father, his
letters to Hugh Mackintosh and most of the manuscripts to his books.

Harry Ransom Research Center in Austin, Texas, holds everything that
was in the library at Combe Florey in 1968 and more, including Dudley
Carew's letters, letters from Evelyn to Alec and from Evelyn to his
sister-in-law Joan. Arthur's letters to Kenneth McMaster are also in
Texas.

The British Library holds 4000 letters of Evelyn Waugh's incoming
correspondence, including most of the letters from his father, mother,
wife and children.

Sherborne School Archive holds the manuscript of *The Loom of Youth* as
well as the collected correspondence concerning it, including letters
from Arthur to Alec (1917) and other material relating to Alec.

OTHER BOOKS CONSULTED

Ackerley, J.R. *My Father and Myself* (1968)
Acton, Harold *Memoires of an Aesthete* (1948)
Blayac, Alain (ed.) *Evelyn Waugh: New Directions* (1992)
Bradbury, Malcolm *Evelyn Waugh* (1964)
Butler, Samuel *Father and Son* [in Butleriana] (1932)
Carew, Dudley *A Fragment of a Friendship: A Memory of Evelyn Waugh* (1974)
Carpenter, Humphrey *The Brideshead Generation: Evelyn Waugh and his
   Friends* (1990)
Davis, Robert Murray (and others) *A Bibliography of Evelyn Waugh* (1986);
   Evelyn Waugh and the Forms of his Time (1989); *Evelyn Waugh, Writer*
   (1981)

Donaldson, Frances *Evelyn Waugh: Portrait of a Country Neighbour* (1967)

Doyle, Paul *A Waugh Companion* (1988)

Gill, Brendan 'Alec Waugh' in *A New York Life of Friends and Others* (1990)

Gosse, Edmund *Father and Son* (1907)

Gourlay, A.B. *A History of Sherborne School* (1971)

Green, G.G (ed.) *The Sherborne School Register 1890–1965* 5th edition (1965)

Greenidge, Terence *Evelyn Waugh in Letters* (1994)

Hare, Steve (ed.) *Father and Son* (1999)

Hastings, Selina *Evelyn Waugh, a biography* (1994)

Hollis, Christopher *Evelyn Waugh* (1954); *Oxford in the Twenties: Recollections of Five Friends* (1976)

Howell, C. *Midsomer Norton and Radstock* (1988)

Laqueur, Thomas W. *Solitary Sex: A Cultural History of Masturbation* (2003)

Lewis, Wyndham *The Doom of Youth* (1932)

Littlewood, Ian *The Writings of Evelyn Waugh* (1983)

Lodge, David *Evelyn Waugh* (1971)

Mackenzie, Ian *Forgotten Places* [with introduction by Arthur Waugh] (1919)

McCartney, George *Evelyn Waugh and the Modernist Tradition* (1987)

McDonnell, Jacqueline *Evelyn Waugh* (1988); *Waugh on Women* (1986)

Myers, William *Evelyn Waugh and the Problem of Evil* (1991)

O'Keeffe, Paul *Some Sort of Genius: a Life of Wyndham Lewis* (2000)

Page, Norman *An Evelyn Waugh Chronology* (1997)

Patey, Douglas Lane *The Life of Evelyn Waugh* (1998)

Powell, Anthony *To Keep the Ball Rolling* (1976–1982) [memoirs in 4 vols]

Powis, Littleton (ed.) *The Letters of Elizabeth Myers* (1951)

Pryce-Jones, David (ed.) *Evelyn Waugh and his World* (1973)

Rolo, Charles (ed.) *The World of Evelyn Waugh* (1958)

Stannard, Martin *Evelyn Waugh: The Critical Heritage* (1984); *Evelyn Waugh: The Early Years* 1903-1939 (1987); *Evelyn Waugh: The Later Years* 1939–1966 (1992)

Stopp, Frederick *Evelyn Waugh: Portrait of an Artist* (1958)

Sykes, Christopher *Evelyn Waugh, a biography* (1974)

Thomsen, Moritz *My Two Wars* (1996)

Trelawny-Ross, A.H. *Their Prime of Life: A Public School Study* (1956)

Watkins, Alan *Brief Lives* (1982)

Wilson, John Howard *Evelyn Waugh, a Literary Biography, 1903–1924* (1996); *Evelyn Waugh, a Literary Biography, 1924–1966* (2001)

Wykes, David *Evelyn Waugh: A Literary Life* (1999)

ESSAYS AND ARTICLES
Relating to the theme of this book:

Cockburn, Claud *Evelyn Waugh's Lost Rabbit*, Atlantic, Dec. 1973

Driberg, Tom *The Evelyn Waugh I Knew*, The Observer, May 20, 1973

Heald, Tim *The Revolutionary Waughs*, Old Shirburnian Society Annual Record (2002)

Hinchcliffe, Peter *Fathers and Children in the Novels of Evelyn Waugh*, University of Toronto Quarterly 35. No 3 (1966)

Waugh, Alec *A Letter to A Father*, Sunday Times, Oct. 26 1924; *Memories*, The Atlantic, Apr. 1974

Waugh, Alexander *Penguin and the Wales*, Penguin Collectors' Society (1999); *My Father the Anarchist*, Daily Telegraph, Nov. 10, 2001

Waugh, Arthur *Sherborne School*, Country Life, Jun. 17, 1916

Waugh, Auberon *And Father Came Too* [Interview with Stephanie Nettell], Books and Bookmen, Jan. 1964; *Death in the Family*, Spectator, May 6, 1966; *My Father's Diaries*, New Statesman, Apr. 13, 1973; *Waugh's World*, New York Times Magazine, Oct. 7, 1973; *Entries and Exits* [Review of Evelyn Waugh's Diaries], Spectator, Sept. 4, 1976; *Father and Son*, Books and Bookmen, Oct. 1973; *Stillingfleet's Revenge* [review of Evelyn Waugh by Sykes], Books and Bookmen, Oct. 1975; *My Uncle Alec*, Spectator, Sept. 12, 1981; *Laura Waugh 1916–1973*, Antigonish Review, 54 (1984); *A Little More Whitewash* [review of Stannard's Evelyn Waugh, vol 1], Literary Review, Dec. 1986

Waugh, Evelyn *The Youngest Generation*, Lancing College Magazine, Dec. 1921; *Myself When Young* [review of Alec's book], Cherwell, Nov. 10, 1923; *What I Think of My Elders*, Daily Herald, May 19, 1930; *Alec Waugh*, Bookman, Jun. 1930; *General Conversation: Myself . . .*, Nash's Pall Mall Magazine, Mar. 1937; *My Father*, Sunday Telegraph, Dec. 2, 1962

Wheatcroft, Geoffrey *Bron and his "Affec. Papa"*, Atlantic Monthly, May 2001

Index

Note: Subheadings are filed in approximate chronological order. A subscript number appended to page numbers denotes a footnote.

Alexander Waugh was born in 1963 and is the grandson of Evelyn Waugh and the son of columnist Auberon Waugh and novelist Teresa Waugh. After reading Music at Manchester University, he became Chief Opera Critic at the *Mail on Sunday* and the London *Evening Standard*. He has written several books on music, including *Classical Music: A New Way of Listening*, which has been translated into fourteen languages. His most recent books, *Time* (Headline, 1999) and *God* (Headline, 2002), were critical and commercial successes.

Also a publisher, a cartoonist and an illustrator, Alexander Waugh composed the music for the award-winning stage musical *Bon Voyage!* He lives in Somerset with his wife and three children.